CONVENTIONAL VALUES
OF THE HELLENISTIC GREEKS

STUDIES IN
HELLENISTIC CIVILIZATION

Edited by Per Bilde,
Troels Engberg-Pedersen, Lise Hannestad,
and Jan Zahle

VIII

CONVENTIONAL VALUES
OF THE HELLENISTIC GREEKS

Edited by Per Bilde,
Troels Engberg-Pedersen, Lise Hannestad,
and Jan Zahle

AARHUS UNIVERSITY PRESS

AARHUS UNIVERSITY PRESS
University of Aarhus
DK-8000 Aarhus C
Fax (+ 45) 8619 8433

73 Lime Walk
Headington, Oxford OX3 7AD
Fax (+ 44) 1865 750 079

Box 511
Oakville, Conn. 06779
Fax (+ 1) 860 945 9468

ANSI/NISO
Z39.48-1992

CONTENTS

ABBREVIATIONS

AA	Archäologischer Anzeiger
Acme	Acme. Annali della Facoltà di filosofia e lettere dell'Università statale di Milano
AbhBerlin	Abhandlungen der Preußischen Akademie der Wissenschaften zu Berlin
AbhMainz	Akademie der Wissenschaften und der Literatur in Mainz. Abhandlungen der Geistes- und Sozialwissenschaftlichen Klasse
AbhWien	Abhandlungen der Österreichischen Akademie der Wissenschaften
ActaHyp	Acta Hyperborea. Danish Studies in Classical Archaeology
AD	Archaiologikon Deltion
AE 1958	Charitonidis, S.I., "Anaskaphi klassikon taphon para tin plateian Syntagmatos", *Archaiologiki Ephemeris*, 1958, 1-152
AXIIIKonKlArch	Akten des XIII. Internationalen Kongresses für Klassische Archäologie (Berlin 1988). Mainz 1990
AeR	Atene e Roma
Agora XII	Sparkes, B.A. & Talcott, L. *Black and Plain Pottery of the 6th, 5th and 4th Centuries B.C. The Athenian Agora* XII. Princeton 1970
AJPh	American Journal of Philology
AM	Mitteilungen des Deutschen Archäologischen Instituts, Athenische Abteilung
AmStP	American Studies in Papyrology
AnalectaBibl	Analecta Biblica, Roma
AnatSt	Anatolian Studies
AncPhil	Ancient Philosophy
AncSoc	Ancient Society
AnnAStorAnt	Annali dell'Istituto universitario orientale di Napoli. Sezione di archeologia e storia antica
AnnNap	Annali della facoltà di lettere e filosofia, Università di Napoli

AnnPerugia	Annali della Facoltà di lettere e filosofia, Università degli studi di Perugia
AnnPisa	Annali della Scuola normale superiore di Pisa
AnPap	Analecta Papyrologica, Messina
ANRW	Temporini, H. & Haase, W. (eds.), *Aufstieg und Niedergang der römischen Welt*. Berlin/New York 1972-
AntCl	L'Antiquité classique
Antichthon	Antichthon. Journal of the Australian Society for Classical Studies
AntJ	The Antiquaries Journal
AntW	Antike Welt
Apeiron	Apeiron. Department of Classical Studies, Monash University
ArchRW	Archiv für Religionswissenschaft
Archéologia	Archéologia, Paris
ARep	Archaeological Reports, London
ARV	Beazley, J.D., *Attic Red-Figure Vase-Painters* (2nd ed.). Oxford 1963
ASAtene	Annuario della Scuola archeologica di Atene e delle Missioni italiane in Oriente
Athenaeum	Athenaeum. Studi periodici di letteratura e storia dell'antichità
Augustinianum	Augustinianum. Institutum Patristicum Augustinianum, Roma
AW	Antike Welt. Zeitschrift für Archäologie und Kulturgeschichte
BAR	British Archaeological Reports
BCH	Bulletin de correspondance hellénique
BEFAR	Bibliothèque des Écoles françaises d'Athènes et de Rome
BiblThB	Biblical Theology Bulletin
BICS	Bulletin of the Institute of Classical Studies, University of London
BIFAO	Bulletin de l'Institut français d'archéologie orientale de Caire
BMC	*British Museum Catalogue of Greek Coins*. London 1873-
BMusFA	Bulletin of the Museum of Fine Arts, Boston
BSA	Annual of the British School at Athens
BSR	Papers of the British School at Rome

Bullép	Bulletin épigraphique
ByzZ	Byzantinische Zeitschrift
CAH	*Cambridge Ancient History* (2nd ed.). Cambridge
CCAG	*Catalogus Codicum Astrologorum Graecorum* (Cumont, F. et al. eds., 1898-1953)
CCCA	Vermaseren, M.J. *Corpus Cultus Cybelae Attidisque*: EPRO 50.1-7, Leiden 1977-1989
CEFR	Collection de l'École française de Rome
Centaurus	Centaurus. International Magazine of the History of Science and Medicine, Copenhagen
CIA	Corpus Inscriptionum Atticarum
CIG	Corpus Inscriptionum Graecarum. Berlin 1825-1877
CIL	Corpus Insciptionum Latinarum
ClJ	The Classical Journal
ClPhil	Classical Philology
ClR	The Classical Review
ClW	The Classical World
ChronEg	Chronique d'Égypte
Corinth XIII	Blegen, C.W., Palmer, H. & Young, R.S. *The North Cemetery. Corinth* XIII. Princeton 1964
CPR	Corpus Papyrorum Raineri
CRAI	Comptes-rendus des séances. Académie des inscriptions et belles-lettres
CronCatania	Cronache di archeologia, Catania
CV	Corpus Vasorum Antiquorum
Dar.-Sag.	Daremberg, Ch. and Saglio, Ed. *Dictionnaire des antiquités grecques et romaines,* Paris 1877-1919
DialHistAnc	Dialogues d'histoire ancienne
Differences	Differences. Journal of Feminist Cultural Studies. Bloomington, Indiana
EntrHardt	Entretiens de la Fondation Hardt. Vandoeuvres/Genève.
EPRO	Vermaseren, M.J. (ed.), *Études préliminaires aux religions orientales dans l'Empire romain*. Leiden 1961-1990
FGrH	Jacoby, F. (ed.), *Fragmente der griechischen Historiker*. Berlin 1923-
FIRA	S. Riccobono, *Fontes Iuris Romani Anteiustiniani* (2nd ed). Firenze 1963
GettyMusJ	The J. Paul Getty Museum Journal

GiornItFil	Giornale italiano di filologia
GRBM	Greek, Roman and Byzantine Monographs
GRBS	Greek, Roman and Byzantine Studies
HSClPh	Harvard Studies in Classical Philology
HAW	Handbuch der Altertumswissenschaft
ID	Inscriptions de Délos
IG	Inscriptiones Graecae
IG Rom.	Inscriptiones Graecae ad res Romanas pertinentes. Paris 1906-1927
IGSK	Inschriften griechischer Städte aus Kleinasien. Bonn 1972-
IJG	Inscriptiones Juridicorum Graecae
IllinClSt	Illinois Classical Studies
Isis	Isis. An International Review Devoted to the History of Science and its Cultural Influences
IstMitt	Mitteilungen des Deutschen Archäologischen Instituts, Abteilung Istanbul
JAOS	Journal of the American Oriental Society
JBrArchAss	Journal of the British Archaeological Association
JdI	Jahrbuch des Deutschen Archäologischen Instituts
JEarlyCSt	Journal of Early Christian Studies
JHistB	Journal of the History of Biology
JHistSex	Journal of the History of Sexuality
JHS	Journal of Hellenic Studies
JNES	Journal of Near Eastern Studies
JPCult	Journal of Popular Culture
JSav	Journal des Savants
Ker	*Kerameikos. Ergebnisse der Ausgrabung.* Berlin
L'homme	L'homme. Revue française d'anthropologie
LibAnt	Libya Antiqua
LIMC	Lexicon Iconographicum Mythologiae Classicae
LSJ	*A Greek-English Lexicon* compiled by H.G. Liddell & R. Scott. Revised and augmented by H. Stuart Jones
MedArch	Mediterranean Archaeology. Australian and New Zealand Journal for the Archaeology of the Mediterranean World
MEFRA	Mélanges de l'École française de Rome. Antiquité
MemAPhilSoc	Memoirs of the American Philosophical Society
MemLinc	Memorie. Atti della Accademia nazionale dei Lincei

Michel	Michel, Ch., *Recueil d'inscriptions grecques*. Paris/ Bruxelles 1900
MusHelv	Museum Helveticum
NSc	Notizie degli scavi di antichità
OGIS	Dittenberger, W., Orientis Graeci Inscriptiones Selectae. Leipzig 1903-1905
OJA	Oxford Journal of Archaeology
ÖJh	Jahreshefte des Österreichischen Archäologischen Institutes in Wien
Olynthus	*Excavations at Olynthus*. Baltimore
Orientalia	Orientalia. Commentarii periodici Pontificii Instituti Biblici. Roma
Page, PMG	Page, D.L., *Poetae Melici Graeci*. Oxford 1962
Pallas	Pallas. Revue d'études antiques, Toulouse
Para	Beazley, J.D., *Paralipomena. Additions to Attic Black-Figure Vase-Painters and to Attic Red-Figure Vase-Painters*. Oxford 1971
PastPres	Past and Present: a Journal of Historical Studies
PCG	Kassel, R. & Austin, C. *Poetae comici Graeci*. Berlin/New York 1984-
PCPhS	Proceedings of the Cambridge Philological Society
PhilWoch	Philologische Wochenschrift
QuadUrbin	Quaderni urbinati di cultura classica
RA	Revue archéologique
RE	Pauly, A. & Wissowa, G. Real-Encyclopädie der classischen Altertumswissenschaft
REA	Revue des études anciennes
REG	Revue des études grecques
RevFSoc	Revue française de Sociologie
RendNap	Rendiconti dell'Accademia di archeologia, lettere e belle arti, Napoli
RevEspLing	Revista española de linguística
RGVV	Religionsgeschichtliche Versuche und Vorarbeiten
RHistRel	Revue de l'histoire des religions
RhM	Rheinisches Museum für Philologie
RM	Mitteilungen des Deutschen Archäologischen Instituts, Römische Abteilung

RM-ErgH	Mitteilungen des Deutschen Archäologischen Instituts, Römische Abteilung. Ergänzungsheft
RPhil	Revue de philologie, de littérature et d'histoire anciennes
Roscher, Lex	Roscher, W.H. Ausführliches Lexikon der griechischen und römischen Mythologie 1-6, 1884-1937
SB	Preisigke, F., Bilabel, F. & Kiessling, E. *Sammelbuch griechischer Urkunden aus Ägypten.* Göttingen/Strasbourg/Berlin 1915-
SBBerlin	Sitzungsberichte der Deutschen Akademie der Wissenschaften zu Berlin
SBHeidelberg	Sitzungsberichte der Heidelberger Akademie der Wissenschaften. Phil.-hist. Kl.
SEG	Supplementum epigraphicum Graecum
SGDI	Collitz, H., *Sammlung der griechischen Dialekt-Inschriften.* Göttingen 1884-1915
SHC	Studies in Hellenistic Civilization- Aarhus 1990-
SIG	Dittenberger, W., Sylloge Inscriptionum Graecarum (3rd ed.). Leipzig 1915-1924
StClOr	Studi classici e orientali
StItFilCl	Studi italiani di filologia classica
SVF	von Arnim, H., Stoicorum veterum fragmenta. Leipzig 1903-1924
TAM	Tituli Asiae Minoris. Wien 1901-1989
TAPhA	Transactions and Proceedings of the American Philological Association
TAPhSoc	Transactions of the American Philosophical Society
TrZ	Trierer Zeitschrift für Geschichte und Kunst des Trierer Landes und seiner Nachbargebiete
Tyche	Tyche. Beiträge zur Alten Papyrologie und Epigraphik
Vichiana	Vichiana. Rassegna di studi filologici e storici
VigilChrist	Vigiliae Christianae. A Review of Early Christian Life and Language. Amsterdam
VisRel	Visible Religion. Annual for Religious Iconography
WSt	Wiener Studien
YaleClSt	Yale Classical Studies
ZA	Zeitschrift für Assyriologie und vorderasiatische Archäologie
ZPE	Zeitschrift für Papyrologie und Epigraphik

INTRODUCTION

The present volume is the latest in a series of proceedings of five international conferences held as part of the Danish interdisciplinary research project on the Hellenistic period sponsored in 1989-1995 by the *Danish Research Council for the Humanities*. At the first three conferences focus was on a blend of a specific theme and a particular geographical perspective: *Religion and Religious Practice in the Seleucid Kingdom* (published 1990, repr. 1996), *Ethnicity in Hellenistic Egypt* (1992), *Centre and Periphery in the Hellenistic World* (1993, repr. 1996). At the last two conferences our focus was exclusively thematic. Here we had chosen two topics intended to cover central parts of the Hellenistic experience, as it were at either end of the spectrum: *Aspects of Hellenistic Kingship* (1996) and the "conventional values" discussed in this volume. The conference on which this last volume is based took place at Rungstedgaard near Copenhagen 25-28 January 1995.

Background

The stimulus for the conference was the realization that the picture of the Hellenistic period given in modern scholarship is full of stereotypes. Who has not heard of the "growing individualism" characteristic of the age, the increase in "anxiety vis-à-vis blind fate", the "breakdown of traditional values", "cosmopolitism" and the like? As always, there is some truth in such stereotypes. Also there is some distortion. The modern stereotypes are of course attempts to formulate what appear to us to be basic features of the period when seen in comparison with what comes before and after. But how did people living in that age understand their world themselves? That was the question we chose to focus on over a wide range of topics and from as many scholarly perspectives as possible.

What we wanted to elucidate were "values" in the sense in which an anthropologist might use the term: perceptions of the world around the individual, and of the individual in relation to that world, which will *eo ipso* be "value-laden" or experienced as having normative force. Basically, how did the various perceptions of the world and the individual over a wide range of issues (see below) hang together so as to produce some kind of coherent world picture? And what were the normative orientations in that picture? Of course, we might expect to find many different world pictures of this kind. Identifying them and determining their location (social or otherwise) would be an important part of the task.

Basically, what we were looking for were the "conventional" world pictures of those people who (because of the nature of the evidence) are literally "the silent majority". Most often their values are reflected only incidentally in the written sources, since these regularly formulate a view that is special, more or less idiosyncratic or at least particularly carefully worked out. In relation to the written sources, we saw the task as twofold: either to follow up on incidental indications of the views of "the many", or else to go for such "special" views which, for one reason or another, would appear to allow for generalization. Not all carefully worked out and distinct views need be idiosyncratic. Some might even be thought to formulate a wider underlying set of perceptions. Still, types of (written or non-written) sources that do not lay claim to being "carefully worked out" in the above sense would, of course, receive special attention.

The Danish research project on the Hellenistic period defined its chronological framework as going from Alexander to Hadrian, though with special emphasis on the period traditionally labelled "Hellenistic", between Alexander and Augustus. This whole period was meant to be a focus at the conference too. But contributors were asked not to concentrate on the period after Augustus *alone*. Instead, they might choose a topic that was either restricted to the Hellenistic period proper or else covered the period both before and after Augustus. In such cases great caution would of course be required in order to avoid anachronism. Still, it was felt that the inclusion of the later period might also help to focus attention on the question of any (gradual) changes between the Hellenistic age proper and the Imperial age.

With this broadening of the chronological frame we combined a restriction of the geographical or, better, cultural frame. The people on whom we aimed to focus, even in the Roman period, were the "Hellenistic Greeks", understood as those living or at least culturally based in the "Hellenistic heartland" that was created by Alexander and his immediate successors and was centred on the Eastern Mediterranean. Writers should not, of course, be left out just because they lived, for instance, in Rome. Rather, irrespective of their geographical location, they might be included to the extent that they belonged basically within the cultural tradition of the Hellenistic heartland. Conversely, they should not be chosen as primary targets of investigation if they did not belong within that tradition. Thus, for instance, Epictetus would belong to the first category, but the younger Pliny writing in Bithynia would belong to the second. Roman writers (to the west) and Jewish writers (to the east) might be included as sources for "Hellenistic Greek" phenomena, but since they would also always have a "Roman" or "Jewish" identity, they were not allowed to be in primary focus. Thus, for instance, Seneca, Josephus and any early Christian writer would be excluded, no matter how "Hellenized" they might otherwise have been.

In our instructions to contributors we proposed to break down the issues that the conference was intended to cover in a number of points.

1. *Issues of basic cultural identity ("We and the others")*
(a) Horizontal: How do we differ from the others?
For example: The perception, on the part of the Hellenistic Greeks, of the Jews. What do the various Hellenistic accounts of the Jews tell us about Greek self-understanding?

Or: The Greek reaction to the Romans. What does, for example, Polybius or Dionysius of Halicarnassus on Romans and Greeks tell us about Greek self-understanding? Can anything be learned from developments in art, city planning and the like, once the Romans had appeared on the Greek scene?
(b) Vertical: How do we differ from our fathers?
For example: Do we meet different types of perception of the cultural products of fifth and fourth century Athens as "classics" throughout the period? Are there similarities in the patterns one can trace in different disciplines?

Or: Is there a pattern in whatever traces we may find in views of the development of civilization as either one of progress or one of decline?

2. *The world view ("Our world")*
For example: How many cosmologies do we find? Is it possible to locate them socially and chronologically?

Or: How widespread was a belief in demons? Can we see a development in this area? The same questions may be raised for astrology and magic. And what about life after death? Was it a widespread belief or the opposite? To be located where?

3. *Political understanding ("Our political system")*
For example: How does our political system compare (a) with that of other people, (b) with that of our fathers?

Or: Were the Hellenistic Greeks defeatist vis-à-vis political issues? Did they have any special views about war? Was it something to be avoided? Or was it rather something to be won?

4. *Social understanding ("We and the others in our world")*
For example: Who is responsible for the situation which poor people are in?
Or: Is poverty bad? Is there anything wrong with wealth? Is "Hellenistic

culture" a culture of the city? Do we see changing views of the countryside and life in it? What is the rôle of the family, the status of women, the status of slaves? What are the social perceptions of sex? Is Hellenistic society an "honour society"? What about patronage and clienthood?

5. *The understanding of the individual ("I and them")*
For example: Are there indications of a heightened perception of "individuality" in the Hellenistic period? In psychological vocabulary? In literary descriptions of individuals? In the rôle allotted to individuals in politics and social relations?

Or: Did individuals feel in some specific way "bound" by extra-individual factors? Do we find indications of an experience of alienation?

Contributors were encouraged to select their topic in the light of these questions, which were meant only as specimens, and of their own scholarly disciplines. They were also encouraged to settle on some fairly sharply defined group of source material, but in the hope that the group would either be relatively large or else with great generalizing potential. The focus should not be on the material treated just as such, but on what it might tell us more generally about the conventional values of the period.

The present volume
Thus our proposal. The present volume catalogues the results. The essays may at first sight appear a very mixed bag. It is also evident that many of the questions we asked have been touched only in passing, or not at all. With eleven papers to cover this field, the result could hardly be otherwise. We have chosen to present the essays here in a manner that reflects some of the main categories in, or underlying, the Hellenistic world view. From the city (Pauline Schmitt Pantel) and the ruler (Burkhard Fehr) we pass to religion (Giulia Sfameni Gasparro, Dale H. Martin) and magic and astrology (Richard Gordon, David Konstan); from there to everyday life (Konstan again, Tomas Hägg) and social relations, including the family and gender questions (Sarah Pomeroy, Sanne Houby-Nielsen, Halvor Moxnes) in order to conclude finally with death (Lise Hannestad). This order has not much more than a specious logic to it. In fact, there are numerous lines of contact crossing from one essay to the other. We would like to pinpoint here some of the overlapping issues.

Whose values? What sources?
A recurrent theme throughout the essays concerns the relationship between the

values of the majority of the population (the "masses") and those of the élite. Almost all the scholars writing in this volume have sought the values of the masses. Throughout, the focus lies on trying to identify majority values, either in contradistinction to those of the élite or else as shared by high and low — but then distinctly also those of the latter. However, in the case of élite groups, too, one may distinguish between conventional, more or less hackneyed views and more individually elaborated ones. This dimension of conventionality is also represented in the volume. In both cases the issue is evidently closely linked with the question of what sources to use.

The essay by Pauline Schmitt Pantel introduces the double problem of conventionality and sources that runs through almost all the other essays. Schmitt Pantel bases her analysis of the public feasts in the Hellenistic Greek cities on inscriptional material, since these give us direct access, she claims, to the values of the majority. She also notes in passing that other types of archaeological material might be of use too, thereby claiming an important rôle for archaeology in helping us to grasp conventional values. In addition to the inscriptions, Schmitt Pantel draws on literary texts, which she takes to express the Greeks' own reflections on the majority values. The texts adduced are those by historians, who in their reconstructions of the past attempted to give meaning to, and so implicitly recognized the existence of, the practices evidenced by the inscriptions. Finally, Schmitt Pantel addresses an individual literary author, Plutarch, suggesting that as a philosopher and a moralist he was no neutral observer but had agendas of his own which discount him as a proper witness to majority values. Three different types of source, then, are being considered. Two are admitted as evidence for conventional values of the majority, one is discounted.

The relationship between inscriptional and literary evidence is in focus in other essays in the volume. Thus in her discussion of demonology and the cults of the Good Daimon and Tuche, Giulia Sfameni Gasparro sees inscriptions as having a popular aspect and as evidence for the beliefs and practices widespread within the population. Literary texts, by contrast, have an intellectual aspect. They express the writers' own interpretations and are a product of reflection or even systematic theory-building by individuals and philosophical schools. Still, Gasparro contends that, at least within her chosen field, the gap is not unbridgeable. There is a perceptible connection, she claims, with popular belief. Indeed, the demonology that she traces back to Hesiod should be seen as a collective representation shared by both ordinary people and the learned. Here Plutarch, too, makes an appearance. In contrast to Schmitt Pantel, however, Gasparro sees him as a representative of the common tradition and the majority view. Both may be right in relation to their specific topics, but this highlights some of the difficulties in using the source material for our purpose.

Another essay that focuses on the relationship between inscriptional and literary evidence is that of Sarah Pomeroy. In her discussion of possible changes in family structures, values and behaviour in the Hellenistic period, inscriptions are taken as evidence for actual changes in the lived reality of ordinary people and hence also for a new set of conventional values and contrasted with official documents such as census reports. These, Pomeroy suggests, reflect a conservative, nostalgic and idealizing influence by certain philosophers who represented either an idiosyncratic view of a single philosopher or else a philosophers' group view that was far removed from that of ordinary people.

The philosophers, indeed, come in for some criticism throughout the volume as providing evidence for conventional values. Halvor Moxnes is the exception, for whom Dio Chrysostom and Plutarch yield much relevant material on the changing understanding of masculinity in the first century AD. Moxnes stresses that the moralist views of Dio and Plutarch were basically conventional in character, but he is specifically interested in the views on masculinity held by the kind of people that were directly addressed in the writings of the two moralists. This audience belonged to the educated élite, not the masses. Thus, what Moxnes examines are not the conventional values of the latter but the values of the former, which in a somewhat different sense may also be called conventional: there are different types of conventionality, and different types of source may be employed to elucidate these.

In the essay by Dale Martin, scepticism towards the philosophers as representing conventional views is very clearly voiced. Indeed, Martin argues that the construal of *deisidaimonia* as "superstition" urged by certain philosophers reflects a basic upper-class social embeddedness of the philosophical discourse as a whole. Martin finds support for this view in a historian (Diodorus Siculus) who, being himself closer to the popular understanding of *deisidaimonia*, consistently portrays philosophers as arguing *against* popular beliefs. Nor is this just an idiosyncratic quirk of the philosophers with respect to *deisidaimonia* alone. It extends, Martin argues, to the whole underlying ideology of the intellectual professionals expressed in such notions as Greek (*hellênikê*) "culture" (*agôgê*) and "education" (*paideia*). Not just the philosophers, but the new medical professionals, too, should be seen as arguing against the beliefs of the rest of the population, including the more popular therapeuts of various sorts: healers, exorcists, root-cutters, magicians, astrologers, omen-readers, seers. Thus Martin's essay focuses on the majority values and the crucial question of which sources to use and how.

This perspective is to some extent shared by Richard Gordon in his discussion of the discursive, dogmatic texts of the Hellenistic period on magic and astrology. Gordon sees these texts as aiming to clear a space between traditional belief and practice, taken to be more or less tacit and incoherent, and trends in Hellenistic cosmology, for instance Epicureanism and scepticism, that tended towards rationalism and agnosticism. Here, too, the views of the philosophers are seen as having been in confrontation with those of ordinary folk, though not necessarily because they were informed by any underlying social agendas, as Martin saw it. On the other hand, Gordon emphasizes the scientific claims to precise and infallible knowledge made by the texts he studies and thinks that they, too, addressed themselves to what was in fact only a fraction of the élite. It is not correct, Gordon thinks, to see their intended readership as consisting of the "not totally uneducated but simply not intellectually trained". On the contrary, a certain level of intellectual training must have been presupposed. The upshot is that while the discursive texts on magic and astrology were in fact directed against certain views of the philosophers, and presumably also of the new medical professionals, they are not just an unproblematic reflection of conventional representations, but a thorough reworking of traditional lore. By seeking to systematize and partially rationalize traditional practices, they took a step from the real world of the root-cutters (etc.), of whom, so Gordon thinks, there were hardly more in the Hellenistic world than before or after, to the (fancied) world of the magi and astrologers. In Gordon's case too, the texts must be used with great caution as evidence for conventional views.

In his discussion of one of these astrological treatises David Konstan, in effect, agrees. Konstan, too, emphasises the interest his text takes in scientific precision as against a need for reassuring superstition. And he considers its function to be that of giving instructions to the novice astrologer, the would-be professional. This presupposes an educated readership for the treatise. But when Konstan looks at the kinds of questions that will be put to the astrologer once he has graduated, he finds that they do not after all reflect only the higher strata of society, but also a broader segment of the population ranging upwards from something like lower middle class. Konstan in fact locates the astrologer's clients centrally in the urban environment of the Greek *polis*: municipal and perhaps commercially minded. Thus Konstan, too, bears witness to the caution with which the literary texts must be used for arriving at the conventional values of this or the other group in the social hierarchy.

A municipal setting is also most appropriate for the main section of the *Life of Aesop* that Tomas Hägg studies. Here we may actually catch a glimpse of the conventional views of people ranging from middle class and downwards. Again we meet the difference between text and audience. While Hägg shows that the author must himself have had a formal schooling, he allows that the audience may have been primarily popular. This is mainly due to the tone of the *Life*, which Hägg compares with Aristophanic comedy. In fact the values expressed in the *Life* on which Hägg focuses — towards slaves, women and intellectuals (philosophers) — may have been shared by high and low — except, presumably, by the philosophers themselves. As for them, we do seem to be presented here with an appreciation of the philosophers, or rather the lack of it, as seen from below. What they are criticized for is not any kind of rationalism that is taken to threaten the religious beliefs of ordinary people. Rather, they are ridiculed, quite conventionally so, for their pomposity and boasted education, their moralizing and their stinginess.

The three archaeological contributions to the volume reflect the complexity of the search for conventional values of the majority even within a single source group. Thus, when Burkhard Fehr looks for the iconographical meaning of one of the major archaeological monuments of the period, the great frieze of the Pergamum Altar, what he finds is certainly a message that will have been congenial to the king who paid for the altar, and so to the élite. But it is also likely, as Fehr shows, that it will have appealed to some very general values that will have been shared by high and low, even cross-culturally. Who did not agree that harmony and co-operation among blood relatives as well as the continuous procreation of numerous and excellent offspring were vitally important for the internal peace, defence and permanent existence of a community? Here, then, we may perhaps take a single source as evidence for an overlap of values at least across social boundaries, not unlike the situation described by Sfameni Gasparro.

Similarly, when Lise Hannestad describes the iconography of grave steles on the funerary island of second to first-century Delos, it is certainly noteworthy (Hannestad's main point) that their iconography is wholly standardized, even though the deceased had widely different ethnic backgrounds and came from widely different places all over the Mediterranean. In contrast to this uniformity in death, the archaeological monuments of Delos of the living suggest that at least larger groups of foreigners tended to organize themselves religiously in separate units.

Another apparent contradiction in the message of the archaeological material — between the iconography of Attic grave reliefs in Athens in the fourth century BC and the actual grave gifts buried with the deceased — is a key issue in Sanne Houby-Nielsen's contribution.

Thus, not only the contributions based on the literary and inscriptional material but also the archaeological contributions highlight some of the difficulties that the source material presents us with in our search for conventional values.

Political, social and mental change

Values are by definition a mental phenomenon. But they need not always be clear to those who hold them, indeed they most often are not. Correspondingly, they are very often expressed in actions and practices, as much as in any explicitly stated beliefs. One result of this state of affairs is that the external situations in which people act — be they socially or politically defined — very often influence people's minds and so contribute to a change in their (mental) values. When one is examining conventional values, it is therefore highly appropriate also to study the social and political situations in which the values are embedded and to try to situate these values in explicit relation to any changes in the social and political context.

This general framework is, explicitly or implicitly, presupposed in all the essays. Indeed, it may even be said to reflect a conventional view of all scholars working on the Hellenistic period, a view that also triggered the search for the conventional values of the period that gave rise to the conference on which the present volume is based. Very briefly, it seems *a priori* likely that the striking political changes brought about by Alexander will also have had important social consequences and that both political and social changes will also have influenced people's values and mentality.

Sfameni Gasparro exemplifies this expectation when she explains a number of phenomena in the fourth century BC relating to the Good Daimon and Tuche (e.g. the increased interest in both figures in that century against a background of interest that stretches back to Hesiod, the development of their cult, their coupling as a pair, etc.), as a result of a crisis of traditional political and social institutions that she takes to have preceded the new politico-cultural order of the Hellenistic age. Similarly, in explanation of the importance attached to public feasts, Schmitt Pantel, too, invokes the new political situation in which, she claims, the city had hardly any means of expressing itself as an entity.

These claims remain at a fairly general level. The relationship between political events and social developments is brought more directly into focus in Pomeroy's discussion of changes in family structures. Some changes that Pomeroy detects are the direct results of the violent political events in the half century after Alexander's rise to power: the migration of widows without kinsmen, the occurrence of bigamy and even trigamy in Egypt among Greek soldiers, etc. But Pomeroy also makes the important observation that changes in social structure often come about slowly following on more rapid and striking political events. To this we may add that changes in the underlying mentalities occur even more slowly. Pomeroy herself gives an example of this in her discussion of a funerary foundation set up by a woman who had apparently no male relatives to help her do so. Still, in the pattern she followed she attempted to adhere to the traditional, androcentric pattern for that kind of institution.

The relationship between political change, social change and mental change is also at the centre of Moxnes' essay. Analysing the views of masculinity as a public virtue that are voiced in the writings of Dio Chrysostom, he connects the issue of manhood very closely with the social category of honour and shame and shows how this social category needed to be filled in in new ways in the Greek cities of the Eastern Mediterranean in the first century AD due, precisely, to the political change for which the Romans were responsible. With manhood at the top of one hierarchy of social values in antiquity and therefore also as one very significant component of the social value of honour, a reinterpretation of manhood was called for when the category of honour itself had to be reinterpreted in response to the new political circumstances. More concretely, the old "hero" ideals of the warrior no longer sufficed to define manhood and male honour when the political circumstances no longer called centrally for war. Instead, Moxnes argues, more peaceful ways to gain honour came to be recognized and masculinity became more a matter of a man's character in terms of a whole number of categories traditionally celebrated by the moralists: self-possession, prudence, self-sufficiency, trustworthiness, etc. One important consequence, Moxnes suggests, was that within marriage, women too got the chance of coming more into their own as independent persons. With manhood now being defined in a way which made it possible for women, too, to attain to it, women became able to enter into a friendship with men in marriage on something like equal terms. In this way, Moxnes concludes, we must allow for subtle, but still recognizable changes in mentality from the classical period to the Hellenistic age.

Houby-Nielsen examines the female and male ideals of the fourth century and the Hellenistic period. In contrast to the old male and female values, she observes that in the grave gifts, which she assumes to be women's work, there is a gradual shift from the strong emphasis on the woman as a mother towards an under-standing of her as a sexual being. The strigil, which had earlier symbolized the man (particularly the young man), is now often found in female graves, and the mirror, which formerly symbolized the bride, is now also found in male graves. Together with the growing importance in the Hellenistic period of the public bath (leading to the Roman thermae), beautification of the body is an aspect of changed conventional values in Athenian society as compared with the early classical period.

Uses of the past

A theme that runs through several essays is the Hellenistic use of the past. Schmitt Pantel shows how in thinking about political structures in terms of manners at table the Hellenistic Greeks made such an emphatic use of their own past that one may well speak of a reconstruction or even invention of it. This seems to be a characteristic feature of the Hellenistic period, one of which innumerable examples might be given in all cultural fields of the period.

In Schmitt Pantel's case it is historians who are thinking of the past in order to throw light on present political ideals. They would presumably primarily represent ideals of the ruling élite. How far down that idealization would be accepted is not clear. In fact, Pomeroy makes a case for ascribing use of the past in political propaganda precisely to the ruling élite (and whichever philosophers served them). Here, as in Martin's essay, the ideological contributions of intellectuals mainly appear to have had the conservative aim of repressing new tentative forms of social practice.

However, there can be no doubt that the past played a crucial rôle more generally in giving the Hellenistic Greeks a sense of their own identity, no matter where in the social hierarchy they belonged. This is of course the "positive" side of the function of public feasting that Schmitt Pantel highlights, the one connected with (re-)constituting the community and (re-)establishing a collective memory. Traces of this non-repressive use of the past make their appearance elsewhere in the volume. An example is that — as shown by Hannestad — the second and first century grave reliefs of the community on Delos all draw on the visual language of fourth century Attic funerary reliefs, no matter of what ethnic extraction the deceased may have been. Similarly, Houby-Nielsen demonstrates the tension between the (new) values expressed "below ground" in the grave gifts and the traditional civic values expressed "above ground" on the grave reliefs. The Greek past was there and it had to be negotiated in one way or the other.

This theme is so important that another conference might well be staged on *Hellenistic Uses of the Past*, but even the present volume contains a sufficient number of pointers to the various perspectives that make it an especially fruitful topic for further exploration.

The Greeks and the others

As already noted, the aim of the conference was to focus specifically on the

Hellenistic Greeks themselves, in contrast to all the other peoples living in the Greek lands during the Hellenistic period. In a way, the distinction is artificial. One thing that makes the Hellenistic period so fascinating is the fact that it was an age of change and cultural fusion which allows the scholar to study the ways in which different ethnic and cultural traditions may become attracted to each other, blend and again reject each other. We feel, however, that the one-sided strategy has paid off well. We did not ask for attempts to look at how Greeks and their non-Greeks neighbours negotiated their shared life.

Interestingly, however, two corners of the issue are in fact illuminated in two of the archaeological contributions (Fehr, Hannestad). Should we take this as a sign that whereas the artificial distinction between the Hellenistic Greeks themselves and the others may well be upheld when one considers, for instance, literary texts, it breaks down when one is looking at the physical surroundings? For here the presence of others was an actual fact that could not be neglected. In any case, Fehr shows how the gigantomachy on the great frieze of the Pergamum Altar may be interpreted as having a meaning fitting propaganda directed at a multicultural population. The medium was of course Greek, but the message of this piece of official propaganda may have been cosmopolitan, with the frieze functioning as a trilingual iconic text. In striking contrast to this, Hannestad shows that whereas Delos of the living may have allowed for ethnic differentiation in its daily life, Delos of the dead apparently did not. Why?

In another respect too, one would like to see more on the relationship of the Hellenistic Greeks with non-Greeks. (Compare, however, *Ethnicity in Hellenistic Egypt*, which focuses on this issue for the limited geographical area of Egypt.) What were the (conventional) views of the Hellenistic Greeks of those closer or more distant "others" with whom they came into contact: how did they think about them? And what light does their way of differentiating themselves from them throw on how they understood themselves? As Schmitt Pantel notes, the Hellenistic Greeks used their own past as the "other" against whom to define themselves. But of course they also continued to use real "others" for the same purpose.

Morality

Ethics and morality are, let us say, not the same thing. Whereas ethics is the name of a philosophical discipline and hence very much a matter of reflection, morality is a name for the normative system, on matters related to the individual and the others, which finds expression in beliefs and practices that are not themselves directly formed by extended, systematic reflection. To a very large extent the

Introduction

normative system of morality is "conventional" and traditional, something people grow into in growing up. It has no doubt been formed by reflection, not just of a philosophical kind but also through the intervention of politicians, historians, educators and (in antiquity) last, but certainly not least, poets. Still, at any particular moment it is first and foremost present as a set of practices and unreflected beliefs. In that form, the "morality" of a given period is a crucially important component of the period's conventional values.

In his essay Konstan focuses on the questions that people will have put to the astrologer, obviously with a view to obtaining a "good life". What is it that determines whether one's life will be a good one? Here is one list: sexual style, wealth or poverty, number of children, success in marriage or business, health or sickness, slavery or freedom, profession, personal continence, character traits. Here is another list extracted from Konstan's discussion: support from kings and nobility, service at the courts of kings, leadership (of men and armies, in business), sickliness and loss of inherited property, generosity, effeminacy, greed, skill in crafts, shamelessness, stammering, self-reliance, stewardship for kings, leadership of the community or city, or position of judge, or secretary for potentates, death of brothers, career as teacher, as magician or thief, overseer for kings, intercourse with one's brothers' wives or one's mother (and conversely for women), love of wine and a swollen liver, poor hearing, eye problems, suicide. A summary of Konstan's findings might look like this: Life revolves around inheritance, marriage, children, business (seafaring), wealth and health. Concerns rarely extend beyond the nuclear family to more distant kin, fellow citizens, or friends. Everything centres upon the patrimonial estate. Marriage is a mutual matter, and sexual excess or romantic involvement play only a minor part, except for their potential effect on the stability of the household. The emphasis is on constancy rather than on "true love". Trade or commerce may take one far from home, but the hope is to return again to the familial domain as soon as possible. What Konstan has captured here is a conventional morality which centres on wealth, health and personal freedom and on a stable relationship within the nuclear family.

The picture of family life that emerges from Hägg's description of the relationships between the philosopher-husband, the wife and the slave in the *Life of Aesop* is closely similar. Both also remind one strongly of the picture of the life of ordinary Athenians given by the speech-writer Lysias in the first decades of the fourth century BC — and then one is reminded of a modern book whose aim with regard to fourth century Athens was not unlike the present search for the Hellenistic conventional values: Sir Kenneth Dover's *Greek Popular Morality in the Time of Plato and Aristotle* (1974). Should we conclude that, in spite of the major political upheavals due to Alexander, the basic understanding of what qualifies as the "good life" of the individual remained essentially the same? Or is it rather that what one might call family values are so (relatively) "timeless" that if one focuses specifically on them under the heading of "morality" one will always come up with something similar?

Another issue that arises is the relationship between the lived morality of family values and the views about the good and moral life that philosophers were putting forward at the very same time. For the Hellenistic period, the Stoics were prominent spokesmen for a form of the good life that was to some extent at variance with the picture of the good life found in those other texts. Similarly, as Dover's title indicates, Plato and Aristotle were themselves around when people were giving expression outside philosophy to the kind of popular morality that Dover depicts. And if we go back to Lysias, that single philosopher was still around who laid the foundation for the whole ethical tradition of the Greeks down to Marcus Aurelius and beyond — Socrates. So, what was the relationship between that reflective tradition and lived morality?

To some extent the reflective tradition saw itself in opposition to the lived morality. When Socrates urged his fellow Athenians to turn their minds from so-called external goods (e.g. wealth, health and social status) to the internal good of the soul, that is, to the virtues, he was attempting to reform them, even though he (and Plato) had little hope of success. This relationship between the philosophers' aim and the conventional views on morality is confirmed in Hägg's essay when the philosopher-husband is shown to be socially debilitated by his own ethical teaching. He teaches self-control and moral conversion (*metanoia*) — and is for that very reason unable to punish his slave by striking him, as everyone expected him to.

In one way, then, the ethicists were in opposition to the kind of lived morality described by Konstan and Hägg. This of course shows only that the latter was what actually guided people's lives. But the ethicists may still be relevant for the search for conventional moral values. For they are perhaps best seen as trying to develop, rather than reform, the ordinary normative views in a direction that both gave them all the credit they could call for and also integrated them into a larger view of the good life that would finally cover all human aspirations. In that case even the texts of the ethicists may be taken to throw light on the ordinary normative views.

Moxnes' essay shows some of the complexity in this area. Discussing the change in the understanding of manhood as a public virtue that one may detect in the works of Dio Chrysostom, Moxnes shows how a large group of states of a man's character, in fact the "moral virtues" so beloved by the ethicists, came to play an important rôle in the construction of manhood that Dio is offering to his addressees as their best bet for the good life. A list of the relevant character states as given by Moxnes runs as follows: civic responsibility, self-sufficiency, independence, trustworthiness, sincerity, liberality, a high-minded nature free from anger, seriousness, education and reason, temperance, modesty, self-restraint, justice and every virtue. What the ethicist Dio is saying is this: Your situation, gentlemen, is now such that letting these states of character form you is your best bet for the good life. This is at present the best way for you to gain honour and to attain to true manhood. In making this claim Dio is obviously engaged in moral exhortation, but what Moxnes brings out is the fact that this particular kind of ("moral") advice was apparently felt by Dio's addressees to be appropriate to the actual situation in which they found themselves. And so they are likely to have adopted the ethicist's values as their own, conventional values.

Again it is possible to be suspicious. Is not Dio, as already noted, addressing people who precisely belonged to the élite? Is it likely that people lower down on the social scale would feel the same set of values to be appropriate to their own situation? And if they did, would that not be because they had been brainwashed by those higher up in the hierarchy to make these values their own? That question should be left hanging. Suffice it to say that the relationship between the normative views of the ethicists and those contained in the moral practices of ordinary people may be considerably more complex than might initially have been expected. Once more we are being reminded of the point from which we began these summarizing remarks: that it matters crucially whose conventional values are being looked for and what sources are being used to bring them out.

It remains to thank the Danish Research Council for the Humanities for support for the conference and for publication of this volume. Thanks are also due to Tobias Fischer-Hansen, MA, for his extensive editorial work on the volume and for compiling the indices; to Dr. Richard Gordon for valuable help with the English and for translating the two essays by Schmitt Pantel and Sfameni Gasparro; and to Dr. Tønnes Bekker-Nielsen of Aarhus University Press for the patience and care with which he has overseen production of the book.

October 1996   *The Editors*

PUBLIC FEASTS IN THE
HELLENISTIC GREEK CITY:
FORMS AND MEANINGS

Pauline Schmitt Pantel

My route into the theme of the conference as set out in the introduction to the volume, that is, the nature of the system of values shared by most Greeks of the Hellenistic period, will be to take an example of a particular social practice, the institution of the public feast.[1] There are several reasons for such a choice.

First, public feasting was an institution that endured at least from the Homeric period until well into the Principate, and through it one can trace the shifts and continuities characteristic of the Hellenistic period: despite what is often said, it is a collective practice with a real history.

Second, the sources for the study of public feasts in the Hellenistic period are very diverse. The archaeological study of private and public spaces for feasting has made considerable progress over the past few years — witness the numerous publications relating to rooms for feasts in sanctuaries.[2] Moreover, archaeologists are tending to revise their views of certain buildings which are now thought to reveal architectural features typical of rooms for feasting. It must also be remembered that there may simply not be any archaeological traces of places where feasts took place, since any building, indeed any reasonably open space within a city, might temporarily be turned into a place for a feast — the prytaneum, the bouleuterion, theatres, agoras, gymnasia, open areas in or close by sanctuaries ... Such use of civic space for collective eating was not an invention of the Hellenistic world. It did exist before; but the inscriptions show that in the Hellenistic cities it became regular.

Archaeology may also reveal evidence of the furniture and equipment needed for feasts. Though the reclining couches (*klinê*) of wood, the cushions, coverlets and hangings have left scarcely any material remains, we know of their existence from the inventory-lists of temples, for example at Delos.[3] Quantities of tableware have sometimes been found on site, for example in the Kabirion near Thebes,[4] or in the Athenian agora.[5] Rubbish of all sorts, but above all the calcined bones of the animals consumed, also witnesses to such feasts.[6] To pursue all this various archaeological evidence in detail would take us too far afield, but there can be no doubt that for our theme the study of the material culture revealed by archaeology is an important facet of conventional values.

My intention is to deal solely with texts. There are two distinct groups, inscriptions and literary texts. They offer different but complementary information concerning the place of public feasts both in public and social life and in the world view (the system of representations) of Greeks in this period. They enable us to grasp both the views of the majority of the population, the masses, and those of the élite.

Third, the practice of feasting in public is rooted in the religious, social and political life of the cities, and for that reason is at the centre of the construction of a system of values characteristic of, and peculiar to, the Hellenistic world.

Before considering the significance of this last theme for my argument, however, I should give a thumbnail sketch of the public feast. A definition first. By "public feast" I mean meals attended by all the citizens or their representatives. That is of course a theoretical and general definition. Refracted through different source-materials, the superficial character of such public meals changed over time: for example, the public meals bestowed by euergetes upon Hellenistic cities are very different from the aristocratic banquets of the Archaic period; but in my view they are both public feasts. It is the community of citizens which in general lays down the rules for participation. Meals taken within the family, among groups of friends and within associations, fall outside my definition.

Throughout antiquity the public feast was closely linked with civic sacrifice, of which it formed the concluding stage. At the public meal people ate meat that had been ritually slaughtered and roasted.[7] The symbolic vision of the world that subtends ritual sacrifice in the Hellenistic world is fully consonant with that of earlier periods. The same holds good for the social function of the ritual, which is to reinforce the sense of belonging to the same community. Even if public feasts do not always take place in the context of a festival in honour of a particular deity, the religious meaning remains dominant. There is no sense at all in which one can discern any sign of disenchantment with civic religion. On the contrary, the rituals, constantly repeated, remained alive throughout the whole period.

Having stressed these two features, the attendance *en masse* of a politically-defined group of people, and the religious underpinning, I now take a closer look at the public feast in the Hellenistic cities. My chronological frame extends from the third century BC to the third century AD. My geographical frame is Greece proper, Magna Graecia, the Black Sea, and Asia Minor. My political frame is that of the Greek city. Numerous inscriptions provide us with information about public feasts. I propose generally to cite as illustration the inscription set out in the appendix to this article (p. 44f.), an honorific decree passed by the city of Cyme in the Aeolid in Asia Minor at the turn of the eras, in honour of an euergete named Cleanax.[8] In its provenance, Asia Minor, its date, and its genre, this document is fully typical of the source-material at our disposal.

1

The epigraphic material includes laws, regulations laid down by cities, dedications and private commemorations; but most usually we find honorific decrees which offer thanks to individuals for benefits conferred upon the city, and in particular for having bestowed a public feast. The character of these sources is germane to our larger topic: the decree is the public utterance of a city, having been passed by vote at an assembly of the citizens. It thus represents the opinion of a fairly large number of people about how public meals should be held. Such documents are without doubt less personal than literary texts, nearer to ordinary opinion. What do we learn from them? First, that the cities went on being concerned about the organisation of public feasts when they created or modified festivals. For instance, a law from Koressos lists in detail the duties of an euergete who gives a feast, including the standard of sacrificial animal required and the amount of meat each participant is to receive.[9] The city has regard for the use made of public funds, but is also anxious that custom shall be properly respected. Temple accounts, such as those from the sanctuary at Delos, also provide details of the number of participants and of the cost of everything to do with the preparation, even to that of the firewood. The Hellenistic inscriptions are the first to provide us with fairly precise information about the actual organisation of such feasts. In sum, the laws and rules make clear both the continuity between the Hellenistic public feast and earlier modes of commensality, and its continuing vitality and importance in the eyes of the cities. This is itself a sign that these public meals responded to a demand that was as much religious as social.

But the honorific decrees allow us to go a little further. Their purpose is to thank benefactors who have paid from their private purse for all kinds of expenses, from embassies to fortifications, from the supply of grain for daily consumption to oil for the gymnasia. One of the very most common types is the expression of gratitude to an euergete for organizing a public feast. That might of course simply be due to the vagaries of survival. But the mass of material may just as well reflect the popularity of this type of euergetic gesture among the city populations. If so, we would be faced with a fact revealed by texts stemming, if not from the population as a whole, at least from the citizen body, a fact requiring interpretation. Historians have hardly bothered themselves with it: for them, feasts are just useless philanthropy. This is to ignore the ideological rôle of the public banquet in the Hellenistic city. Far from distinguishing between useful and useless benefactions, that is, creating a hierarchy based on utility, the decrees show that the honour is bestowed by the city in consideration of the euergetic gestures as a whole.[10] The work of Paul Veyne, who takes the "thirst for feasts" as an aspect of the ludic character of Hellenistic society — people love festivals[11] — and of Oswyn Murray, stressing that pleasures, including that of drinking, exist independently of their social functions and are irreducible to these,[12] foregrounds an element too often neglected in ancient history. But if it cannot be denied that feasting offered pleasure and relaxation in a society in which daily life was often extremely penurious, we must in my view go further. Detailed attention to the occasions, the guests and the procedures reveals that banquets had a key place in the formation and reproduction of the social and political system. The decrees, public documents voted by a political community, give us an insight into the dominant collective view of the place of banquets in Hellenistic cities. This type of source is indispensable for the historian trying to reconstruct the value-system of a society as a whole.

This is not the place for a detailed account of the organisation and course of public feasts as revealed by the epigraphic evidence. Rather, I want to select a small number of characteristic features specially relevant to the subject of the colloquium. We may take the decree in honour of Cleanax as our starting point.

There is nothing unusual in the euergetic rôles assumed all through his life by Cleanax, nor in the honours decreed him by Cyme. Rather more so is the fact that he seems at one period of his life to have given public feasts whenever the opportunity arose: the inscription provides a good summary of several hundred inscriptions on the same topic. Cleanax naturally paid for all these feasts out of his own purse. The document does not say much about their actual organisation — that is not its main purpose, since the euergete himself saw to everything — in other cases, in which the community itself did the organizing, there are detailed prescriptions. Our decree names three places where the banquets were held, the sanctuary of Dionysus, the prytaneum and the agora, but, as noted above, any public area might be used for a banquet, while some cities possessed buildings for the purpose. Another venue, on the occasion of the marriage of his daughter, was probably his own house. Each location corresponds to a different type of banquet: the temple of Dionysus was used for the mysteries of Dionysus Pandemos, the prytaneum for more civic rituals such as entry into a public office, the agora for the *Caesarea*, the civic festival in honour of the emperor Augustus, when crowds of people from all over the province of Asia attended.

A sacrifice always took place before the banquet. The guests received meat, bread and wine, which is also normal. One odd dish is mentioned, in the context of the celebration of a festival for the dead, a porridge made from barley grains. There is no mention of presents being distributed, though this was sometimes done at banquets.

Most of the document is devoted to describing the euergete's qualities and benefactions, certain features of the banquets associated with the public office Cleanax held at the time, and the beneficiaries: in each case the list of those invited is different. This document, and the others like it, gives us an insight, through a quite commonplace institution, the invitation to a public meal, into a feature of Hellenistic social history which is quite different from the classical period. Thus Cleanax was priest of Dionysus Pandemos over several years, and held a banquet in that connection. He was *prutanis* and celebrated his entry into the office on the first day of the civic year with a distribution of wine and a feast. He also gave feasts at the religious festival of Corydon ("Day of the Lark"); after the solemn Laurel Procession; and on the occasion of the *Caesarea*. He showed the same open-handedness on the occasion of an event in his private life, the marriage of his daughter. Banquets might thus be given on a wide variety of occasions, and the inscriptions show that, though there are regularities, the circumstances and details depended upon the generosity of the benefactor.

The new phenomenon of euergetism had a profound influence on the rôle of public meals in the Greek city.[13] Until the late fourth century BC, public meals were the responsibility of the community of citizens: the administration of the liturgy of the *hestiasis* at Athens, for instance, was controlled entirely by the city. In the Hellenistic cities, the initiative in offering public feasts passed to individuals. They did so, admittedly, in the context of holding public offices — a priesthood, the agonothesia, gymnasiarchy, any sort of magistracy in fact. But it is the individuals who are thanked. These euergetes do not give just to be "kings of the feast" in Veyne's phrase, for the sheer pleasure of giving, but because this type of benefaction fosters their recognition as members of the city's ruling élite. The decrees often stress the political status of the giver; but of course behind that is his economic status, the wealth that was a precondition for this type of benefaction. For the city to recognise this openly is new by contrast with the classical period, and makes plain the shift in the means of defining the political élite. But at the same time, and here the Hellenistic city shows itself conservative, the euergete operates solely within the frame of the religious festival and public sacrifice. He is dependent upon this traditional expression of the community's identity.

Examination of the categories of guests, which are often, as in our text, carefully listed, offers a concrete image of Hellenistic sociability. At Cyme an anonymous crowd jostles at the marriage feast — this is a private event, so status and rank, the social distance between each individual, are not important. But rank is specified in the case of the other feasts. All free persons and even slaves — this is exceedingly uncommon — were invited to the feast in honour of the dead, which was in effect a festival of the *oikoi*, the households conceived as extending through time — a domestic rather than a political feast. Citizens, Romans, the *paroikoi* (resident foreigners) and *xenoi* (non-resident foreigners) were invited to the feasts in honour of Dionysus, on the Day of the Lark, and at the Caesarea. These three feasts are not truly political, since they are found widely in the Greek world, and were thus open to all free persons in the city. When Cleanax assumes office, he does not invite the same sets of people to the *glukismos* (light refreshments) and the feast. The guests at the *glukismos* are all free persons in the city; the feast in the prytaneum is attended only by numerous citizens and the Romans. The hierarchy is clearly set out, and extends symbolically also to the food that is eaten and the venue where it is eaten. A *glukismos*, at which one drank sweet wine and perhaps nibbled something, had not the same status as a feast at which one partook of sacrificial meat. This means of expressing social and political hierarchy through differentiated guest lists is not unique to Cyme: Priene, Stratonicea, Akraiphia, Eresus and other cities offer comparable examples.[14] Finally, at the celebration of the solemn Laurel Procession in honour of Apollo, only the priests, victors at the games, the magistrates and "numerous citizens" are present.

In the course of a few phrases, therefore, the decree makes clear that, in the city's eyes, the euergete has acted in a fitting manner; and that the rules of inclusion are different from one feast to another. The document is to an extent unusual in making such distinctions explicit; and we must be on our guard against generalizing from a single instance — knowing who was invited to one feast does not necessarily tell us who was invited to the whole set of feasts of a given city. But our text does hint at the complexity of the system of invitations in a single city, a complexity which fits neatly with local religious custom and its civic reflection.

The actual means by which the invitation was made known is often specified. An undertaking made in the assembly, a proclamation shouted by the herald through the streets of the city, bills posted on the walls of public buildings: all three means are mentioned in the Cyme inscription. Cleanax had bills posted to announce a feast (*ek prographas*, l.16-17 and 44); he had the herald proclaim the invitation for the Day of the Lark (*apo karugmatos*, l.36-37); and he gave a solemn undertaking in the presence of the assembly to offer sacrifice and a feast at the Caesarea (*katôs epangeilato*, l.41).

Given a corpus of such texts, we can give an account of society in a Hellenistic city thanks to this scrupulous concern for the status of the guests. The feast-inscriptions are especially interesting in this context — this degree of precision is lacking when it comes to distributions of oil or other benefactions. First come the citizens and, holding pride of place, the magistrates. Foreigners are frequently invited, resident foreigners more often than non-resident. Slaves are not normally invited. Nor are women and children; but if they are, they are hived off to a separate location. This picture of a city at feast complements, while sometimes modifying, the familiar image of the city at assembly. Thinking of people attending a feast together may perhaps help us to grasp the social relations at play, to understand the sociability which underpinned the Hellenistic city, which is not simply a matter of legal status nor limited to a narrow circle of citizens. Being neighbours, working together, everyday life — all fostered the bonds unacknow-ledged by formal political status, bonds which made for a more open sense of community than in previous periods. Invitations to public feasts thus faithfully mirror the evolution of social relations in the Hellenistic city.

The *boulê* and people of Cyme resolved to grant Cleanax a golden crown and to have this resolution made known at the festivals of Dionysus and at the civic deliberations at which the magistrates were chosen — in other words, at the religious festival where the greatest crowds were to be expected, and at the most "political" moment of the civic calendar, the point at which the office-holders were renewed. At Cyme, as in other Hellenistic cities, the gift of a public feast contributes to the creation of civic memory. Let me explain briefly. The institution of euergetism seems to me to have been one of the major sources of collective memory in the Hellenistic city, taking the place of other institutions of earlier ages, such as heroic death in single combat in the time of the Homeric heroes, or the anonymous death of the citizen hoplite who remained at his place in the ranks in the classical city-state.[15] The community remembers the euergetic gesture ("the city walls have finally been repaired ...") and at the same time the name of the euergete ("X repaired the walls"), and that of his family. To be remembered is essential if one is to be a member of the élite, to enjoy enduring political weight. The group of benefactors, by perpetuating itself in the collective memory, creates, and then reinforces, its hold over the city. Feasts are only one link in this

chain of memory, but an important one, I think — not merely because banquets
are more frequent than other types of benefaction, but because they catch the civic
community at a propitious moment. People remember the feast's occasion and
also name of the person who gave it. The banquet is simultaneously an expression
of the social order at a given instant (there is nothing less revolutionary than a
list of people invited to a public feast) and a means of legitimizing that order —
to participate in the feast is to assent to the social power of the euergetes. In short,
at a period and in a world in which the city had hardly any means of expressing
itself as an entity — no victories, no politics of prestige — the public feast was
one of the few occasions at which one could still experience a sense of collective
existence, and perhaps even affirm a cultural identity. Which leads me to the other
type of document on feasts, the literary texts.

2

Cultural identity: I am concerned here with a single strand of the much wider
process of constructing cultural identity, namely how the Greeks of the Hellenistic
age made use of the public feast to represent cultural history to themselves, how
they used a discourse about others the better to define themselves. I would argue
in fact that in this context too we can point to a development peculiar to the Hellenistic period by comparison with earlier periods, and specifically the Classical.

At least since Homer, the Greeks made use of manners at table, in the wide
sense of the cultural rules for eating, as a criterion for distinguishing men from
gods, and Greeks (or rather civilised beings) from those who were not. In the
Odyssey, the cultivation of grain and the consumption of its products is one of
the main yardsticks by which Odysseus judges whether a community is civilised,
and so whether he can in principle expect a friendly welcome.[16] The Cyclops
Polyphemus and the Lotus-eaters, for example, do not cultivate grain, as Odysseus
and his companions learn to their cost. In the fifth century, and quite
systematically in Herodotus for example, the staple diet of a people enables them
to be located somewhere on the continuum between the savage — the bestial —
and the civilised. Now the peoples described by Herodotus do not know the
institution of the meal. They eat, they nourish themselves, but this act does not
give rise to formalised social exchange. The absence of the meal as an institution
is a mark either of the complete absence of communal (social and political)
organisation, as in the case of the Androphagi and Ichthyophagi; or of a nomadic
way of life, as with the nomadic Libyans or the Scyths. In either case it denotes
ignorance of city-organisation.[17] Conversely, non-Greek peoples whose way of
life is presented positively have types of meal comparable with those of the

Greeks. Finally, excess with regard to meals, which is a recurrent feature of the Persian way of life, for example, is evidence of a fault in their political organisation. We can say that the meal is a gauge not only of manners and customs but also of the structure of an entire social and political régime.

This way of thinking about political structures in terms of manners at table can be found in Herodotus, and continues in numerous authors into the fourth century and the Hellenistic period. We can cite Xenophon on the Persians[18] and Thracians,[19] Theopompus on the King of Kings[20] and on Thys, king of Paphlagonia,[21] Theophrastus again on the King of Kings;[22] and later, in the third century BC, Phylarchus on the Galatians,[23] and, in the early first century, Posidonius on the Celts.[24] Tellingly enough, most of these (and many others) are cited by Athenaeus in Book 4 of the *Deipnosophistae*.[25] Alertness to the meal-customs of non-Greek peoples produced both an account of the diversities of practice and an examination of how power functioned in these societies. There thus developed a means of thinking not only about culture or civilisation but also about *politeia*, which, though it existed already in the fifth century, becomes amplified and diversified during the Hellenistic period.

But what seems to me peculiar to the fourth century, and then the Hellenistic period, is the use not of non-Greek peoples but of the Greeks' own past as a means of constructing an analogous thematic. Public banquets play a part in a grand scenario depicting human history as a series of significant moments. I will just take three of these moments: In the Beginning, the Heroic Age, the Age of Decadence.

In the evolutionary scheme of human history developed by Theophrastus, Dicaearchus and others, meals are not mentioned in the account of the state of primitive savagery, nor in the transition from savagery to civilisation. They are absent from the phase of pastoralism and the beginnings of agricultural life. Neither the accounts of the emergence of humanity nor of the beginnings of social life mention them. They only occur in the early stages of civic life. I have examined three such accounts elsewhere:[26] the story of Sopatros told by Theophrastus and preserved by Porphyry;[27] the case of Italus who according to Aristotle in Book 7 of the *Politics* founded the *sussitia*;[28] and the first city described by Plato in the *Republic*.[29] These texts make clear (1) that the meal presupposes the practice of sacrifice followed by the eating of the flesh (the burden of the story of Sopatros according to Theophrastus), (2) that it is the institution on which the social group is based (Aristotle), and (3) that the shared meal is the leaven of sociability (Plato). The institution of the meal marks the moment when the group creates rules, laws, for itself, and becomes a true civic community. In their

accounts of human origins, the Greeks thus connected banquets with the beginnings of the *polis*, of the political community. But they also allowed the banquet
to evolve, giving it a history analogous to their own, from the sobriety of the
ancients to the excesses of the city or kingdom that rejects all due limit. There
is a very long passage in the first Book of Athenaeus devoted to the Homeric
banquet.[30] Its core seems to be borrowed from a book by Dioscurides of Tarsus
(c. 150-100 BC) on the manners of the Heroic Age, onto which have been hung
quotations from different writers. The passage's main theme is that a simple mode
of eating is an indication of temperance in all walks of life. Every facet of
Homeric manners at table illustrates the theme. Everyone, kings and commoners,
young and old, ate the same fare; meat was always roasted; neither fish nor fowl
was served; artifice in cooking was banned; no honey-cakes, no fruit, but great
quantities of bread; no unguents, no crowns, no couches — one sat down to eat.
(The later writers of course often quote and comment upon the actual text of
Homer.) The consequence of such restrained and simple habits was *euphrosune*,
the good cheer produced by the feast.

But there is another theme too in this account of the heroic, Homeric, age, the
motif of the equal division of food and drink at the banquet. On this view,
division, and especially equal division, are inventions of the Homeric age. They
come about after a period when food was eaten in common, when there was no
process of division at all. A passage of Dicaearchus, commenting on the proverb
"One portion doesn't choke", explains the change:

At these meals it was not the custom among the Ancients to divide the food into separate
portions. The custom of dividing it up prevailed because it was claimed that there was not
enough food to go round — that is the origin of the proverb. When, in the beginning, the
food was served in common and not divided into portions, the stronger used to grab the
food of the weaker — and choked, and no one was able to save them. That was the reason
for inventing the individual portion.[31]

Athenaeus offers an analogous account, followed by a discussion of the Homeric
word for feast, *dais*.[32] The ancestral period serves as a model for and a contrast
with present-day customs: there is even a passage in Book 8 in which Then and
Now are systematically contrasted.[33]

The positive evaluation of the feast in the Homeric age by the Greeks of the
Hellenistic period thus rests on two rather different main arguments. One
emphasizes an idea, division and equality, which has direct political implications.
The other dwells on a style of behaviour, restraint and simplicity, and makes a
moral judgement. These two kinds of argument are never fused, as though there

were two ways of thinking about banquets in the past, two types of argument
corresponding to different phases of Greek thinking.

Finally, banquets play a rôle in the specifically Hellenistic debate about *truphê*,
luxury. It has been shown convincingly that it is in the fourth century, with
Isocrates and Xenophon, but above all Plato, that a concern with mode of life
(*diaita*) becomes a theme in political thought.[34] In this context, *truphê* becomes
one of the possible explanations for the decline of institutions. It may corrode
tyrannies as well as oligarchies and democracies. It is a stage of development
which any people, any city, may reach, producing rapid, and usually disastrous,
political change. In short, *truphê* is a principle of historical change.

It is not difficult to see why the banquet should have been used as a mark of
truphê, though it is not the only — not even the primary — mark of a life of
luxury (clothing seems to be even more important). Moreover, many examples
of banquets concern individual behaviour, which is irrelevant here. Public feasts
are invoked when it is the *truphê* of an entire city or people, such as the cities
of the Archaic period (Sybaris, Tarentum, Samos, for example), or the Etruscans,
that is at issue. I will take just one example, the feasts ascribed to Sybaris.

Athenaeus presents life in Sybaris as follows:

Of the peoples of Italy, the Sybarites were particularly friendly with the Etruscans, and
among peoples overseas,with the Ionians, because they too lived a life of *truphê* ... They
used to hold public feasts thick and fast and honoured their euergetes with golden crowns:
they proclaimed their names at the public sacrifices and competitions, making a special point
not of their philanthropy in general but of their banquet-liturgies.[35]

He then cites Phylarchus:

The Sybarites, when they allowed themselves to drift into a life of *truphê*, adopted a law
according to which the women were to be invited to public feasts. Their hosts at the
sacrifice were to inform them a year in advance, so that they might be able to prepare their
clothes and other finery in a manner befitting the long notice.[36]

One of the manuscripts of this passage bears a marginal note to the effect that
most of Athenaeus' material on *truphê* comes from a second-century AD treatise
On the truphê of the ancients by Alciphron.[37] This book was probably just a tissue
of excerpts from earlier authors; since Phylarchus wrote in the second half of the
third century BC, we may take it that the theme of Archaic *truphê* was created
early in the Hellenistic period. Athenaeus' account of the banquets of Sybaris is
interesting from several points of view. Its tone is evidently Hellenistic: the

passage employs the form of words usual in the decrees of Greek cities at that time. We certainly do not here have to do with a documentary account of real banquets in Archaic Sybaris — that city was razed by her neighbour Croton in 511 BC. The reconstruction or invention of the past is put together from contemporary materials and it will be obvious that we cannot use such texts as evidence for real practices in the Archaic period. In the mention of public banquets given by euergetes who were in turn thanked by having their names announced at the following banquets, we simply find what I described earlier in this paper on the basis of the Hellenistic inscriptions. No detail of this account can be referred to to the sixth-century city without risk of gross anachronism. On the other hand, it is of interest to note that the description of the alleged *truphê* of Sybaris is based on a critique of habits contemporary with the writers who created the theme. Phylarchus' mention of the law of Sybaris admitting women to public sacrifices sets that city on a footing with the barbarian nations who alone allow their womenfolk to attend banquets. The theme of *truphê* is a form of the theme of the Other — only here the Others are not non-Greeks but the ancestors of the Greeks.

The *truphê* of the Archaic cities is regularly contrasted with the sobriety of a number of Greek cities, chiefly Sparta. This theme helps to define more precisely the rules to be followed in order to avoid the fate of all the cities bloated by *truphê*, such as outright destruction in the case of Sybaris, or the loss of political freedom in the case of Samos, subjected to the Persian yoke.[38] But in their exploration of the link between extravagance in the banquet and political excess, the Hellenistic texts also cite contemporary examples of princes and kings who, instead of carrying on the civic tradition of public feasts, behave in the manner of barbarian potentates.[39]

This criticism of banquets is directed at excess, not at the pleasures of the table as such. The same period witnessed the discovery, if not the full development, of gastronomy as a topic. The earliest books on cooking, in the fifth century, were related to medical knowledge and especially treatises on diet: they just list and classify different types of food. In the poetry of Archestratus (*The Life of Luxury*, second half of the fourth century BC) and Matro (end of the same century), descriptions of dishes and recipes rub shoulders with advice and instruction about the proper treatment of food.[40] Gastronomy becomes an art.

To sum up: In the overall process of constructing a past and thinking about the criteria of civilisation and the good *politeia* or constitution, collective eating was used by Hellenistic writers as a yardstick for gauging the beginnings of city-life, the successful working of egalitarian societies, and the failure of cities where luxury reigned instead of policy. This account of their past is no less constructed — invented one could almost say — than the fifth-century account of non-Greek nations. But just as difference is a means of thinking about the inhabited world, the *oikoumene*, so it is a means of thinking about the past.

3

One last passage will allow us to juxtapose practice and reflection more directly. I will be brief about it, because Plutarch, its author, has been used by several other contributors to this book. It comes from the *Convivial Questions*. Plutarch's question is: "Is the practice of the Ancients in each eating his own portion better than the modern custom of eating from a common dish?"[41] Plutarch's starting point is the simple fact that his contemporaries, the Chaeroneans of the first and second centuries AD, no longer understood the significance of the *dais*, the division and collective consumption of the sacrificial meat, which was still practised at public sacrifices. Plutarch, a highly educated man, and himself the provider of such feasts, simply saw in the practice the survival of an ancient custom without any real meaning for the present. This is a very dense text,[42] but I think one can show that neither of the two main interlocutors in the dialogue, Hagias and Lamprias, one of whom argues in favour of equal division at the banquet, every participant receiving his portion, and the other in favour of shared food, each participant taking what he wants from a great central dish, supposes for a moment that the public banquet, organised by the archon in his own city in his own day, has anything to do with these models. Lamprias, who speaks in the dialogue in favour of separate shares, does not in fact defend the banquets with equal division that take place in his city. After defining equality in political terms, he describes meals which are quite evidently private — the preparations in the kitchen, the host, the couches, the place-settings, the crowns and so on; and he justifies the equal portion that everyone is to receive in terms of private property, just as everyone at the banquet has his own place and his own courtisan. By the end of his chain of reasoning, the stress is not on equal shares but on the individual share. As for Hagias, right from the start he supports the banquet-symposium and the value of private entertainment. He criticizes the custom of giving shares and contrasts it with the most elementary laws of food-consumption: division becomes rationing equals starving. The usages which make sense in the public sphere are simply comical in the private sphere of the symposium.

The confrontation between the virtues of the sacrificial banquet with equal shares (*dais*) and those of the banquet-symposium never actually takes place: for the models offered by Hagias and Lamprias are in fact oddly similar. Their dif-

ference is purely sophistic, and ends up in complete agreement. The two interlocutors, forgetting all about individual shares and common dishes, the original
point of debate, both emphasise what in their view is essential to create a feeling
of common well-being, namely shared conversation, shared music and song. Both,
in fact, have the same institution in mind as their model, an institution casually
familiar to them, in which sharing and equality are both to be found: the symposium, the private banquet. Both agree that the meal where equal division took
place is past and gone; neither makes any attempt to find a place for, or give
meaning to, the *dais* in their own city.

If we take Plutarch at face value, we would have to conclude from his
contemporaries' lack of response to the banquet with equal shares, fossilized in
the public sacrifices of Chaeronea, that they no longer understood the significance
of such a meal, that for them the institution belonged to the city of their
forefathers, not their own. The ritual modelling of egalitarian social relationships
would have no bearing on the city of the second century AD. The sense of civic
unity would be derived from other institutions, such as the private banquet, where
philanthropia reigns. In other words, in this Convivial Question, the sacrificial
meal, the public banquet, has ceased to be model and reflection of civic life —
that rôle, itself now altered, has been taken over by the symposium.

As is well known, Plutarch devotes several dialogues to the best way of con-
ducting a symposium. The meal must reflect a certain order in all its component
parts: the basis of that order can be debated, but order itself is a prerequisite of
the symposium's success. Here too we find argument. One view maintains that
the divisions and hierarchies of political and social life are the best possible ones,
indeed the only possible ones. Consequently, they should also inform the rules
of the banquet, for instance regarding where the guests should be placed in the
hall. The alternative view is that we should construct a different model, of
koinônia, of community, whose principles would be different from those of the
city. Far from reproducing the civic rules, the banquet should have its own, aimed
at creating cohesion within the group, a sense of shared identity among the guests.
This form of banquet is similar to that imagined by Plato and Aristotle. Only the
symposium, in the form of the Philosophers' Banquet, can offer the guests the
model of a way of life.

A number of questions arise if we compare Plutarch's reflections with the
euergetic institutions discussed in the first part of the paper. On the one hand, the
epigraphy, inasmuch as it records both public acts, the decrees, and private
initiatives, such as commemorations and foundations, testifies to the importance
of public banquets in the life of the city. On the other hand, Plutarch, who himself

organised such banquets in his own city, sees in them merely traditional customs which have no real significance in the contemporary city. Between these two positions slide the Hellenistic texts that construct an anthropology and a history of their world, and stress the place of the public banquet in the construction of that past. Common sense suggests that these two versions of the same world are not so much contradictory as complementary. The historian must be cautious: exclusive reliance upon one type of source runs the risk of distorting our view of that world. And it is a truism to acknowledge the part played in the Hellenistic city, as of course elsewhere, by the private sphere in the construction of identity. Another way of putting the point is to say that, at least for those who had attained a modest station in life, civic life was composed of both public banquets and private ones.

But if we are interested in the majority view, Plutarch is probably misleading. What is he actually up to? He uses private values, values belonging to his own imaginative world, to judge public life. He is no neutral observer, but a man — a philosopher, a moralist — whose conception of a good citizen is the fruit more of his own reflections than of observation of public conduct. He does not try to represent the thoughts of the citizens of second-century Syros, for example, when they heaped praise on the benefactors who gave them public banquets.[43] It is surely not a matter of rejecting what Plutarch says, but of putting it in its correct context. His ideal symposium is as irrelevant to civic practice as were those of Plato and Aristotle.

That brings us back to the difficulty of defining the idea of "conventional values". We must study both the values of the majority and the Greeks' own reflections upon their value-system, or, more simply, both the values of the Hellenistic world and the representations of those values. Working from this angle, we can take account of the multiplicity and diversity of the available sources, and so of the types of discourse. In choosing to work on a social institution, I am of course confronted by the question of the relation between the different types of discourse offered by our sources, a difficulty not faced, or not in the same degree, by scholars who focus on a single text or a homogeneous group of texts. In the case of public banquets, the archaeological and epigraphic sources make possible a spatial, social and ritual account, but they also provide insight into the Hellenistic Greeks' values. As we have seen, the honorific decrees dispense praise and commemoration according to the terms of this particular system of values. The literary sources, on the other hand, show how banquets served as markers in the construction of a particular cultural system. The relation between the two is clear: it was the salience, the importance, of public banquets in the life of the

Hellenistic Greek cities which caused them to become markers, crawling-pegs in the measurement of the degree of civilisation and constitutional excellence of nations and cities. Conversely, the literary discussion of banquets testifies to their continued vitality in the Hellenistic period. Plutarch seems to provide evidence of a certain warping of the perceived value of the institution. But we should see this view of Plutarch's not so much as evidence of a general shift of values among the Hellenistic Greeks — after all, at the very same moment cities by the score were continuing to heap honours on euergetes who provided them with banquets — as an indication of the exceptional nature of this sort of moral-philosophical discourse, which had remained tangential to "conventional values" ever since the fourth century BC, deliberately distancing itself from them and thereby guaranteeing its own intellectual status.

There is then no simple answer if we try to descry the values of a society through the medium of a collective social institution. But it must surely be clear that a proper historical analysis requires that we take account of, and seek to relate, distinct types of discourse about that institution.

Translated by Richard Gordon

53 rue Planchat
F-75020 Paris
France

Appendix

The decree of Cyme in the Aeolid in honour of Cleanax the *prutanis*, *c.* 2 BC – *c.* AD 2 (from Hodot 1982).

On the motion of the generals, recorded by the Three chosen by lot, viz.: Asklapon son of Dionysus, Hegesandros son of Herakleidas, Athenagoras son of Dionysus, and the secretary to the Assembly, Heraeus son of Antipater:

Whereas Cleanax son of Sarapion, but issue of Philodamus, *prutanis*, possessed both of noble birth through his ancestors on either side and of unsurpassably ambitious benevolence towards the city of his fathers, has all through his life been a generous benefactor to the city, permitting himself no momentary neglect of his solicitude for the people, in act and utterance true counsellor to the city; for which reasons <not only> does the people now pay tribute to him in respect of the zealous execution of his present office of *prutanis*, its gratitude is expressed also in numerous official minutes and through earlier decrees: for example, his contribution as priest of Dionysus Pandamos to the associated mysteries instituted by the city; his disbursements for the quadrennial celebration of the mysteries, where the scale of his outlay pays witness both to his determination to put on a fitting spectacle and to his piety, as the very first to discharge the office; and (when) he caused bills to be posted inviting the citizens of Cyme, the Italian residents, the resident and non-resident foreigners to a public feast in the precinct of Dionysus Pandamos, and regaled them sumptuously — a feast he provides each year; and (when) he gave a feast to the whole population on the occasion of the marriage of his daughter:

And whereas the people, mindful and cognisant of these benefits, has not forgotten the other splendid entertainments he has provided over the years; — Cleanax the *prutanis* is also worthy of praise and honour in that, becoming the father of a fine son, he had him trained in rhetoric, and gave the people in Sarapion not merely a man worthy of his family but also a protection and shield, who has already manifested his zeal for the city in many acts of personal benevolence; a man of "true filial piety", who has well merited the title voted him by public consent, his love of his father being attested for ever by a vote of the people;

In view of all which, the people pays tribute to Cleanax the *prutanis* for his constant, unremitting public benevolence: first, as *prutanis* now, he has performed the traditional sacrifices to the gods for New Year's Day; served a *glukismos* to everyone in the city; provided lavish games; performed the traditional New Year ceremonies and sacrifices; entertained many of the citizens and the Italians over several days in the prytaneum; second, he has performed the traditional offerings to the dead on the appointed day, and distributed milk gruel to all persons, free and slave, in the city; and on the Day of the Lark on his own initiative invited the citizens, Italians, resident and non-resident foreigners by public proclamation to lunch in the prytaneum; and provided Bounty as generously as other *prutaneis* have provided it; and paid for the processions on Laurel Day, and provided the priests, the victors in the games, the magistrates and many of the citizens with lunch; and at the Caesarea of the province of Asia, he provided the sacrifices and festivities, as he had promised, sacrificing oxen to the emperor Caesar Augustus and his children and the other gods — from which sacrifice he entertained the Greeks, the Italians and the resident and non-resident foreigners <lavishly?> in the agora, announcing the invitation by handbills, providing <...> in abundance; and he performed the other rites <...>; Wherefore the people and council resolved: that he be presented with a crown after the sacrifice <at the festival of Dionysus> before the altar of Zeus, and at all the <...> and the elections of magistrates after the prayers, and at the <...>, the presentations being announced in the following form of words:

The People presents <Cleanax, son of Sarapion, but issue
of> Philodamus with a crown of gold, for having performed
his *prutaneia* <...>.
<The generals?> are to be responsible for (providing) the crown <...>.

Notes

1. See my synthesis in Schmitt Pantel 1992. On Greek banquets in general, see Murray 1990 with full bibliography; also Murray and Tecuşan 1995.

2. On rooms for ritual meals in sanctuaries, see Goldstein 1978.
3. See in particular *IG* XI 161a, 203a, 287a; *ID* 401, 406b, 440, 442a, 445, 452, 461, 464, 1400, 1403b, 1417b, 1894.
4. Heyder and Mallwitz 1978.
5. Rotroff and Oakley 1992.
6. Jameson 1988.
7. See Detienne and Vernant 1979, with the bibliography on sacrifice at the end of the book.
8. Published by Hodot 1982; see also the important remarks of J. and L. Robert, *Bullép* 1983, no. 323.
9. *IG* XII 5, 647.
10. Schmitt Pantel 1992, 411-15.
11. Veyne 1976.
12. "Yet it seems to me clear that pleasures exist independently of any social function they may possess, and cannot be wholly reduced to such functions" (Murray and Tecuşan [eds.] 1995, 6). For a slightly different view, see my article in the same volume, 93-105, at 102-5.
13. On euergetism, see, apart from L. Robert's entire oeuvre, Veyne 1976; Gauthier 1985.
14. For Priene, for example, see *I. Priene* 108, 109, 111.
15. On the commemoration of the dead, see the articles by J-P. Vernant, Nicole Loraux and the present author in Gnoli and Vernant 1982.
16. Cf. Vidal-Naquet 1981, 39-68.
17. Schmitt Pantel 1992, 425-38.
18. Xen. *Ages.* 9.3.
19. Xen. *An.* 7.3.21.
20. *FGrH* 115 F113 = Athen. *Deipn.* 4.25 (145a).
21. *FGrH* 115 F179 = Athen. *Deipn.* 4.25 (144f).
22. Theophr. frg. 125 Wimmer = 603 Fortenbaugh (Athen. *Deipn.* 4.25 (144ef) = Sosibios the Laconian, *FGrH* 595 T3); the story was widely circulated, see Fortenbaugh's apparatus ad loc. (2:454).
23. *FGrH* 81 F9 and 2 = Athen. *Deipn.* 4.34 (150d-f).
24. *FGrH* 87 F15 = Ath. *Deipn.* 4.36 (151e-152d).
25. See Bruit & Schmitt Pantel 1986.
26. Schmitt Pantel 1992, 443-49.
27. Porph. *Abst.* 2.29-30.
28. Arist. *Pol.* 7.10 (1329b5-23).
29. Pl. *Resp.* 2 (372a5-e1).
30. Athen. *Deipn.* 1.15-18 (8e-11b) = *FGrH* 594 F8.
31. Dicaearchus frg. 59 Wehrli (= Porph. *Abst.* 4.2).
32. Athen. *Deipn.* 1.21 (12d-13a).
33. Athen. *Deipn.* 8.65-66 (363d-364d).
34. Passerini 1931; Bordes 1982.
35. Athen. *Deipn.* 12.17 (519b-d).
36. Athen. *Deipn.* 12.20 (521c) = *FGrH* 81 F45. [The meaning of this obscure passage is made clear by Plut. *Conv. sept. sap.* 2.147e. Tr.]
37. See the note in the Loeb edition of Athenaeus, 5, p. 333.
38. Athen. *Deipn.* 12.57 (540d-541a).
39. Some examples: Alexander feasting the entire population of Babylon (Diod. Sic. 17.95.6); the banquet given by Ptolemy II Philadelphus and described by Callixenus (Kallixeinos) of Rhodes in Athen. *Deipn.* 5.25-35 (196a-203b) = *FGrH* 627 F2; the banquet of Ptolemy VIII

Euergetes II at Cyrene in Athen. *Deipn.* 12.73 (549e-550b) cf. *FGrH* 87 F26; or again Cleopatra's banquet for Antony in Cilicia, described by Socrates of Rhodes in Athen. *Deipn.* 4.29 (147e-148b) = *FGrH* 192 F1. On the feasts of Hellenistic kings, see Schmitt Pantel 1992, 457-66.

40. See Degani 1990 and 1991; Wilkins and Hill 1994.
41. Plut. *Quaest. conv.* 2.10 (642e-644d).
42. See Schmitt Pantel 1992, 471-82 for a detailed analysis.
43. *IG* XII 5, 659, 660, 662-65, 667, 668; *IG* XII Suppl. 238.

Bibliography

Bordes, J. 1982. *Politeia dans la pensée grecque jusqu'à Aristote*. Paris.

Bruit, L. & Schmitt Pantel, P. 1986. "Citer, classer, penser: à propos des repas des Grecs et des repas des Autres dans le livre IV des Deipnosophistes d'Athénée", *AnnAStorAnt* 8, 203-21.

Degani, E. 1990. "On Greek Gastronomic Poetry, I", *Alma Mater Studiorum* 1990, 51-63.

Degani, E. 1991. "On Greek Gastronomic Poetry, II", *Alma Mater Studiorum* 1991, 164-75.

Detienne, M. & Vernant, J.-P. (eds.) 1979. *La Cuisine du sacrifice en pays grec*. Paris.

Gauthier, P. 1985. *Les Cités grecques et leurs bienfaiteurs* (BCH Suppl. 12). Paris.

Gnoli, G. & Vernant, J.-P. (eds.) 1982. *La Mort, les morts dans les sociétés anciennes*. Cambridge/Paris.

Goldstein, M. 1978. "The Setting of the Ritual Meal in Greek Sanctuaries, 600-300 BC", PhD dissertation, University of California, Berkeley.

Heyder, W. & Mallwitz, A. 1978. *Die Bauten. Das Kabirenheiligtum bei Theben* II. Berlin.

Hodot, R. 1982. "Décret de Kyme en l'honneur du prytane Kleanax", *GettyMusJ* 10, 165-80.

Jameson, M.H. 1988. "Sacrifice and Animal Husbandry in Classical Greece", In: Whittaker (ed.) 1988, 87-119.

Murray, O. (ed.) 1990. *Sympotica: a Symposium on the Symposion*. Oxford. [With a thematic bibliography].

Murray, O. & Tecuşan, M. (eds.) 1995. *In Vino Veritas*. London.

Passerini, A. 1931. "La *truphê* nella storiografia ellenistica", *StItFilCl* 9, 35-56.

Rotroff, S.I. & Oakley, J.H. 1992. *Debris from a Public Dining Place in the Athenian Agora* (Hesperia Suppl. 25). Princeton.

Schmitt Pantel, P. 1992. *La Cité au banquet. Histoire des repas publics dans les cités grecques* (CEFR 157). Rome/Paris.

Veyne, P. 1976. *Le Pain et le cirque: sociologie historique d'un pluralisme politique*. Paris.

Vidal-Naquet, P. 1981. *Le Chasseur noir: formes de pensée et formes de société dans le monde grec*. Paris.

Whittaker, C.R. (ed.) 1988. *Pastoral Economies in Classical Antiquity* (PCPhS Suppl. 14). Cambridge.

Wilkins, J. & S. Hill (eds.) 1994. *Archestratus, The Life of Luxury*. London.

SOCIETY, CONSANGUINITY AND THE FERTILITY OF WOMEN

The Community of Deities on the Great Frieze of the Pergamum Altar as a Paradigm of Cross-Cultural Ideas

Burkhard Fehr

Archaeologists who analyse the great frieze (pl. 1a/b) of the Pergamum altar delight in discovering its subtle meanings and allusions accessible to only a small number of well-educated members of ancient society.[1] But no one would deny that the great frieze — like the Pergamum altar as a whole — contained some important messages also for the less learned, for those who enjoyed only a basic or "grade-school" knowledge of Greek mythology.[2] Three features that characterize the gigantomachy on the great frieze may well have attracted such persons' attention, even if they considered it in haste and superficially. Though the frieze is now rather damaged and lacunate, these characteristics, which do not occur in other representations of the gigantomachy, are still clearly recognizable. Often mentioned in archaeological publications, they are rarely discussed in detail. They may be outlined as follows:

1) As a rule the deities on the great frieze fight in groups of blood relatives.[3] Sometimes these groups include several generations, as for instance at the southeast corner, where we can trace back the female ancestors of Apollo and his sister Artemis over two generations.[4]

2) On the great frieze considerably more goddesses than gods are represented.[5] The ratio seems to be about 3:2.[6] The impression that this majority is not incidental is confirmed by the fact that a series of over thirty larger-than-life female statues was found in the altar area.[7] They may originally have stood either in the outer colonnade (pl. 2) of the altar itself[8] or on a very long *bathron* bordering the north side of the altar temenos (pl. 3).[9] In this area there was no series of male statues comparable with the female ones in number or coherence. To this evidence we may add another remarkable fact: on the eastern side of the gigantomachy (pl. 2), that is to say, on that part of the great frieze which the visitor saw upon entering the altar temenos, the central position is *not* held by

a male deity, as one might expect. As M. Pfanner has pointed out, this side of the frieze is composed symmetrically.[10] So its centre should have some relevance. It is generally agreed that a female deity occupies this prominent place: Hera. The now very fragmentary figure of the goddess, vigorously attacking a giant, was given additional emphasis by a mighty quadriga with four winged horses (pl. 4).[11] This dominant motive must have been the most effective eye-catcher on this side of the great frieze before its destruction and mutilation.[12]

3) The mothers of the fighting gods and goddesses are rarely omitted on the great frieze.[13] Yet we search in vain for the fathers of a considerable number of important deities taking part in the battle: we miss Kronos, the father of Zeus, Hera and Poseidon; Koios, the father of Leto and Asterie; Perses, the father of Hekate.[14] Thus, at least three divine mothers — Rhea (wife of Kronos), Phoibe (wife of Koios), Asterie (wife of Perses) — who can be seen on the great frieze with their sons or daughters lack a male partner. Among the preserved figures, however, there is no instance of a divine father represented with his offspring but without the offspring's mother. If we compare the number of mothers on the frieze with the number of fathers, the ratio will be about 2:1.[15] In any case, the mothers by far outnumber the fathers. Wenning calls this a "Dominanz der Mütter".[16] These mothers' "reliable" fertility is indirectly but effectively demonstrated by the representation of four divine generations on the frieze (e.g. Gê/Rhea/Zeus/ Athena), the youngest generation being particularly emphasized on the east frieze facing the entrance of the sanctuary (pl. 1 and 2). Finally, the importance of the mothers is once more stressed by the Telephus frieze, where Telephus' mother Augê plays a prominent part.[17]

It seems that these three evidently interconnected characteristics — the co-operation of consanguineous deities, the preponderance of female figures and the emphasis on motherhood and fertility — were essential for the concept of the great frieze and probably also of the Pergamum altar as a whole. But in what regard were they essential? This question can be put more precisely if we take into account that in Greek art, the battle between deities and giants had always been a symbol of the victory of "civilization" over lawlessness, hybris and chaos.[18] Are our three characteristics perhaps to be linked to a specific notion of "civilization" which is represented and defended by the divine society on the great frieze? Is the victory of the deities on the great frieze of the Pergamum altar possibly to be regarded first of all as a consequence of their embodying certain principles and values of that "civilization"? For, regarded from a purely practical point of view, the divine army is physically and militarily inferior to its enemies. Many giants are equipped with hoplite weapons, and all of them are powerful men. In

the divine armed forces considerably more women than men are fighting.[19] There
are few hoplites among the gods. Some male deities are old men, one — Eros
— is a boy, to say nothing of the two little satyrs fighting alongside Dionysus.
Thus, less than twenty gods would be eligible for military service and they face
at least 64 giants.[20] The divine superiority cannot be based on material or physical
resources, but only on the power of an idea — or ideology. What kind of
ideology? And what was its purpose?

Among the publications I have consulted pursuing these questions is a
particularly helpful and stimulating article by W. Neumer-Pfau on the fighting
goddesses of the great frieze.[21] Pointing to an aspect that will also be important
for my own reasoning, she argued convincingly that the imagery of the Pergamum
altar must have had a meaning not only for Greek beholders but also for the
numerous non-Greek inhabitants of the Pergamene empire.[22] The latter could
accept what they regarded as the message of that imagery only if it was in
accordance with their own religious and cultural traditions. Neumer-Pfau thinks
that this condition was actually fulfilled. She assumes that a connection existed
between the importance given to the divine mothers on the great frieze and the
support granted by the Pergamene kings to various old indigenous cults of the
Great Mother. In order to strengthen her argument Neumer-Pfau also recalls
matrilinear elements from some societies of Asia Minor.

As for the Greek viewers, she presumes a link between the prominent rôle of
the maternal deities on the altar and the Attalids' well-known love and veneration
for their mother Apollonis.[23] These were not only private feelings. They were
repeatedly demonstrated in public and should therefore be regarded as a political
— perhaps one could even say propagandistic — phenomenon. Unlike other
Hellenistic queens, Apollonis was to be considered a paragon of the Greek wife,
mother and educator, one result being the much-praised unanimity among her four
sons. Thus, the Pergamene dynasty presented itself as embodying an ideal also
found (according to Neumer-Pfau) in the theories of contemporaneous Stoic
philosophers, especially Panaetius.[24] In their eyes, the solidarity between relatives
and friends belonged to the foundations of the state.

All the same, some questions remain which cannot be answered by Neumer-
Pfau's arguments. It seems plausible that the importance of the divine mothers
on the great frieze was acceptable to non-Greek spectators rooted in the indigenous
traditions of Asia Minor. As to the Greek point of view, however, one might ask
how the numerical and visual preponderance of women and mothers could be
harmonized with traditional Greek patriarchy, particularly the position of the *kyrios*
in the *oikos*. The Attalids were no feminists. Finally, the Stoic Panaetius: For him

marriage is "the first social connection",[25] whereas the Pergamum frieze — as well as the Attalids' behaviour toward their mother — emphasizes the biological ties between blood relatives much more than the institutional ties between husbands and wives.[26]

The contribution of Neumer-Pfau has shed light on important aspects of the problems outlined at the beginning, but it does not offer a coherent solution. In order to clarify which part the three characteristic features described above played in the concept of the Pergamum altar, we should look at some traditional Greek ideas: first, on consanguinity and second, on the fertility of women as a precondition for the durability of *oikos* and *polis*.

Consanguinity — be it real or fictitious, as in *phulai* or *phratriai* — was always an essential component of Greek social thinking.[27] It will suffice to mention some well-known facts. The popular and deeply-rooted conviction that harmony and solidarity between blood relatives were indispensable for the coherence, safety, and prosperous future of a society could be supported particularly by citing the authority of Hesiod: in his *Works and Days*, discord and strife between brothers, or between children and parents, are characteristics of a society perishing because of its lack of justice and shame.[28] The solidarity of brothers was a popular theme in Greek literature and philosophy.[29] In Athens laws regulated the obligations of children to their parents.[30] Solidarity between blood relatives was commemorated by public monuments, such as the famous statues of Cleobis and Biton[31] whose exemplary behaviour toward their mother served as a model for the veneration of Apollonis by her sons.[32] One could add the numerous representations of the inseparable Dioscuri, along with many other examples.

So much for consanguinity and the social norms and values connected with it. As to the second point, ancient literature abounds in assurances that no man's life can be called fortunate in the absence of the children necessary for the continued existance of *oikos* and *polis*.[33] As examples for this conviction we may cite Herodotus' well-known story of Tellus[34] or, in the realm of sculpture, the representation of several generations of a dynasty by the Daochos monument at Delphi or by the statues in the Philippeion at Olympia.[35] The same concerns are also displayed by the anxiety that was aroused when a family seemed about to die out. One is reminded of a famous passage in Polybius, where the author bemoans the depopulation of Greece caused by an aversion against marriage and child-rearing.[36] Even more momentous is Hesiod's comment on the subject. Again according to his *Works and Days,* good and just societies are rewarded not only by economic prosperity but also by women bearing "children similar to their parents." Inversely, women will not bear children any more and the *oikoi* will perish if people injure each other.[37] This is the first appearance of a theme often repeated in later times: the obedience of a society to ethical principles — whether of divine origin or otherwise — is a precondition for the successful contribution of women to the continuance of *oikos* and *polis* by giving birth to numerous and auspicious offspring.[38]

Let us now return to the Pergamum altar. Since the end of the 19th century most specialists have agreed that the genealogical relations among the deities on the great frieze are influenced by Hesiod's Theogony.[39] This suggests that the solidarity of consanguineous deities and the stress laid on the divine mothers and female fertility on the Pergamum altar should be interpreted along the lines of Hesiod's ethical principles described above. Brothers and sisters, as well as parents and their children, fight side by side. Furthermore, many mothers are represented along with their famous daughters who, in their turn, have become mothers of "children similar to their parents," and so on. Thus, the united divine clans on the frieze show exactly those features from which, according to Hesiod, one can conclude that a society is founded on justice. In other words, in this way the community of deities on the Pergamum altar is characterized indirectly as a just, good, and civilized one. The "Hesiodic" values embodied by that community enable it to overcome the giants in spite of the latters' physical and military superiority.[40]

There is nothing merely academic in these values. We are therefore confronted with simple and conventional ideas that can be traced back to the earliest phase of Greek culture — ideas which presumably were communicated to a broader public mainly at school, where Hesiod's works belonged to the standard literature.[41]

Moreover, beyond the positive aspects of Hesiodic morality, the great frieze includes also the negative ones: while the deities represent the solidarity of blood relatives in a paradigmatic way, the battle as a whole is an example of pernicious discord between such relatives, because deities as well as giants are descendants of their common mother Gê. Her huge figure emerging on the east frieze (pl. 5)[42] seems not only to plead for mercy for her sons, the giants, but also to exhort these aggressive offspring to live in concord with the peaceful and civilized ones. She is given a cornucopia as an attribute which promises prosperity[43] as a reward for those who follow her admonition.

This view of the great frieze also explains the above-mentioned central position of Hera on the eastern side of the great frieze. As wife of Zeus, she was the divine prototype of the Greek citizen's wife.[44] In the Argive Heraion, her main sanctuary, she carries the epithet *Eileithyia*,[45] and Homer as well as Hesiod made her the mother of the *Eileithyiai*, the midwife-goddesses.[46] Hence she was also the protectress of child-bearing citizen-wives.[47] That is to say, she guaranteed the successful procreation of legitimate offspring on which the continuity of *poleis* and *oikoi* depended. This responsibility of Hera is underlined by the fact that Hebe, the incarnation of the rising generation's youthful vigour, is her daughter.[48] Some have suggested Hebe as Hera's charioteer on the great frieze.[49] Unfortunately this cannot be proven.

A basic message of the whole great frieze is therefore summarized by the figure of Hera. Additional support for this assumption comes from the fact that the first and only temple to Hera (pl. 6a) to be erected in Pergamum was situated prominently above the great gymnasium (pl. 6b) where the youth of the city met.[50] This temple was built in the mid-second century BC by order of King Attalus II. When work on it started, the Pergamum altar had been just completed or, more probably, was in its last building phase.[51] Hera's cult image in the temple was framed, as the archaeological context suggests, by statues of Attalus II and his wife Stratonice.[52] In Pergamum there are no traces of a cult of Hera earlier than this temple.[53] Thus, Hera had in a rapid career become the patroness of the royal family — she was called *Hera Basileia* — and at the same time the most important protectress of the rising generation of Pergamum. Hence it appears reasonable to argue that the prominent position of Hera on the great frieze, as well as the founding of her cult above the gymnasium, resulted from similar intentions based on values of "Hesiodic" stock. Perhaps the decision to found Hera's cult was made at the same time and in close connection with that planning phase of the great frieze in which Hera's figure was placed in the centre of the altar's eastern front.

Up to now my argument has been centered on the great frieze. I would suggest that the "Hesiodic" aspects of its message also played an essential part in the story of Telephus told on the frieze in the peristyle on top of the altar podium. As mentioned above, Augê — likewise a mother who deserved glory for having produced a child "similar to its parents" — was, together with her son Telephus, one of the main figures on this frieze. Possibly, the close emotional connection of mother and son was expressed in scenes which are not preserved, as for instance in their mutual recognition of one another, which is to be postulated in that version of the myth on which the narration is based.[54] This event was represented on one of the nineteen sculptured columns of a temple devoted to the deified Pergamene queen mother Apollonis in her hometown of Cyzicus.[55] In these reliefs one could see mythical scenes in which sons demonstrate their love sometimes to both their parents, sometimes just to their fathers, but mostly to their mothers by honouring, liberating or avenging them. The monumental Dirke group in Naples showing the brothers Amphion and Zetos as avengers of their mother Antiope — a myth also represented on the Cyzicus temple[56] — seems likewise to be connected with the Pergamene dynasty.[57] The mythical scenes on the reliefs of the Cyzicus temple as well as the Dirke group have been paralleled with the public veneration of Apollonis by her concordant sons.[58] These two works and the friezes of the Pergamum altar have in common the old ideas and values I have called "Hesiodic": the solidarity of blood relatives and the durable existence of social micro- and macrostructures secured by mothers who give birth to excellent and numerous children from generation to generation.

But why did this prevalence of women on important public monuments not alarm the Greek partisans of patriarchy? There was a very old and respectable element in epic poetry which might well have given rise to the idea of representing so many impressive mothers on the great frieze of the Pergamum altar as well as on the sculptured columns of the Cyzicus temple. I am referring to the so-called catalogue of women, enumerations of beautiful women who were made mothers of outstanding descendants by a god or a hero. Homer catalogued such women in the Nekyia of the Odyssey, and — at least according to the *communis opinio* of the ancient scholarly world — so did Hesiod (once again!) in a famous poem which was popular still in Hellenistic times.[59] The reliefs of the Cyzicus temple and the great frieze show, it seems to me, at least a remarkable affinity with the literary catalogues of women. The series of over thirty larger-than-life female statues, which, as mentioned at the beginning, belongs either to the decoration of the Pergamum altar itself (pl. 2) or to that of the altar temenos,[60] can perhaps be explained in a similar way: they may have been a counterpart in stone to those literary catalogues of Homer and Hesiod — perhaps mothers of heroes of the empire's cities.[61]

There must have been a special motive for reminding the viewers of the Pergamum altar of this literary scheme. This implies that in addition to the well-known relation of the altar to the Attalids' victorious wars against the Gauls,[62] there was a further motive for erecting this monument. It has been suggested that by enumerating and glorifying heroines in the Nekyia, Odysseus is paying homage to his royal listener and protectress, Queen Aretê,[63] and that the social background and motivation for Hesiod's catalogue of women was some kind of "Frauen-verehrung".[64] Is it too daring to look in this direction for an explanation of the numerical and visual preponderance of women and mothers on the Pergamum altar? Some years ago K. Stähler[65] pointed out that the architectonic structure of the Pergamum altar not only continues the tradition of archaic Ionic monumental altars, but also relates typologically and structurally to the Mausoleum of Halicarnassus and to heroa; Stähler, therefore, entertained the hypothesis that the heroon of Telephus is to be recognized in the Pergamum "altar".[66] Another interpretation related to the sepulchral sphere is suggested by a lemma in Suidas' lexicon,[67] where we are told that Attalus II had his mother Apollonis interred (*katetheto*) in the greatest sanctuary (*hieron*) of Pergamum which "he had himself built." Is this "*hieron*" perhaps to be identified with the Pergamum altar? This monument might well be termed "the greatest *hieron* of Pergamum". Begun in Eumenes' time, in the 160's BC at the latest, work on the altar was probably not finished before 156 BC, i.e. in the first years of the reign of Attalus II — or even considerably later, as has recently been argued.[68] Thus, Attalus may well have been considered in later times as the king who "had himself built" the Pergamum altar. As to his mother Apollonis, we do not know the year of her death. The last inscription to mention her as living dates from 175 BC,[69] when she was between sixty and seventy. We do not know how long she lived afterwards. It seems possible that the planning, and also a good deal of the construction, of the Pergamum altar took place while the grand old lady was still alive, and that she found her last resting-place in its podium, but only some time after her death. The few fragments of the dedicatory inscription[70] would not support objections to this hypothesis: a queen (*basilissa*) is mentioned, and an unknown person is thanked for benefits bestowed — Apollonis?

The hypothesis just outlined is not merely of biographical interest. It stimulates reflections on the function of the Pergamum altar and its temenos. Like others, I doubt whether the altar was really used for burnt-offerings.[71] But it offered an excellent architectural background for processions or similar ceremonial movements of large groups in the altar temenos, which, after all, does not seem to have contained anything to obstruct such celebrations. These movements could be continued by stepping up to the platform of the altar podium. If one of the main purposes of the Pergamum altar was to serve as a grave monument and memorial for Apollonis[72], the meritorious mother of four magnificent princes, and if at the same time it symbolized the idea of and the hope for a secured continuity of *oikoi* and *polis* by generations and generations of vital offspring, then we may imagine its civic function: the building and its temenos would have provided a fitting scene for the performance of sacred rites and ceremonies in which the organisations of boys, youths, young men and unmarried young women (*parthenoi*) — organisations keenly promoted in Pergamum as well as in other Hellenistic cities[73] —

presented their *hebe* to the public.[74] Spectacles such as these may have strengthened the confidence of the citizen body in its ability to regenerate itself continually by vital progeny.

Thus, the meaning of this monument seems to be associated with rather primitive patterns of social thinking (coming uncomfortably close to *Blut-und-Boden* ideology). These patterns originated in an early Greek context and were based to a considerable extent upon the alleged importance of blood relationship. Evidently the concept of the altar is far from the complex reality of the highly developed Pergamene society. Why this looking back to a past supposed to be better and simpler? Although I cannot here fully answer such an intricate question, I would like however to point to two *political* aspects which should be taken into account.

First, some demographic observations and considerations in the written sources deserve our attention. In the fourth century BC, Aristotle reflects on the problem of whether and how the number of descendants of citizens in a *polis* could be regulated in order to avoid over-population.[75] As opposed to this, in the second century BC Polybius, as mentioned above, complains that the Greek cities are deserted, poor, and powerless because the number of children and the population in general are diminishing.[76] In his opinion, this is caused by those people who on account of their mad ambition, their avarice, and their wantonness fail to marry or, if they do, are unwilling to rear all the children born, keeping only one or two in order to let them grow up in luxury and to avoid quarrels about the division of the inheritance. He calls for laws to enforce the bringing up of progeny (here Polybius seems to allude indirectly to the ancient practice of exposing infants).[77] A second testimony: according to a passage in Livy's Roman history[78] referring to the year 185 BC, a decrease of the population seems to have induced King Philip V of Macedonia to force the inhabitants of his empire (by means not described in detail) to procreate and rear children. He further settled many Thracians on his territory. Together with other provisions, both of these measures were to prepare Macedonia for a future war.

Thus, actions taken by the state to stimulate the growth of the citizen population[79] do not appear to have been far from the thoughts of second-century intellectuals and politicians. From the contents of these passages in Polybius and Livy, one can draw the conclusion that two goals were thought desirable: first, to secure a sufficient number of well-situated citizen families to serve the economic welfare and social stability of the Greek cities; second, to provide sufficient manpower for the armed forces. The Pergamene kings must have been particularly interested in both of these ends. The staff for government and administration was recruited mainly from the citizenry of the *poleis*.[80] Moreover, the kings had to secure the defence of their state from continual threats by the Gauls. A considerable part of the armed forces consisted of expensive mercenaries.[81] Therefore, every able-bodied son of a citizen potentially lessened the treasury's burden, aside from the fact that he was probably more reliable than a mercenary.

We do not know if in the Pergamene cities of the second century BC the number of Greek citizens had diminished to such a degree that for the two reasons just mentioned a greater number of citizen marriages and an increasing rate of children reared became politically desirable.[82] In any case, the many wars in which Pergamum was involved must have cost a lot of blood, not only of mercenaries, but also of the younger citizens. Furthermore, it may be significant that the greatest gymnasium of the Greek world was erected here in Pergamum. This seems to indicate that the rising generation of youths (an important concern everywhere in Hellenistic Greece) was paid special attention[83] by the royal Pergamene government, particularly with regard to the demographic aspects discussed above. In such a political context the complex message of the great frieze may have contained another important aspect: the man- (and women-) power of the fighting community of deities remains stable from generation to generation, thanks to the faithfully bearing divine mothers; therefore this community could be recommended to the subjects of the Pergamene king as an example to be followed in order to secure the internal welfare of the empire as well as its military efficiency which protected it from external enemies.

There may have been a second and possibly even more weighty political motive for the altar's dual emphasis on harmony among blood relatives and politically important procreation. Pergamene internal politics had to balance relations between Greek and non-Greek parts of the empire's heterogeneous population. As to external affairs, Pergamum often had to rely on co-operation with mighty states whose cultural background was at best superficially Greek or non-Greek, like Rome. For both of these reasons it was in the empire's interest to develop and present an image of itself that was not only convenient for the Pergamene and non-Pergamene Greeks, but could also be understood and accepted by other peoples as an expression of their own cultural identity and traditional value systems. To adapt the visual arts to these ends required symbols and structures which, on the one hand, were rooted in the traditions and conventions of Greek sculpture and painting, but could, on the other hand, also be "read", i. e. decoded, and approved by non-Greeks coming from various countries. Let us now consider the Pergamum altar from this point of view.

As mentioned above, W. Neumer-Pfau has argued convincingly[84] that Mysians,

Carians, Lydians, Phrygians, and other peoples living in Asia Minor could relate the emphasis the great frieze laid on the divine mothers and on the maternal line of the deities' descendance to their indigenous religion and matrilinear elements in their social systems.

As far as Rome is concerned, the Pergamene empire always tried to cultivate the friendship — or at least neutrality — of this powerful partner, even at the price of occasional humiliations.[85] Therefore (and also for other reasons), I doubt the hypothesis put forward recently by T. Mathias-Schmidt that the sculptural decoration of the Pergamum altar has an anti-Roman tendency.[86] There are several features of Pergamene art and architecture which might have appeared familiar to a Roman visitor. Some decades ago, H. Drerup pointed out, for instance, that the Italic temple podium and the Tuscan column seem to have influenced the architecture of Pergamum before it became part of the Roman empire.[87] Moreover, among the mythical scenes on the sculptured columns of the temple of Apollonis at Cyzicus was also a representation of the brothers Romulus and Remus liberating their mother Servilia.[88] Hence one should consider the possibility that one motivation for the Pergamene praise for mothers of merit and concordant blood relatives was the knowledge that such values were highly esteemed — and, as we shall see, much debated — in Rome as well.[89]

The *gentes* of the Roman aristocracy were interconnected by numerous marriages, that is to say, the members of the upper class clans were linked by a complicated network of consanguineous persons. From this point of view, conflicts of these *gentes* — which had been intensifying since the end of the third century[90] — could be regarded as discord among blood relatives. *Concordia* of those *sanguine coniuncti* was urgently required. Furthermore, the continuity of noble houses was often endangered by a lack of legitimate sons, necessitating adoptions to obtain male heirs.[91] There may have also been a shortage of marriageable daughters, caused by the practice of exposing female babies more often than male ones.[92] This situation has been seen as an explanation for the increasing economic and social autonomy of Roman women in the middle and late republic.[93] The riot caused by the lex Oppia in 195 BC[94] indicates that the self-assured attitude of such women in public was perceived by Roman conservatives like Cato as a provocation. Apparently, such people were afraid that the noble ladies would no longer care about their traditional duties as wives, mothers, and educators. This conservative ideal of the Roman woman found its most famous incarnation some decades later in Cornelia,[95] the famous mother of the two Gracchi — in a way the younger Roman counterpart to Apollonis.

Thus, the traditional Greek values communicated by the sculptural decoration of the Pergamum altar may well have found the approval of Cato-minded Romans who came to Pergamum as respectable guests or diplomats and paid visits to the monument, perhaps accompanied by a well-informed native guide. Particularly the prominent position of Hera (and perhaps her daughter Hebe) in the centre of the east frieze might have seemed appropriate to a Roman.[96] Just like Hera, her Roman equivalent Juno was the protectress of citizens' legitimate progeny.[97] Indeed, Juno's name, belonging to the same family of words as *iuvenis, iuventus* etc., indicates her responsibility for the vitality of the young generation. Furthermore, the fighting Juno, with the chariot as her attribute, was familiar to the Romans and was often represented in Roman art (pl. 7).[98] As opposed to this, Greek artistic depictions of a warlike Hera are rare,[99] her iconography being dominated by matronly features. Nevertheless, the bellicose Hera on the Pergamene Great frieze did not run counter to Greek tradition. In some cults she bore the epithet *hoplosmia*.[100] Moreover, the beholder of the great frieze may have felt reminded of a famous passage in the Iliad, where Hera is described as a pugnacious goddess whose horses fly under the starry sky pulling her magnificent chariot.[101] Thus, one of the motives for the decision to emphasize just this aspect of Hera on the great frieze may have been the consideration that it was compatible with religious notions and traditions of both Greek and Roman viewers.

To sum up, the selection and arrangement of the deities on the great frieze was guided by the traditional conviction, first attested by Hesiod, that harmony and co-operation among blood relatives as well as the continuous procreation of numerous and excellent offspring are vitally important for the internal peace, defence, and permanent existence of the community. Since these simple patterns of thinking were just as popular among Greeks as amongst the people of Asia Minor and Rome, their translation into the visual medium of sculpture on the Pergamum altar could be deciphered by members of all these cultures in accordance with their own specific traditions and values: a trilingual iconic text, so to speak. An essential motive for the decision to base the conceptualization of the altar sculptures just on those rather trivial notions may have been the assumption that ideas of this kind were something like an international currency to be used for communication between all civilized peoples. Thus, they appeared well-suited for promoting the Pergamene kings' popularity among non-Greek inhabitants of their empire and at the same time for securing good relations with mighty neighbouring states, particularly Rome.

As some studies of the last two decades indicate,[102] this function of the Pergamum altar is not an isolated phenomenon in Hellenistic art: Ptolemaic and Seleucid monuments show similar "bilingual" or "multilingual" tendencies. They are composed of visual symbols which could be perceived by Greeks as well as non-Greeks as expressing their own traditional notions of, for example, "The king (god) and his vanquished foe", or "The permanence of the monarchy", or "The containment of destructive natural forces by the superior virtues of human civilization (the divine order);" etc. Perhaps we meet here a general characteristic of official art in the Hellenistic monarchies, a characteristic which seems to correspond to the cosmopolitism of this age. But a price had to be paid for that innovation. Such works of art offered spectators a more or less superficial presentation of some cross-cultural commonplaces. They could receive from them no deep insights into the essentials of their own cultural identities, bound as they were to the social and religious structures, the norms and values of specific regions and peoples. Visualizing such particularities had once been one of the great achievements of pre-Hellenistic Greek art. But now, in an era of high mobility and manifold cultural contacts and mixtures, this former merit was in danger of being disregarded as provincialism.

Archäologisches Institut
Johnsallee 35
D-20148 Hamburg
Germany

Notes

1. I am grateful to Dale Martin for revising my English. For the supposed impact of ancient scholarship, especially Stoicism, on the altar sculptures see e.g. V. Salis 1912, 23f; Schober 1951, 88; Simon 1975, 56-59; Pfanner 1979, 57; Schalles 1986, 77-80. More sceptical: Onians 1979, 88-94 and Stewart 1993a, 153-59.
2. The inscriptions giving all the names of deities and giants, even well-known ones, may have been very helpful to such people. Cf. also Schalles 1986, 80.
3. See e.g. Neumer-Pfau 1983, 75; Schalles 1986, 77; Stewart 1993a, 163.
4. Neumer-Pfau 1983, 80. Cf. also the juxtapositions Poseidon/Triton/Amphitrite/Nereus/Doris/Oceanus/Tethys at the north-west corner and Herakles/Zeus/Athena/Ares/Aphrodite/Eros/Dione at the north-east corner.
5. Neumer-Pfau 1983, 75.
6. I have counted 32 goddesses and 21 gods (fragments of frieze sculptures and/or inscriptions). Simon 1975, filling the lacunae of the frieze with conjectural deities, has 38 goddesses and 24 gods.
7. Winter 1908, 74-127.
8. Cf. the reconstruction Hoepfner 1989, 625 Abb. 24-26.
9. See Hoepfner 1989, 624-27; Hoepfner 1993, 114-16; Kunze 1993, 133-35.
10. Pfanner 1979, 49-51.
11. H. Winnefeld 1910, 128, 48; Kähler 1948, 39-42, 44; Pfanner 1979, 50.
12. Cf. also the impressive description of Hera's chariot with flying horses in Hom. *Il.* 5.720-32, 748-52, 755, 767-76.

13. The identifications of 33, i.e. over 50 % of the ca. 60 fighting deities, are assured and/or not controversial since more than half a century. The mothers of 26 of these 33 deities can be found among the very same 33 (the mothers of five of the surely identified deities were probably not represented for the following reasons: the origin of *Gê*, the mother of all, was the Chaos; *Athena, Zeus'* daughter, was brought by him into the world after he had devoured Metis pregnant with Athena; *Herakles'* mortal mother Alkmene, never searched for or identified by anyone on the frieze, was married to the judge of the dead, Rhadamanthys, after her death but never became a member of the Olympic community; the two *Satyrs* were the sons of an anonymous human mother, the daughter of the Argive king Phoroneus, according to Hes., frg. 123 M.). This group of 33 includes also the mothers of a good deal of the deities who were tentatively identified or whose existence was postulated on the frieze.

14. I mention just the fatherless deities whose identification on the frieze is certain. Probably we have to add Kronos' daughter Demeter (cf. Simon 1975, 29f.; Stewart 1993a, 157). Vian's identification (Vian 1951, 22) of Hyperion, father of Helios, Selene and Eos, has found no followers; thus these three astral deities, whose identifications on the frieze are undoubted, may well have lacked a father. Cf. Simon 1975, 30 who noticed an "'Unterdrückung' der männlichen Mitglieder einer Sippe."

15. Among the deities whose identifications are assured or at least not controversial I have counted 12 mothers and 6 fathers (not including those gods and goddesses whose progeny is mentioned in written sources but cannot be identified on the great frieze). As regards the other deities, the proposed identifications, though very numerous and diversified, do not leave a chance for a substantially higher percentage of fathers.

16. Wenning 1979, 360.

17. Cf. the list of scenes in Bauchhenß-Thüriedl 1971, 72-74.

18. See e.g. Thomas 1976, 19-28.

19. Cf. above note 6.

20. See Schober 1951, 84.

21. Neumer-Pfau 1983.

22. Neumer-Pfau 1983, 81-84.

23. Neumer-Pfau 1983, 84-86.

24. Neumer-Pfau 1983, 85.

25. See Cic. *Off.* 1.54 excerpting Panaetius: "prima societas in ipso coniugio est."

26. Only the marine deities Nereus/Doris and Oceanus/Tethys (to the left of the great staircase) are represented as couples, as husband and wife fighting side by side, whereas the more prominent Olympians Zeus and Hera as well as Poseidon and Amphitrite are separated by a considerable distance.

27. See e.g. Arist. *Eth. Nic.* 1161b; Arist. *Eth. Eud.* 1241b.

28. Hes. *Op.* 180-200.

29. See for instance, Hes. *Op.* 707; Xen. *Cyr.* 8.7.14f.; Xen. *Mem.* 2.3. Arist. *Eth. Nic.* 1161a-1162a.

30. Lacey 1968, 116f.

31. Lullies & Hirmer 1979, 46f. pl. 18.

32. For the story of Cleobis and Biton see Hdt. 1.31. For the comparison with the sons of Apollonis see Polyb. 22.20, cf. Stupperich 1990, 108.

33. Cf. the passages of ancient authors collected in Haedicke 1937, 39f. This book is mainly useful as an example of the influence of Nazi racism and Blut-und-Boden ideology on German scholars after 1933.

34. Hdt. 1.30.

35. See recently Hintzen-Bohlen 1990, 131-37.
36. Polyb. 36.17. Cf. Vatin 1970, 229f.
37. Hes. *Op.* 235-44.
38. See the ancient statements in Haedicke 1937, 37 nn. 53-55.
39. For references to earlier publications see Simon 1975, 2.
40. See above n. 20.
41. Cf. Christ 1912, 128f.
42. Simon 1975, pl. 14.
43. See the description in Hes. *Op.* 230-37.
44. Nilsson 1967, 427-33; Pötscher 1987, 110-25.
45. Hesych. s.v. *Eilethyias... Hera en Argei.*
46. Hom. *Il.* 11.270f.; Hes. *Theog.* 922. — Cf. an unpublished statuette of a parturient woman in the Heraion of Samos (mentioned by Pötscher 1987, 115 n. 261).
47. Artemis also helps women in childbirth — but all of them, not only the married.
48. See Pötscher 1987, 115-23.
49. This possibility mentioned e.g. by Simon 1975, 20.
50. For the gymnasium see Schazmann 1923 and Radt 1988, 131-54. For the Hera temple Radt 1988, 214-16, 375.
51. The dedication by Attalus II (159-138 BC) was mentioned in the inscription on the architrave of the temple, see Schazmann 1923, 105 and Ohlemutz 1940, 252. The dating of the Pergamum altar is discussed by Schmidt 1990, 141-62; idem 1994, 1-6. The traditional date for the beginning of the project (*c.* 180 BC) is rejected by Schmidt. He supposes — like others before him — that work on the altar started in the sixties and was stopped by King Attalus II shortly after 156 BC for political reasons, see Schmidt 1994, 5. Cf. Kunze 1990, 135-38 and Hoepfner 1993, 117f. For the possibility that the building activities lasted from *c.* 165 BC until the beginning of the reign of Attalus III (138-133 BC) see Börker 1990, 592. I would prefer a late date, too. Hence the building periods of the altar and of the Hera temple may well have overlapped.
52. See Radt 1988, 215f, 375.
53. Ohlemutz 1940, 258.
54. See Bauchhenß-Thüriedl 1971, 56.
55. The only source is the 19 epigrams in the third book of the *Anthologia Palatina*, see Stupperich 1990, 101 (with further references in n. 2). The mutual recognition of Auge and Telephus is described in epigram 2.
56. Epigram 7.
57. Heger 1986, 642f. Heger's hypothesis that the Dirke group is a Pergamene original is rejected by Andreae 1993, 111-17.
58. Simon 1975, 49f; Neumer-Pfau 1983, 85; Heger 1986, 643; Stupperich 1990, 108f.
59. Hom. *Od.* 11.226-332. For the Hesiodic (?) Catalogue of Women, see Schwartz 1960, 265-625; West 1985.
60. See above nn. 7-9.
61. P. Zanker suggested that these statues embodied the cities of the Pergamene empire, see Hoepfner 1989, 627.
62. The great frieze seems to allude not only to the Gauls but also to the Macedonian and Seleucid opponents of the Pergamene empire, see Yfantidis 1993, 230-35 and Schmidt-Dounas 1993, 16.
63. Marg 1970, 399f.
64. Rzach 1913, 1205.
65. Stähler 1978.

66. The foundations of the Pergamum altar enclose the remnants of an apsidal building which, according to Stähler 1978, sheltered the hero cult of Telephus before the Pergamum altar was built. Rheidt 1992, 259f. regards the function of this building as uncertain; Hoepfner 1993, 113 n. 15 rejects Stähler's hypothesis in favour of an interpretation as nymphaeum.

67. Suid. s.v. *Apollonias limne*. Cf. Stupperich 1990, 109.

68. See above n. 51.

69. Hopp 1977, 32f; Stupperich 1990, 101.

70. Fraenkel 1890, 54f. no. 69.

71. Cf. also Hoepfner 1989, 629; Hoepfner 1993, 117; Kunze 1990, 130.

72. This does not necessarily exclude the hero cult of Telephus in the altar precinct, as pointed out by Stähler 1978.

73. Cf. recently v. Hesberg 1995.

74. Entering the altar precinct the young people were confronted with the figure of Hera in the centre of the east frieze (see pl. 1-4), the same goddess who, looking down from her temple (see pl. 6), watched their activities in the great gymnasium.

75. Arist. *Pol.* 1265a-b.

76. Polyb. 36.17.

77. Generally on the subject Brulé 1992.

78. Liv. 39.24.1-4.

79. Cf. Günther 1993, 318f. (dowries granted by Greek city-states and by queen Laodice, wife of Antiochus III, to penniless female orphans and to poor families with marriageable daughters in order to increase the number of marriages and thereby the number of descendants with citizen status), 322f. (enfranchisement of women without husbands in Miletus as potential candidates for marriages with Milesian citizens and as future mothers).

80. See Kertész 1992.

81. For the Pergamene army see Hansen 1971, 224-33.

82. Cf. above n. 79.

83. For the relationship of the Hellenistic gymnasia of the second century BC to the young generation see recently v. Hesberg 1995.

84. Neumer-Pfau 1983, 81-84.

85. MacShane 1964, 92-176; Gruen 1984, 529-610; Habicht 1989, 324-34.

86. Schmidt 1990, 147-62; Schmidt 1994, 3-6; Stewart 1993b, 716 is sceptical.

87. Drerup 1966, 189 n. 15.

88. *Anth. Pal.* 3, epigram 19.

89. Cf. Neumer-Pfau 1983, 86f. who suggests that the Attalids' veneration of their mother Apollonis should be understood "als Verkörperung des traditionellen griechischen (und wohl auch römischen) Familienideals."

90. See e.g. Alföldy 1984, 48f.; Astin 1989, 174-96.

91. Alföldy 1984, 46.

92. Brunt 1987, 148-52; cf. Gardner 1986, 157f.

93. Brunt 1987, 152. Cf. also Flaig 1995, 139f., 144 (importance of daughters in the context of Roman familial strategies).

94. Livy 34.1-8. See Schuller 1987, 35-37.

95. Schuller 1987, 39f.; Dettenhofer 1992, 791 n. 44 (further references); Bauman 1992, 42-45.

96. I believe that the anticipated view of potential Roman beholders was an important factor in the conception of many figures and scenes of the two friezes on the Pergamum altar. I am preparing a contribution centred on this aspect.

97. See recently La Rocca 1990, 814-18 (with further references).

98. La Rocca 1990, 814-18 and especially 819-22 (Iuno Sospita), 835f. (Iuno Curitis). Cf. Simon 1990, 98-100.
99. See Kossatz-Deißmann 1988, 702-4.
100. Jessen 1913, 2299.
101. Hom. *Il.* 5.720-76. For Hera's love of fighting cf. especially v. 732.
102. Kyrieleis 1973 and 1975; Neumer-Pfau 1983; Fehr 1988 and 1990.

Bibliography

Alföldy, G. 1984. *Römische Sozialgeschichte* (3rd ed.). Wiesbaden.

Andreae, B. et al. 1990. *Phyromachos-Probleme* (RM-ErgH 31). Mainz.

Astin, A.E. 1989. "Roman Government and Politics, 200-134 B.C.", In: *CAH* VIII (2nd ed.), 163-96.

Bauchhenß-Thüriedl, C. 1971. *Der Mythos von Telephos in der antiken Bildkunst*. Würzburg.

Bauman, R.A. 1992. *Women and Politics in Ancient Rome*. London/New York.

Börker, C. 1990. "Zur Datierung des Pergamon-Altares", In: *AXIIIKonKlArch*, 591-92.

Brulé, P. 1992. "Infanticide et abandon d'enfants. Pratiques grecques et comparaisons anthropologiques", *DialHistAnc* 18.2, 53-90.

Brunt, P.A. 1987. *Italian Manpower 225 B.C. — A.D. 14* (2nd ed.). Oxford.

Büsing, H. & Hiller, F. (eds.) 1988. *Bathron. Beiträge zur Architektur und verwandten Künsten für Heinrich Drerup zu seinem 80. Geburtstag von seinen Schülern und Freunden*. Saarbrücken.

Christ, W. v. 1912. *Geschichte der griechischen Litteratur. I. Klassische Periode der griechischen Litteratur*. Unter Mitwirkung von Otto Stählin und Wilhelm Schmid (HAW VII.1. 6th ed.). München.

Crawford, M.H. 1974. *Roman Republican Coinage*. Cambridge.

Dettenhofer, M.H. 1992. "Zur politischen Rolle der Aristokratinnen zwischen Republik und Prinzipat", *Latomus* 51, 775-95.

Dörpfeld, W. 1912. "Die Arbeiten zu Pergamon 1910-1911, I. Die Bauwerke", *AM* 37, 1912, 233-76.

Drerup, H. 1966. "Architektur als Symbol. Zur zeitgenössischen Bewertung der römischen Architektur", *Gymnasium* 73, 181-96.

Eckstein, F. (ed.) 1973. *Antike Plastik* XII. Berlin.

Fehr, B. 1988. "Zwei Lesungen des Alexandermosaiks", In: Büsing and Hiller (eds.) 1988, 121-34.

Fehr, B. 1990. "Lectio Graeca – Lectio orientalis. Überlegungen zur Tyche von Antiocheia", *VisRel* 7, 83-97.

Flaig, E. 1995. "Die Pompa Funebris. Adlige Konkurrenz und annalistische Erinnerung in der römischen Republik", In: v. Oexle (ed.) 1995, 115-48.

Fränkel, M. (ed.) 1890. *Die Inschriften von Pergamon. Altertümer von Pergamon* VIII 1. Berlin.

Gardner, J.F. 1986. *Women in Roman Law and Society*. London/Sydney.

Gruen, E.S. 1984. *The Hellenistic World and the Coming of Rome*. Berkeley/Los Angeles/London.

Günther, L.M. 1993. "Witwen in der griechischen Antike – zwischen Oikos und Polis", *Historia* 42, 308-25.

Habicht, C. 1989. "The Seleucids and their rivals", In: *CAH* VIII (2nd ed.), 324-87.

Haedicke, W. 1937. *Die Gedanken der Griechen über Familienherkunft und Vererbung*. Halle.

Hansen, E.V. 1971. *The Attalids of Pergamon* (2nd ed.). Ithaca/London.

Heger, F. 1986. s.v. Dirke. In: *LIMC* III 1, 635-44.

Hesberg, H. v. 1995. "Das griechische Gymnasion im 2. Jh. n. Chr.", In: Wörrle & Zanker (eds.) 1995, 13-27.

Hintzen-Bohlen, B. 1990. "Die Familiengruppe – ein Mittel zur Selbstdarstellung hellenistischer Herrscher", *JdI* 105, 129-54.

Hoepfner, W. 1989. "Zu den großen Altären von Magnesia und Pergamon", *AA*, 601-34.

Hoepfner, W. 1993. "Siegestempel und Siegesaltäre. Der Pergamonaltar als Siegesmonument", In: Hoepfner & Zimmer (eds.) 1993, 111-25.

Hoepfner, W. & Zimmer, G. (eds.) 1993. *Die griechische Polis. Architektur und Politik.* Tübingen.

Holliday, P.J. (ed.) 1993. *Narrative and Event in Ancient Art.* Cambridge.

Hopp, J. 1977. *Untersuchungen zur Geschichte der letzten Attaliden* (Vestigia 25). München.

Jessen, O. 1913. s.v. Hoplosmios. In: *RE* VIII, 2299.

Kähler, H 1948. *Der große Fries von Pergamon.* Berlin.

Kertész, I. 1992. "Zur Sozialpolitik der Attaliden", *Tyche* 7, 133-41.

Kossatz-Deißmann, A. 1988. s.v. Hera. In: *LIMC* IV 1, 659-719.

Kunze, M. 1990. "Neue Beobachtungen zum Pergamonaltar", In: Andreae et al., 1990, 123-39.

Kyrieleis, H. 1973. "Kathaper Hermes kai Horos", In: Eckstein (ed.) 1973, 133-47.

Kyrieleis, H. 1975. *Bildnisse der Ptolemäer.* Berlin.

Lacey, W. K. 1968. *The Family in Classical Greece.* London.

La Rocca, E. 1990. s.v. Iuno. In: *LIMC* V 1, 814-56.

Lullies, R. & Hirmer, M. 1979. *Griechische Plastik* (4th ed.). München.

Marg, W. 1970. *Hesiod. Sämtliche Gedichte.* Zürich/Stuttgart.

McShane, R.B. 1964. *The Foreign Policy of the Attalids of Pergamum* (Illinois Studies in the Social Sciences 53). Urbana, Illinois.

Neumer-Pfau, W. 1983. "Die kämpfenden Göttinnen vom großen Fries des Pergamonaltars", *VisRel* 2, 75-94.

Nilsson, M. 1967. *Geschichte der griechischen Religion I: Die Religion Griechenlands bis auf die griechische Weltherrschaft* (HAW 5.2.1). München.

Oexle, O.G. v. (ed.) 1995. *Memoria als Kultur.* Göttingen.

Ohlemutz, E. 1940. *Die Kulte und Heiligtümer der Götter in Pergamon.* Würzburg.

Onians, J. 1979. *Art and Thought in the Hellenistic Age. The Greek World View 350-50 B.C.* London.

Pfanner, M. 1979. "Bemerkungen zur Komposition und Interpretation des Großen Frieses von Pergamon", *AA*, 46-57.

Pötscher, W. 1987. *Hera. Eine Strukturanalyse im Vergleich mit Athena.* Darmstadt.

Radt, W. 1988. *Pergamon. Geschichte und Bauten, Funde und Erforschung einer antiken Metropole.* Köln.

Rheidt, K. 1992. "Die Obere Agora. Zur Entwicklung des hellenistischen Stadtzentrums von Pergamon. Mit einem Beitrag von C. Meyer-Schlichtmann", *IstMitt* 42, 235-306.

Rzach, A. 1913. s.v. Hesiodos. In: *RE* VIII, 1167-1240.

Sahin, S., Schwertheim, E. & Wagner, J. (eds.) 1978. *Studien zur Religion und Kultur Kleinasiens. Festschrift für Friedrich Karl Dörner* II. (Études préliminaires aux religions orientales dans l'empire Romain 66). Leiden.

Salis, A. v. 1912. *Der Altar von Pergamon. Ein Beitrag zur Erklärung des hellenistischen Barockstils in Kleinasien.* Berlin.

Schalles, H. 1986. *Der Pergamonaltar. Zwischen Bewertung und Verwertbarkeit.* Frankfurt a.M.

Schazmann, P. 1923. *Das Gymnasion. Der Tempelbezirk der Hera Basileia Altertümer von Pergamon* VI. Berlin.

Schmidt, T.M. 1990. "Der späte Beginn und der vorzeitige Abbruch der Arbeiten am Pergamonaltar", In: Andreae et al. 1990, 141-62.

Schmidt, T.M. 1994. "Der Pergamonaltar – Weltwunder oder Investitionsruine?", *Gymnasium* 101, 1-6.

Schmidt-Dounas, B. 1993. "Anklänge an altorientalische Mischwesen im Gigantomachiefries des Pergamonaltares", *Boreas* 16, 5-17.

Schober, A. 1951. *Die Kunst von Pergamon*. Vienna/Innsbruck/Wiesbaden/Bregenz.

Schuller, W. 1987. *Frauen in der römischen Geschichte*. Konstanz.

Schwartz, J. 1960. *Pseudo-Hesiodeia. Recherches sur la composition, la diffusion et la disparition anciennes d'oeuvres attribuées à Hésiode*. Leiden.

Schwertheim, E. (ed.) 1990. *Mysische Studien* VIII. Bonn.

Simon, E. 1975. *Pergamon und Hesiod*. Mainz.

Simon, E. 1990. *Die Götter der Römer*. München.

Stähler, K. 1978. "Überlegungen zur architektonischen Gestalt des Pergamonaltares", In: Sahin, Schwertheim & Wagner (eds.) 1978, 838-67.

Stewart, A. 1993a. "Narration and Allusion in the Hellenistic Baroque", In: Holliday (ed.) 1993, 130-74.

Stewart, A. 1993b. Review of Andreae et al. 1990, *Gnomon* 65, 710-16.

Stupperich, R. 1990. "Zu den Stylopinakia am Tempel der Apollonis in Kyzikos", In: Schwertheim (ed.) 1990, 101-9.

Thomas, E. 1976. *Mythos und Geschichte. Untersuchungen zum historischen Gehalt griechischer Mythendarstellungen*. Köln.

Vian, F. 1951. *Répertoire des gigantomachies figurées dans l'art grec et romain*. Paris.

Vatin, C. 1970. *Recherches sur le mariage et la condition de la femme mariée à l'époque hellénistique*. Paris.

Wenning, R. 1979. Review of Simon 1975. *Gnomon* 51, 355-61.

West, M.L. 1985. *The Hesiodic Catalogue of Women. Its Nature, Structure and Origins*. Oxford.

Winnefeld, H. 1910. *Die Frieze des großen Altars. Altertümer von Pergamon* III 2. Berlin.

Winter, F. 1908. *Die Skulpturen mit Ausnahme der Altarreliefs. Die Altertümer von Pergamon* VII 2. Berlin.

Wörrle, M. & Zanker, P. (eds.) 1995. *Stadtbild und Bürgerbild im Hellenismus*. München.

Yfantidis, K. 1993. "Beobachtungen an zwei pergamenischen Köpfen in Schloß Fasanerie bei Fulda", *AM* 108, 225-38.

DAIMÔN AND *TUCHÊ* IN THE HELLENISTIC RELIGIOUS EXPERIENCE

Giulia Sfameni Gasparro

The contribution of Cleombrotus to the discussion in Plutarch's *On the disappearance of oracles* centres on the rather thorny issue of Providence. In his view, the introduction of the category of *daimones* between gods and men has resolved a good many difficulties, for we have thus "in a sense discovered the common bond that links us, joins us, to the gods".[1] Without lingering to determine the origin of the idea,[2] Cleombrotus continues:

Of the Greeks, we can see Homer using both words indiscriminately, and sometimes calling the gods *daimones*. Hesiod was the first to draw a clear distinction, setting out four classes of sentient beings: gods, *daimones*, heroes and finally men.[3]

Plutarch here appeals first to the two poets recognised as the creators of the entire Greek religious tradition; in *On Isis and Osiris* he also appeals to the authority of Plato, Pythagoras, Xenocrates and Chrysippus, each of them in his turn supposedly a "disciple of the ancient writers on the gods" (*hepomenoi tois palai theologois*). All these thinkers believed that *daimones* exist:

stronger than men, and easily surpassing our nature in might, yet they do not possess unmixed, pure divinity; it is instead joined together with the nature of the soul and bodily sensation – which is capable of perceiving pleasure and pain, and whatever subjective sensations are bound up with change, affecting different individuals differently: for *daimones*, like men, are good and bad.[4]

In these two passages we find the notion of *daimones* understood as a class of beings intermediate between gods and men,[5] a notion particularly valuable to Plutarch in *On Isis and Osiris*, in which it plays a central part in the theological argument.[6] For without rejecting traditional beliefs or cult practices, he argues there in favour of a theodicy compatible with his Platonist metaphysical and ethical leanings.[7]

Plutarch was also familiar with the idea, developed in numerous different forms at different points in the *Moralia* and the *Lives*, of a personal *daimôn*, the individual's guardian[8] and/or the superior, divine, element of the soul.[9] Moreover, he often — especially in the dense context of the contingencies faced by the heroes of the *Lives* — introduces the resistless power of Tuchê, "chance" or "fortune", but at the same time a divine being who presides over the destinies of men and nations.[10] Thus, the great Sicilian venture of Timoleon is from first to last directed by Tuchê: Timoleon's military career "appears, to those who judge truly, the product, not of Tuchê, but of virtue favoured by Tuchê".[11]

The moralizing tone betrays the narrow perspective on this issue that Plutarch reveals throughout his work, and not merely in rhetorical exercises such as the *On the Fortune of Alexander* or *On the Fortune of the Romans* which discuss in school terms whether virtue and chance operate concurrently or in opposition.[12] But he does remark that Timoleon himself:

used to attribute all these successes to Fortune (Tuchê), and, in letters to his friends in Corinth and in his speeches at Syracuse, often used to say that he was grateful to the divinity for ascribing to him her own decision to save Sicily. In his private house he even dedicated a shrine to Chance (*Automatia*), and sacrificed to her; the house itself he dedicated to the *hieros daimôn*.[13]

Automatia may be taken as another form of Tuchê; and in two other parallel contexts, Plutarch himself uses *Agathos Daimôn* instead of *Hieros Daimôn*.[14] For the moment I do not propose to touch on any of the various problems raised by the ideas underlying the passages I have cited. What I want to stress here is the paradigmatic value of Plutarch's usage, evoking as it does the grain of the religious experience I propose to explore. Plutarch stands, as it were, at one extremity of a notional arc representing the entire religious history of the Greeks from the Archaic period up to the early decades of the second century AD. He thus occupies a privileged position, and his writings offer an excellent vantage-point from which to observe the different strands of that complex amalgam we may call Greek daemonology. This set of notions turns out in several ways to be closely linked to the notion of *tuchê*, a term whose values and connotations are themselves extremely dense.

Some preliminary points first. The term daemonology denotes neither a clearly-defined doctrine nor a coherent and finished system of ideas: Greek religion implies a "national" tradition that developed in parallel with the evolution of Greek culture. It lacked official normative institutions as well as dogmas. Rather, daemonology is a more or less homogeneous and articulated set of ideas and beliefs, sometimes associated with ritual practice, relating to the category of the divine which the Greeks, from the time of Homer, denoted by the term *daimôn/daimones*. It is also difficult, if not downright misleading, to split the process of history into distinct phases, isolating autonomous periods within the continous flux of religious belief of such a "national" tradition. Hellenistic daemonology must therefore be set off against earlier traditions if we are to be able to gauge possible continuities, shifts, and innovations. At the same time, we must eschew anachronism and avoid interpreting Archaic and Classical texts in the light of later developments and in terms of ideological schemes belonging to a different historical and cultural context.

There are, moreover, numerous problems stemming from the nature of the source-material. Literary texts easily outnumber direct documents, such as inscriptions. It is difficult, sometimes indeed quite impossible, to differentiate within the literary texts between material deriving from the writers' own interpretation, and their ideological options, and that which might reflect more directly beliefs and practices widespread within the population. But the gap between the two, between learned speculation — or more simply personal or school positions (in the case of those writing within the intellectual framework of one of the main philosophical schools) — and the broader level of the mentalities and religious experience of Greek communities and numerous Hellenised peoples within the Mediterranean *oikoumene* (the inhabited world), is not unbridgeable. It may be reduced considerably if we consider the stability of religious cultures in the ancient world, and of the Greek tradition in particular. Within that world, in the absence of official normative authority, there was a deeply conservative attitude with regard to beliefs: in particular, both in the case of the individual *polis* with its own traditions and at the level of the Greeks seen as a cultural whole, we find a faithful observance of traditional cult practices. None of those who deal with religious themes, be they poets, historians, philosophers or simply writers, innovates in a radical fashion, except in the confessed defence of a critical position: rather, in greater or lesser degree they draw on the common tradition, which also nourishes their own ideological and cultural roots. Such methodological considerations notwithstanding, my question here is whether, in relation to daemonology and the notion of Tuchê, there is a specifically Hellenistic juncture within the *longue durée* from the Homeric age to that of Plutarch.

It is useful to start with Plutarch, since his dense oeuvre can be seen as a kind of pandect, in which almost all the various themes broached by the notions *daimôn* and *tuchê* are brought together. Together with several other contemporary authors,[15] he provides a lively *chiaroscuro* of late-Hellenistic daemonological ideas. The basic lineaments are well-enough known. One view, which we may term theological, denotes by *daimôn* a superhuman being occupying a specific division of a graduated continuum, often including heroes, whose poles are occupied by gods and men. Within this continuum, the *daimones* constitute a group wielding specific powers and competence, usually as a direct consequence of this intermediate status. A second view is anthropological. The *daimôn* is conceived as in various modes equivalent to the soul of a person, living or dead. This view correlates to some extent with the protective function often ascribed to the *daimôn*, which is probably the oldest conception, and the one most deeply rooted in the Greek ethical and religious tradition. This function is linked to the notions of the individual's destiny (*moira*) and his lot or fortune (*tuchê*). On a third view, daemonology has a cosmological function, since the *daimones* belong to one or other of the spheres which compose the graduated structure of the cosmos.

I cannot analyse here in detail this entire "inherited conglomerate", whose basic themes are related, and often profoundly interwoven. I have chosen in principle to examine the material in the light of the distinction, where it can be made, between a popular aspect of a notion or belief, and an intellectual aspect, that is, the product of reflection or even systematic theory-building by individuals and philosophical schools.

The connection between the notions *daimôn* and *tuchê*, already strong in the Classical period, must be viewed in the context of specifically Hellenistic religious experience, that is, in the context of the cults of Agathos Daimôn and Agathê Tuchê, which begin to appear in the first half of the fourth century BC. Before tackling this question, however, there are two preliminary issues to be discussed. First, the extent to which Agathos Daimôn, as a divine persona with appropriate iconography and specific attributes and functions, is linked to ideas about *daimones* as a category of beings intermediate between gods and men. Second, we must ask whether the well-nigh universal view of Tuchê as a personification is actually justified: this will involve some discussion of the history of the term, and a concurrent examination of the main features of the complex relation, already in the pre-Hellenistic period, between the notion of *tuchê* and the nuanced concept of the daemonic (*to daimonion*).

According to Cleombrotus:

Hesiod was the first to draw a clear distinction, setting out four classes of sentient beings: gods, *daimones*, heroes and finally men.[16]

Some modern scholars have denied that the men of the race of gold, who become *daimones* after death, could have been a distinct category for Hesiod. In other words, they understand *daimones* in the Homeric sense of "gods", beings of divine status without special connotation.[17] There are two main difficulties in holding such a view: not merely does it contradict the entire ancient tradition, which always understood Hesiod's *daimones* as beings of special status within his general theological scheme,[18] but it makes a nonsense of the deeper import of the myth of the four races. There have been numerous rewarding interpretations of that myth, which lends itself to different — even contradictory — readings generated by the inexhaustible wealth of meanings it implies or suggests.[19] It certainly reflects its author's attempt to construct a coherent framework for the disorderly religious inheritance which he was trying to rethink in terms of his own ethical views. Among the various meanings of the myth, we may insist here upon its vocation as a classification, in terms of nature and functions, of beings which operate at different levels of reality, levels that are notionally distinct but do not imply any sudden break within a homogeneous and continuous chain of being. The history of man is linked to that of the gods by virtue of the metamorphosis into *daimones* of the "golden race of mortal men".[20] The word *daimôn* retains, throughout Greek tradition from the Homeric poems to the very end, its meaning as a synonym for *theos*;[21] but it also has its own specific nuances, which are deployed here to define a status which is certainly divine but also, in view of the connection with an aboriginal human condition, idiopathic. So much is evident from the attributes and functions characteristic of Hesiod's *daimones*, "by will of great Zeus good spirits of the earth, guardians of mortal men, bestowers of wealth".[22] Acting as guardians is quite appropriate to the *daimones*: the poet's moralising perspective represents them as operating at the level of justice ("they keep watch over the good and evil deeds of men");[23] but they are also *ploutodotai*, bestowers of wealth (126). This is their *geras basilêion*, their royal privilege, which characterizes their position in the scale of divine beings.

We can see in Hesiod's scheme here a whole series of ideas, familiar from different levels of Greek religious thinking, neatly imbricated into a consistent whole. The *daimones*, as an ancient race of men "hidden beneath the earth", are related to the souls of the dead. The rôle of watchers over the good and evil deeds of living men may be evoked in either of two directions. On the one hand, it suggests a notion familiar from the Homeric poems, and recurrent in later Greek tradition: in lyric[24] and gnomic[25] poetry, tragedy,[26] the historians[27] and the orators,[28] the *daimôn* appears as a divine agent intervening at will in human affairs, positively or negatively, for good or ill, often in revenge for crimes (we may think of the *daimôn alastôr* in tragedy),[29] invariably exercising a decisive influence upon human fate. On the other hand, the guardians "by will of great

Zeus" appear here as a well-defined category of beings, midway between gods and men, and acting as intermediaries between them.

Does this scheme of Hesiod's derive from his own poetic imagination, or does it reflect a fund of popular belief? There is no need here to insist on the basic congruence between the poet's own ethical and theological reflection and the traditional material that composes the two poems, the *Theogony* and the *Works and Days*, which, together with Homer, constitute at once the founding charter and the summa of Greek myth and religious belief. Hesiod's view of *daimones* may also derive from such a congruence.[30] We may test this conclusion by examining the various contexts in which *daimones* occur as a specific category of divine (superhuman) beings, related to but distinct from the gods, and in particular as intermediaries.

According to a doxographic tradition reported by the Christian apologist Athenagoras (second century), Thales of Miletus was the first to establish a systematic classification of *theos*, *daimones* and *hêrôes*: god was supposedly the intelligence (*nous*) of the world, the *daimones* were psychic essences (*ousiai psuchikai*), while the heroes were human souls separated from the body and good or bad according to the moral quality of the relevant soul.[31] The value of this late report is undecidable, but we know from Aristotle that according to Thales, soul was intermingled in the universe, such that "all things are full of gods" (*panta plêrê theôn*).[32] This view is echoed in a report by Aetius (also second century AD), that, according to Thales, "the sum of things is besouled, and full of *daimones*".[33] *Daimones* here corresponds to Aristotle's *theoi*, and we have here an attempt to express in philosophical terms the conceptual categories of religious tradition. But on the question of the identification with gods or *daimones* of the psychic stuff that constitutes the vital principle of the universe,[34] we cannot say whether in Thales' cultural and religious context the two terms carried different connotations.

However, as Marcel Detienne has shown, such a distinction does appear relatively clearly within Pythagorean tradition.[35] I will stress here just two relevant points selected from the mass of material he collected in support of the thesis. One is the relation between the views of Pythagorean writers on this topic and popular belief — the clear inference is that these writers are steeped in Greek inherited tradition. The second is the number of sources concerning *daimones* deriving from the fourth century BC and the Hellenistic period.[36]

It is a truism that the two major difficulties in the study of Pythagoreanism are of establishing a reliable chronology of Pythagorean teachings and of distinguishing between the doctrines of Pythagoras himself, whose legend took hold very early, and the numerous tendencies that developed within the school during the course of its long and complex history.[37] Among the numerous senses of *daimôn* to be found in Pythagorean sources, as analysed by Detienne, I stress here that of a category of beings with a particular function in relation to human beings, to whom they are anyway linked, inasmuch as they are souls detached from their bodies. We read in the *Pythagorean Commentaries* cited by Alexander Polyhistor:

The whole air is full of souls. We call them *daimones* and heroes, and it is they who send dreams, signs and illnesses to men – and not only to men, but also to sheep and other domestic animals. It is toward these *daimones* that we direct purifications and apotropaic rituals, all kinds of scrying, kledonomancy and other things of a similar kind.[38]

The date of the *Pythagorean Commentaries* is uncertain. Some scholars have seen in it an early Pythagorean document;[39] others consider it a late work, an expression of second or first-century BC Neo-pythagoreanism, and certainly not earlier than Speusippus (the second head of the Academy, d. 340/39).[40] Detienne saw in the detail that domesticated animals, as well as humans, might be the object of daemonic attack an indication of an Archaic view of *daimones*, reflecting a society of small agricultural communities prior to the sixth century BC "in which animals and humans were indivisible and formed a unity whose parts had equal value" (1963, 32). In my view, the question cannot be resolved with complete assurance. It would also be possible to suppose that the text contains different strata of conceptions, especially as the *Pythagorean Commentaries* drew upon sources diverse in age and origin. The idea that *daimones* and heroes are equivalent to the souls that pullulate in the air, analogous to the doctrine attributed to Thales, might go back to an Archaic stratum, just like that of the daemonic influence upon sheep. The oracular function of these beings, on the other hand, and in particular the ascription of purificatory and apotropaic rituals as well as scrying and kledonomancy to the daemonic world, evidently derives from "intellectual" speculation in a Pythagorean milieu, analogous to that represented by Plato's *Symposium*, and then in the Platonic tradition from Xenocrates (d. 314 BC) to Plutarch.

Everyone is familiar with the myth of the birth of Erôs that Diotima, female sage of Mantinea, tells Socrates in the *Symposium* in support of her view that Love is a *daimôn*: "he is a powerful *daimôn*, and *daimones* as a class are half-way between god and man".[41] She introduces her narrative with the statement that the rôle of *daimones* is

to ply between heaven and earth, flying upwards with our worship and our prayers, and descending with the heavenly answer and commandments ... They form the medium of the prophetic arts, of the priestly rites of sacrifice, initiation, and incantation, of divination and of sorcery.[42]

The theological crux of the argument is revealed in the very next sentence:

The divine will not mingle directly with the human, and it is only through the mediation of the daemonic world that man can have any intercourse, whether waking or sleeping, with the gods (203a1-4).

The introduction concludes with the observation that "there assuredly are many *daimones*, and many kinds of *daimones*".[43] This is probably a collective representation shared both by ordinary people and by the learned, a view supported by the fact that the same idea is to be found in progressively more texts from the fourth century BC. Plato himself in several dialogues develops the notion of a personal *daimôn* who protects the individual during this life and guides him in the life to come,[44] or actually is the superior, divine part of the soul (*Ti.* 90a2-c8). But he also makes use of the traditional tripartite scheme gods-*daimones*-heroes to define the category superhuman.

Of the several cases, it will be enough to cite an important passage of the *Laws* in which the scheme is closely linked to ritual practice. The context is the establishment in the newly-founded city of the rules for religious observation, that "fairest and best and most effective means to happiness".[45] The Athenian proposes that different honours (*timai*) be paid to different categories of divine being:

Well, first, I say, the mark of godliness will be hit if the chthonic gods are held in honour next to the Olympian gods and the civic gods ... After these gods a man of good sense will pay cult to the *daimones* too, and then to the heroes.[46]

The allocation of *timai* among the different categories of beings that collectively constitute the level of *to theion*, the divine, goes back beyond philosophers' need of schemes to civic cult-practice, particularly at Athens. Plato and his contemporaries could there discern not merely the well-defined category of heroes, but also gods and *daimones*. But it is difficult for the historian of religions to grasp exactly what was intended by this latter term in the context of civic cult; and in practice, when Plato describes the different ritual prescriptions, he makes no distinction between rites for gods and rites for *daimones*.[47]

The author of *Epinomis*, whether Plato in his old age[48] or, more plausibly, his follower Philippus of Opus,[49] is following a precise scheme when he sets out a hierarchy of beings that compose the All, closely linked with the five physical elements. In first place comes "the divine host of the stars", visible, immortal and composed of fire (981e4); in last place comes the creature "made of earth, entirely mortal" (984b3-4). Once the poles are defined, the author can proceed to "try to give the most faithful account warranted by reasonable conjecture of the three intermediate sorts out of the five, which lie between these extremes".[50] Without bothering to specify the precise relationship between the Olympian gods and the three elements, aithêr, air, and water, that fall between the poles,[51] he places the *daimones*, of which he distinguishes two kinds, aetherial and of the air, in second and third place after the stars.[52] Both are invisible, but

of a kind that is quick to learn and of a retentive memory: they read all our thoughts and regard the good and noble with signal favour, but the very evil man with deep aversion. For *they* are not exempt from feeling pain, whereas a god who enjoys the fullness of deity is clearly above both pain and pleasure, though possessed of all-embracing knowledge and wisdom.[53]

The intermediate beings, who are subject to pain, thus form the copula between the poles of the universe, acting "as interpreters, and interpreters of all things, to one another and to the highest gods, since the middle-ranking beings can flit so lightly over the earth and the whole universe" (985b1-4). Their agency is at work in dreams and oracles, and they are the sources of all sorts of city cults (985c).

This passage of the *Epinomis* is a systematisation of the Pythagorean and Platonic doctrine of the intermediate, and mediative, status of the *daimones*. It also foreshadows a theme developed later by Xenocrates and Plutarch by turning the notion of *daimôn* into a portmanteau reinterpretation of Greek myth and cult. Whereas god is perfect and impassible, the *daimones* are capable of experiencing suffering. In this intellectual context, it follows that mutability and vicissitude must also be characteristic of the lower orders of divine being. This then becomes the definiens of the notion *daimôn*, which allows writers such as Xenocrates and Plutarch to reinterprete the adventures of the gods of traditional mythology, as well as the ecstatic and violent phenomena of orgiastic cult, with reference not to the higher gods but to *daimones*, who belong to a level close to human beings, susceptible to suffering, and on occasion ambiguous or downright wicked.

According to Plutarch, Xenocrates accepted the compound nature of *daimones*, and considered that

unlucky days and such festivals as involve scourgings or lamentations or fastings or blasphemies or foul language belong to the honouring neither of gods nor of good *daimones*, but that there are great and strong beings in the atmosphere, malevolent and morose, who rejoice in such things.[54]

This is the distinction, between good, beneficent, *daimones* and malevolent *daimones*, harmful to mankind, that Plutarch often deploys, and sometimes attributes to the Stoic Chrysippus.[55] In all these learned contexts, the idea is developed as part of a much more extensive reinterpretation of the "inherited conglomerate", subtended by a stratified view of divinity. But there is a perceptible connection, near or remote, with popular belief in the power, sometimes dangerous, always cloven, of the *daimôn*.

As for other learned conceptions of *daimones*, it is just worth noting the views of certain Stoics, to whom Diogenes Laertius attributes a doctrine of guardian *daimones*.[56] Aetius records that *daimones* were equated with the *ousiai psuchikai*, the psychic essences.[57] Stoics, like the Pythagoreans and the Platonists, also attributed the working of oracles to them.[58] Later, Posidonius accepted that the spirits of the dead become *daimones*.[59] This is the view that comes nearest to Greek popular belief through the centuries from the Hesiodic myth of the races, and which we still find among the Greeks and the Hellenised populations of the Mediterranean *oikoumene* during the Hellenistic period.

We turn now to some texts which reveal more clearly the nature of traditional popular beliefs and rituals. My purpose is to trace the process by which Greek religious thinking came to distinguish firmly between the words *theoi* and *daimones* so as to define two categories of divine being.

Arguing for a close link between the Pythagorean and Platonic division between gods-*daimones*-heroes and older levels of Greek popular belief, Victor Goldschmidt invoked the inscriptions from the oracular site of Dodona.[60] In one of these texts, from the fourth century BC, two individuals enquire "to which of the gods, heroes or *daimones*" should they address their prayers and oblations to gain prosperity for themselves and their families, "now and for all time".[61] Two inscriptions of the same period offer an analogous formulation, while others mention only gods and heroes.[62] We can accept Goldschmidt's conclusion that "the hierarchy of divine beings is implicit in popular belief and that it is by no means an exclusively learned invention" (1950, 32).

This inference is supported by the text of one of the gold leaves from the two tomb-mounds at Thurii in Magna Graecia, likewise fourth-century BC (or possibly early third). The dead man addresses the powers of the Underworld, distinguishing between the "queen of the chthonic, Eukles, Eubouleus and you other immortal gods and *daimones*".[63] Moreover, Plutarch tells us that at Opuntian Locris there were two priests, "one of them in charge of the worship of the gods, the other that of the *daimones*".[64] In an unknown city on Crete, the *katakautai* were officials responsible for the cult of the *daimones chthonioi*, the underworld *daimones*.[65] Clear evidence for a true cult of *daimones*, conceived as a category of superhuman beings separate from the gods, is to be found on a white marble herm from Thespiae in Boeotia. The herm carries a phallos and is dedicated by the *hierarchai*, the responsible priests, to the *daimones, tois daimonessi*.[66] The inscription can be dated to the fourth century (c. 300 BC), and is clearly an official document belonging to public cult: the *hierarchai* were the most senior official priests in the state.[67] The significance of the monument lies in its iconography, which evidently has to do with fecundity, and in its provenance — Boeotia, homeland of Hesiod and Plutarch. It seems to confirm the existence of a direct and close link within Greek religious tradition between learned theological speculation and popular belief.

Several texts addressed to a broad public at the very beginning of the Hellenistic period make clear that the distinction between gods and *daimones* was by then traditional. We need do no more than recall an exclamation by a character in Menander's *Arbitrator*, "by the gods and *daimones*",[68] or the orator Aeschines' invocation of "the earth, the gods, the *daimones* and mankind" as witnesses (*In Ctes*. 137). But it is the defunctive inscriptions which provide the clearest proof of the lively presence of *daimones* within popular religious consciousness.

It is quite unnecessary here to list the numerous references in these inscriptions to the idea that death is caused by daemonic intervention: the malevolent *daimôn* brusquely "snatches" the man, woman or child and carries them off to Hades.[69] Scenario and language are already fixed in the Archaic and Classical periods. But with the Hellenistic period, and then right into the Late Empire, the evidence increases noticeably. There is a particularly interesting series of homogeneous texts from Asia Minor, mainly Caria, which may well have ritual implications even though they are expressly defunctive. These are the stelai and mortuary altars whose inscriptions mention the "Good *Daimones*", generally as an introductory formula in the genitive: *daimonôn agathôn*. In most cases this formula is followed directly by the names of the dead, from which we may infer that the *daimones* are the souls of these people, that is, that the dead have become *daimones*.[70] This would be documentary evidence of the idea, familiar from literary sources, of the *daimôn* as a human soul that has departed from the body. The funerary monument is dedicated to the dead conceived in their new rôle of beneficent *daimones*. But occasionally the phrase *daimonôn agathôn* is absolute, without direct relation to the rest of the inscription. At Mylasa, where there are particularly large numbers of such monuments, some altars carry the formula followed by the phrase *to mnêmeion* or *to mnêmeion touto*, (this is) the monument, with the names of the commemorated in the genitive.[71] We may conclude that the beneficent *daimones* have become detached in some measure from the person of the deceased and reached the status of autonomous divine beings, members of a particular category of superhuman entities, reverenced, and possibly worshipped, by the living.

There is in fact plenty of epigraphic evidence from Carian Olymos of a public cult of the *daimones agathoi*. One of them can be dated to the first century BC.[72] An inscription of the previous century, from Hyllarima, inscribed on a stele beneath another text of the fourth century BC, lists the priests of several city cults, including the *daimones agathoi* of two individuals, Arrhisis, son of Imbrasis, and Hermias, son of Arrhisis. The original editor of this monument, A. Laumonier, at first considered it to be part of a defunctive cult, though he remarked that it was strange to find it "in the context of public cults" (1934, 345-376 no. 39). In his later study of the local cults of Caria, however, he revised his opinion, on the grounds that while "we should be wary of reading the Mylasian formula *daimonôn agathôn* as a mere calque upon the Latin *dis manibus*", we should equally not undervalue the religious import of these texts. He concluded that "this public cult of the *daimones* as protectors of the living and the dead must attest a belief local to Caria".[73] At any rate, these Carian documents, defunctive and cultic, suggest a local form of belief and worship directed towards a specific category of superhuman beings distinct from the gods, and in receipt of divine honours and public cult. The undeniable association between the *daimones agathoi* of these Hellenistic Carian communities and chthonic-mortuary beliefs and practices does not mean that these beings cannot have enjoyed a specific status within the sacred hierarchy. On the contrary, it serves strongly to reinforce the argument.

Alongside the undifferentiated plethora of these Carian *daimones*,[74] and of the other texts we have examined,[75] we must now set the Agathos Daimôn in its religio-historical context. The cult was widespread throughout Greece and the Mediterranean from the fourth century BC until the Late Empire. Both divinity and cult came into being earlier, but the period of their dynamic success is the Hellenistic age, when Agathos Daimôn has its own part to play in the development of the daemonic as a specific domain within a stratified representation of the divine order.

From Aristophanes to Plutarch[76] and Athenaeus,[77] the literary evidence suggests that Agathos Daimôn was linked to the good cheer arising from the collective meal, at the end of which it was customary to pour a libation in his honour:

"Come", says Nicias in the *Knights*, "now pour a libation to Agathos Daimôn".[78] That does not mean that the divinity is nothing more than a "personification", a mere epiphenomenon, of a formula of complaisant bonhomie, as Richard Ganszyniec claimed.[79] Here, as in the case of Tuchê, the modern notion of "personification" is wholly inappropriate for understanding the operation of ancient polytheistic religious thinking, which bestows on every event, and every phenomenon in nature or in human life, a pregnant meaning, such that subjective and objective aspects combine and fuse. In this mode of thought, with its vivid individualism and its personalisation of the totality of human experience, the Agathos Daimôn is the happy juncture, the "right moment", at which a divinity intervenes, manifests itself. But at the same time it is also a divine person, precisely an Agathos Daimôn, who can be invoked, to whom one may offer a libation.[80] The fact that it is a *daimôn* and not a *theos* marks, in this mode of religious thinking, the recognition that the divine world is more or less sharply differentiated, but also that there is a functional continuity in relation to ideas such as unforeseeability, chance, sometimes arbitrariness, associated with the term *daimôn*, which the predicate *agathos* seeks to manage and direct to human advantage. The frequent coupling of Tuchê with Agathos Daimôn in a single formula confirms my interpretation of the underlying meaning of this divine entity which, as the precipitate of a long and complex evolution, condenses on the cusp of the Hellenistic age several different religious trends and movements.

There are no literary sources to shed light on the personality of Agathos Daimôn. Some representations and inscriptions do, however, allow us to chart the spread of the cult in time and space; and they provide us with a few hints concerning popular conceptions of his attributes and powers. A pillar with a rounded top evoking a phallus, and bearing the inscription Agathos Daimôn, was found in the sanctuary of Artemis near Doliane at Tegea.[81] This is probably an aniconic representation of the familiar type of Zeus Meilichios and other chthonic Zeuses.[82] In fact, this early Hellenistic monument occurs in a context that offers several chthonic forms of Zeus: dedications to Zeus Pasios (= Ktesios),[83] Patrôos, Storpaos and to an Agathos Theos (*IG* V(2) 60), this latter also in the form of a pillar, but with a bearded human head (*IG* V(2) 67), have all been found in the vicinity. There is a broken limestone bas-relief from Thespiae with the anthropomorphic figure of Agathos Daimôn holding a sceptre and cornucopia and seated on a throne with a bird beneath it. Two worshippers, a man and a woman, stand before the divinity, whose name is inscribed below the scene.[84] (Not far away, a *temenos* of Agathos Daimôn was dedicated in the third century BC by one Theophestos, son of Dallês.)[85] This iconographical scheme is virtually canonical for the representation of the different forms of chthonic Zeus, especially Zeus Meilichios, Ktesios and Philios, all three of whom are closely associated with fecundity and the domestic hearth.[86] This anthropomorphic version of Agathos Daimôn is probably the most common, though the sceptre is sometimes replaced by a *patera* (libation dish).[87]

There is also a third iconic stereotype for Agathos Daimôn, a third way of understanding his nature and function. This is a theriomorphic mode, in the shape of a serpent. This form is of course familiar among the stock of Greek religious images, representing a beneficent chthonic power, itself often in turn identified with one or other manifestation of chthonic Zeus, usually Meilichios, but also Ktesios and Philios.[88] A relief from Eteonos in Boeotia, of the fourth century BC, probably represents Agathos Daimôn as a large bearded snake.[89] The same animal occurs on a complex scene on a Delian bas-relief, between two human figures who may be identified as Agathê Tuchê and anthropomorphic Agathos Daimôn.[90] The snake is doubtless a parallel representation of the latter. We may accept Françoise Dunand's conclusion that "the god may be represented simultaneously in his two aspects, as an old man with a cornucopia and as a large bearded serpent".[91] There are no grounds for assigning these three different modes to different chronological periods, or to different ritual contexts. The iconographies are all ways of emphasising his chthonic associations and his close link with fecundity, in perfect harmony with the ancient Hesiodic *daimones ploutodotoi*, guardians of mankind, and intimately related to the world below.

During the fourth and third centuries BC the cult of Agathos Daimôn appears in many sites in mainland Greece,[92] and still more commonly in the Aegean, on Thera,[93] Thasos,[94] on Delos (in association with Agathê Tuchê),[95] Teos,[96] and Cyprus.[97] It is found in a special form on Cos and, perhaps most important of all, on Rhodes. There, Agathos Daimôn enjoys a significant place in the religious world of the three cities Lindos, Camiros and Rhodes. From Camirus there is only one small altar dedicated to him;[98] but at Lindos[99] and at Rhodes itself we find, during the second and first centuries BC, associations of *Agathodaimoniastai*, associations of worshippers with a special status, often also named after their founder or their current president. For example, one association is twice mentioned in inscriptions as *Philôneiôn koinon*,[100] the association of the followers of Philo;[101] another is called the *Agathodaimonistan Menekrateiôn tôn sun Menekratei koinon* — in this case Menekrates was evidently the president of the association.[102] Likewise, the *Agathodaimoniastai* on Cos are called "(those belonging to) Apollonios son of Nikios".[103]

I cannot enter here into the very complex problem of the types, functions and aims of Greek religious associations.[104] G. Pugliese Carratelli has made a close study of the associations on the island of Rhodes (1939-1940), of which there was an astonishing variety during the Hellenistic and Roman periods. He distinguished between clan- and "tribal"-associations of citizens, and those in which foreigners were predominant; these latter were generally dedicated to foreign divinities, mostly oriental. What the two types had in common was their double purpose, religious and funerary. We know neither the names nor the social status of the *Agathodaimoniastai*, to give us a hint of where they came from — just the names of the three presidents, all Greek. We cannot know whether the members were citizens or foreigners, though the link with Zeus Atabyrios suggests a close link with one of the oldest and most traditional local cults. But we may certainly stress the local religious and social significance of Agathos Daimôn, who was no less capable than the most important Greek and oriental gods of attracting a cult-association.[105] This probably included a shared feast, usual in such religious groups, but of course especially fitting in this case given his traditional connotations.[106]

The cult of Agathos Daimôn is also found in Asia Minor,[107] on Sicily,[108] in Italy,[109] and in Africa at Cyrene[110], and above all in Egypt. Here he has one feature that is typically Greek, since he is associated with the foundation of Alexandria.[111] But the cult soon became inextricably entangled with local religious belief and practice. Already in the Hellenistic period he was identified with one of several Egyptian divinities with similar attributes — Sobek/Sebek, Sokonôpis, Shai.[112] And from the first century BC he was regularly identified with Sarapis, forming a couple with Isis-Agathê Tuchê, who herself, as is clear from early Hellenistic sources, reproduces an ancient identification of Isis with Greek Tuchê, especially at Alexandria and Delos.[113]

It is not possible here, in the course of an article, to trace this process of expansion, which requires all due attention to local inflections and tonalities. We need merely stress that the cult of Agathos Daimôn had an autonomous status and a specific character. On the other hand, a proper assessment of its connotations and implications needs to take account of its close relation to the cult of Agathê Tuchê. This cult has, of course, larger dimensions than the rather modest sphere of Agathos Daimôn — the importance of the notion of *tuchê* (chance, fortune) and the goddess Tuchê for the whole of Hellenistic religion, to the very end of the Roman Empire, hardly needs dwelling upon.[114] Nonetheless, the relation between the two provides a good means of exploring the significance of Tuchê herself in the context of the religious culture of the Hellenistic world.

The historian of religion notes two points at the outset. First, the process of "personalising" Agathos Daimôn and Tuchê proceeds in parallel, and sometimes convergently (e.g. in the formula coupling them). We do not here have to do with the banal and battered notion of the "personification" of mere mental representations, whose inadequacy we have already noted. Far from it: such a view would imply the emergence of a specific *daimôn* based on a homogeneous and articulated set of attributes and qualities already associated with divinity in Archaic and Classical tradition. Rather, we have to do with a *daimôn* and a *tuchê*, with all their many associations and diverse manifestations, who elude complete human understanding. The process of condensation and amalgamation of older elements that led to the simultaneous production of individualised Agathos Daimôn and Agathê Tuchê, and their coupling as a pair, took place only in the fourth century BC.

Secondly, we may note the parallel — probably implying a historical connection — between the Hellenistic pairing of Agathos Daimôn and Agathê Tuchê and the idea, already Classical, but especially vivid on the cusp of the Hellenistic period, of a close and determinate association between *daimôn* and *tuchê*. We should understand the first term in its wider sense of a powerful superhuman presence, whose intervention cannot be foreseen and whose identity is unclear; while *tuchê* here has an ambivalent — occasionally ambiguous — denotation as a superhuman entity who is at the same time an abstract notion, namely fate, chance or fortune. Such a blending of elements is typical of Greek religious mentality all through its history, with different inflections depending on period and cultural context, but essentially continuous from the Archaic period until the late Hellenistic period and the Roman Empire, when Tuchê becomes the Fortune of the Emperor, but also fragments into Tuchai, patron goddesses and symbols of the various cities.

Tuchê makes her first appearance in the history of Greek religion as a specific individual in Hesiod, as daughter of Oceanus and Tethys, one of the "holy race of daughters, who, with Lord Apollo and the Rivers, have charge of young men (*andras*) all over the earth, for Zeus appointed them to do this work" (*Theog.* 346-349). As one of the divine entities responsible for the up-bringing of children until adolescence, Tuchê, with the young Oceanids who accompany Korê, takes part in the "anthology", the scene of picking flowers which, in the Homeric hymn to Demeter, precedes the Rape of Persephone — a rite of passage between childhood and the *telos*, consummation, of the marriage of the young Divine Child (417-432). The figure of Tuchê is thus linked in myth to life and fecundity — whose typical metonym is water — and to the maturation of youth, whose term is reached, in the Greek view, at the celebration of marriage. She acquires a cosmic dimension in Empedocles' poem *On Nature*, where Tuchê is the power "by whose will all creatures may acquire full understanding."[115]

Pindar brings out the aspects of Tuchê that belong to the notion of human fortune or destiny. She is "one of the Moirai" — indeed the most powerful of them (frg. 41 Snell). She is *sôteira*, "saving daughter of Zeus Eleutherios" (*Ol.* 12.1-2) and *pherepolis*, "protector of cities" (frg. 39). She is the goddess "who cannot be turned by entreaty" (*apeithês*), and who holds the "twin steering-oars" (frg. 40).[116] Both the connection with Zeus and that with the Moirai become one of the constant features of the Hellenistic cult of Tuchê.[117] The association with Zeus is not confined merely to the "conceptual" dimension of *tuchê* as fortune, in keeping with the idea of "the will of Zeus" (*boulê Dios*) which controls the fortunes of the world and of mankind, and is therefore linked with the idea of *moira* as the "portion" assigned each person. For, given the strongly-marked personality of Zeus and of the Moirai themselves, who of course have chthonic attributes,[118] it serves to lend colour and definition to the figure of Tuchê herself.

I cannot here adduce all the Classical texts which testify to an individualised Tuchê[119] among the even larger number of occurrences of the word in its general meaning of lot/chance/fortune. One of the most powerful is certainly Aeschylus' image of "life-saving Tuchê", who "gladly sat" in Agamemnon's ship and saved it from wreck (*Ag.* 664-666). Aside from literary texts, which are apt to afford too much latitude to the personal views of their authors, there are several others in which Tuchê appears with strongly marked personal traits. These provide the basis of the image of a mighty, ubiquitous deity that appears at the very beginning of the Hellenistic period and thereafter predominates throughout the history of Greek, and indeed Mediterranean, religious experience. Beginning in the late fifth century, a series of inscriptions from widely scattered cities — Petelia and Krimisos in Magna Graecia,[120] Panormus in Sicily,[121] Dodona,[122] Corcyra[123] and above all in Boeotia, where the habit continues into the Hellenistic and Roman periods[124] — carries the formula *theos Tucha* or its analogues as a heading in official documents relating to private individuals — contracts, gifts and wills — and in public decrees. In some Hellenistic cases (third century BC), the goddess is actually called *agathê*. We may conclude that in these latter cases all those who made use of the formula were aware of the living presence of Tuchê. (It is however true that public documents from this period onwards tend to bear a stereotyped dedication "to Good Fortune", *agathêi tuchêi*.)

But the problem with our fifth- and fourth-century series is to understand the true significance of the expression *theos Tucha*. In his commentary on the Archaic inscription from Petelia, Boeck took the first word as an appellative of *Tucha*, meaning that *Tucha* was evoked as a *theos* (*CIG* I 4). Without necessarily sub-scribing to this view, we may discern in the linking of the two words a strong sense of the sacred attaching to *Tucha*, which leads to her being invoked alongside the power of "god" in order to sanction deliberations or agreements among humans that have social import. This Tuchê, established alongside "god", clearly has personality and thus shares fully in the honour bestowed upon, and the efficacy ascribed to, the deity. The formula surely suggests a profound synergy, and the same is true of its later variant in the dative case (*tuchêi agathêi*). This unites the notion of good omen inherent in the general meaning of the word *tuchê* (lower case), lot or fortune, with the sense of a personal Tuchê (upper case) as an auto-nomous power who can intervene as she wishes in the affairs of men and regulate them according to her own impenetrable will, just like a *theos* or a *daimôn*.

There is actually an Arcadian monument, from the first half of the fourth century BC, which bears witness to the convergence between these two aspects. It is an inscription from Tegea, dated 362/1, in honour of the Athenian Philarchus, which opens with the formula *theos Tucha*. The document is an official resolution by the *boulê tôn Arkadôn*, the Council of the Arcadian League, in recognition of Philarchus' political services as benefactor (*euergetês*) of the peoples of Arcadia. The stela is decorated with a bas-relief showing a female figure holding a steering oar in her left hand and touching a trophy with her right.[125] The honours bestowed upon Philarchus are thus placed under the aegis of a Tuche who is no longer merely "good fortune" but now a true divinity, with her own individuality recognised in the creation of an anthropomorphic iconography.[126] This monument is exceptionally important, in that it shows directly the essential connection between the two levels. As one of the earliest representations of Tuchê, it confirms the fusion between the two aspects which we rationally distinguish, between abstract idea and mythical person. But in the subjective religious experience of Hellenistic man, it is simply a matter of the same reality presenting two faces: the reality of a superhuman being who exercises powerful sway over the day-to-day lives of individuals and communities.

Around the middle of the fourth century BC, on the cusp of the Hellenistic period, there occurs a considerable increase in the evidence for the cult of Tuchê, who can now be said to be a well-defined divine person[127] with a more or less marked element of abstraction, deriving from the wider notion of *tuchê* as chance or fortune. We may, with Aristoxenus of Tarentum, define this aspect as "daemonic". In his *Pythagorean Sentences*, he described how the Pythagoreans "used to say of *tuchê* that it had a daemonic side — the *daimon* nudges men (impelling them) now towards the good, now towards ill".[128] Numerous documents testify to a wide diffusion of the cult all over mainland Greece, in the Aegean and Asia Minor, but especially prevalent in the Peloponnese and Boeotia.

We may quickly resume the most important early evidence for the cult.[129] There is a fifth or fourth-century BC dedication to Tuchê and Nemesis from Epidaurus.[130] From Gordion in Phrygia comes the base of a statue dedicated to Tuchê between 350 and 300 BC.[131] She is also known to have been worshipped at Mistra, Laconia, and at Heraclea on the Lucanian coast. In these two places the close relation between Tuchê and Demeter and Korê/Persephone confirms her ancient association with fertility, already clear from her status in Hesiod as a daughter of Oceanus. The first document is a *lex sacra* relating to a cult analogous to the Thesmophoria at Athens, in which a male piglet and some bread are offered to Tuchê in association with Demeter, *Despoina*, Persephone and Pluto.[132] At Heraclea, a woman deposited in the sanctuary of Demeter a piece of metal foil and her own portrait, dedicated to Demeter, Korê and Tuchê Agathê (fourth or third century BC).[133] There is also a fourth-century BC altar from Troezen where several other texts document the cult into the Roman period.[134]

In the Aegean, there are a number of early Hellenistic monuments,[135] especially at Delos, where there was a temple dedicated to Tuchê from the second century BC.[136] There is also evidence from Thera,[137] in particular an inscribed altar from the rock-cut sanctuary created by Artemidorus of Perge manifesting the wealthy owner's devotion to the goddess.[138] At Syracuse in Sicily one of the city wards was known as Tycha, because, as Cicero puts it, "there was an ancient shrine to her there" (*Verr.* 4.119).[139] An altar dedicated *Dii kai Tuchêi* by a certain Markianos underscores the association already remarked on between Zeus and Tuchê (Bernabò Brea 1948). I mentioned at the beginning Timoleon's dedication of a shrine in his house to Automatia, an entity similar to, if not identical with, Tuchê, as well as Agathos Daimôn: this practice of domestic worship of the goddess in Sicily is confirmed by Cicero's allusion to "an ancient wooden statue of good Fortune" kept by Heius of Messana in his private shrine (*Verr.* 4.7). And finally there is a late-third or early-second century bronze coin from Syracuse bearing the image of Tuchê "standing l., wearing mural crown, holding rudder and leaning on sceptre".[140]

In Martin Nilsson's view, the earliest figurative representation of Tuchê was the cult-statue in her temple at Thebes, by Xenophon of Athens and Callistonicus of Thebes.[141] Pausanias informs us that they took as their model the statue at Athens of Eirene (Peace) with the infant Ploutos (Wealth) by Cephisodotus (9.16.1-2). In adopting this view, Nilsson rejects another notice by Pausanias, to the effect that Bupalus of Chios made the first statue of Tuchê, with *polos* and the horn of Amalthaea, for the city of Smyrna, in the second half of the sixth century.[142] Even if we do not accept this claim, Nilsson's view must be wrong. For the stela of Philarchus at Tegea, discussed above, demonstrates the existence of the iconographic type of Tuchê with the steering-oar already in the second quarter of the fourth century, whereas the Theban statue belongs, according to Ch. Picard (1941, 204-226) to the third quarter (between 346 and 338 BC). In fact, Panathenaic amphorae from the first decade of the fourth century carry representations of Tuchê,[143] whose iconography was thus well-established by the beginning of the Hellenistic period, even if it does not go back to the Archaic period.[144] An Argive coin, datable between 350 and 328 BC, shows Tuchê with patera and cornucopia.[145]

This conclusion is perfectly consistent with the development of the personality and cult of Tuchê, which reaches maturity in the fourth century BC after a long and complex history. During the Hellenistic period, in keeping with the new psychological climate created by the changes in socio-economic, politico-military and cultural affairs, the cult of Tuchê flourished exuberantly — became indeed one of the determining features of the religious life of the Greeks and Hellenised populations of the Mediterranean *oikoumene*. We may take the situation at Athens as paradigmatic in this respect. From the early fourth century until the Late Empire, Tuchê was both recipient of popular cult and the object of learned speculation on the part of philosophers, historians, orators and play-wrights. One individual, in the dedication of a base of Pentelic marble to the gods who sustained the life of the *polis*, brings the Twelve Gods, the main representatives of the official pantheon, into association with Agathê Tuchê (mid-fourth century).[146] There is another dedication to her from the end of the century by a certain Kallides.[147] Just by the *prytaneum*, symbolic centre of city life, there stood a statue of the same goddess by Praxiteles, that was so alluring and beautiful that a young man fell in love with it.[148] Dedications to Tuchê continue into the third century AD. Throughout the whole period, we have evidence of an intense relationship with the goddess.

A law of Lycurgus dated between 336-334 BC regulated the cult and specified the duties of the *epistatai* (the board of curators) and the working of the temple treasury (*IG* II² 333c19-20). More or less contemporaneously, animal sacrifices are attested in the city[149] and in the deme Kallytos, where there may have been another temple.[150] Twenty years later, we hear of sacrifices performed by the tribe Akamantis in honour of the city goddess Athena Nikê, Agathê Tuchê and the saviour gods (*theoi sôtêres*) Demetrius Poliorcetes and Antigonus Monophthalmos.[151] There is a close connection between Agathê Tuchê and the main actors in the vertiginous political and military events of the period down to the battle of Ipsus (301 BC), such that the individual conceives himself as having a personal relationship with *tuchê*, analogous to the personal relationship between self and *daimôn*. As a result, there emerge, alongside Tuchê as a superhuman being, goddess among the gods, numberless *tuchai* of groups and communities, cities, states and individuals, each enjoying his own.

A bas-relief from the temple of Asclepius in Athens (*IG* II² 4644), again from the fourth century, shows the goddess with a cornucopia, which is the most widespread iconographical type during the Hellenistic period and the Principate. The common association between Tuchê, alone or with Agathos Daimôn, and healing cults and oracular sites accounts for the monument's provenance: she is found in the precincts of Asclepius at Epidaurus[152] and Pergamum,[153] and in the oracle of Trophonius at Lebadeia in Boeotia (Paus. 9.39.5). The vigour of the cult at Athens right up to the third century AD is confirmed by other reliefs[154] and inscriptions, as well as by the existence of a temple of Tuchê in the Piraeus, and another outside the city.[155] And Menander in the *Shield* has her come on stage proclaiming her status as god, arbiter and sovereign mistress of human life — wholly in accord with the sentiments of his audience.[156]

The stela from Tegea, which displays a perfect congruence between the opening formula of the inscription and the image of Tuchê, the divine patron of the decree, confirms the view advanced by S.V. Tracy, that the increasing frequency of the inaugural formula "to good fortune" on Athenian inscriptions from the early fourth century BC is to be related to the contemporary expansion of the cult of Tuchê as a distinct figure.[157] In several occurrences of the formula, the *agathê tuchê* is qualified as that of "the Athenian people". The claim to possession reflects the process of particularisation of Tuchê already remarked upon — the universal divinity is skirted by the numberless *tuchai* of individuals and communities, of kings,[158] cities and nations. Demosthenes gives expression to the idea, already familiar to his audience, in *On the Crown*. His opponent, Aeschines, had urged the Athenians to dissociate themselves "from this man, the dangerous *daimôn* of Hellas", and from the *tuchê* attached to him as if it were a Doppelgänger (*In Ctes.* 157). In rebutting this sally, Demosthenes formulates a scheme of three related levels at which Tuchê operates. He deftly sketches the idea of a play of forces, sometimes opposing and contrary, sometimes convergent, which directs the course of history. On one side is the individual's determination, exertion and technical competence; on the other a group of superhuman powers, *theos*, god, *daimôn* and Tuchê, "the mistress of all" (*De Cor.* 192-195). The key configuration is clearly that between *daimôn* and *tuchê*. The sovereign power of

Tuchê operates on three distinct but co-articulated levels: there is a *tuchê* of the individual, which determines the course of every man's life from birth in relation to his family background and his social and moral behaviour; there is a *tuchê* of the city, which determines its happiness and success in international affairs, and sometimes its conflicts with other cities and states; and there is a universal Tuchê who operates at a cosmic level and directs the entire history of mankind. Given this scenario, Demosthenes compares his personal *tuchê* with that of his opponent, and the *tuchê* of Athens with that of King Philip of Macedon and his allies, and concludes: "in my view, the *tuchê* of our own city is good, ... but that of the generality of mankind at the moment is harsh and terrible" (253). Athens, though her *tuchê* is happy, has suffered a set-back and in that respect he accepts that the city "has suffered its due share of the general *tuchê* of mankind" (254).

This passage is just one of a much larger number of texts, albeit important because it refracts Greek perceptions during the crisis of traditional political and social institutions that preceded the new politico-cultural order of the Hellenistic age. It is both impossible and unnecessary here to examine in any depth the literary tradition — from Theognis to the tragedians, from Pindar to Herodotus and Thucydides, from Aristophanes to Xenophon, Plato, Lysias and Isocrates (just to mention some of the most typical authors in this connection) — which, in a variety of ways, associates *daimôn* with *tuchê* as a pair of divine agents able dialectically to determine human destiny and the evolution of history.[159] *Daimôn* is sometimes used loosely to mean "divine", "that comes from the gods", but often also in a specific sense referring to the realm of *daimones* as distinct from that of *theoi*. We need simply note here that the term is employed to express the idea of divine intervention in human life, and that it is closely linked with *tuchê*. The usage indicates how Greek religious thought from the Archaic period onwards was actively aware of the opaque, aleatory, element in the divine allotment of "portions" (*moirai*), in the assignment to each individual of a personal destiny. And it is in fact precisely this element which the word *daimôn* etymologically suggests, over against the word *theos*.[160]

A new phenomenon, intimately related to the set of themes we have been discussing, becomes apparent during the fourth century BC. This is the association of Agathos Daimôn with Agathê Tuchê as a pair of the kind traditional in polytheisms structured on the dynastic principle, that is, according to genealogical and conjugal relationships. They are thus manifest as individual figures with specific attributes, a constituent of the unwearying permutation of divine associations within the pantheon familiar to many Greek peoples. But occasionally there seems to be an awareness in popular religious feeling of a special link between these two. The cult of Tuchê flourished on Thera from the third century BC, when we have seen her worshipped in the rock sanctuary of Artemidorus, into the first century. An inscription relating to sacrifices in honour of the Mother of the Gods offers an introductory locution which recalls the formula we have already discussed, and also couples the two divinities: "The god: to the good fortune of the good *daimôn*".[161] This very unusual heading underscores the closeness of the association between Agathos Daimôn and Agathê Tuchê, the latter being thought of as a predicate of the former. We catch a glimpse of a religious perception that asserts the individuality of the two divine entities, while at the same time recognising that the *daimôn* is the effective agent who assigns "good fortune" to the believer.

The wide diffusion of the cult of the pair Agathos Daimôn and Agathê Tuchê is attested by a good deal of epigraphical evidence, from Athens[162] to Epidaurus[163] and Lebadeia[164] in Greece proper, at Rhodes,[165] Cos,[166] Delos,[167] and Thasos[168] in the Aegean, at Pergamum[169] and Philadelphia[170] in Asia Minor, and above all in Egypt, where they are often fused with Sarapis and Isis.[171] Among all these texts, it will suffice here to single out a fourth- or third-century BC inscription from Halicarnassus which is richly suggestive.[172] This text documents the lived experience of the sacred of an individual and his family. Though unique, it is grounded in the traditional usages, known from elsewhere, associated with the foundation of a domestic cult. It contains the reply of the oracle of Apollo at Telmessus in response to an enquiry by a certain Posidonius, the provisions of his will relating to the institution of a domestic cult in accordance with the oracle's requirements, and finally the resolution by Posidonius and his heirs concerning the cult.

Posidonius had consulted the oracle to find out how he could obtain happiness and prosperity for himself and his family by fulfilling his religious obligations. The god replied that he would do well if he — just like his parents — paid honour to "Zeus Patrôios, Apollo of Telmessus, the Moirai and the Mother of the Gods". At the same time he should worship "the Agathos Daimôn of Posidonius and Gorgis", that is, of himself and his wife. Agathos Daimôn is associated here with the gods of the official pantheon, with the tutelary Zeus of Halicarnassus, the patron god of the famous oracle at Telmessus, the Moirai, goddesses of destiny, and the asiatic Great Goddess, long since hellenised as the Mother of the Gods. At the same time, it is clearly also a "guardian angel" in that it is qualified as being the *agathos daimôn* of the married couple.[173] We can thus recognise, in a funerary and cultic context, the *daimones* sometimes called *agathoi* whom we encountered earlier, and in precisely the same area, Caria. But in this text we find a unique figure that stands out from the anonymous crowd of *daimones* who are both the guardians of the dead and the daemonic avatars of their souls, namely the Agathos Daimôn. The Agathos Daimôn here is an independent person, with his own separate divine identity, but who at the same time enjoys a special relationship with human beings, in this case the husband and wife.

In the regulations for the cult laid down in the third section of the inscription and binding upon Posidonius' heirs, mention is made of the cult of the Agathê Tuchê of Posidonius' parents, alongside that of the Agathos Daimôn. After the death of the donor, his descendants are to follow a ritual calendar: there is to be a sacred area (*temenos*) held in common by all the members of the family, where on specific days each year sacrifice is to be offered. On the first day a ram is to be sacrificed "to the Agathê Tuchê of the father and mother of Posidonius", and another to the "Agathos Daimôn of Posidonius and Gorgis". On the second day offerings are to be made to Zeus Patrôios, Telmessian Apollo, the Moirai (a ram each) and the Mother of the Gods (a goat). All participants, male and female, present and absent, are to receive equal shares of the offerings.

This unusual document provides an insight into a religious world which we can take as paradigmatic for the wider Hellenistic world, rooted as it was in ancestral tradition, yet open to new experience. The turbulence of that age, in politics, society, culture and religion, certainly encouraged the rise of belief in the idea of a divine power with sway over the universe as a whole, yet at the same time capable of intervening in the daily life of the individual: in a word, the realms of *tuchê* and of *daimôn* respectively. Both terms have a long history, in part separate, in part more or less symbiotic. In the course of this development each aggregated new meanings. To the religious sensibility of those living in a world distracted by the conquests of Alexander and the struggles of the Diadochi, they appeared excellent material for constructing a new conceptual framework, for redrawing the map of the sacred. The term *daimôn* could be used to represent a graduated conception of the divine. On the one hand, the notion distanced divinity, immutable and impassible, from the world and the vicissitudes of a troubled humanity, ever prey to passions and vices. On the other hand, some form of mediation had to be found between the world of man and the higher world of the divine. The philosophers used the idea of *daimôn* to reinterpret traditional beliefs in a theological sense and to adapt them to new ideological frameworks, rather than reject them outright. They stressed the already traditional conception of *daimones* as intermediate beings so as to turn them into mediators between a transcendent god, far above all material reality, and mankind. As for Tuchê, her identity developed in accordance with a tradition by which a divinity came to be individuated from the bundle of significations — in this case fortune, chance, luck, destiny — offerred by the appellative. She thus appears in the context of Hellenistic religion as a personal, "daemonic" power, actively intervening in the lives of individuals and nations, often unforeseeably, now for good, now for ill. But at the same time, thanks to this progressive individualisation, she became, as it were, the prisoner of the men and the communities who offered her private or public cult. For thereby they established a bond, a relation of reciprocity, between themselves and the sovereign Mistress of the Universe; and were no longer the hapless victims of fumbling chance.

Translated by Richard Gordon

Via Protonotaro Is. 204
I-98123 Messina
Italy

Notes

1. Plut. *De def. or.* 10.415a1-5. For the problems of the date of the dialogue and of its relation to the other 'Pythian' dialogues, see Flacelière 1947, and 1974, 3-11; Goldschmidt 1948, 298-302; Ogilvie 1967; Babut 1981; 1992; Rescigno 1995, 10-21.
2. "Perhaps the doctrine derives from the *magi*, followers of Zoroaster, or perhaps it is Thracian, and derives from Orpheus — or it may be Egyptian — or Phrygian ...": 415a5-7.
3. Plut. *De def. or.* 10.415a9-b3.
4. Plut. *De Is. et Os.* 25.360d8-e5, with Griffiths 1970, 383-86 (commentary).
5. On Plutarch's daemonology, which is not a rigid system but combines several different views and solutions, see Soury 1939, and more esp. 1942; Babut 1994b; Brenk 1969, 1973; 1977; 1986, 2117-30; 1987, 274-94; also Vernière 1977, 38-40; 249-62; Moreschini 1989.
6. On the dualist interpretation of the Egyptian myth in the *De Is. et Os.*, see Bianchi 1986; 1987.
7. On Plutarch's philosophical grounding, see recently Donini 1986a, b; Froidefond 1987; Dillon 1988; Moreschini 1990; his links with Stoicism and the Peripatetics are discussed by Babut 1969; 1994c. Light has been shed on the issue of the mutual influence of his two basic interests, philosophy and religion, by numerous studies, in particular Babut 1988; 1994c; Valdés 1994. On Plutarch's close relation to the sanctuary at Delphi, see Sfameni Gasparro 1996a.
8. We may simply recall the *De genio Socratis* (cf. Corlu 1970; Döring 1984) and the numerous allusions to the personal *daimones* of the heroes of the *Parallel Lives* (cf. Brenk 1977, 145-83), often in relation to the idea of *tuchê*.
9. See the three elaborate myths, of Sulla (*De fac.* 940f-945d), of Timarchus (*De gen.* 589f-592e), and of Thespesios (*De sera* 563b-568f), whose religious content has been exhaustively analysed by Vernière 1977. The identification of *nous* and *daimôn* is of course Platonic (*Ti.* 90a-c).
10. Cf. Brenk 1977, 145-83; Swain 1989a; most recently, Torraca 1996.
11. Plut. *Tim.* 36; cf. Swain 1989b.

12. Cf. Ziegler 1951, 719; Flacelière 1966; Forni 1989.

13. Plut. *Tim.* 36.5-6.

14. *De laude ipsius* 11.542e; *Praecept. ger. reip.* 20.816f.

15. The most important of these is Apuleius, whose daemonology, clearly inspired by Plato, is set out systematically in *De dog. Plat.* and *De deo Soc.* On the problem of the attribution of the former, and in general on their significance, see Beaujeu 1973. Of the relevant literature, I cite only Barra 1966, 1972; Barra and Pennuti 1960-1961, 1962-1963; Moreschini 1978, 19-42; 51-132. On the daemonology of the Middle Platonists, Dillon 1977; Donini 1990; Bianchi 1990.

16. Plut. *De def. or.* 10.415b1-4, referring to Hesiod, *Op.* 121-26. The continuation of the passage has Cleombrotus emphasise the lability of the scheme, involving possible transitions from one category to another: "and on this basis, evidently, he has the golden race turn into a plethora of beneficent *daimones*, separate from the demi-gods, who become heroes".

17. Heinze 1892, 78-123; cf. Boyancé 1935, 197; Brenk 1990.

18. The earliest evidence for this interpretation is Pl. *Cra.* 397e-398a. But it seems to go back to the Pythagoreans, whose interest in Hesiod (for them almost holy writ) is well-known: Delatte 1915, 136; Boyancé 1935, 197; Detienne 1962.

19. Cf. for example Vernant 1960/1965, 19-47; 1966; Defradas 1965; Hofinger 1981; Rudhardt 1981.

20. *chryseon genos meropôn anthrôpôn*: Hes. *Op.* 109.

21. On the Homeric sense of *daimôn*, see Untersteiner 1939/1971; Bianchi 1953, 115-32; Chantraine 1954, with the discussion on pp. 80-94; Wilford 1965; Brenk 1986, 2071-82; Schenkeveld 1988.

22. Hes. *Op.* 122-23, with West ad loc.

23. Mazon, Solmsen and West all bracket ll.124-25.

24. For example Pind. *Ol.* 13.105; *Pyth.* 5.122-23.

25. *Theog.* 149-50; 161-66; 402-6; 637-38; cf. Wilamowitz-Moellendorf 1931-32, 1:364 n. 1; Festugière 1950, 270.

26. Aesch. *Pers.* 158; 354; 473; 601; 724-25; 825 (*ton paronta daimona* = "your present fortune"); 942, cf. Edsman 1967; Soph. *OC* 76; frg. 653 Pearson/Radt; Eur. *Med.* 1347; *Alc.* 499; 561; *Andr.* 98; 974; *Phoen.* 1653; cf. on the theme in Euripides, Busch 1937. There is a full discussion of the literary evidence for *daimôn* in Andres 1918; cf. Wilamowitz-Moellendorff 1931-32, 1: 362-70. For the differing meanings of the term *daimôn* and its relation to human destiny, see Festugière 1950, 268-88.

27. Xen, *An.* 5.2.25.

28. Lys. 2.78-79.

29. E.g. Aesch. *Pers.* 353-54.

30. Goldschmidt 1950, 33-39; Brenk 1990, 24.

31. Athenag. *leg.* 23: *Thalês diairei hôs hoi ta ekeinou akribountes mnêmoneuousin eis theon, eis daimonas, eis hêrôas*. The passage is rejected by Heinze 1892, 85, on the grounds that Xenocrates was the first to systematise the doctrine of *daimones*.

32. Arist. *De An.* A5.411a7-8 = Diels *Vorsokr.* 11 A22; cf. Pl. *Leg.* 10.899b9.

33. Aetius *Plac.* 1.7.11 (Dox. 301.20-22) = Diels *Vorsokr.* 11 A23: *Thalês noun tou kosmou ton theon, to de pan empsuchon hama kai daimonôn plêres*; cf. also *Schol. Platonis in Remp.* 600a, ap. Diels *Vorsokr.* 11 A3: *ton de kosmon empsuchon ephê kai daimonôn plêrê*.

34. Cf. Kirk, Raven, Schofield 1983, 95-98; Guthrie 1962, 47-72.

35. Detienne 1963, cf. his earlier essays, 1958; 1959a,b. On the Pythagorean roots of daemonology, in the sense of a 'system' and a mode of representing the relations between

men and gods, cf. Jensen 1966, esp. 77: "the conception of *daimôn* as *metaxu* (intermediate) was a product of the theological speculation of the Pythagorean mathematici."

36. Detienne 1963, 171-77, Appendix: *Pythagoricorum fragmenta de daemonibus.*

37. Kirk, Raven and Schofield 1983, 214-38; Guthrie 1962, 146-340; Burkert 1962/1972; von Fritz 1963; de Vogel 1966.

38. Alexander Polyhistor (first century BC), *Philosophôn Diadochai* ap. Diog. Laert. 8.32 (Delatte 1922, 129.12-130.3; commentary, 198-237) = Jacoby, *FGrH* 273 F93 §32 = Detienne 1963, 171 frg. 3.

39. Wellmann 1919; Delatte 1922, 198-237; Detienne 1963, 32-37.

40. Heinze 1892, 110-12, who thought the view of *daimones* was influenced by Xenocrates; Festugière 1945/1971.

41. Pl. *Symp.* 202d13-202e1.

42. Pl. *Symp.* 202e3-203a1 (tr. Michael Joyce).

43. 203a6-7: *outoi dê hoi daimones polloi kai pantodapoi eisin.*

44. Cf. Pl. *Phd.* 107d5-108c5; 113d1-4. The *daimôn* is assigned to each individual during his or her life (107d6-7), and acts as *hêgemôn* of the person. But note also, however, *Leg.* 4.713c4-e2 where it is "the tribe of *daimones*", as a specific category of divine being, that acted as guardians of men during the age of Kronos: this was a "tribe better than us" (713d6-7).

45. *Leg.* 4.716d8-9.

46. 717a3-b4; the last sentence reads: *meta theous de tousde kai tois daimosin ho ge emphrôn orgiazoit'an, hêrôsin de meta toutous.*

47. Cf. however *Leg.* 5.738b-d: when it is a matter of the temples to be founded in different communities, and the gods and *daimones* they are to be dedicated to, the directions of the "ancient oracles" – Delphi, Dodona, Ammon – are to be followed. The lawgiver "shall assign each district its patron god, or *daimôn* or *hêrôs*" (738d1-2). From such a passage we must conclude that there was a perceptible difference at the level of cult between gods and *daimones.*

48. des Places 1931; 1956, 97-109.

49. Tarán 1975.

50. Pl. *Epin.* 984b4-6, tr. A.E. Taylor.

51. Pl. *Epin.* 984b6-c4; d3-5.

52. 984d8-e1.

53. 984e5-985a7.

54. Xenocrates frg. 25 Heinze (1892, 168) = Plut. *De Is. et Os.* 25, 361b1-5, tr. J.G. Griffiths; cf. also *De def. or.* 14, 417c. Plutarch attributes the same doctrine of the *phauloi daimones* to Xenocrates in *De Is. et Os.* 25, 360d and *De def. or.* 17, 419a = frg. 24 Heinze (cited n. 4 above).

55. See the last two references in the preceding note; also Sext. Emp. *Math.* 11.27, p. 381 Mutschmann (*hypoth.* 3 §171, p. 180 M.).

56. Diog. Laert. 7.151: *phasi d'einai kai tinas daimonas anthrôpôn sumpatheian echontas, epoptas tôn anthrôpeiôn pragmatôn.*

57. Aetius *Plac.* 1.8.2 (Dox. 307a9-14) = *SVF* 2.1101: *Thalês Puthagoras Platôn hoi Stoikoi daimonas huparchein ousias psuchikas*; cf. Heinze 1892, 96 n. 2.

58. Stob. *Ecl.* 2.6.5b.12, p. 67 Wachsmuth.

59. Sext. Emp. *Math.* 9.71-74, p. 231 Mutschmann = frg. 400b, p. 317 Theiler (omm. Edelstein and Kidd[2]): *ei oun diamenousin hai psuchai, daimosin hai autai ginontai.* On Stoic demonology, see Heinze 1892, 96-110.

60. Goldschmidt 1950, 31; cf. already Delatte 1915, 48.
61. Parke 1967, 263 no. 1: "Gods, Good Fortune (*theoi. tuchên agathan*). Evandros and his wife enquire of Zeus Naios and Dione by praying and sacrificing to what of the gods or heroes or supernatural powers (*tini ka pheôn ê hérôôn ê daimonôn*) they may fare better and more well, themselves and their household both now and for all time" (tr. Parke); cf. *SGDI* 1582a; Michel no. 845.
62. *SGDI* 1585Bb; 1566A.
63. Kern, *Orph. Frag.* 32d and e.1-2 = Zuntz 1971, 299-343 texts A3 and 4: *ch{th}oniôn bas{i}l[ê]ei{a} / Eukle kai Eubouleu[i] kai {hosoi} theoi daimo{n} /e{s} alloi*. Zuntz (302-27) attempts to resolve the difficulty of the separate listing of *theoi* and *daimones* by equating the latter with the *theoi chthonioi*, as distinct from the Olympians.
64. Plut. *Quaest. Graec.* 6.293b9-c4: *duo d'êsan hiereis par'autois, ho men peri ta theia tetagmenos, ho de peri ta daimonia*.
65. Plut. *Quaest. Graec.* 21.296c5-9: privileges are accorded to two categories of sacred functionaries, *tas men tois hiereusi tôn theôn, tas de tois tapheusi tôn teteleutêkotôn, epiphêmisanta kai tautas daimosi chthoniois*. Here the reference is to a defunctive cult.
66. Michel no. 1102 = Cook 1914-1940, 2, 1150 n. 9.
67. Schachter 1981, 149 stresses the cult's public character: "There are several clues: first, this is an official dedication by a part of the civic government; second, the hierarchs are identified not only by name, but also by date (they are the hierarchs in office in the archonship of Hippon): the stone may therefore record an annual rite (although this does not necessarily follow); third, the hierarchs are accompanied by a herald: there must therefore have been a public gathering if not a procession." In his view, the context must be a defunctive cult: "I would interpret our stone as commemorating one of these regular public rituals in honour of the dead of the polis." The conclusion is not irresistible; but in any case the text's interest remains unimpaired, since it provides evidence of precisely that transition from one category (man) to another of higher status (the *daimones* now the object of cult), which we find in the literary sources from Hesiod to Plutarch. As we shall see later, there is evidence at Thespiae itself, and elsewhere in Boeotia, of a lively cult of Agathos Daimôn.
68. Men. *Epitr.* 1083 Sandbach (frg. 8, p. 128 = 184 Kock) = 725 Körte-Thierfelder.
69. Cf. Nowak 1960. I cite simply *SEG* 23:148 (Attica, 4th cent. BC); *CIG* 3344b: *daimôn eis Haidên pempsen ameilichios*; 3627: *tuchê daimôn*; 3715: *baskanos hêrpase daimôn*; 6261: *kakos hêrpase daimôn*; 6858: *tôi phthonerôi daimoni memphometha*; *IG* VII 1882-1883; XII(8) 441: *dusmoros harpase daimôn* (1st cent. BC).
70. Blümel 1987, nos. 428-29; 433; 437; 442; 446; 450; 452; 454-55; 458; 463-64; 471; 477; 479-80; 483-84; 486-89; *SEG* 36:1005. In two instances, 433 and 472, the formula is in the genitive singular, *daimonos agathou* + the name of the deceased.
71. Blümel 1987, nos. 436; 439; 444; 449; 453; 456 (*to hérôon*); 470 (*thêkain = thêkaion*); 473; 478.
72. Blümel 1988, no. 870 (*hiereus Daimonôn Agathôn*); 806; 810-12; 819; 869; cf. Buckler 1916-1918, 190-215; Persson 1922, 394-426.
73. Laumonier 1958, 138-39. There is an interesting parallel to the Carian cult of the dead/*daimones* in the defunctive monuments cut into the rock at Akrai, the colony of Syracuse. In this little town, a cult of the dead addressed as *hêrôs agathos* or, quite often, *daimôn agathos*, in the quarries worked by chain gangs, is attested by numerous painted or carved niches and inscriptions (3rd-2nd cents. BC) (Bernabò Brea 1956, 59-88).
74. The same formula occurs at Iasos in a funerary inscription (c. 200 BC) commemorating

mercenaries: *SEG* 17:450; cf. Blümel 1985, no. 116, a decree detailing funerary honours for one Isocrates, *daimôn agathos*.

75. Some other examples of defunctive dedications: *daimonôn agathôn*: altar by a married couple, Rhodes, 1st cent. BC (Maiuri 1925, 88, no. 163); *daimones hêsuchioi*: Cyprus, 2nd cent. BC (*SEG* 18:574); *daimosi chthoniois*: Athens, 2nd-3rd cent. AD (*IG* II² 4820); *theois daimosi*: Minoa, Amorgos (*IG* XII(7) 385 = *IG Rom.* IV 1020); offering to the *daimôn* of the deceased: Paros (*IG* XII(5) 305); *theois daimosin*: Patara, Lycia (*IG Rom.* III 675-76); Saqqara, Egypt (*SEG* 8:530); *A(gathois) D(aimosin)*: Arabia (*SEG* 7:993); *theoi daimones*: Macedonia, 2nd cent. AD (*SEG* 18:274); dedication to *agathôi daimoni Teoklôi*, Rome (*IG* XIV 1653).

76. *Quaest. conv.* 3.7.1, 655e: after invoking the Athenian festival of the new wine, *Pithoigia*, in the eleventh month, Anthesterion, Plutarch mentions that "the same month among us is called Prostaterios, and on the sixth day we are accustomed to sacrifice to *agathos daimôn* (*thusantas agathôi daimoni*), and then to taste the wine, after the West wind has set in"; cf. *Quaest. conv.* 8.10.3, 735d, and Diod. Sic. 4.3.4: "it is the custom, they say, when unmixed wine is served during a meal to toast it by saying '*agathôu daimonos*'".

77. 15.47-48, 692f-693f: "After that discussion ended, most of the guests called for a cup in honour of *agathos daimôn* ... ". There follow citations from several authors, including Nicostratus, Xenarchus, Eriphus, Theophrastus and Philochorus; note esp. 693b1-3: "In the same play (Nicostratus) also mentions the 'mixture for the *agathos daimôn*', as do practically all the Old Comic poets". Also 11.73, 487b4-6: "Antiphanes in *The Torch* (frg. 137): 'table, pastries, salted sprats, tuna-fish, after-dinner glass *daimonos agathou*'". Athenaeus also cites the work *On Perfumes and Wreaths* by the physician Philonides, who equated this Agathos Daemon with Dionysus: "For this reason when the unmixed wine is poured during the meal, the Greeks invoke *agathos daimôn*, in honour of the *daimôn* who discovered wine – Dionysus" (15.17, 675a-b). This is of course a learned interpretation of a ritual custom.

78. Ar. *Eq.* 106-8, cf. 85; *Pax* 300 with the schol.; *Vesp.* 525 with schol.

79. Ganszyniec 1919; cf. idem 1918a. The literary texts and principal monuments and inscriptions are to be found in Hild 1892; Roscher 1884-1886; Andres 1918; cf. already Lehrs 1856/1895, 151-74 (Dämon und Tyche); Gerhard 1868.

80. A number of archaeological finds confirm that it was customary to dedicate wine-vessels to Agathos Daimôn, though also to other divinities. I confine myself to citing a few Sicilian vases with the name *daimôn* or Agathos Daimôn in the genitive: *daimonos*, sanctuary of Demeter at Morgantina (*SEG* 34:964); Monte Iato (*SEG* 34:938 = *SEG* 35:104 (350-300 BC); Centuripae (*IG* XIV 2406, 109). For these and further cases with the names of other divinities, cf. Manganaro 1985, 150-53.

81. *IG* V(2) 59. Several uninscribed pyramidal shafts were found on the same site, *IG* V(2) 61-66, and probably relate to the same cult; cf. Nilsson 1955-1961, 1, 206 n. 4; Dunand 1981, 278 no. 1 with plate ("later than 4th cent. BC").

82. Cf. Harrison 1903/1922, 12-31; Nilsson 1955-1961, 1, 201-7; 402-6; 411-14; Picard 1942-1943; Picard 1943. For the identification of Zeus with *Agathos Theos*, see Paus. 8.36.5.

83. *IG* V(2) 59; 61-66.

84. *IG* VII 1815: the inscription mentions the names of four dedicators, a man and three women: cf. Harrison 1903/1922, 357 fig.107; Nilsson 1955-1961, 2, 214-15 fig.1; Dunand 1981, 278 no. 2; Schachter 1981, 146-47.

85. *SEG* 25:511, "two sanctuary boundary-stones from Koraki, at or near Ellopia". This

Boeotian town was evidently an important centre of the cults of Agathos Daimôn and the *daimones* from early in the Hellenistic age.

86. Cf. Nilsson 1955-1961, 1, 411-15. Some Athenian examples of images of Zeus Meilichios are to be found in *IG* II² 4569; 4618 (both 4th cent.); Zeus Philios seated on a throne: ibid. 4623.

87. E.g. Dunand 1981, 278, no. 3-5a; pl. 203.

88. At Athens, image of a snake with dedication to Zeus Meilichios: *IG* II² 4617; 4619-21, all 4th cent.; to Zeus Philios: 4624, 4th cent.

89. Harrison 1912/1926, 282 with fig. 273 (p. 283); Dunand 1981, 287 no. 6.

90. Picard 1944-1945, 265-68 and fig. 14; Nilsson 1955-1961, 2, 216 n. 1 with pl. 3.1; Marcadé 1969, 187; 436; Bruneau 1970, 300; 303-4; 641; Dunand 1981, 287 no. 3.

91. Dunand 1981, 280. There may be an analogy to such a double representation in a relief from Epidaurus of Roman date, showing the full bust of some chthonic Zeus holding a sceptre and a cornucopia, with a snake writhing below, and inscribed *Agathou Theou* (Harrison 1912/1926, 285 fig. 75).

92. A marble statue from Delphi (3rd cent. BC) of a cloaked and bearded Agathos Daimôn holding a cornucopia (inv. no. 11424: Dunand 1981, 278 no. 5a, pl. 203); sanctuary of Asclepius at Epidaurus, 4th-3rd cent. BC: *IG* IV 1160; fragmentary base from Athens, *Aga]thon Daimon[a*, 2nd-3rd cent. AD (*IG* II² 4819 = III 215).

93. Several dedications and altar bases of 3rd cent. BC (*IG* XII(3) 1319) and 2nd-1st cent. (1320-1322); cf. 1366, *Dios Sôtêros kai Agathou Daimonos*.

94. A dedication *Agathôi Daimoni* by the seven *Apologoi*, the city magistrates, in the *temenos* of Dionysus, c. 300 BC (Daux 1926, 283 no. 14).

95. See n. 90 above.

96. *IG Rom.* IV 1566 (1st cent. BC), in association with Zeus Ktesios, Zeus Kapetôlios and the goddess Roma.

97. Some dedications on vase fragments from the nymphaeum of Kazifin: Mitford 1980, no. 122; no. 144c; *SEG* 30:1608; Masson 1981, 635; J. and L. Robert, *Bullép* 1981, no. 636.

98. Segre and Pugliese Carratelli 1949-1951, 250 no. 134.

99. Blinkenberg 1941, 546-66 no. 253 1.251, a stela of 115 BC, listing contributors to the temple of Lindian Athena and Zeus Polieus.

100. *IG* XII(1) 161,5 = *SGDI* 3842,5; cf. Foucart 1873, 230 no. 48.

101. Pugliese Carratelli 1952-1954, 266 no. 17: the association also has another name, *Dio-sataburiastan Agathodaimonistan*. It thus combines the cult of Agathos Daimôn with that of Zeus Atabirios, the Zeus whose temple was on Mt. Atabirios, one of the oldest and most important cult-centres of the island, cf. Morelli 1959, 46-49; 136-47.

102. Pugliese Carratelli 1939-1940, 151 no. 6 ll.12-13, 1st cent. BC. For the cult of Agathos Daimôn on Rhodes, see Morelli 1959, 1; 77-79.

103. Maiuri 1925, 181 no. 494, a *horos thêkaiôn*, the boundary-marker of a burial plot reserved for the members of the association.

104. See Foucart 1873; Poland 1909.

105. A priest of Zeus Megisteos (i.e. of the island Megiste), and perhaps also of Agathos Daimôn is mentioned in a fragmentary inscription from Rhodes, *CIG* III Add. 4301d.

106. The only two literary references to *Agathodaimoniastai* emphasise the custom of drinking little but eating well: Hesych. s.v. *Agathodaimoniastai hoi oligopotountes*; Arist. *Eth.Eud.* 3.6, 1233b3; cf. Ganszyniec 1918b.

107. Eumenia in Phrygia, a priest of Zeus Sôtêr, Apollo, Men Askaenus, Agdistis, Isis, *Eirenê Sebastê* and Agathos Daimôn, 2nd cent. AD: *IG Rom.* IV 739 = *CCCA* 1, 32, no. 84;

Gordion, graffito *agathou daimonos* on a kantharos, 350-275 BC: *SEG* 37:1107, cf. Roller 1987, 111 no. 4; Moschakoum, Lydia: *TAM* V(2) 1409; *SEG* 40:1053; Ephesus, altar to Artemis and Agathos Daimôn: J. and L. Robert, *Bullép* 1981, no. 467. Vetters 1978 discusses a third-century monument from Ephesus with an image of a snake, possibly relating to a domestic cult of Agathos Daimôn.

108. At Syracuse, *IG* XIV 5a; Tauromenium, *IG* XIV p. 685 add. 5; cf. Manganaro 1985, 155-56 with pl. 46.6, fig. 7; *SEG* 34:988.

109. At Tibur (2nd cent. AD), *IG Rom.* I 374 = *CIL* XIV 3533 = *IG* XIV 1123; *SEG* 38:1018.

110. A cult regulation on a stele (1st-2nd cent. AD) mentions a *hiereus Agathou Daimonos*, a priest of Agathos Daimôn: *SEG* 20:721.

111. [Callisthenes] *Hist. Alex. Magni* 1.32.6-7 (p. 32 Kroll); cf. Visser 1938, 65; Fraser 1972 1, 209-12.

112. Dunand 1981, 277-82, with the catalogue of Egyptian monuments (nos. 10-43). Among the inscriptions, note the dedication to Agathos Daimôn and Souchos (Arsinoe, Fayyûm, 44/5 AD), *SEG* 40:1562; dedication by an *eques* to *theôi megalôi Agathôi Daimoni* (Alexandria, 69-79 AD), *SEG* 2:850. The Canopic mouth of the Nile was called the *potamos agathos daimôn*: *OGIS* 672 (80/1 AD) with Ptol. *Geog.* 4.5.16, p. 699.16 Müller-Fischer.

113. On Agathos Daimôn-Sarapis, Dunand 1969; Pietrzykowski 1978; on Isis-*Tuchê/Fortuna*, Tran Tam Tinh 1990, 784-86 with pl. 520-23; Vidman 1969, index s.v. For Isis-*Tuchê* at Alexandria, Fraser 1972, 1:240-45 (in relation to the dynastic cult of the Ptolemies); Jentel 1978. See also Sfameni Gasparro 1997 for a discussion of this aspect of the goddess as mistress of destinies, which is fundamental to her rôle in the Graeco-Roman world.

114. There exists no recent monograph on the cult of Tuchê based on the history of religions approach. There is an old book by Allègre 1889, on which note the review by Bouché-Leclercq 1891; and encyclopaedia-articles by Hild 1896; Ruhl 1916-1924; Waser 1916-1924; Herzog-Hauser 1948a; cf. also Wilamowitz-Moellendorff 1931-1932, 2, 298-308; Strohm 1944; Buriks 1948; Nilsson 1956-1961, 2, 200-10; Hamdorf 1964, 37-39, 97-100. Champeaux 1982-1987, 1, 92-94, 455-60 and *passim*; 2, 38-59, has remarks on the Greek cult; further on the similarities and differences between Tychê and *Fortuna* see Herzog-Hauser 1948b; Kajanto 1981 (who in my opinion exaggerates the "negative" cast of Tuchê compared with the "beneficent" character of *Fortuna*). On the broader and more stippled sense of "destiny", see Greene 1948; Bianchi 1953; Dietrich 1965/1967.

115. DK 31 B103 = 46 Gallavotti: *têide men oun iotêti Tuchês pephronêken hapanta*.

116. On the symbolism of the steering-oar, Göttlicher 1981.

117. There is an intimate connection, expressed in a "couple formula" between Zeus Sôtêr and a Tuchê *prôtogeneia* in a Hellenistic inscription from Itanus in Crete: *IG Rom.* I 1020, cf. Reinach 1911, 411-15; Spyridakis 1969. Other documents of different periods provide a number of further divine associations, including Zeus and Tuchê: Agathê Tuchê of Zeus Dionysus Gingylos, Sarapaeum at Thessalonika, 1st cent. AD (*IG* IX 259); dedications to Zeus and Agathê Tuchê, and Agathê Tuchê in association with Zeus Hypsistos, Hera and Hekate Sôteira, sanctuary of Zeus at Panamara, Caria (Deschamps and Cousin 1888, 256 no. 36; 264 no. 49; Hatzfeld 1927 no. 42, no. 103; cf. Laumonier 1958, 266); dedication by a priest to Tuchê and Zeus Kapetôlios, the Moirae, the Charites, the Muses and Mnemosyne at Stratonicea, 2nd cent. AD (Deschamps and Cousin 1888, 272 no. 59); also with Zeus Ktêsios and Asclepius, 2nd-3rd cent. AD (Deschamps and Cousin 1888, 269 no. 54); dedication to *Iuppiter Optimus maximus, Minerva Zizimmene* and Tuchê at Iconium (*IG Rom.* III 1471 = *CIL* III 13638); also a priest of Zeus *Egainetos* and of the *Tuchê Sebastôn* (*IG Rom.* III 407); cult of Zeus and other gods including Agathê Tuchê and Agathos

Daimôn in the *oikos* of Agdistis at Philadelphia (*CCCA* 1 no. 489); dedication to Agathê Tuchê and Zeus *Sureanos* at Cotiaeum or Nakoleia, Phrygia (*SEG* 27:1380; Drew-Bear 1976, 251 no. 8); statue of the Tuchê of the Mother of the Gods and of Zeus *Batenos* at Saittai, Lydia, 1st cent. AD (*SEG* 35:1232). A dedication in Arabia to *Dii olympiôi sôtêri kai Tu[chêi]*, 2nd cent. AD (*SEG* 7:840). At Halicarnassus and at Statonicea the Moirae are associated with Zeus and Tuchê. An inscription from Aegilae (Amorgos) mentions Tuchê with the Mother of the Gods and the Moirae (*IG* XII(7) 432). Tuchê is invoked with Phanes and the Moirae in one of the gold leaves from Thurii (Kern *Orph. frag.* no. 47), cf. Zuntz 1971, 344-54.

118. Cf. Dietrich 1965/1967, 59-90.

119. Some examples: Archil. frg. 8 Diehl = 16 West: *panta Tuchê kai Moira, Periklees, andri didôsin*; the personal character of Tuche/tuchê in Bacchyl. 10.115-116 is not certain: the poet says to Artemis *sun de tuchâi/naieis Metapontion*. Alcman is said to have known a string of Tuchê's family relationships – "the sister of Order (Eunomia) and Persuasion (Peithô), daughter of Forethought (Promêtheia)" (frg. 62 Bergk = 64 Page, *PMG*).

120. Petelia: *CIG* I 4; Comparetti 1916, 230-36; Krimisos: Comparetti 1916, 220-24.

121. *SEG* 27:657, 2nd half of 5th cent. BC, cf. Manganaro 1977, 1329-35, citing numerous analogous texts from the Peloponnese. Also, in Thessaly, Crannon (Pelasgiotis), 3rd cent. BC (*IG* IX(2) 458); Phayattos (490.11); Hypata (Ainis) (9).

122. Comparetti ibid. 259-62; *SEG* 23:475 (4th cent. BC). A lead lamella (4th-3rd cent. BC) from the sanctuary mentions a Tuchê Agathê with Zeus and Dione: *Hêrakl[e]idas aitei ton Dia kai tên Diônên tuchên agathên kai ton theon eperôtai peri ge<i>neês, ê esta[i] ek tês gunaikos A[i]glês, tês nun echei* (the text of Dittenb. *SIG* 1160). In my view we should probably consider Agathê Tuchê a divine person here; on the other hand, Parke's (rather tortured) translation runs: "Heracleidas requests Zeus and Dione for good fortune, and asks the god concerning offspring, whether there will be any from his wife Aigle, whom he has now" (1967, 265 no. 7). A fifth-century inscription gives a list of divinities to whom libations (*loiban*) are made, and Tuchê is among them (*SEG* 15:391, cf. J. and L. Robert, *Bullép* 1956, 135 no. 143.22). The formula *theos/theoi – Tucha agatha* occurs frequently among the Dodona lead slips: e.g. Michel 1898 nos. 843, 845, 847; also Parke 1967, 259 no. 1,3; 263 no. 1-2; 266 no. 9; 267 no. 13; 269 no. 18,21; 271-72 no. 24-26; J. and L. Robert, *Bullép* 1956, 135 no. 143.21. Sometimes the tablet invokes *Tuchê agathê* alone: Michel 1898, 849; Parke 1967, 261 no. 5; 269 no. 19; 270 no. 22; 272 no. 28.

123. *CIG* 1850; cf. Comparetti 1916, 262-65.

124. Orchomenus, *Thios tiuchan agathan*, 3rd cent. BC: *IG* VII 3167-68; Dendra, 2nd half 3rd cent. BC: *IG* VII 2809; Copaea, 2nd cent. BC: *SEG* 22:432; sanctuary of Trophonius, Lebadeia, *Theos tychêi agathêi, Thios tiouchan agathan, Thios Toucha agatha*, 1st-2nd cent. AD: *IG* VII 3077; 3082-83; Thebes: Dittenb. *SIG* 179; Thespiae, *Theos Tucha* in a 4th cent. temple inventory relating to the Heraeum and other temples of the city and the surrounding area (Platon and Feyel 1938; cf. J. and L. Robert, *Bullép* 1967 no. 292).

125. Dittenb. *SIG* 183. Other texts provide evidence of the cult of Tuchê at Tegea (*IG* V(2) 98-99, both *Tuchai Agathai*) into the Roman period (*IG* V(2) 100, statue in her honour, 2nd cent. AD).

126. The opening formula, *Theoi: Tuchêi Agathêi tou dêmou*, of an inscription from Eretria containing a law against tyranny, may have a similar import (*IG* XII(9) 190; cf. 211, early 3rd cent. BC). The *Tuchê Agathê* is closely linked to the people, whose freedom she upholds. Many examples of such a usage are known from the Hellenistic period, e.g. a stela from Imbros, *Tuchêi dêmokrateiai*: *IG* XII(8) 80; Carystus, *Agathêi Tuchêi tou dêmou Karustinôn*:

IG XII(9) 3; Delos, *Agathêi Tuchêi tou dêmou tou tôn Athênaiôn* (108/7 BC): *SEG* 35:887.

127. Note already Alexandrides frg. 4 Kock (2:137): "It is Tuchê who alters our fortune ... the goddess steers the rudder of our destiny" (2nd quart. 4th cent. BC). In Philemon's (d. 264/263 BC) *Apokarterôn* we find several Tuchai linked to each individual (frg. 10 Kock 2:481); note also the unattributed comic frag. cited by Stob. *Ecl.* 1.6.6 (p. 85.1-4 Wachsmuth) = 4:358 no. 693 Meinecke (cf. Wilamowitz-Moellendorff 1931-1932, 2, 299 n. 2).

128. Frg. 41 Wehrli = Diels *Vorsokr.* 1, 478.23ff. = Detienne 1963, 176 no. 30 (from Stob. *Ecl.* 1.6.18, p. 89.10-14 Wachsmuth): *Peri de tuchês tad'ephaskon: einai men ti kai daimonion meros autês, genesthai gar epipnoian tina para tou daimoniou tôn anthrôpôn eniois epi to beltion ê epi to cheiron, kai einai phanerôs kat'auto touto tous men eutucheis, tous de atucheis.* The "daemonic" character of Pythagorean Tuchê is well expressed in the maxim cited by Plutarch in *Consol. ad Apollon.* 29 (116e-f): "The Pythagoreans used to give the following excellent advice: Whichever of the innumerable sufferings inflicted on mankind by divine whim (*daimoniêisi tuchais*) falls to your share, accept them – do not complain" (cf. Hani 1972, 132-33).

129. Pausanias mentions several temples of Tuchê whose distribution is of interest, though they can hardly be dated. At Megara there was a *hieron* and a statue "by Praxiteles" (1.43.6); at Corinth a *naos* and statue (2.2.8); a temple of Tuchê *Akraia*, "of the rock" on the acropolis at Sicyon (2.7.5), and in the Asclepium near the town a *xoanon* (2.11.8); a shrine at Argos (2.20.3); a temple with a *kolossos* at Hermione (2.35.3); a temple and very old statue at Pharae (4.30.3); a statue in the temple of Asclepius at Messene (4.31.10); an altar to Agathê Tuchê at the horse-race track (5.15.6) and an ancient statue in the temple of Hera (5.17.3) at Olympia; a shrine and *xoanon* at Elis with a neighbouring shrine to Sôsipolis as a small boy (6.25.4); small temple and statue with an Eros beside it at Aigeira in Achaea (7.26.8); shrine and statue at Megalopolis (8.30.7); temple and statue with Wealth as a child at Thebes (9.16.1-2); a statue at Thespiae (9.26.8); and a small temple of Agathos Daimôn and Agathê Tuchê in the oracle of Trophonius at Lebadeia (9.39.5).

130. *IG* IV 1326. Several inscriptions from the sacred precinct document the cult into the Roman period: *IG* IV 765; 948; 1045; 1046; 1051.1; 1327-28; *SEG* 11:442 (3rd cent. AD); also a dedication *Tuchai* from the *temenos* of Apollo Meleatês: *IG* IV 1536. For the similarities to Nemesis, with whom Tuchê is sometimes associated (e.g. *IG Rom.* III 739, xix = *TAM* II(3) 905.xixa, Rhodiapolis, 124-153 AD), see Perdrizet 1912; Chapouthier 1924; Volkmann 1928; Seyrig 1932; Hornum 1993.

131. *SEG* 37:1106, cf. Roller 1987, 110 no. 3. There is also a drinking cup inscribed *Agathê Tuchê* among the offerings deposited by Seleucus I Nicator and Antiochus (290-280 BC) in the temple of Apollo at Didyma (*OGIS* 214 l.30). The cult was very widespread in the cities of Asia Minor, especially in the form of the official cult of the city Tuchê, *Tuchê poleôs.* Among many examples (cf. n. 142 below), note the inscription from the statue of the *Tuchê sôteira* of Antioch in Pisidia at Ephesus (Engelmann 1977).

132. *IG* V(1) 364 = Sokolowski 1969 no. 63; cf. Sfameni Gasparro 1986, 299. There is a good deal of evidence for the cult of Tuchê in Laconia, and esp. Sparta: *IG* V(1) 242; 250; 259.

133. See Sartori 1980, 408-9 no. 15 with pl. 75.13; Ghinatti 1980, 139 no. 5; Pianu 1988, 105-7.

134. *IG* IV 765, 4th cent. BC; *Tuchê philanthrôpos*, 778 (undated); *T. autokratoros* 779; a *hiereus* of *T. Sebastê*, 799, 2nd cent. AD.

135. There are two altars dedicated to Agathê Tuchê from Camirus on Rhodes, where she is paired with Agathos Daimôn, whose cult was particularly favoured (cf. p. 80-81 above): Segre and Pugliese-Carrattelli 1949-1951, 244 no. 117; 256 no. 145. In one of them Tuchê

has the epithet *euetêria*, wealth, prosperity. At Rhodes itself, Tuchê is associated with Isis on an altar (Pugliese Carratelli 1952-1953, 264 no. 11) and there was a priest in her name (*IG* XII(1) 67. There may be an association too with Helios: *IG* XII(1) 23 and Corr. p.207 = *IG* Rom. IV 1121; cf. Morelli 1959, 1; 70; 77; 176-77.

Some other Aegean documents: at Mitylene : *IG* XII(2) 270; 67; Paros: XII(5) 249-51; Aegiale (Amorgos): XII(7) 432 (4th cent. BC); Thasos: XII(8) 369, *Tuchê Thasou* (2nd cent. AD); Samothrace: XII(8) 150 (decree of 288/7-281/0 relating to building work in the sanctuary, esp. line 9: *Agathêi Tuchêi basileôs Lusimachou kai tês poleôs*); Imbros: XII(8) 80; Carystus: XII(9) 3; Eretria: XII(9) 190 (4th cent. BC); 211 (3rd cent. BC); Minoa (Amorgos): XII(7) 247 = *IG Rom.* IV 1011 (*agalma* of Tuchê, 2nd cent. AD); XII(7) 257; Melos: an inscription *Agathê Tuchê Mêlou* on a 2nd-3rd cent. AD relief showing the goddess with a child on her arm, dedicated by the association of the *mustai* of Dionysus, cf. Bosanquet 1898, 60 fig. 1; Harrison 1912/1926, 284 fig. 74 = *IG* XII(3) 1908; also Suppl. 1669; Nisyros: XII(3) 97. As for Cyprus, there is a good number of Hellenistic sealings representing Tuchê and Isis-Tuchê (Michaelidou-Nikolaou 1993; Nicolau 1978). The cave-*nymphaeum* of Kafizin was dedicated both to Tuchê and to the Nymph (Mitford 1980 no. 47, 104 = *SEG* 1980:1608; Masson 1981, 638-39; J. and L. Robert, *Bullép* 1981, 474-76 no. 636). At Paphos, a husband and wife, the *archiereis dia biou tês Tuchês*, erected a shrine to her, a *tuchaion* (E. Gardner et al. 1888, 237 no. 40 = *OGIS* 585).

136. Bruneau 1970, 534-43; cf. Plassart 1928, 222-28. The Delian *tuchaion* may have replaced the *philadelpheion*, the temple dedicated to Arsinoe Philadelphe, in which case her cult will have been linked to the Alexandrian cult. A small Tuchê, probably for domestic cult, was found in the 'house of Hermes' (Marcadé 1953, 558-63).

137. These date from the Hellenistic period into the Empire: *IG* XII(3) 325; 326 (*naos tês Tuchês*); 446-47 (statue-bases); 448, 1375-77 (altars).

138. *IG* XII(3) 1338: *Pergaios Artemidôros ephêne Tuchên episêmo[n]/ tois epiginomenois onom' athanaton kataleipôn.* The other inscriptions are no. 1333-48; see also Hiller von Gaertringen 1899, 166; 1904, 89-102 with figs. 73-81, noting that there was a seated statue of the goddess near the inscription, though all that survives is the traces of the feet. Another statue was found in the town, in a house by the market.

139. Confirmed by other evidence: Diod. Sic. 11.68, cf. Steph. Byz. s.v. *Tuchê*; Ziegler, 1948.

140. *BMC Sicily* 226 no. 688-89; on the type and the question of the date, see Sfameni Gasparro 1995.

141. 1955-1961, 2, 207; cf. already Wilamowitz-Moellendorff 1931-1932, 2, 304.

142. Paus. 4.30.6. Several documents show that the cult was known into the Roman period, cf. Petzl 1987 no. 760 (dedication in Smyrna of a statue of *Tuchê Thessalonikeôn*, imperial date); 761 (1st cent. AD); 762; no. 613 mentions a tower of Agathê Tuchê (3rd-2nd cent. BC); and the *prutanis* Smaragados erected a shrine to her (*IG Rom.* IV 1431: Hadrianic). An inscription found outside the city tells us that one Rufinus built a sacred building for Agathê Tuchê (*CIG* 3171).

In Asia Minor we can just cite the temple of Tuchê at Lagina (Hatzfeld 1920, 95 no. 32); Stratonicaea and Panamara (n. 117 above; cf. Laumonier 1958, 193-340); texts from Daedala (dedication to Agathê Tuchê and Aphrodite: *TAM* II(1) 163); Termessus (*hiereus dia biou tês Tuchês poleôs*: *TAM* III(1) 134; prayer for help to *Tuchê poleôs*: 881; Tuchê of the gymnasium: 31; dedication *Eutuchêi*: 880); Selge (priestess *Tuchês kai Arês dia biou*: *IG Rom.* III 383); Syllium (*hieron*: *IG Rom.* III 800); Colossis (*IG Rom.* IV 870); Thyateira (priestess of the city Tuchê, 2nd cent. AD: IV 1233; cf. 1231); Sardis (Hellenistic coins and Roman inscription in honour of *Tuchê Sardeôn*: Hanfmann 1983, 130 fig. 201.2; 269 n.30

and 33a); Rhodiapolis (shrine of Tuchê and Nemesis, gilded statue and a festival for *Tuchê poleôs*: *IG Rom*. III 739, xix = *TAM* II(3) 905, xix a-b); Phrygian Hierapolis (*Megalê Tuchê tês poleôs*: *CIG* 3906 = *SEG* 35:1388; *Agathêi Tuchêi theôi epiphanestatôi*, on two fragments of an architrave: *SEG* 35:1373a-b); Ephesus (dedication *Agathêi Tuchêi* on a mosaic: Engelmann and Knibbe 1978-1980, 39 no. 47; dedication to *Sôteira Tuchê*: *SEG* 38:949); Saghir in Pisidia (dedication of a bronze Tuchê by the *xenoi Tekmoreioi*, the resident foreigners from Tekmoreia, Roman: *IG Rom*. III 298).

143. Picard 1941, 212 fig. 2; 225; Hamdorf 1964, 98 no. 287g.

144. It has been suggested that several statues of Roman date go back to a prototype "of the late third quarter of the fourth century BC": Palagia 1982, 102; cf. P. Gardner 1888.

145. *BMC Peloponnese* 144 no. 109, pl. 27.24. Pausanias mentions that there was a very old temple of Tuchê in the city of Argos (2.20.3).

146. *IG* II² 4564 = Wycherley 1957, 122 no. 376: "Philippos son of Iasidemos of Kolone dedicated this to the Twelve Gods and Agathê Tuchê." We may recall that the *tuchaion* at Alexandria contained statues of the Twelve Gods as well as those of Alexander and Ptolemy I Soter (Libanius p. 529.31 Förster, cited by Visser 1938, 99 n. 2).

147. *IG* II² 1610; 4852 (undated) is a dedication to Agathê Tuchê and Apollo; 4510 (304/3 BC) is an inscription in honour of the goddess by an orator; a graffito from the Agora (Lang 1976, G9) mentions Agathê Tuchê with Dionysus and Zeus.

148. Ael. *VH* 9.39 = Wycherley 1957, 166 no. 542; cf. Effenberg 1971. The widespread custom of erecting statues of the goddess in the most prestigious sites in cities harks back to the rôle of Tuchê as protectress of cities and their people. At Cyrene, for example, during the 1st cent. BC, the ephors and other magistrates dedicated a statue of Tuchê, together with that of Apollo, the city's chief god, in the agora (Marengo 1988, 98). The inscriptions in honour of Agathê Tuchê, Apollo and Aphrodite in the same city are Augustan (*SEG* 9:131-35).

149. *IG* II² 1496 lines 76, 107, 148 = Dittenb. *SIG* 1029, lines 13, 43, 83.

150. *IG* II² 1195, cf. Walbank 1994.

151. Woodhead 1981 (304/3 BC); cf. Tracy 1994.

152. See n. 130 above. At both Titane (Paus. 2.11.8) and Messene (2.31.10) the statue of Tuchê was in the temple of Asclepius.

153. Habicht 1969, 167-90 no. 161; cf. Ohlemutz 1940, 263-64.

154. An example from the Piraeus (*IG* II² 4589, mid-fourth cent. BC) shows Tuchê with a cornucopia together with two worshippers, a man and a woman; the dedication, by Puthonikos, is to *agathêi theôi*. There is another Athenian relief from the same century on which Tuchê appears with other gods and three worshippers. She is described as wife of *Zeus epiteleios philios*: "Aristomachês, Theôris and Olumpiodôros dedicated (it) to Zeus epiteleios philios and to Philia, the mother of the god, and to Agathê Tuchê, the wife of the god" (*IG* II² 4627; cf. Harrison 1922, 354-56, fig. 106: "this interesting relief came from a precinct of Asclepius in Munuchia down at Peiraeus, the same precinct which yielded the snake reliefs dedicated to Meilichios").

155. *IG* II² 1035.44-48, cf. Culley 1975; *SEG* 26:121. Dedications of 1st-2nd cent. AD: *IG* II² 1076; 3703; 4761; *SEG* 21:816, cf. Merritt 1961, 274 no. 116.

156. Men. *Asp*. 147-148, p. 7-8 Sandbach: *tis eimi? pantôn kuria toutôn brabeusai kai dioikêsai: Tuchê*; also *Epitr*. 351, Sandbach = 175: and frgs. 295 and 417 Körte-Thierfelder, cf. p. 315 Sandbach. On Tuchê in Menander, cf. Webster 1960, 198-201.

157. Tracy 1994; cf. Mattingly 1974.

158. A decree from Mylasa from the period of Persian domination is dedicated *Tuchêi epiphanêi basileôs* (*CIG* 2693b); in later times oaths were sworn by Zeus, Gê, Helios, some other

gods, and the Tuchê of Seleucus II Callinicus (ibid. 3137; cf. P. Gardner 1888, 74). The Agathê Tuchê of Lysimachus is mentioned in *IG* XII(8) 150 (Samothrace, 288/7-281 BC).

159. See the ample materials collected in the bibliography listed in n. 79 and n. 114 above, esp. Herzog-Hauser 1948a.

160. Cf. Festugière 1950, 268-69 on the probable link between *daimôn* and the verbs *daiomai, dainumi*; *daimôn* would mean etymologically "distributor of a lot or portion".

161. *IG* XII(3) 436 = Dittenb. *SIG*. 1032: *theos agathai tuchai agathou daimonos*. There is an altar of Roman date dedicated to the pair: 1323.

162. Relief from the Acropolis with representations of the two gods together with a (human) woman (Dunand 1981, 278 no. 4). The inscription is fragmentary: *Agathos Dai[môn Agathê] Tuchê*. There is also an altar of Roman date, *CIG* 371.

163. *IG* IV 1160 (temple of Asclepius, 4th-3rd cent. BC); cf. 1045; 1051.

164. The *oikêma* of Agathos Daimôn and Agathê Tuchê in the oracular sactuary of Trophonius (Paus. 9.39.5; 13).

165. Altar with dedication: Maiuri 1916, 138 no. 7.

166. The dedication by a private individual of a horologium associates the two divinities with the *demos*: *Philippos Autophôntos to hôrologion Tuchai agathai kai Agathôi Daimoni kai tôi dêmôi* (*SGDI* 3650). There is also a Hellenistic dedication of an altar in the temple of Asclepius to Agathos Daimôn and Agathê Tuchê together with Helios and Hemera (Sherwin-White 1978, 362). Statue of Tuchê from 1st cent. BC: Laurenzi, 1955-1956, 71-73 no. 4.

167. Relief with a large snake between the two divinities cited n. 91 above; also a 2nd cent. BC dedication to Agathos Daimôn and Agathê Tuchê "by order of (Sarapis)" from Sarapaeum A (*IG* XI(4) 1273).

168. Fragmentary early 4th cent. inscription on an altar or libation-trench (*IG* XII Suppl. 378). Daux' restoration takes it that a distinction is made between the two divinities in respect of the offerings they are to receive (1926, 236-37).

169. Dedication of a base by a *skoutlarios*, a mosaicist (Dittenb. *SIG* 1124, ?1st cent. AD). Agathos Daimôn and Agathê Tuchê in the temple of Asclepius: Ael. Arist. p. 378.10ff. Keil.

170. A dream caused Dionysius to dedicate a shrine (*oikos*) to Agdistis in which there are to be several altars to other divinities, including one to Agathos Daimôn and Agathê Tuchê (Dittenb. *SIG* 985 = *CCCA* 1:147 no. 489, 1st cent. BC); cf. Weinreich 1919.

171. We may recall the 1st cent. BC hymn of Isidorus at Medinet Madi in which the speaker invokes Isis-Tuchê and Agathos Daimôn-Sokonôpis: *Chaire, Tuchê Agathê, megalônyme Isi megistê* (2.1); *ho Agathos Daimôn Sokonôpis* (2.9) (cf. Vanderlip 1972, 34-40). A 2nd cent. AD dedication at Antinoopolis to Isis Thermouthis mentions Agathê Tuchê and Agathos Daimôn (*SEG* 8:635 = 18:659). For representations, see Dunand 1969; 1981, 278-80.

172. Dittenb. *SIG*. 1044 = *CCCA* 1:211-13 no. 715.

173. Weinreich cites (1919, 34) as an analogy to the religious conception here a passage of Proclus: *enioi touto kat'apeiron oiontai ton idion hêmôn daimona kai tên toutôi sustoichon tuchên tou Agathou Daimonos kai tês Agathês Tuchês diapherein ouden*. Some wrongly believe that the individual's own *daimôn* and the fate linked with it are the same as the Agathos Daimôn and Agathê Tuchê (*In remp.* 619b, 2:299.7 Kroll).

Bibliography

Allègre, F. 1889. *Étude sur la déesse grecque Tyché. Sa signification religieuse et morale, son culte et ses représentations figurées.* Paris.

Andres, F. 1918. s.v. Daimon, in: *RE* Suppl. 3, 267-322.

Babut, D. 1969. *Plutarque et le stoïcisme.* Paris.

Babut, D. 1981. "Unité et diversité dans l'oeuvre de Plutarque: à propos d'une édition récente de quatre traités des Moralia", *RevPhil* 55, 319-24.

Babut D. 1988. "La part du rationalisme dans la religion du Plutarque: l'exemple du *De genio Socratis*", *IllinClSt* 13.2, 383-408 (repr. Babut 1994a, 431-56).

Babut D. 1992. "La composition des Dialogues pythiques de Plutarque et le problème de leur unité", *JSav* 189-234 (repr. Babut 1994a, 457-504).

Babut D. 1994a. *Parerga. Choix d'articles de Daniel Babut (1974-1994).* Paris.

Babut D. 1994b. "Le rôle de Cléombrote dans le *De defectu Oraculorum* et le problème de la 'démonologie' de Plutarque", in: Babut 1994a, 531-48.

Babut D. 1994c. "Plutarque, Aristote et l'aristotélisme", in: Babut 1994a, 504-29.

Babut D. 1994d. "Du scepticisme au dépassement de la raison: philosophie et foi religieuse chez Plutarque", in: Babut 1994a, 549-81.

Barra, G. 1966. "La questione dell'autenticità del *De Platone et eius dogmate* e del *De mundo* di Apuleio", *RendNap* 41, 127-88.

Barra, G. 1972. "Apuleio e il problema del male", *Vichiana* n.s. 1, 102-13.

Barra, G. & Pennuti, U. 1960-1961. "Il valore e il significato del *De deo Socratis* di Apuleio", *AnnNap* 9, 67-119.

Barra, G. & Pennuti, U. 1962-1963. "Il *De deo Socratis* di Apuleio. Tradotto e annotato col testo a fronte", *AnnNap* 10, 81-141.

Beaujeu, J. (ed.) 1973. *Apulée. Opuscules philosophiques (Du Dieu de Socrate, Platon et sa doctrine, Du monde) et Fragments.* (Coll. Budé). Paris.

Bernabò Brea, L. 1948. "Siracusa. Cippo con dedica a Tyche", *NSc* Ser. 8.1, 202-3.

Bernabò Brea, L. 1956. *Akrai.* Catania.

Bianchi, U. 1953. ΔΙΟΣ ΑΙΣΑ. *Destino, uomini e divinità nell'epos, nelle teogonie e nel culto dei Greci.* Rome.

Bianchi, U. 1986. "Plutarco e il dualismo", in: *Miscellanea Plutarchea. Atti del 1 Convegno di studi su Plutarco (Roma, 23 novembre 1985)*, 111-20. (Quaderni del Giornale Filologico Ferrarese). Ferrara.

Bianchi, U. 1987. "Plutarch und der Dualismus", in: *ANRW* II.36.1, 350-56.

Bianchi, U. 1990. "Sulla demonologia del medio- e neo-platonismo", in: Corsini & Costa (eds.) 1990, 51-62.

Blinkenberg, C. 1941. *Inscriptions. Lindos. Fouilles de l'Acropole, 1902-1914* 2. Berlin/Copenhagen.

Blümel, W. (ed.) 1985. *Die Inschriften von Iasos* 1: *Nr. 1-218.* (IGSK 34). Bonn.

Blümel, W. 1987. *Inschriften der Stadt. Die Inschriften von Mylasa* 1. (IGSK 34). Bonn.

Blümel, W. 1988. *Inschriften aus der Umgebung der Stadt. Die Inschriften von Mylasa* 2. (IGSK 35). Bonn.

de Boer, M.B. & Edridge, T.A. (eds.) 1978. *Hommages à M.J. Vermaseren* 1-3. (EPRO 68). Leiden.

Bosanquet, R.C. 1898. "Excavations of the British School at Melos. The Hall of the Mystae", *JHS* 18, 60-80.

Bouché-Leclercq, A. 1891. "Tyché ou la Fortune. À propos d'un ouvrage récent", *RHistRel* 23, 273-307.

Boyancé, P. 1935. "Les deux démons personnels dans l'antiquité grecque et latine", *RPhil* 9, 189-202.

Brenk, F.E. 1969. "Le songe de Brutus", in: *Actes du VIII Congrès de l'Association Guillaume Budé (Paris, 5-9 avril 1968)*, 588-94. Paris.

Brenk, F.E. 1973. "'A most strange Doctrine': daimon in Plutarch", *CIJ* 69, 1-11.

Brenk, F.E. 1977. *In Mist Apparelled: religious themes in Plutarch's Moralia and Lives*. Leiden.

Brenk, F.E. 1986. "In the Light of the Moon: demonology in the early Imperial period", in: *ANRW* II.17.3, 2068-145.

Brenk, F.E. 1987. "An Imperial Heritage: the religious spirit of Plutarch of Chaironeia", in: *ANRW* II.36.1, 249-349.

Brenk, F.E. 1990. "I veri demoni greci 'nella nebbia ammantellati'? Esiodo e Plutarco", in: Corsini & Costa (eds.), 1990, 23-35.

Bruneau, P. 1970. *Recherches sur les cultes de Délos à l'époque hellénistique et à l'époque impériale*. (BEFAR 217). Rome.

Buckler, W.H. 1916-1918. "Documents from Mylasa", *BSA* 22, 190-215.

Buriks, A.A. 1948. ΠΕΡΙ ΤΥΧΗΣ. *De ontwikkeling van het begrip tyche tot aan de Romeinse tijd, hoofdzakelijk in de philosophie*. Leiden.

Burkert, W. 1962. *Weisheit und Wissenschaft: Studien zu Pythagoras, Philolaos und Platon*. Nuremberg. (Eng. trans. *Lore and Science in Ancient Pythagoreanism*, Cambridge, Mass. 1972).

Busch, G. 1937. *Untersuchungen zum Wesen der Τύχη in den Tragödien des Euripides*. Heidelberg.

Caccamo Caltabiano, M. (ed.) 1995. *La Sicilia tra l'Egitto e Roma: la monetazione siracusana dell'età di Ierone II: Atti del Seminario di studi, Messina 2-4 dicembre 1993*. Messina.

Cambiano, A. (ed.) 1986. *Storiografia e dossografia nella filosofia antica*. Turin.

Champeaux, J. 1982-1987. *Fortuna. Recherches sur le culte de la Fortune à Rome et dans le monde romain des origines à la mort de César*. (CEFR 64). Rome/Paris.

Chantraine, P. 1954. "Le divin et les dieux chez Homère", in: *La notion du divin depuis Homère jusqu'à Platon*, 47-94. (EntrHardt 1). Vandoeuvres.

Chapouthier, F. 1924. "Némésis et Niké", *BCH* 48, 287-303.

Comparetti, D. 1916. "Tabelle testamentarie delle colonie achee di Magna Grecia", *ASAtene* 2, 219-66.

Cook, A.B. 1914-1940. *Zeus. A Study in Ancient Religion*. Cambridge. (Repr. New York 1964-1965).

Corlu, A. (ed.) 1970. *Plutarque: Le démon de Socrate*. (Études et Commentaires 73). Paris.

Corsini, E. & Costa, E. (eds.) 1990. *L'autunno del diavolo* 1. Milan.

Cousin, A. 1898. "Voyage en Carie", *BCH* 22, 361-404.

Cousin, G. & Diehl, C. 1888. "Inscriptions de Mylasa", *BCH* 12, 8-37.

Culley, G.R. 1975. "The Restoration of Sanctuaries in Attica: *IG* II² 1035", *Hesperia* 44, 207-23.

Daux, G. 1926. "Nouvelles inscriptions de Thasos (1921-1924)", *BCH* 50, 213-49.

Defradas, J. 1965. "Le mythe hésiodique des races. Essai de mise au point", *L'Information Littéraire* 4, 152-56.

Delatte, A. 1915. *Études sur la littérature pythagoricienne*. (Bibliothèque des Hautes Études, Sciences historiques et philologiques 217). Paris.

Delatte, A. (ed.) 1922. *La Vie de Pythagore de Diogène Laërce: édition critique avec introduction et commentaire*. (Mémoires de l'Académie Royale des Sciences, des Lettres et des Beaux-arts de Belgique, Classe des lettres et des sciences morales et politiques sér. 2, 2). Brussels.

Deschamps, G. & G. Cousin 1888. "Inscriptions du temple de Zeus Panamaros. Ex-voto et dédicaces", *BCH* 12, 249-73; 479-90.

Des Places, É. 1931. "Sur l'authenticité de l'*Epinomis*", *REG* 44, 153-66.

Des Places, É. (tr.) 1956. *Platon. Oeuvres complètes*, 12.2: *Les Lois (XI-XII); Epinomis*. (Coll. Budé). Paris.

Detienne, M. 1958. "Xénocrate et la démonologie pythagoricienne", *REA* 60, 271-79.

Detienne, M. 1959a. "La 'démonologie' d'Empédocle", *REG* 72, 1-17.

Detienne, M. 1959b. "Sur la démonologie de l'ancien pythagorisme", *RHistRel* 78 (155), 17-32.

Detienne, M. 1962. *Homère, Hésiode et Pythagore. Poésie et philosophie dans le pythagorisme ancien*. (Coll. Latomus, 57). Brussels.

Detienne, M. 1963. *De la pensée religieuse à la pensée philosophique. La notion de daimôn dans le pythagorisme ancien*. (Bibliothèque de la Faculté de Philosophie et Lettres de l'Université de Liège 165). Paris.

Deubner, L. 1902-1909. s.v. Personifikation (griechisch), in: Roscher, *Lex.* 3.2, 2142-45.

Dietrich, B.C. 1965/1967. *Death, Fate and the Gods: the development of a religious idea in Greek popular belief and in Homer*. London.

Dillon, J. 1977. *The Middle Platonists: a study of Platonism, 80BC to AD 222*. London.

Dillon, J. 1988. "Plutarch and Platonist orthodoxy", *YaleClSt* 13, 357-408.

Döring, K. 1984. "Plutarch und das Daimonion des Sokrates (Plut., *de genio Socratis*, Kap. 20-24)", *Mnemosyne* 37, 376-92.

Donini, P.L. 1986a. "Plutarco, Ammonio e l'Accademia", in: *Miscellanea Plutarchea. Atti del I Convegno di studi su Plutarco (Roma, 23 novembre 1985)*, 97-110. (Quaderni del Giornale Filologico Ferrarese). Ferrara.

Donini, P.L. 1986b. "Scetticismo academico, Aristotele e l'unità della tradizione platonica secondo Plutarco", in: A. Cambiano (ed.) 1986, 203-26.

Donini, P.L. 1990. "Nozioni di *daimôn* e di intermediario nella filosofia tra il I e il II secolo d.C.", in: Corsini & Costa (eds.) 1990, 37-50.

Drew-Bear, T. 1976. "Local cults in Graeco-Roman Phrygia", *GRBS* 17, 247-68.

Dunand, F. 1969. "Les représentations de l'Agathodémon. À propos de quelques bas-reliefs du Musée d'Alexandrie", *BIFAO* 67, 9-48.

Dunand, F. 1981. s.v. Agathodaimon, in: *LIMC* 1.1, 277-82; plates, 1.2, 203-7.

Edsman, C-M. 1967. "Divine and demonic Necessity in the *Oresteia*", in: Ringgren 1967, 19-34.

Effenberger, A. 1971. "Die drei Tyche-Statuen des Praxiteles: ein neues archäologisches Märchen", *Klio* 53, 125-28.

Engelmann, H. 1977. "Zu Inschriften aus Ephesos", *ZPE* 26, 154-56.

Engelmann, H. & Knibbe, D. 1978-1980. "Aus ephesischen Skizzenbüchern", *ÖJh* 52, 19-62.

Farnell, L.R. 1909. *The Cults of the Greek States* 5. London.

Festugière, A.-J. 1945/1971. "Les *Mémoires Pythagoriques* cités par Alexandre Polyhistor", in: idem, *Études de philosophie grecque*, 371-435. (Repr. from *REG* 58,1-65).

Festugière, A.-J. 1950. *Contemplation et vie contemplative chez Platon*. Paris.

Flacelière, R. (ed.) 1947. *Sur la disparition des oracles*. Paris.

Flacelière, R. 1966. "Plutarque, *De Fortuna Romanorum*", in: *Mélanges d'archéologie, d'épigraphie et d'histoire offerts à Jérôme Carcopino*, 367-75. Paris.

Flacelière, R. (ed.) 1974. *Plutarque. Oeuvres morales 6: Dialogues pythiques*. (Coll. Budé). Paris.

Forni, G. (ed.) 1989. *Plutarco: La fortuna dei Romani*. (Corpus Plutarchi Moralium 4). Naples.

Foucart, P. 1873. *Des associations religieuses chez les grecs: thiases, éranes, orgéones*. Paris.

Fraser, P.M. 1972. *Ptolemaic Alexandria*. Oxford.

Fritz, K. von. 1963. s.v. Pythagoras, Pythagoreer, in: *RE* 25, 171-267.

Froidefond, C. 1987. "Plutarque et le platonisme", in: *ANRW* II.36.1, 184-233.

Gallo, J. (ed.) 1996. *Plutarco e la religione. Atti del VI Convegno plutarcheo (Ravello, 29-31 maggio 1995)*. Naples.

Ganszyniec [Ganschinietz], R. 1918a. s.v. Agathodaimon 1, in: *RE* Suppl. 3, 37-59.

Ganszyniec R. 1918b. s.v. Agathodaimoniastai, in: *RE* Suppl. 3, 59-60.

Ganszyniec R. 1919. *De Agathodaemone*. (Travaux de la Société des Sciences de Varsovie, Cl. 2,17). Warsaw.

Gardner, E.A. et al. 1888. "Excavations in Cyprus, 1887-1888", *JHS* 9, 147-271.

Gardner, P. 1888. "Countries and cities in ancient art", *JHS* 9, 47-81.

Gerhard, E. 1868. "Über Agathodaemon und Bona Dea", in: Gerhard, E. 1868. *Gesammelte akademische Abhandlungen und kleine Schriften* 2, 21-57. Berlin.

Ghinatti, F. 1980. "Nuovi efori in epigrafi di Eraclea Lucana", in: *Forschungen und Funde. Festschrift Bernhard Neutsch*, 137-43. (Innsbrücker Beiträge zur Kulturwissenschaft 21). Innsbruck.

Goldschmidt, V. 1948. "Les thèmes du *De defectu oraculorum* de Plutarque", *REG* 61, 298-302.

Goldschmidt, V. 1950. "Théologia", *REG* 63, 20-42.

Göttlicher, A. 1981. "Fortuna gubernatrix. Das Steuerruder als Glückssymbol", *AW* 12, 27-33.

Greene, W.C. 1948. *Moira: fate, good and evil in Greek thought*. Cambridge, Mass.

Griffiths, J.G. (ed.) 1970. *Plutarch's De Iside et Osiride*. Cardiff.

Guthrie, W.K.C. 1962. *A History of Greek Philosophy* 1: *The earlier Presocratics and the Pythagoreans*. Cambridge.

Habicht, C. 1969. *Die Inschriften des Asklepieions. Altertümer von Pergamon* 8.3. Berlin.

Hamdorf, F.W. 1964. *Griechische Kultpersonifikationen der vorhellenistischen Zeit*. Mainz.

Hanfmann, G.M.A. 1983. *Sardis from Prehistoric to Roman Times*. Cambridge, Mass./London.

Hani, J. (ed.) 1972. *Plutarque. Consolation à Apollonios*. (Coll. Budé). Paris.

Harrison, J.E. 1903/1922. *Prolegomena to a Study of Greek Religion*. Cambridge.

Harrison, J.E. 1912/1926. *Themis: a study of the social origins of Greek religion*. Cambridge.

Hatzfeld, J. 1920. "Inscriptions de Lagine en Carie", *BCH* 44, 70-100.

Hatzfeld, J. 1927. "Inscriptions de Panamara", *BCH* 51, 57-122.

Heinze, R. 1892. *Xenokrates: Darstellung der Lehre und Sammlung der Fragmente*. Leipzig. (Repr. Hildesheim 1965).

Herzog-Hauser, G. 1948a. s.v. Tyche, in: *RE* 7A, 1643-89.

Herzog-Hauser, G. 1948b. "Tyche und Fortuna", *WSt* 63, 156-63.

Hild, J.A. 1892. s.v. Daemon, in: *Dar.-Sag.* 2.1, 9-19.

Hild, J.A. 1896. s.v. Fortuna, in: *Dar.-Sag.* 2.2, 1264-77.

Hiller von Gaertringen, F. 1899. *Die Insel Thera in Altertum und Gegenwart mit Ausschluß der Nekropolen. Thera: Untersuchungen, Vermessungen und Ausgrabungen in den Jahren 1895-1898* 1. Berlin.

Hiller von Gaertringen, F. & Wilski, P. 1904. *Stadtgeschichte von Thera. Thera: Untersuchungen, Vermessungen und Ausgrabungen in den Jahren 1895-1902* 3. Berlin.

Hofinger, M. 1981. "Le logos hésiodique des races: les Travaux et les Jours, vers 106 à 201", *AntCl* 50, 404-16.

Hornum, M.B. 1993. *Nemesis, the Roman State, and the Games*. (Religions in the Graeco-Roman World 117). Leiden.

Jensen, S.S. 1966. *Dualism and Demonology: the function of demonology in Pythagorean and Platonic thought*. Copenhagen.

Jentel, M.-O. 1978. "Isis ou la Tyché d'Alexandrie?", in: de Boer & Edridge (eds.) 1978, 2, 539-60.

Kajanto, I. 1981. "Fortuna", in: *ANRW* II.17.1, 502-58.

Kirk, G.S., Raven, J.E. & Schofield, M. 1983. *The Presocratic Philosophers: a critical history with a selection of texts*. Cambridge.

Lang, M.L. 1976. *Graffiti and Dipinti. The Athenian Agora* XXI. Princeton.

Laumonier, A. 1934. "Inscriptions de Carie", *BCH* 58, 291-380.

Laumonier, A. 1958. *Les Cultes indigènes en Carie.* (BEFAR 188). Rome/Paris.

Laurenzi, L. 1955-1956. "Sculture inedite del Museo di Coo", *ASAtene* 33-34, 59-156.

Lehrs, K. 1856/1895. *Populäre Aufsätze aus dem Alterthum. Vorzugsweise zur Ethik und Religion der Griechen.* Leipzig.

Maiuri, A. 1916. "Nuovi iscrizioni greche dalle Sporadi meridionali", *ASAtene* 2, 133-50.

Maiuri, A. 1925. *Nuova silloge epigrafica di Rodi e Cos.* Florence.

Manganaro, G. 1977. "Tavolette di piombo inscritte della Sicilia greca", *AnnPisa* NS 3,7, 1329-49.

Manganaro, G. 1985. "Per la storia dei culti nella Sicilia greca", in: *Il tempio greco in Sicilia. Atti della 1a riunione scientifica della Scuola di perfezionamento in Archeologia classica dell'Università di Catania* (CronCatania 16 , 1977) 148-64. Catania.

Marcadé, J. 1953. "Les trouvailles de la maison dite de l'Hermès, à Délos", *BCH* 77, 497-615.

Marcadé, J. 1969. *Au Musée de Délos: étude sur la sculpture hellénistique en ronde bosse découverte dans l'île.* (BEFAR 215). Rome/Paris.

Marengo, S.M. 1988. "L'agorà di Cirene in età romana alla luce delle testimonianze epigrafiche", *MEFRA* 100, 87-101.

Masson, O. 1981. "À propos des inscriptions chypriotes de Kafizin", *BCH* 105, 623-49.

Mattingly, H.B. 1974. "The language of Athenian imperialism", *Epigraphica* 36, 33-53.

Merritt, B.J. 1961. "Greek inscriptions", *Hesperia* 30, 205-92.

Michaelidou-Nikolaou, I. 1993. "Nouveaux documents pour le syllabaire chypriote", *BCH* 107, 343-47.

Mitford, T.B. 1980. *The Nymphaeum of Kafizin: the inscribed pottery.* (Kadmos Suppl. 2). Berlin/New York.

Morelli, D. 1959. "I culti in Rodi", *StClOr* 8, 1-184.

Moreschini, C. 1978. *Apuleio e il platonismo.* (Studi dell'Accademia Toscana di Scienze e Lettere 'La Columbaria' 51). Florence.

Moreschini, C. 1989. "Divinazione e demonologia in Plutarco e Apuleio", *Augustinianum* 29, 269-80.

Moreschini, C. 1990. "Plutarco e la tradizione platonica", in: *La tradizione: forme e modi. XVIII Incontro di studiosi dell'antichità cristiana, Roma 7-9 maggio 1989*, 223-34. Rome.

Nicolau, K. 1978. "Oriental divinities represented on the clay sealings of Paphos, Cyprus", in: de Boer & Edridge (eds.) 1978 2, 849-53.

Nilsson, M.P. 1955-1961. *Geschichte der griechischen Religion* (2nd ed.). (HAW 5.2.1-2). Munich.

Nowak, N. 1960. *Zur Entwicklungsgeschichte des Begriffes Daimon. Eine Untersuchung epigraphischer Zeugnisse von 5. Jh. v. Chr. bis zum 5. Jh. n. Chr.* Diss. Bonn.

Ogilvie, R.M. 1967. "The date of the *De defectu oraculorum*", *Phoenix* 21, 108-19.

Ohlemutz, E. 1940. *Die Kulte und Heiligtümer der Götter in Pergamon.* Würzburg/Aumühle.

Palagia, O. 1982. "A colossal statue of a personification from the Agora of Athens", *Hesperia* 51, 99-113.

Parke, H.W. 1967. *The Oracles of Zeus: Dodona, Olympia, Ammon.* Oxford.

Perdrizet, P. 1912. "Némésis", *BCH* 36, 248-74.

Persson, A.W. 1922. "Inscriptions de Carie", *BCH* 46, 394-426.

Petzl, G. 1987. *Die Inschriften von Smyrna*, 2.1. (IGSK 24,1). Bonn.

Pianu, G. 1988-1989. "Il santuario di Demetra ad Eraclea di Lucania", *AnnPerugia* 26 (n.s. 12), 103-37.

Picard, C. 1941. "Le sculpteur Xénophon d'Athènes à Thèbes et à Mégalopolis", *CRAI*, 204-26.

Picard, C. 1942-1943. "Sanctuaires, représentations et symboles de Zeus Meilichios", *RHistRel* 126, 97-127.

Picard, C. 1943. "Sur le Diasia d'Athènes", *CRAI*, 158-75.

Picard, C. 1944-1945. "Statues et ex-voto du '*Stibadeion*' dionysiaque de Délos", *BCH* 68-69, 240-70.

Pietrzykowski, M. 1978. "Sarapis-Agathos Daimon", in: de Boer & Edridge (eds.) 1978 3, 959-66.

Platon, N. & Feyel, M. 1938. "Inventaire sacré de Thespies trouvé à Chostia (Béotie)", *BCH* 62, 149-66.

Plassart, A. 1928. *Les sanctuaires et les cultes du Mont Cynthe.* (Exploration archéologique du Délos). Paris.

Poland, F. 1909. *Geschichte des griechischen Vereinswesens.* Leipzig.

Pugliese Carratelli, G. 1939-1940. "Per la storia delle associazioni in Rodi antica", *ASAtene* 16-17 (n.s. 1-2), 147-200.

Pugliese Carratelli, G. 1952-1954. "Supplemento epigrafico rodio", *ASAtene* 30-32 (n.s. 14-16), 247-316.

Reinach, A.J. 1911. "Inscriptions d'Itanos", *REG* 24, 377-425.

Rescigno, A. (ed.) 1995. *Plutarco, L'eclissi degli oracoli.* (Corpus Plutarchi Moralium 19). Naples.

Ringgren, H. (ed.) 1967. *Fatalistic Beliefs in Religion, Folklore, and Literature.* (Scripta Instituti Donneriani Aboensis 2). Stockholm.

Roller, L.E. 1987. "Hellenistic epigraphic texts from Gordion", *AnatSt* 37, 103-33.

Roscher, W.H. 1884-1886. s.v. Agathodaimon, in: Roscher, *Lex.* 1.1, 98-100.

Rudhardt, J. 1981. "Le mythe hésiodique des races et celui de Prométhée", in: Rudhardt, J., *Du mythe, de la religion grecque et de la compréhension d'autrui,* 245-81. Geneva. (Revue européenne des sciences sociales 19, no. 58).

Ruhl, L. 1916-1924, s.v. Tyche, in: Roscher, *Lex.* 5, 1309-57.

Şahin, S., Schwertheim, E., & J. Wagner (eds.) 1978. *Studien zur Religion und Kultur Kleinasiens: Festschrift für F.K. Dörner zum 65. Geburtstag.* (EPRO 66). Leiden.

Sartori, F. 1980. "Dediche a Demetra in Eraclea Lucana", in: *Forschungen und Funde. Festschrift Bernhard Neutsch,* 401-15. (Innsbrücker Beiträge zur Kulturwissenschaft 21). Innsbruck.

Schachter, A. 1981. *Cults of Boiotia,* 1. *Acheloos to Hera.* (BICS Suppl. 38.1).

Schenkeveld, D.M. 1988. "Ancient views on the meaning of δαίμων in *Iliad* Θ 166", *Hermes* 116, 110-15.

Segre, M. & G. Pugliese Carratelli 1949-1951. "Tituli camirenses", *ASAtene* 27-29 (n.s. 11-13), 141-318.

Seyrig, H. 1932. "Antiquités syriennes, 4: Monuments syriens du culte de Némésis", *Syria* 13, 50-64.

Sfameni Gasparro, G. 1986. *Misteri e culti mistici di Demetra.* (Storia delle Religioni 3). Rome.

Sfameni Gasparro, G. 1995. "Le attestazioni dei culti egiziani in Sicilia nei documenti monetali", in: Caccamo Caltabiano (ed.) 1995, 79-156.

Sfameni Gasparro, G. 1996. "Plutarco e la religione delfica: il dio 'filosofo' e il suo esegeta", in: Gallo (ed.) 1996, 157-88.

Sfameni Gasparro G. 1997. "Iside Fortuna: fatalismo e divinità sovrane del destino nel mondo ellenistico-romano", in: *Le Fortune dell'età arcaica nel Lazio e in Italia e la loro posterità. Atti del 3. Convegno internazionale di Studi archeologici sull'antica Preneste (Palestrina 15-16 ottobre 1994),* 3-25. Palestrina.

Sherwin-White, S.M. 1978. *Ancient Cos: an historical study from the Dorian settlement to the Imperial period.* Göttingen.

Sokolowski, F. 1969. *Lois sacrées des cités grecques.* (Travaux et Mémoires de l'École Française d'Athènes 18). Paris.

Soury, G. 1939. "Le sens de la démonologie de Plutarque", *REG* 52, 52-69.

Soury, G. 1942. *La démonologie de Plutarque: Essai sur les idées religieuses et les mythes d'un platonicien éclectique*. Paris.

Spyridakis, S. 1969. "The Itanian cult of Tyche Protogeneia", *Historia* 18, 42-48.

Strohm, H. 1944. *Tyche. Zur Schicksalsauffassung bei Pindar und den frühgriechischen Dichtern*. Stuttgart.

Swain, S.C.R. 1989a. "Plutarch: chance, providence, and history", *AJPh* 110, 272-302.

Swain, S.C.R. 1989b. "Plutarch's Aemilius and Timoleon", *Historia* 38, 314-34.

Tarán, L. 1975. *Academica: Plato, Philip of Opus, and the pseudo-Platonic Epinomis.* (MemAPhilSoc 107). Philadelphia.

Torraca, L. 1996. "I presupposti teorici e i diversi volti della *tyche* plutarchea", in: Gallo (ed.) 1996, 105-55.

Tracy, S.V. 1994. "*IG* II² 1195 and Agathe Tyche in Attica", *Hesperia* 63, 241-44.

Tran Tam Tinh, V. 1990. s.v. Isis, in: *LIMC* 5, 761-96.

Untersteiner, M. 1939/1971. "Il concetto di δαίμων in Omero", in: Untersteiner, M., *Scritti minori: studi di letteratura e di filosofia greca*, 117-64. Brescia. (Repr. from *AeR* 41, 93-134).

Valdés, M.G. (ed.) 1994. *Estudios sobre Plutarco: ideas religiosas. Actas del III Simposio internacional sobre Plutarco, Oviedo, 30 de abril a 2 de mayo de 1992*. Madrid.

Vanderlip, V.F. 1972. *The Four Greek Hymns of Isidorus and the Cult of Isis*. (AmStP 12). Toronto.

Vernant, J.-P. 1960/1971. "Le mythe hésiodique des races: essai d'analyse structurale", in: Vernant, J.-P., *Mythe et pensée chez les grecs: études de psychologie historique* (2nd ed.) 1, 13-41. Paris. (Repr. from *RHistRel* 57, 21-54).

Vernant, J.-P. 1966/1971. "Le mythe hésiodique des races: sur un essai de mise au point", in: *Mythe et penseé chez les grecs*, 42-79. (Repr. from *RevPhil* 40, 247-76).

Vernière, Y. 1977. *Symboles et mythes dans la pensée de Plutarque: essai d'interprétation philosophique et religieuse des Moralia*. Paris.

Vetters, H. 1978. "Der Schlangengott", in: Şahin, Schwertheim & Wagner (eds.) 1978 2, 967-79.

Vidman, L. 1969. *Sylloge inscriptionum religionis Isiacae et Sarapiacae*. (RGVV 28). Berlin.

Visser, E. 1938. *Götter und Kulte im ptolemäischen Alexandrien*. (Archaeologisch-Historische Bijdragen 5). Amsterdam.

de Vogel, C.J. 1966. *Pythagoras and Early Pythagoreanism*. Assen.

Volkmann, H. 1928. "Studien zum Nemesiskult", *ArchRW* 26, 296-321.

Walbank, M.B. 1994. "A *lex sacra* of the State and of the deme of Kollytos", *Hesperia* 63, 233-39.

Waser, O. 1916-1924. s.v. Tyche in bildlicher Darstellung, in: Roscher *Lex.* 5, 1357-80.

Webster, T.B.L. 1960. *Studies in Menander*. Manchester.

Weinreich, O. 1919. "Stiftung und Kultsatzungen eines Privatheiligtums in Philadelphia in Lydien", *SBHeidelberg* 16, 3-68.

Wellmann, M. 1919. "Eine pythagoreische Urkunde des IV. Jhdts. v.Chr.", *Hermes* 54, 225-48.

Wilamowitz-Moellendorff, U. von 1931-1932. *Der Glaube der Hellenen*. Berlin.

Wilford, F.A. 1965. "Δαίμων in Homer", *Numen* 12, 217-32.

Woodhead, A.G. 1981. "Athens and Demetrius Poliorketes at the end of the fourth century BC", in: *Ancient Macedonian Studies in honor of C.F. Edson*, 357-67. Thessalonica.

Wycherley, R.E. 1957. *Literary and Epigraphical Testimonia The Athenian Agora* III. Princeton.

Ziegler, K. 1948. s.v. Tyche, 2: Stadtteil von Syrakus, in: *RE* 7A, 1689-96.

Ziegler, K. 1951. s.v. Plutarchos, in: *RE* 21, 636-962.

Zuntz, G. 1971. *Persephone: Three Essays on Religion and Thought in Magna Graecia*. Oxford.

HELLENISTIC SUPERSTITION:
THE PROBLEMS OF DEFINING A VICE

Dale B. Martin

In a series of lectures, published as the now classic *The Greeks and the Irrational*, E.R. Dodds posed the question: "Whatever happened to Greek rationality?" The Greeks of classical Athens, or at least the most important of them, had boldly stared down the fears and insecurities of primitive religious beliefs and practices. The Ionians had dismissed the myths and offered naturalist accounts of the universe. Aristotle rejected religious origins and interpretations of dreams and offered a theory of dreams that was "coolly rational" (Dodds 1957, 120). At the beginning of the Hellenistic period, Hippocratic medical writers were dismissing "the old magico-religious catharsis" formerly practiced in a "religious context", and substituting in its place "purely physical treatment" subject to "rational criticism" (Dodds 1957, 80; 115). But then something happened. By the end of the Hellenistic period and the beginning of the Roman Empire, the cool rationalism of the early thinkers disappeared or at least became polluted by reemerging irrational beliefs and practices — indeed, antirationalism — even among theorists and philosophers. Religious therapeutics became popular again; irrational beliefs about divine causation of disease recurred; supernatural intervention in nature was again accepted; primitive fears of pollution reemerged — and all this even among philosophical writers. Dodds asks: "What happened? Why did the promising beginnings of Greek rationalism never mature?" If rationalism is such an obviously compelling advance over irrationalism — science over superstition — why the failure of rationalism and the retreat into superstition?

Interestingly, though not surprisingly, Dodds never defines *rationality*. Nor does he define or systematically describe what he means by superstition, though he does give examples of it. Magic and its therapeutics are superstitious. So is the belief that people are compelled to do something by a personal daemon. The projection of one's own psychological impulses onto an external agent, like a god or daemon, is superstitious. So too the belief that gods send dreams (121; 130 n. 81). Other things, while not explicitly called "superstitious" by Dodds, fall under the label of the "irrational", and thus were probably considered by him to be superstitious: the belief that guilt can be inherited (34); the notion that madness has supernatural origins (65); religious purification (80; 154); augury and hepatoscopy (217); and the belief that the gods could be made jealous (221). Sometimes Dodds substitutes "religion" for "superstition", as when he relates the retreat of the people of the early Roman Empire from science, rationality and freedom to astrology, magic, Mithraism and Christianity (251).

Indeed, the phrase "retreat from freedom" provides the kernel of Dodds's thesis. Internal political problems and external military threats shook the confidence of the Greek people. We can discern this failure of nerve beginning about 432 BCE, when "disbelief in the supernatural and the teaching of astronomy were made indictable offences" (189). Due to political and social setbacks, most Greeks turned away from the individualism nurtured by democracy and began again to fear that the impiety of some would provoke divine anger upon all. They turned tail and fled from freedom. In Dodds's words, "The old religious dualism of mind and matter, God and Nature, the soul and the appetites, which rationalist thought had striven to overcome, reasserts itself in fresh forms and with a fresh vigour" (247).

I have no interest in criticizing Dodds's broad historical thesis. What is important here for my project is Dodds's construal of superstition. Dodds assumes an unquestioned dichotomy: superstition, irrationality, and the supernatural are combined on one side; science, rationality, and nature on the other. What makes something "superstitious" is that it proposes the intervention of a supernatural force or agent into the closed nexus of cause and effect known to exist in nature. Belief in such intervention is irrational.

I am picking on Dodds here not because he is idiosyncratic, but because he is not. The long, and now old, article on "Aberglaube" by Riess (1894) in Pauly-Wissowa starts out with a discussion of *deisidaimonia*, defined as "fear of the gods or demons". As the article progresses, however, *Aberglaube* comes to refer to any belief in the efficacy of supernatural (*übersinnlich*) power or agency; and it ends up referring simply to "Volk" belief and practice, from magical therapeutics, to the belief that bees are generated from the carcasses of cattle, to the belief that magical materials operate by means of a sympathy of the elements.[1] These assumptions and the lack of rigorous definition occur also in recent publications. In a book published in 1993, medical historian James Longrigg portrays "Greek rational medicine" as the rational rejection of divine origin of disease and the attribution of disease instead to "natural causes" (Longrigg 1993; see also Longrigg 1963, 149-50).[2] Contemporary historians have not invented these assumptions, of course. Since the beginning of the modern period, superstition has generally referred to "misplaced assumptions about causality stemming from a faulty understanding of nature" (O'Neil 1987).

For the interpretation of ancient culture, these definitions and assumptions are inadequate. In the first place, they suffer from insufficient theoretical reflection about "rationality". Lately, the very category of "rationality" has come under severe critique by philosophers, cultural anthropologists, historians of science and medicine, literary theorists, and cultural critics. Many scholars of my generation, including myself, simply have no idea what "rationality" means anymore, except insofar as it may refer to locally situated, historically contingent, usually presupposed grammars or structures of thinking and acting (Wilson 1970; Hollis and Lukes 1982; Rorty 1989, esp. 32-34, 47-54; MacIntyre 1988; B.H. Smith 1988; Peukert 1984; Latour and Woolgar 1979). In other words, though I have no problem talking about "rationality" in something like a "local" sense — meaning sensibility within the context of specific beliefs, presuppositions, or assumptions — I do not find sensible the use of "rationality" to refer to some abstract or universal epistemological category or criterion. But all that theoretical stuff aside, the traditional account of superstition simply never tells us what exactly is *irrational* about certain beliefs, to whom such things are irrational, and why. Certainly, we can agree that kissing the nose of a donkey to cure a cold seems irrational, but that's because we agree that donkeys' noses do not belong in pharmacies. And we will probably agree that we need not fear the jealousy of Athena, but if we really believed Athena existed and that she was the jealous type, we would be irrational *not* to fear her. In any case, for the study of ancient super-stition, the category of rationality is simply not going to get us anywhere, mainly because the question will send us down the probably endless road of philosophical debate currently being travelled by others. Of course, it could be helpful to explain why a particular belief or practice was considered irrational in the ancient world. But then we need to indicate, "irrational to whom?", "why?", "informed by what kinds of assumptions?" and "supported by what kinds of rhetoric?"

If the rational/irrational dichotomy is problematic, its supernatural/natural partner is more so, although modern medical and classical historians have not been loath to invoke it. The ancient medical writers did reject popular ideas that blamed the gods and other superhuman beings for diseases. But it is misleading to portray this as a rejection of supernatural intervention into a closed system of nature. The author of *The Sacred Disease*, for example, notes that "the masses" ascribe epilepsy (or madness) to divine attacks, thus its label "the sacred disease". In arguing against these beliefs, however, he does not deny divine activity and attribute the disease to other "natural" sources; rather he argues that *all* diseases are divine in the sense that all disease is part of nature, which is imbued with divinity (or divinities). Diseases are all part of natural processes, which include divine processes (*Sacred Disease* 1.4.21). The author rejects, in fact, the therapies and prescriptions of popular healers by saying that such therapists are *im*pious; they dishonour the gods. The author argues that the gods occupy a legitimate realm *in nature*, but not as *direct agents* of disease causation or cure. The writer does not remove the gods from nature or consign them to some supernatural realm; he just denies them an active rôle as personal tormentors in disease (see esp. chapter 3).

Moreover, the Hippocratic authors have no intention of completely excluding divine activity from the mechanisms of disease and healing. Indeed, they sometimes allow the gods benevolent rôles in healing. As another Hippocratic text states: "The gods are the real physicians, though people do not think so. But the truth of this statement is shown by the phenomenon of disease".[3] Other educated authors also allow gods a rôle in disease treatment. Herophilus, to cite an example from our period, calls drugs "the hands of the gods".[4] Whatever the ancient scientists find objectionable about popular practices, it has nothing to do with something called "supernatural intervention".

This is mainly because the supernatural didn't exist in the ancient world. The category itself is a distinctly modern phenomenon. It can be traced to early modern thinkers and the philosophical precursors of the Enlightenment who attempted to develop a scientific method independent of the constraints of Christian dogma. Elsewhere I go to some length to describe what may, with hyperbole, be called the "invention" of the supernatural by René Descartes (Martin 1995, 4-6). To summarize briefly, the ancients had no conception of the "supernatural" because the "natural" was not the kind of closed, mechanistic system assumed by early modernism — a system that excluded the gods or "spiritual" forces. The forces that modern scholars, whether theologians, philosophers, or scientists, would label as "supernatural" were included in the category of *phusis* . For my purposes, this means that in seeking to define and delimit "superstition" in the ancient world, we must begin by rejecting any account that links "superstition" to "the supernatural".[5]

When the ancients actually got around to defining *deisidaimonia*, they defined it as "fear of the gods or daemons", or sometimes qualified as "*unreasonable* fear of divinities".[6] While better than the modern definition, this is still not sufficient. In the first place, it doesn't fit those instances where a particular belief or practice is labelled as a case of *deisidaimonia* even though fear seems not to be involved (see below). In the second place, the ancient definition does not explain what is "unreasonable" about the fear and why? Is *all* fear of divinities unreasonable? Does this extend to respectful awe? Why is it unreasonable to fear divine forces? We need an account of ancient superstition that is hostage neither to the misleading categories of modernism such as the "supernatural" nor to the simplistic definition of the ancient theorists themselves. We need a grammar of ancient superstition.

As a small step in this direction, I offer here a very limited study. I have examined the use of just one word, *deisidaimonia* (and those of the same word group, such as *deisidaimôn*) in only two authors: Theophrastus, from the beginning of the Hellenistic period, and Diodorus Siculus, who wrote in the first century BCE. This brief survey suggests that charges of "superstition" made sense in the ancient world because they drew on ancient sensibilities concerning proper social rôles and practices. For certain educated writers "superstition" broke accepted rules of upper-class social etiquette or infringed on practices and epistemologies claimed by philosophers. "Superstition" went beyond the bounds of "proper" behaviour — either demanding inappropriate behaviour of human beings or attributing it to the gods.

We have no evidence that *deisidaimonia* was taken to be a problem by anyone before the late fourth century BCE. Xenophon uses the term to refer simply to what we might call "piety", respect that is appropriate toward the gods. Aristotle likewise uses the term only in this rather approving sense.[7] Aristotle's pupil and successor, Theophrastus, however, included a very negative portrait of the "Superstitious Man" (*Deisidaimôn*) in his book of character sketches (*Char.*, ch. 16). We haven't enough information to say what happened — how a philosophical virtue became a philosophical vice so quickly — but Theophrastus is apparently not the innovator, at least not in this book.[8] In it Theophrastus can assume the "superstitious man" to be a negative character type. If he were here being innovative in his use of the term, he would doubtless have had to defend it in some way. Theophrastus seems able to assume, at least for his audience, that they also find *deisidaimonia* a vice.

What does Theophrastus label as superstitious? Washing one's hands too often, sprinkling oneself with water from a shrine, walking around with a piece of laurel in one's mouth all day. If a weasel crosses the path, the superstitious man won't walk on until someone else goes by or he has thrown three stones across the road. Seeing a snake in his house, he invokes the god Sabazios; if it is a holy snake, he builds a hero-shrine on the spot, right there in his living room if necessary. It is superstitious to drench every pile of anointed stones one sees with more oil and prostrate oneself before them. If a mouse gnaws a hole in a sack of barley, the superstitious man performs an expiation instead of simply repairing the sack. He repeatedly purifies his house in case Hekate has possessed it. When he hears an owl hoot he invokes Athena. He is afraid of becoming polluted by stepping on a gravestone, viewing a corpse, or visiting a woman in childbirth. The list goes on: purifying houses with boiled wine and spices on prescribed days; consulting dream interpreters, *manteis*, or bird-omen readers; being initiated often in mysteries; sprinkling oneself with seawater; avoiding polluted persons; avoiding a madman (or epileptic), and spitting down one's chest for protection against catching the madness.

How do we make sense of this conglomeration of condemnations? We need what I call a "logic" or "grammar" of superstition that shows how these various behaviours Theophrastus condemns fit together and are differentiated from other acceptable behaviours and beliefs. To illustrate what I mean by "grammar" here, I will take a rather lengthy detour to another of Theophrastus's writings, the *De Causis Plantorum*.

Theophrastus here discusses how one can discern the relative heat of plants. Menestor, an earlier writer on botany, had put forward several positions that Theophrastus wants to correct, partly by employing empirical observation and partly by logic, that is, "rationality" (*eis logon*).[9] Menestor's position is as follows.

(1) Hot plants, like hot animals, are more fruitful than colder plants. Hot animals, for instance, bring forth live births whereas colder animals produce eggs.

(2) Plants thrive in regions of opposite temperature to that of their own nature. Plants that grow in water are hot and therefore do not freeze. Evergreens are hotter than other plants and thus thrive in cold regions. This is supported by Empedocles' observation that animals that dwell in water are more fire-like in their nature.

(3) Hotter plants, due to hotter sap, sprout and fruit earlier than cooler plants.

(4) Hotter plants retain their leaves longer: witness again evergreens which more successfully hold onto their leaves.

(5) Hotter plants catch fire quicker and burn faster. "Trees with the most fire in them catch fire quickest".

Theophrastus answers Menestor with various arguments. (1) As proof that hotter plants are not the most fruitful, Theophrastus points out that female trees produce more than male trees, just like female animals produce more than male animals. But, since everybody knows that females, of any species, are colder than males, their greater fecundity must not be due to higher temperature.[10] In animals also, hotter species do not bear more young. Of the hotter animals, only dogs and pigs produce a lot; the rest bear fewer young than inferior species. It is not simply greater heat that correlates with fecundity, but the proper balance of heat. As

Theophrastus says: "What is required not only for the generation of animals but for the production and ripening of fruit is a right amount of heat, and no excess of it, since the excess leads to too much dryness and too close a texture" (22.2). (2) Menestor's second point that plants thrive in regions of opposite nature to their own is also false. Rather, living things of all sorts partake of the essence of their region. Thus, fish are moister and cooler; land animals are warmer; hot-natured trees thrive in warmer climates, and cold-natured plants in cold. All things are constituted of the materials and natures of their own appropriate place. (3) To the claim that wood of a hotter nature burns easier, Theophrastus answers that "firesticks" burn easily not because they are hotter but because of their loose structure, which makes them "better able to vaporize the fluid". Theophrastus ends by urging observation to supplement logic. We know that oily and pungent plants are hotter; pungent because fragrance operates by a mechanism of heat. And we know that oily plants are hotter because pine is an oily wood and easily ignited. We can tell that others are hot by other means; for example, the lime tree is hot because it can dull the temper of iron. Some plants must be hot because when used as medicines or food they produce reactions of heat in the body, such as concoction of internal substances. Finally, we can tell that some plants partake of a hotter nature because they quite simply *feel* hot or *taste* hot.

   Now, I'm not sure this kind of thinking is what modern historians of science or medicine are referring to when they talk about ancient Greek "rationality". It doesn't look particularly rational to me — which is to say, I cannot imagine myself being persuaded by it. But I'd not want to call it *irrational* either. With a little imagination we can see how these different positions, both Menestor's and Theophrastus's, reflect a certain grammar of assumptions and argument, thus revealing not some "universal rationality" but the *local* rationality shared by Menestor and Theophrastus. The different arguments can be abstracted to a few basic rules and "facts" assumed by both parties. Without invoking some sort of rationality that is available (theoretically) to all "reasonable" persons of all times, we can see how a "reasonable" person could share such views given certain assumptions.

   First, the cosmos is a hierarchical spectrum. Everything in the universe occupies a place in that gradual hierarchy. The hierarchy is one of ontology and axiology: human beings are higher (and in general better) than beasts; animals are higher than fish; fish are higher than plants; plants are higher than rocks, etc. Gender is almost always inscribed in this hierarchy, with male over female whether we are speaking of plants or animals (Martin 1995, 32-34). The hierarchy *may* also be one of temperature; hotter is better than colder. Whereas Menestor uses the hierarchical principle to argue that plants that are more productive (better, stronger) must also be hotter, Theophrastus responds with a different twist on the same principle: the male-female spectrum, in which females are obviously colder yet produce more, demonstrates that production does not relate to greater heat; otherwise, women would be hotter than men, and thus better, which, of course, is impossible. Both arguments depend on the same basic principle of hierarchy, but apply it somewhat differently because they are using slightly different corollary assumptions.

The second basic grammatical principle has to do with balance and the function of sympathy and antipathy in the cosmos.[11] The cosmos is a state of equilibrium; that equilibrium is maintained because the different parts of the universe are made up of basically the same elements; the different parts of the universe are able to act and react to one another due to the identity of basic elemental structure. Menestor claims that plants thrive in the region opposite that of their own nature, demonstrating the balance aspect of the principle. Opposites are necessary in order to maintain equilibrium. This is quite similar to the ancient medical principle *contraria contrariis curantur*, "opposites are cured by opposites" (Hippoc., *Breaths* 1.30; Martin 1995, 149). To cure a hot disease the doctor administers a cold therapy, and vice versa. Opposites are necessary; only an *imbalance* of them is harmful. Theophrastus responds to Menestor by emphasizing the "sympatheia" rather than "antipatheia" aspect of the principle. He insists that "like produces like", thus entities partake of the region of their origin. This principle later became explicit in Stoic theory about the different levels of the cosmos and the nature of the bodies that exist in those levels. The stars are bodies made primarily of ether or *pneuma*, or whatever is taken to be the material of the highest sphere; the bodies of animals are more earthy; the bodies of fish are more watery, etc. (Scott 1991; Martin 1995, 118-19). Thus the rationale for Theophrastus's argument against Menestor: hot plants are those that thrive in hot regions because "like produces like". Menestor himself uses this part of the principle when he argues that hot plants catch fire quicker: heat produces heat. Thus, by emphasizing different aspects of what is basically a shared rule of discourse, Menestor and Theophrastus come to different positions using the same grammatical principles.

The third principle plays a rôle in Theophrastus's argument alone: the principle of the microcosmic body. The cosmos is a body and each body in the cosmos is a microcosmos. This means, for one thing, that the mechanisms of the cosmos can be discerned in the body and vice versa. Disease is the internal weather of the human body. The mechanisms of disease reflect the mechanisms of surrounding nature, including fires, winds, the refinement of elements like *pneuma* in the body, and so forth. Thus Theophrastus can urge that if we want to discern the heat of a plant in nature, we should observe the effect that plant has on the internal weather in the body. The principle also emphasizes that since the body is a microcosm, made up of the same substances that surround it, an absolutely firm boundary between the human body and its environment would be unhealthy. The medical doctrine of "pores" was one expression of this principle (Martin 1995, 15-18). Materials (moisture, *pneuma*) must be able to pass into the body and from the inside out. If the body's surface becomes too impenetrable, illness will result. Theophrastus assumes the same principle when he says that wood that burns easily is not necessarily hotter but has a looser structure. Burning is a natural and good mechanism. "Better" wood is wood that is porous enough to allow easy passageway for the elements, in this case, fire, air, and moisture. Wood whose surface is too constricted won't burn as easily, just like a patient whose body is too constricted will become ill. Both arguments depend on the principle of the microcosmic body.

Thus the rationality of Theophrastus's argument with Menestor depends on three basic principles: (1) the cosmos is a hierarchical spectrum and everything in it has its proper place; (2) the cosmos is a system of balance whose equilibrium is maintained by relationships of "like" and "unlike" among its different parts; and (3) the cosmos is a body and the body is a microcosm. The structures of both arguments, that by Menestor and that by Theophrastus, are ruled by these basic principles. By understanding these basic principles, we can see the rationality of their arguments, the grammar assumed by their discourse.

But how does this relate to superstition? Here too, there are certain overriding principles that inform what Theophrastus accepts and what he rejects. For example, a sense of "balance" is very important to him. Just as he argued (in *De Causis Plantorum*) that not a lot of heat but the right amount of heat is best for fecundity, so in the *Characters* he often condemns any kind of "excess". Some men are overly scrupulous (2.10). Some characters have no shame and dance even when they aren't drunk or dance the first time they're asked (6.3; 12.14); others, however, are too proud and unwilling to dance even when drunk (15.10). Although a gentleman shouldn't be excessively pious, neither should he tastelessly curse the gods (19.8). It is perfectly fine to devote a bronze ring at a shrine, but it is excessive to polish it often (21.10). Even the love of honour, *philotimia*, often taken as the highest virtue by many upper class Greeks, can be done to excess; a man can look petty by trying too hard to be honourable (21).

This emphasis on balance and the mean, therefore, is important for Theophrastus's account of *deisidaimonia*. Theophrastus has nothing against the traditional public cult. He seems to accept, for instance, the legitimacy of becoming an "initiate" of some god or mystery, dedicating votive offerings to gods or goddesses, or paying one's respects at a shrine of Heracles (27.5.8). Theophrastus does condemn what he considers *excessive* attention to any of the traditional cults. So superstition sometimes consists of too much of a good thing (Koets 1929, 36). Theophrastus assumes a classical ideal of hellenistic upper-class etiquette: the golden mean. Of course, this doesn't answer the question of how one knows when enough is enough. But it is precisely that sort of subtlety that is a regular mark of élite etiquette.

Many of Theophrastus's concerns about superstition relate to the principle of hierarchy. For example, when Theophrastus rejects fear of the gods, he is not concerned with the "irrationality" of divine intervention, but rather the hierarchical system of honour and shame. Quite often in his *Characters* Theophrastus criticizes behaviour that an upper class gentleman should be ashamed to be seen doing: debasing himself with flattery (2), answering the door himself (4), behaving too familiarly with the servants, playing games with children (5.5), putting up with abuse (6), shopping for himself (11.7), walking behind his slave (18). The vice of stinginess concerns Theophrastus so much that he offers portraits of four different kinds of "cheapskates" (see 30).

The rejection of fear of the gods participates in this rationality of hierarchy and honour. Cringing before anyone, whether Alexander the Great, the Great King of Persia, or a god or goddess, is behaviour that belies the honour appropriate for an upper-class, free Greek man. Thus, any religious posture or activity that makes the gentleman look less than honourable is condemned. Moreover, fear of the gods is dishonourable because it ascribes to the gods, who are the most honourable members of the cosmological hierarchy, passions and behaviours that would be branded as petty and low-class if manifested by an educated gentleman. If it is inappropriate for a philosopher to be controlled by anger, desire, or jealousy, how much more a god?

Just as every plant or element of the cosmos has its appropriate place, so religious observations have theirs. Thus Theophrastus, though never rejecting the public cult, does not approve of its being privatized. Building a hero shrine in one's home, besides being excessive, is in bad taste because *eusebeia* of that sort is a public thing, belonging to the *polis*. The public cults belong in public. It is a sign of the tasteless brand of piety, *deisidaimonia*, to appropriate them to oneself inappropriately.

The expression of these general principles in the particulars of specific behaviour shows that there is structure to Theophrastus's account of *deisidaimonia*, even if it is more complex and nuanced than either the modern or ancient definition suggests. But other aspects of *deisidaimonia*, though more easily noted, are perhaps less easily explained. For example, Theophrastus seems to reject any notion that pollution from external forces might affect one's person. All concerns about pollution seem to be condemned. As I have shown elsewhere, whether or not one was concerned about pollution seems in this period to have divided philosophers from most of the rest of the population, at least from the uneducated. Diogenes, for example, went out of his way to eat apples from a tree on which a man had hanged himself and to visit so-called "polluted" areas in order to demonstrate to the masses that pollution does not occur (Diog. Laert. 6.61; Martin 1995, 153-59).

To some extent, the rejection of pollution can be explained again by recourse to honour and shame. Those who fear pollution by daemonic forces are compelled to cringe before invisible, and therefore invincible, powers. They also thereby ascribe those dishonourable polluting activites to divine beings, who, for one thing, are certainly not so concerned about the everyday details of human life — just like a gentleman is not concerned about the details of his cook's life. For another, even if divine beings could be bothered with those of lower status, they would not be divine if they went around maliciously polluting people and causing disease. So notions of pollution are rejected, to some extent, because they entail dishonourable behaviour on the part of both mortals and gods.

But the situation seems more complex than that. Elsewhere, I have argued that there existed in the ancient world two conflicting etiologies of disease, one that ascribed disease to the invasion of the body by foreign hostile elements or agents, and the other that ascribed it to an imbalance of the body's constituent elements and parts. The former, more popular belief feared pollutions and strove to protect the vulnerable boundaries of the body from invasion and thus disease. The latter belief was advocated by all sorts of medical theorists from Alcmaeon to the Hippocratics to Galen. It attributed disease to a disruption of a normal equilibrium; it made no attempt to solidify rigidly the boundaries of the body; and it rejected any etiology that posed invasive agents or hostile pollutions (Martin 1995, 139-62). The social forces that brought about the coexistence of these conflicting disease etiologies are at this time unclear to me. But apparently there was some sort of "turf war" between the emerging medical profession in the philosophical and Hippocratic tradition on the one side and more popular therapeutics practiced in healing sanctuaries and by healers, exorcists, root-cutters, and magicians on the other.[12] Some of Theophrastus's rhetoric reflects a related turf war. He explicitly ridicules those who seek out the advice of dream interpreters, seers (*manteis*), and omen-readers. What exactly was the relationship between people who occupied such rôles and those who were developing systematic philosophies and a new medical professionalism? I now have no answer to these questions, but it strikes me that rejections of "superstitious" professions sometimes sound remarkably personal and invested.

Perhaps Diodorus Siculus may be of some help. Diodorus wrote his *Library of History*, no less than a history of the world, in the first century BCE, probably over a period of some 30 years. Diodorus is more difficult and yet more helpful than Theophrastus for our purposes precisely because his subject is not *deisidaimonia* in particular. He presents unguarded, and indeed contradictory statements about it. Diodorus's modern reputation as an uncritical "compiler" or even plagiarist of others' histories, however, presents no problem for my use of his writings here. Indeed, because he includes others' accounts so freely, and sometimes uncritically, his own history provides a range of ways in which his predecessors and contemporaries were using *deisidaimonia*.[13] By looking at the occurrence of the word in Diodorus Siculus, we may observe not just his views of it but the views of other authors as well.

Usually for Diodorus *deisidaimonia* refers to piety and reverence towards the gods and sanctuaries. The piety of some people may look strange; the Egyptians' piety toward cats led them to kill a Roman soldier because he had accidentally killed a cat (1.83.8). But generally, Diodorus does not condemn *deisidaimonia*. It motivates people to take their oaths seriously (1.79.1; 11.89.5-6); it teaches them to respect the votive offerings in sanctuaries (5.27.4; 5.63.1-3); it guards against arrogance and the impiety of *hubris* (14.76.4); and it sometimes makes people at least hesitate before doing something they know to be wrong (20.43.1). Obviously, fear is an issue here. *Deisidaimonia* functions as social control because it instills fear of punishment in people, and according to Diodorus, that's not bad.[14]

But Diodorus himself appears to believe that this fear is not *just* social control — it is quite well-founded. Indeed, often the *deisidaimonia* of people saves them from certain disaster; and acting *against* its promptings sometimes *leads* to disaster. The kinds of beliefs and practices most condemned by Diodorus are impiety (disbelief in the gods), tomb destruction, temple robbing, interfering with the Delphic oracle, and *hubris* that the gods find offensive.[15] The gods themselves punish people directly for these misdeeds. Indeed, Diodorus seems to relish passing on stories of the gods' excruciating punishment of those who have not respected the property of sanctuaries.[16] Therefore, though sometimes in Diodorus *deisidaimonia* is an unfounded and exaggerated fear of divinities, elsewhere it seems quite well-founded indeed. Diodorus is simply not consistent on the issue.

But the element of fear is not always present in his accounts of *deisidaimonia*. In a few instances, the word refers to the acceptance of a belief that brings confidence, not fear. For instance, one day during the seige of Tyre when Alexander the Great was building the causeway to the city, a great monster sprang out of the sea and foundered on the causeway under construction. After a few moments, it freed itself and swam away. Both sides, the Macedonians and the Tyrians, were overtaken with *deisidaimonia* and took the occurrence as an omen *in favour of themselves* (17.41.5-6). Here *deisidaimonia* refers to the *false* belief that a freak occurrence is a *good* omen.[17] To cite another example, after the death of Alexander, it falls to Eumenes to try to get the other commanders to cooperate in leading the large army. He invents a cult of Alexander, complete with new rituals during which the dead Alexander is said to be present among the generals. This *deisidaimonia*, which here apparently refers neither to false belief nor fear, inspires the generals with new joy, confidence, and a willingness to cooperate (18.61.3).[18] It is hard to say exactly what *deisidaimonia* is here except religious reverence for Alexander, which is certainly not considered inappropriate by Diodorus.

Thus, though Diodorus sometimes presents *deisidaimonia* as due to *false* belief — sometimes prompted by the tricks of kings, priests, or generals[19] — he generally accepts it as appropriate fear of the gods or as simply confident belief in the gods. It is therefore especially interesting to note the few cases in which *deisidaimonia* is openly criticized. Importantly, in each case philosophy is involved.

According to Diodorus, until the third century Ethiopian kings had been under the control of the Ethiopian priesthood. The priests would even tell the kings when it was time to die, and the kings would submit, convinced by specious arguments of priestcraft, their *logismoi* being overpowered by *deisidaimonia*. King Ergamenes, however, disdained the command, entered the holy sanctuary unlawfully, and killed the priests. It is important to notice the vocabulary used in this story. The previous kings had been fooled because of their "simple understanding" (*haplê dianoia*); they accepted "ancient" traditions because they did not have the wherewithal of critical thinking; they were thus overpowered by *deisidaimonia*. Ergamenes, however, had been formed by Greek education (*hellênikês agôgês*) and had studied philosophy. He therefore assumed the *phronêma* (state of mind) worthy of a king, and thereafter conducted things according to his own will (*proairesis*, 3.6.3). This is clearly a philosophical moral story about how

Greek education and philosophy can liberate anyone, even the barbaric Ethiopian, from *deisidaimonia* that keeps him shamefully controlled by priestcraft and potentially fatal ignorance.

A similar story occurs about the Theban general Epameinondas, who is attempting to rouse the Thebans to attack the invading Spartans. The people, especially the "older folk", are hesitant because of certain ill omens. Epameinondas advocates "nobility" and "justice" over attention to omens. He had been, we are told, "trained in philosophy and [now] applied sensibly the principles of his training" (*paideia*, 15.52.6). Later, in order to convince the army to ignore certain omens, he manufactures several other omens. He finally succeeds in liberating the soldiers from their *deisidaimonia* (even though he has had to resort to deception) and getting them to stand for battle "emboldened in their souls". Here, as was the case with the Ethiopian king, Greek philosophical education and "noble values" prevail over *deisidaimonia*, referring here to belief in omens that paralyze. Of course, Epameinondas, as an educated man, must himself resort to false belief to rid the masses of their *deisidaimonia*. The term *deisidaimonia*, therefore, doesn't refer *simply* to false belief about divine signs and omens since Epameinondas is said to use false belief about omens to liberate the soldiers from their *deisidaimonia*.

This kind of story, about philosophy liberating people from *deisidaimonia*, may have been used by Anaxarchus of Abdera, the philosopher who, according to Diodorus, convinced Alexander to enter the city of Babylon. The term *deisidaimonia* does not occur here, but the account is worth attention. Having been warned by the Chaldean astrologers that if he entered Babylon he would die, Alexander camped outside. But then Anaxarchus, of the school of Democritus, convinces Alexander to ignore the astrologers. Alexander's change of heart is portrayed as the "healing" of the "soul" by philosophical discourse, a well-known topos of moral philosophy.[20] Up to this point, this story sounds just like the other two: philosophy brings liberation from bondage brought on by attention to omens and astrologers.

Actually, however, the astrologers prove to be right. After Alexander enters Babylon, according to Diodorus, all sorts of portents presage his death. And sure enough, Alexander dies, angry at the philosophers who had convinced him to ignore the warnings of the astrologers. As this and several other stories show, Diodorus himself takes things like omens, prophecies, and astrology quite seriously. So it is especially interesting when he passes on philosophical moral stories that portray philosophy as that which liberates people from *deisidaimonia*, which here refers to paying attention to astrologers, seers, and omen-readers.[21]

I am suggesting that Diodorus is historically useful precisely because he is not consistent in his portrayal of popular beliefs and practices or of *deisidaimonia* in particular. Although philosophers like Theophrastus condemn *deisidaimonia*, even well-educated men like Diodorus are not completely convinced.[22] Yet they know the arguments. Philosophers are consistently portrayed by Diodorus as arguing against popular beliefs. They do not argue, however, against the cult itself, against belief in the gods, nor even against the idea that the gods may heal someone. Rather they argue against relying on particular kinds of epistemological sources: Chaldean astrologers, omen-readers, seers (*manteis*). Though he obviously does not always buy the arguments of the philosophers, Diodorus is quite familiar with them. He knows the debate is going on. I only wish we knew more particularly the specifics of and reasons for this turf battle between philosophers and popular practitioners over epistemology and *deisidaimonia*.

E.R. Dodds was certainly right about many things. The ancient Greek world did produce important upheavals and revolutions relating to healing practices, nature, myths, and scientific epistemologies. But to characterize those complex upheavals as a single revolution in which "scientific rationality" overturned "religious or superstitious irrationality" is simplistic and anachronistic. Indeed, that narrative better fits the autobiography of modernity in its battles against those enemies of, to a great extent, its own construction: Religion and the Medieval Mind. Rather than viewing the ancient arguments as analogies to or precursors of modern rationality, we will be better served by sketching — however tentatively — the more complex logics and grammars of *ancient* rationalities and superstitions.

Duke University
Department of Religion
Box 90964
Durham, NC 27708-0964
USA

Notes

* The research and writing of this essay were supported by a fellowship from the Alexander von Humboldt Foundation, Federal Republic of Germany. I wish to thank the foundation and my host in Tübingen, Professor Hubert Cancik, for their generous hospitality.

1. For similar uncritical uses of the category of "rationality", see Hamilton 1942, 289-90. The article by Gladigow (1988, 1, 387-88) is much better, pointing out that accusations of "superstition" relate not to some kind of discernible phenomenon but to "interreligious polemic".

2. Even a leading expert on ancient moral philosophy, Martha Nussbaum, freely uses the category of "rationality" to differentiate ancient philosophy from ancient superstition and

religion but without ever precisely defining the concept. One searches her recent book in vain for a clear account of this abstract notion or an explanation of why ancient popular religious beliefs were "irrational", except in the sense that they were just "wrong". For example, Nussbaum assumes that it is "rational" to believe in free will or the innate human ability of moral choice, but she never explains *why* such a belief is "rational" or why it is irrational to believe in an unstable self or accept the idea that gods or other forces may act to destabilize the self. See Nussbaum 1994, e.g. 197, 318, 328, 353.

3. *On Decorum* 6 (trans. W.H.S. Jones). This translation is based on a conjecture (the text is in a state of confusion), but the writer is, in any case, at pains to insist that medicine is not in opposition to or independent of the gods. Rather, it works in harmony with or even subservient to them.

4. Quoted in Plut., *Mor.* 663B-C and Gal. *De compositione medicamentorum secundum locos* 6.8 (XII, pp. 965-966K); see von Staden 1989, 417-18. For fuller discussion and other relevant references, see Martin 1995, 154-56.

5. It is important in this regard to recognize how it was in modernism, since say the Enlightenment, that the supernatural was first invented and then rejected. More and more, modernist rationality implied a rejection of past "superstitions" and "orthodoxies" — including the supernatural — in support of a notion of individual freedom. See the portraits of modernism, for example, in Craig 1991, 27; and Toulmin 1990, 107.

6. Thus Chrysippus and later Stoics: *SVF* 3.394, 408, 409, 411. The central issue for Plutarch is also fear; see *Mor.* 164E-171F and M. Smith 1975, 2-3.

7. Xen., *Ages.* 11.8; *Cyr.* 3.3.58; Arist., *Pol.* 1314b40; see also Bolkestein 1929, 5. For *deisidaimonia* from a variety of chronological periods, see Koets 1929. For similar fluctuations in the meaning of *superstitio*, see Salzman 1987, 172-88; Grodzynski 1974, 36-60.

8. Koets suggests that the change from Aristotle's positive to Theophrastus's negative use of *deisidaimonia* was due to the criticism of traditional piety by "the different post-Socratic schools, more especially those of Cyrenaics and Cynics" (Koets 1929, 8). He admits, though, that this is just a guess.

9. The full discussion is found in *Caus. Pl.* 1.21.4-22.7.

10. Not all scientists and physicians accepted the notion that females were colder than males; thus Theophrastus may be building his argument on a belief that Menestor does not share. For the ancient debate about temperature and sex, see Horowitz 1976; Allen 1985, 95-97; Lloyd 1964, 92-106; Dean-Jones 1991.

11. I am judiciously warned by Richard Gordon against anachronistically reading a Stoic doctrine (*sumpatheia*) back into pre-Stoic sources. I am referring here, however, not to the full presence of a *doctrine* of sympathy, but to the cultural assumptions, presuppositions, and "common sense" that helped produce the later expression of Stoic *sumpatheia*. After all, the notion that "like is friend to like" occurs in the "natural science" (*peri phuseôs*) of Plato's *Lysis* (214B), along with corresponding concepts that prefigure *antipatheia*: "everything draws its opposite" (*Lys.* 215E). Pre-Stoic notions of sympathy and antipathy are reflected also in the Hippocratic *The Nature of Man* (*peri phusios anthrôpou*) 6-9, in spite of the fact that neither an explicit doctrine nor such explicit terminology occurs there.

12. Several writings from the Hippocratic corpus indicate a rising "professionalism" (an attempt to create something like an informal "guild") among at least some healers/doctors as well as "turf battles" in which the Hippocratic practitioners delineate themselves from other healers and discredit the latter. See, e.g., *On the Sacred Disease* 3-4, et passim; *Oath* 7-8, 10, 13; *Ancient Medicine* 1, 21; *Regimen in Acute Diseases* 2, 6, 8; *Art* 8-9; *Law* 1-2;

Decorum 5, 17; *The Physician*. Especially in these last four small pieces, the concern is to distinguish the *real* physician from charlatans, magicians, ignorant imposters, and sometimes even rivals of another school of thought. The legitimacy of the "profession" is at issue, and lines are being drawn and defended.

13. For Diodorus's use of sources see Hammond 1983, 12; Perl 1957. Koets attributes the presence of both positive and negative meanings of *deisidaimonia* in Diodorus to the possibility that he copied his sources uncritically (1929, 9). But see also Sacks (1990, esp. 11), who argues that Diodorus is not so slavish in his appropriation of others' writings.

14. There are some quite explicit statements about the salutary effects on the masses of *deisidaimonia*. According to these statements, such people are unlikely to be virtuous for the right reasons, so must be kept in line by laws, threats, and fear of divine retribution (34/35.2.47). These statements occur in the fragments of Diodorus found in other authors; this, for instance, comes from Eusebius. I have not made use of the fragmentary materials because I believe the wording may not preserve that of Diodorus. These statements on *deisidaimonia*, for example, sound distinctly "un-Diodoran" in their more negative portrayal of *deisidaimonia*. Robert Drews notes Diodorus's usually pietistic editing of his sources; he sometimes *changes* his sources (such as Polybius) to emphasize traditional pious beliefs about divine retribution for sacrilege (Drews 1962). The exact wording in these less "pious" fragments, therefore, may reflect the sentiments and terminology of other later scholars who are here excerpting Diodorus.

15. Impiety: 6.6.3ff; the impiety of taking a suppliant from an altar: 14.4.7; tomb destruction: 13.86.1-3.

16. Diod. Sic. 14.63; 14.69.2-3; 14.70.4; 15.14.4; 15.16.3; 16.56; 27.4.3.

17. This is actually closer to the *modern* notion of "superstition" than the ancient "fear of the gods". From the modern point of view, the belief is superstitious (i.e. "false") because it takes chance, irrelevant occurrences as having extremely relevant meanings. The belief is "false" because it is rejected by modern science. Note, however, that in this same section, *deisidaimonia* refers to fear on the part of the Tyrians, who believed a crazed prophet's pronouncements that the god Apollo was about to leave the city. Fearful that he would desert them, they tied down his statue with ropes. Diodorus seems to think of this as ridiculous.

18. Unfortunately, Koets, who is careful to address the different meanings of *deisidaimonia* in Diodorus, does not give sufficient attention to these texts in which the element of fear is absent.

19. Diod. Sic., 1.62.4; 4.51.1-3; similar accounts without the explicit occurrence of *deisidaimonia* are 20.7.3; 20.11.2.

20. See especially Nussbaum 1994.

21. *Deisidaimonia* is elsewhere explicitly connected with *manteis*: e.g. 13.12.6; 13.86.1-3.

22. On Diodorus's social class and position, see Sacks 1990, 184-85.

Bibliography

Allen, P. 1985. *The Concept of Woman: The Aristotelian Revolution 750 BC-AD 1250*. Montreal.

Betz, H.D. (ed.) 1975. *Plutarch's Theological Writings and Early Christian Literature*. Leiden.

Bolkestein, H. 1929. *Theophrastos' Charakter der Deisidaimon als religionsgechichtliche Urkunde*. Giessen.

Craig, G.A. 1991. *The Germans*. New York.

Dean-Jones, L. 1991. "The Cultural Construct of the Female Body in Classical Greek Science", in: Pomeroy (ed.) 1991, 111-37.

Dodds, E.R. 1957. *The Greeks and the Irrational*. Boston.

Drews, R. 1962. "Diodorus and His Sources", *AJPh* 83, 383-92.

Gladigow, B. 1988. "Aberglaube", in: Hubert Cancik et al. (eds.) 1988, *Handbuch religionswissenschaflicher Grundbegriffe*. Stuttgart.

Grodzynski, D. 1974. "Superstitio", *REA* 76, 36-60.

Hamilton, E. 1942. *The Great Age of Greek Literature*. New York.

Hammond, N.G.L. 1983. *Three Historians of Alexander the Great*. Cambridge.

Hollis, M. & Lukes, S. (eds.) 1982. *Rationality and Relativism*. Oxford.

Horowitz, M.C. 1976. "Aristotle and Women", *JHistB* 9, 183-214.

Koets, P.J. 1929. *Deisidaimonia: A Contribution to the Knowledge of the Religious Terminology in Greek*. Purmerend.

Latour, B. & Woolgar, S. 1979. *Laboratory Life: The Social Construction of Scientific Facts*. Beverly Hills.

Lloyd, G.E.R. 1964. "The Hot and the Cold, the Dry and the Wet in Greek Philosophy", *JHS* 84, 92-106.

Longrigg, J. 1963. "Philosophy and Medicine: Some Early Interactions", *HSclPh* 67, 149-50.

Longrigg, J. 1993. *Greek Rational Medicine: Philosophy and Medicine from Alcmaeon to the Alexandrians*. London.

MacIntyre, A. 1988. *Whose Justice? Which Rationality?* Notre Dame.

Martin, D.B. 1995. *The Corinthian Body*. New Haven.

Nussbaum, M. 1994. *The Therapy of Desire: Theory and Practice in Hellenistic Ethics*. Princeton.

O'Neil, M.R. 1987. "Superstition", in: Mircea Eliade (ed.) 1987, *The Encyclopedia of Religion*. New York.

Perl, G. 1957. *Kritische Untersuchungen zu Diodors römischer Jahrzählung*. Berlin.

Peukert, H. 1984. *Science, Action, and Fundamental Theology: Toward a Theology of Communicative Action*. Cambridge.

Pomeroy, Sarah B. (ed) 1991. *Women's History and Ancient History*. Chapel Hill.

Rorty, R. 1989. *Contingency, Irony, and Solidarity*. Cambridge.

Sacks, K.S. 1990. *Diodorus Siculus and the First Century*. Princeton.

Salzman, M.R. 1987. "'Superstitio' in the Codex Theodosianus and the Persecution of Pagans", *VigChrist* 41, 172-88.

Scott, A. 1991. *Origen and the Life of the Stars*. Oxford.

Smith, B.H. 1988. *Contingencies of Value: Alternative Perspectives for Critical Theory*. Cambridge.

Smith, M. 1975. "*De superstitione (Moralia* 164E-171F)", in: Betz (ed.) 1975, 1-35.

Toulmin, S. 1990. *Cosmopolis: The Hidden Agenda of Modernity*. Chicago.

Von Staden, H. 1989. *Herophilus: The Art of Medicine in Alexandria*. Cambridge.

Wilson, B.R. (ed.) 1970. *Rationality*. Oxford.

QUAEDAM VERITATIS UMBRAE:
HELLENISTIC MAGIC AND ASTROLOGY

Richard Gordon

Every classicist has surely dreamed that some lost work or other might one day miraculously be recovered from the sands of Egypt. But there can be few in the modern age who have longed to recover one of the occult books on Nature, that is on natural magic, put out in the "Long" Hellenistic period down to Nero,[1] some under the names of Democritus, Pythagoras, the Egyptians Hermes Trismegistus, Apollobeches (or Apollobex) and Manetho, Zoroaster and Ostanes of Persia, the Jewish Dardanus, or Mochus of Phoenicia, but also some, such as the books of Demetrius *ho phusikos* (Pliny *HN* 8.59), Nigidius Figulus, Anaxilaos of Larissa, Apollodorus *adsectator Democriti* (Pliny *HN* 24.167) or Xenocrates of Aphrodisias, written in proprio nomine.[2] Their flavour can be inferred from a list compiled by one Asclepiades, who had evidently drunk deep of these muddy waters. He recounted how the plant *aethiopis* dries up streams and ponds; that the mere touch of another whose name is mangled "causes locks to spring open"; and that a certain *latace* used to be given by the Persian kings to their satraps to ensure that wherever they went they would have supplies (Pliny *HN* 26.18). Different in idiom, but quite as difficult for the modern observer to engage with, is the discourse of astrological handbooks, of which the melothesia, the scheme of planetary influences upon the human body, of the anonymous treatise known as *PMich* 149 may provide an example:

But at 130′ we must mark off the portion of the Moon; and it will include the calves; and somehow, whenever we see a noteworthy face, we go around and straightway see the calf of the leg, since naturally the portion of the Moon which is akin to it leads to all this. Afflictions, fractures, and amputations of the leg come about through the Moon's influence.[3]

It has long seemed natural in modern scholarship to treat the occult discourse on Nature and the astrological treatises as evidence for the same Hellenistic phenomenon, the rise (or perhaps return) of irrationality. This may be termed the classic reaction, typified by the exasperated tone of Hermann Diels in his *Antike Technik*, who described the pseudo-Democritan literature as:

A cloudy scientific and gnostic mysticism, full of religious formulae, bogus quotations from philosophers, occult conjuring and magic — in sum, a real witch's brew of sense and nonsense, of Greek gnosis and oriental superstition (1920, 130).

The return of the irrational is also the burden of the last chapter of E.R. Dodds, *The Greeks and the Irrational* (1951), and, insofar as it has a single theme at all, of the second volume of Martin Nilsson's *Geschichte der griechischen Religion* (1961). It has recently been forcefully restated by Peter Green (1990). His version of the argument is framed in terms of the political contrast between the classical polis and the Hellenistic kingdoms. The key problem is seen as the loss of a "special sort of confidence that only self-determination can produce", a confidence created in the classical period by the existence of democratic and autonomous states. The destruction of these states in the period 350-300 BC prompted people, unsettled by the disruption of old certainties, to turn in one of two directions. Those with education and leisure turned inward on themselves, in quest of the familiar values of Hellenistic philosophies. The other route was open dependence — on divinized, palpable kings who might take the place of the absent gods, but more often on symbolic satisfactions, ecstatic or mystery cults, astrology and magic (Green 1990, 52-64; 586-681). "The age was hungry for visions, for miracles, for knowledge of what lay beyond the boundaries of nature and reason: Plutarch's Timarchus was told he would die in three months, and did" (595).

This account of what was happening at the religious level during the Hellenistic age is so well-known that it has the air of a fixed and immutable truth. And, though it is easy to see how it is based on a scarcely-mediated opposition between an idealised Classical polis and the Hellenistic age, and how it minimises the numerous continuities between them, it may not for all that be entirely wrong. A standard work on the rise of the occult in nineteenth-century France, for example, shows how the origins of that revival lie in the mid-eighteenth century, when the old order, court power and enlightenment philosophy, was crumbling, and claims roundly: "The human mind abhors the absence of irrational belief" (McIntosh 1972, 18). On that reading, irrationalism would be the natural child of scientistic and progressive philosophies or world views, and its appeal would be to those excluded from these philosophies.[4] And Foucault has taught us, in more general terms, to be prepared for precisely such a reading, to see intellectual and cultural history as a battleground between those with a "right" to discourse, and those refused it.

There is a casual sense in which the claims of Asclepiades and of the melothesist of *PMich* 149 are "irrational", that is, educated twentieth-century westerners are likely to find them absurd. If that is all that is being said, we may simply note that the Greeks are once again failing to fulfil the rôle of cultural heroes thrust on them by a certain tradition of Romanticism. If the claim is more substantial, it must be that "people" in the Hellenistic period chose to embrace what they themselves considered irrational beliefs. But before we as historians accept this version, it would be as well to take a second look at the character of the evidence offered.[5] On the question of the character of mystery cults, Walter Burkert has surely said enough (1987) to make the thesis of irrationalism seem oddly by the way: if anything, it was in the mystery cults, certainly not in civic cult, that an attempt was made to expound the intentions and significance of religious rituals. To claim ecstatic cults as a typically Hellenistic phenomenon is simply to elide the history of the cults of Dionysus and Bendis. But in this essay I want to take a closer look solely at the cases of magic and astrology.

For Green, restating the traditional view, it is self-evident that "astrology and magic" somehow belong together in one breath and that we are talking about widespread, indeed newly vigorous, belief — even if the social location of that belief remains strangely imprecise. In my view, the casual coupling of magic and astrology, a product of the dismissive view that sees them as symptoms of the decay of a heroic Greek rationalism, is to be resisted: their social contexts and rôles, their Sitz im Leben, are in fact quite sharply distinct.[6] It is true that Pliny the Elder's account of magic, which goes back to Hellenistic sources, presents it as possessing "quasdam veritatis umbras", "shadows of truth as it were", one of which is astrology.[7] But this is not a formulation which gives much encouragement to those who believe in the irrationalist thesis.

Second, the very terms magic and astrology in this context are notoriously elusive. Now they mean "general belief in" certain claims about the world, now "frequent consultation of practitioners" of one sort or another, now "discursive texts which provide us with evidence of the beliefs that were around". It bears stressing that we possess very little direct evidence for either strong commitment to or practice of magic and astrology in the Hellenistic period — Green, for example, is reduced to citing late antique evidence for malign magic from the magical papyri, and, as we shall see, the documentary evidence for astrological practice in the Hellenistic world is extremely poor — but for the most part only evidence for books about these topics. The existence of discursive texts on magic and astrology in the Hellenistic world is interpreted as evidence for a new intensity of popular belief and practice. This inference seems to me at best unargued, and in all probability quite doubtful — at any rate, in need of considerable nuance. But before we can talk about the place of magic and astrology among the conventional values of the Hellenistic world, which I come to in the third section, we need to examine the character of the texts which are offered as evidence. That is my purpose in the first two sections of the article.

Some prefatory remarks linking the Hellenistic discourses of natural magic and astrology to wider contemporary themes are perhaps in order. For there are at least three contexts in which Hellenistic magic and astrology do indeed converge, namely as discursive dogmatic texts, as examples of "alien wisdom" and as pseudepigrapha. All of these have their place among the inventory of conventional values in the Hellenistic world.

The occult writings on Nature and the books of early astrologers[8] were essentially compilations of reference material, lists of reported facts and procedures whose significance was not so much individual as cumulative. These materials required to be written down in systematic order, whether alphabetic, topical or schematic, because their inherent connections were extremely meagre. Both kinds of text depended upon the prior existence of a tradition of natural-scientific enquiry and of an audience able to place their claims and procedures in context (cf. Lloyd 1979, 59-125). There can for example be little doubt that the facts and supposed facts ("factoids") listed by the occult writers were mainly drawn from work put in hand by the Peripatetic tradition, above all Theophrastus' works on nature; from geographies of the Orient, such as the works of Ctesias, Callisthenes, and Onesicrates;[9] and from the characteristically Hellenistic genre of the agricultural manual (Oder 1910, 1221-22; Gabba 1984, 28-29).

As texts, the books on natural magic and astrology exemplify an advanced stage in the development of pre-incunabular literacy, in which writers specializing in the accumulation of a complex mixture of empirical facts and factoids arranged in terms of explicit higher-order conceptions about the world, and claiming practical utility of a restricted kind, could find an audience furnished "con una mentalità e un bagaglio libreschi" (Cavallo 1983, 172). The existence of such highly specialized, and not at all entertaining, texts correlates with the Hellenistic phenomenon of slight extension of reading ability among the free inhabitants of cities, with foundations being set up in cities such as Teos, Miletus and Rhodes to pay teachers of writing, combined with markedly greater reliance upon reading and writing among the élite (Harris 1989, 116-46). For such texts were not a component of the public culture of the Hellenistic cities; but rather a component of the construction of an all-but-private world at the disposal of a tiny leisured group, a fraction of the élite as a whole, whose avocation was scholarly learning.[10] We shall return later to the issue of readership.

The issue of discourse and reception is inseparable from that of "alien wisdom", the Hellenistic negotation with complex foreign cultures made necessary by Alexander's conquest of the Achaemenid empire.[11] "Democritus" wrote works expounding Babylonian and Nubian sacred texts (or perhaps hieroglyphs, i.e. non-Greek scripts), and a *Chaldaios logos*, probably a book of syncretistic religious speculation, which have been dated as early as the third century BC (Diels *Vorsokr.* 68 B298b, 299a,d).[12] Other Hellenistic occult books on Nature reveal some access to the material contained in the Seleucid cuneiform šikinšu-lists of plants and stones, themselves resting upon much earlier exorcists' "tablets about stones" and "tablets about plants" (cf. Reiner 1985, 593).[13] Again, Seleucid Babylonian lists are either the direct source or the ultimate inspiration both of Greek interpretations of astral and meteorological phenomena (Pingree 1987, 620-23) and of the characterological classifications employed by the Greek astrological writers. Although Berosus' "school" on Chios (Vitruv. *De Arch.* 9.6.2 = Jacoby *FGrH* 680 T5a) has rightly been scouted,[14] Epigenes reportedly used observations recorded on clay tablets, which must have carried cuneiform writing (Pliny *HN* 7.193 = *FGrH* 680 F16b).[15] Accurate information regarding the schools of "Chaldaean astrologers", that is Babylonian interpreters of non-hepatoscopic omens and principally the stellar motions, is to be found in Strabo and Pliny the Elder.[16] Indirect transmission through speakers of Aramaic, once suggested by A.L. Oppenheim, is to some degree confirmed by the discovery of texts in Palestinian Aramaic closely analogous to Babylonian exemplars (Greenfield and Sokoloff 1989).[17]

As borrowings, such elements were open to furious recasting: "alien" wisdom in the Hellenistic world was, even more than in the fifth and fourth centuries, as much Greek as it was foreign (Piccaluga 1987). But whereas in the Archaic and Classical periods the barbarian Other constituted a stock of tropes for the exploration of the hierarchy of Hellenic norms, appeal to alien wisdom in the Hellenistic world often was a means of legitimating new values in the broadest sense religious. What the "wise nations" in general had to offer the Greeks was privileged access to a whole spectrum of non-civic religiosity. They were a significant element in the Hellenistic reinterpretation and transformation of traditional religious meanings (cf. Bilde 1993).

The appeal to the alien justified the third feature common to the two types of text: recourse, frequent though by no means universal, to pseudonymous authorship (Festugière 1950, 309-54). The very names of the occult writers, Zoroaster, Ostanes, Dardanus, Hermes, Apollobeches, Mochus, are so many appeals to the fascination of the obscure; and the still more favoured names Democritus and Pythagoras are mere disguises for the same appeal — for everyone knew that both had learned their wisdom from the Egyptians, or the Persians, Chaldaeans or even the Gymnosophists.[18] Whatever the place of named historical individuals in the astrological tradition, the most famous Hellenistic astrological texts were those ascribed to an Egyptian god, Hermes Trismegistus — 20,000 by one enthusiastic account, 36,525 by another[19] — and to two quasi-historical persons, Nechepso, an all-but-imaginary Pharaoh, and Petosiris, "Gift of Osiris", a priest.[20] Pseudonymity registers another feature of Hellenistic literate culture, the tendency to turn great names from the past into authority-figures, "to whom appeals could be made as some kind of guarantee of the validity of the ideas associated with them" (Lloyd 1987, 105). As in the ancient Near East, the written text becomes a vehicle for the transmission of authority, the name of the author serving to bracket the claims contained in the text from the kind of pragmatic doubt both writers and readers commonly applied in their everyday experience. "As the quality of the data falls, so the stature of the sanctioning authority rises" (Beck 1991, 502).

In each of these contexts, the Hellenistic literature on natural magic and astrology can be considered products of convergent tendencies in Hellenistic literate culture. We turn now to a closer examination of the characteristics of each of the two bodies of texts. My general claim is that each discourse, taken as a whole, basing itself on the natural-philosophical category Nature, sought to supplement or complete traditional practices in the same general area, rhizotomist practice in the case of the discourse on Nature, traditional divination in the case of astrology. If modern occultism represents a flight from the domination of science and technology, Hellenistic occultism and astrology attempted to systematize and partially rationalize prior praxeis whose assumptions were almost wholly tacit. This process of supplementation amounts sometimes to no more than what Geoffrey Lloyd has called "the literate representation of Greek folklore" (1983, 202). But sometimes, especially in the case of the discourse on Nature, it implied the occlusion or pre-empting of less articulate and self-conscious knowledge-practices. Literate discourse, as Pauline Schmitt Pantel has urged elsewhere in this volume, cannot simply be opposed to "conventional" representation; but neither is it, at least in these cases, an unproblematic reflection of such representations.

1. The discourse on Nature: Bolus of Mendes

First, the Hellenistic discourse on Nature, *ta phusika*, which I propose to term, for the sake of convenience, the "Democritean" tradition. There is no space here to deal with the whole range of this fragmentary and hopelessly obscure material, and I propose to confine myself exempli gratia to the figure of Bolus of Mendes in the Egyptian Delta, who was active *c.* 200 BC. This is not because I share Max Wellmann's hypothesis that Bolus was the sole source of the entire "Democritean" tradition, but because he is the only one of these authors, apart from Nigidius Figulus, who is more than a shadow.[21]

But not, it must be confessed, very much more than a shadow.[22] The basic problem is the nature of the relationship between Bolus and the Greek philosopher Democritus of Abdera (active *c.* 430 BC), with whom he is associated in the doxographical tradition.[23] Bolus evidently put out at least one of his works under the pseudonym Democritus. Columella and Pliny, who were contemporaries writing in the mid first century AD, make it clear that he wrote at least one book, the *Cheirokmeta*, "the book of artificial remedies", under the name Democritus. Pliny evidently knows of a controversy about the matter,[24] while Columella roundly states that the book was a forgery whose real author was Bolus (*Rust.* 7.5.17 = Diels *Vorsokr.* 68 B300.3). On the other hand Vitruvius, writing in the 30s and 20s BC, who ascribes the book without ado to Democritus, apparently knew nothing of the dispute (*De Arch.* 9.1.14 = Diels *Vorsokr.* 68 B300.2). The most probable explanation of this discussion in the early Empire is to be found in the cataloguing work of Ti. Claudius Thrasylus, the astrologer of the Emperor Tiberius. Thrasylus (or Thrasyllus) catalogued the works ascribed to Democritus of Abdera, and in the course of this task came to consider that some were spurious.[25] The list cited by Diogenes Laertius names in an appendix eight such works, one of which has been conjectured to conceal *Cheirokmeta* (Diog. Laert. 9.45-9 = Diels *Vorsok.* 68 A300.33) .

There has been a general reluctance to describe Bolus' work as forgery.[26] One recent suggestion is that we should imagine the relationship between the two as analogous to that between the Socrates of the dialogues and Plato. Bolus' residence in the Delta would have given him access to the Alexandrian library, and he may have begun by compiling authentic material from Democritus' writings, but gradually suffused them with his own views (Laurenti, 1985). This seems naive. In my view, the best solution is to take Bolus as indeed a forger, that is, as intentionally publishing books under a false name in order to give his own views greater authority, but that the choice of Democritus was quite appropriate to his purpose in promoting a theory of natural magic. Without denying the frequent impenetrability of forgers' motives, Grafton has lately stressed that the forger commonly sees his invocation of a name as giving a sense of probability and importance to what he has to say (1992, 48).[27] Forgery is one among several ways of coming to terms with the past, which is subjectively recast in the mould perceived by the forger, and then, as the forgery wins acceptance, also objectively — the forgery actually remakes the past (96). The succession of references to "Democritus" (and the rest of the pseudonymous tracts) by Clement of Alexandria, Hippolytus and others, long after after the impact of Thrasylus' discovery had worn off, shows that the gamble paid off handsomely.

Of the several books ascribed to Bolus by the Suda's two entries (Diels *Vorsokr.* 68 B300.1), mention may be made of three to give an idea of the kind of material they contained.

His book of marvels, *Peri tôn ek tês anagnôseôs tôn historiôn eis epistasin hêmas agontôn*, or *Peri thaumasiôn* in brief, is not known to have been ascribed to Democritus.[28] Bolus' contribution to the paradoxographical tradition seems to show some awareness of the rules for the genre established by Callimachus' *On every variety of marvel topographically arranged* (Giannini, 1964, 105-9), in that he cites named authors for example; on the other hand its subject matter is quite at odds with post-Callimachean naturalism. The book seems to be the source of the first six entries in Apollonius, *Historiai thaumasiai*, a work probably of the first half of the second century BC.[29] These items describe six famous early *andres theoi*, holy men, Epimenides of Crete, Aristeas of Proconnesus, Hermotimus of Clazomenae, Abaris, Pherecydes and Pythagoras. The stories stress soul journeys, presence in two places at once, and second sight: the gulf between heaven and earth has repeatedly been crossed by exemplary historical individuals. The citation of historical authors certifies the authenticity of the claims, and thus the inference to be drawn from them, namely that divinity, if not the divinities of civic religion, is immanent in the world. It is its overtly religious intention that marks this work by Bolus off from the main Hellenistic paradoxographical tradition.

Though the other two works I wish briefly to discuss are not strictly paradoxo-graphical, there is a dilute sense in which they also belong to the genre, if to an entirely un-Callimachean conception of it. For a second book by Bolus, certainly written under Democritus' name, is the *Phusika dunamera*, "(Remedies of) natural potency", also called more descriptively *Peri sumpathôn kai antipathôn*. Columella cites one account from it, namely the belief that caterpillars will be killed if a woman walks round the field three times, barefoot, with her hair down and while she is menstruating, "and afterwards all the caterpillars fall off and so die" (*Rust.* 11.3.64 = Diels *Vorsokr.* 68 B300.3). Another probable fragment concerns among other topics, the relation between the ferret and the fox: "The domesticated ferret is antipathetic (*antipathês esti*) to the fox, which cannot endure its smell or sight, but dies at once".[30] In this book Bolus evidently collected and recast popular lore about the animal world, systematically selecting material that could be made to illustrate a thesis about inherent powers of opposition and attraction. A traditional, unsystematic and informal representation of relations between animals, that of friendships and enmities, picked up already by the fourth-century writer on gardening, Androtion, has been rigorized and turned into an explicit, privileged account of the working of Nature.[31] It is also clear from the most common title for the book, *Peri antipathôn*, that it was mainly not about sympathy but about natural remedies based on the idea of inherent contrariety. The choice of natural facts both illustrates a claim, essentially the Stoic claim that nature is a self-regulating, living being; and insinuates a thesis, that traditional lore, though it contains substantive truths about the manner in which that natural order works, must be reworked by the occultist in order to reveal its message.

The third book is the pendant to the *Phusika dunamera*, the *Cheirokmêta*, the "Artificial remedies". If the sources are to be relied upon — by no means to be taken for granted — it contained some material drawn from traditional farming practice: Columella cites it, for example, for a remedy against *ignis sacer* in sheep. The sheep with the disease is to be buried alive, belly up, at the entrance of the sheep pen and the other sheep made to walk over the spot (*Rust.* 7.5.17 = Diels *Vorsokr.* 68 B300.3). By inference, this is an "artificial remedy" in that the farmer intervenes into the processes of nature by constructing a liminal point analogous to that used in malign magic, and referring to other deliberate infringements of the normal rules for sacrifice, such as those for averting disaster presaged by omens. But other parts of this text owed more to the paradoxographical tradition. The elder Pliny cites a section in which a herbarium of the exotic marvellous was evidently listed in alphabetical order: all the plants, except for one from Cappadocia and Mysia, are alleged to come from the orient or Ethiopia, and they all have miraculous properties:

Arianis comes from Ariana (the satrapy) and is fire-coloured. It is gathered when the Sun is in Leo. If you soak sticks in oil and put them in contact with the plant, they catch fire.

And:

The theangelis ... is taken by the Magi as an infusion so that they can foretell the future (*HN* 24.160-66).

Magic is here equated with the practice of the Persian Magi, in the agreed terms of the Hellenistic pseudo-historical aetiology (Gordon 1987, 74-79). But it is at the same represented as entirely natural, a matter of exploiting knowledge of properties inherent in certain constituents of nature. Incantation, the second leg of actual magical practice, has mysteriously disappeared from view. More generally, such lists, which occur repeatedly in the "Democritean" tradition, create a textual site in which the world becomes an Alician Wonderland, a place in which marvellous events are commonplace, in which one extraordinary fact presses breathlessly against the next until the reader has no choice but to concede that the commonsense boundary between actual and impossible, between what I know to be true and what I know to be false, is hopelessly uncertain. Per contrarietatem, the appeal to empirical facts — factoids of course, but who was to insist on the hard facts of so many cases in far off Arachosia, Persia or even in the local woods? — amount to an attack upon the validity of a mechanistic, especially an Epicurean, physics. For every one of these facts offers a challenge, composes an implied entry in a *Problemata*, a book of knotty natural problems.

We turn now to the more general question of the function of the occult discourse on nature typified by the work of Bolus. I would urge that the redescription of selected natural facts as marvels strung together on an occult string had the effect of clearing a space between the tacit, incoherent quality of traditional belief on the one hand, and those trends in Hellenistic cosmology, particularly Epicureanism and scepticism, which tended towards rationalism and agnosticism on the other. That space the occultists attempted to fill with a demonstration of the superabundant strangeness of nature. The variety of the occult texts and their fragmentary state — the fact that no programmatic statements survive — naturally make one cautious about making such a claim. And Pliny's observation: "I imagine that they can only write such rubbish because they despise mankind and want to make fun of it" (*HN* 37.124), is so exactly our immediate reaction that we are excused from wondering whether there might not be alternative views, whether the discourse on nature might not have had a serious intent of this kind.

There seem to me to be two main reasons for thinking so. One is the occult tradition's total lack of interest in ordinary conceptions of magic and magical procedure, to which I have already alluded. But the point bears expansion. First, although Bolus and the other Hellenistic occultists were at least partly concerned with the lore of traditional magical healers, *rhizotomoi*, "root-cutters" and wise women (Kingsley 1995, 337), there is no evidence that they concerned themselves with first-hand collection of such material. Their facts or factoids were taken from earlier books, and some no doubt even invented. Such a procedure meant that the contextual meaning of magical practices as well as the ritual underpinning was lost. What survived was a mere claim, an extravagant statement of automatic effectiveness. Second, occult literature typically made sense of magical "facts" in a quite different way from its practitioners. Competence for a root-cutter lay in two directions, in the knowledge of rules for collection and preparation of plant and animal materials (Delatte 1938; Martini 1977) and in the construction of elegant recipes in keeping with the tradition he or she had learned. By contrast, the occult tradition had interest neither in the rules nor in the elegance. Its "magicians" are not humble root-cutters but the Magi, the exotic representatives of a class of wonder-workers. The transfer of magical action out of the real world of the rhizotomists into the world of the Magi serves to transform the character of belief in magical effects. Magical beliefs were redescribed under the rubric of marvels, free from the messy and tedious practicalities of collection, preparation, and application. The "Democritean" tradition was not primarily, if at all, practical in intention.[32] But it does form an essential part of an emergent Hellenistic concept of magic far removed from the actual practice of root-cutters and wise women.

The second reason for thinking that the "Democritean" tradition was working, perhaps fitfully, towards a middle ground is its use of perfectly respectable Classical and Hellenistic explanatory terminology. The principal terms for occult influence, *dunamis* in Greek, *vis* in Latin, are taken from the language of Greek natural speculation, both Hippocratic and Peripatetic.[33] There is no question here of a metaphorical extension by the "Democritean" tradition of a clear or determinate concept in natural philosophy: one can hardly even allow *dunamis* a "focal meaning" of the Aristotelian type, with other secondary meanings clustering around it (Lloyd 1987, 198-203). But occult *dunamis* does draw upon the implication frequently present in natural scientific contexts of "specific property", represented by the noun with an adjectival complement — the Aristotelian nose for example has a "power of smelling", a *dunamis osphrêtikê*. It combines this notion with the second main implication of *dunamis*, "the effect one thing has upon another", as in the "powers" of the humours that play such an important part in *On Ancient Medicine*. These natural-philosophical usages are then applied in a quite mechanical fashion to provide an account of the marvellous: the wolf has the power to induce sleepiness in a horse that steps on its tracks (Pliny *HN* 28.157).

The notion of sympathy was likewise taken over from the natural-philosophical tradition: it was a central element already in Zeno's cosmology (Long 1982, 167-68), and traces of the notion, limited to the internal relations of parts of the body, are already to be found in the Hippocratic *De alimento* §23. But there are important differences between the typical Stoic *exempla* that proved that the cosmos was thoroughly ordered, the appeals to the influences of the Sun and Moon, the power of the magnet and so on, and the usages found in the "Democritean" tradition. In particular, the latter hardly uses the notion of sympathy at all (Röhr 1923-24, 34-38), let alone the common Hippocratic idea of like curing like (Müller 1965). It is antipathy, more usually in the verbal form *antipathein*, that is made to do the work of explanation, acquiring a useful double sense, that of reciprocal or corresponding passive affect, and secondly rejection or intolerance. It is by means of this semantic slide that the notion of an occult force at work in healing or in relationships between plants and animals could be made plausible.

Explanation was in fact not the occultists' main intention. Their slogan was that the natural world ought not to be subjected to rationalistic enquiry: "seek not the cause but the will of Nature", *nec quaerenda ratio in ulla parte naturae, sed voluntas* (Pliny *HN* 37.60, cf. Beagon 1992, 63-8). The will of Nature was expressed directly in its myriad unpredictabilities and astonishments. The occultists claimed simply to be recording hundreds of cases in which Nature's inherent force might be recognised and celebrated. The implication of their combination of the marvellous with the language of natural philosophy is that they saw themselves as working against the "atheism" and scepticism of Epicureanism. This raises once again (see p. 131-32 above) the question of their intended or actual readership. It has been suggested that this was a new class in the Hellenistic world of modest reader, "not totally uneducated but simply not intellectually trained" (Cavallo 1983, 179). This seems doubtful on two counts. Pliny the Elder and other commentators in the early Principate evidently considered the "Democritean" literature part of a wider discourse on nature — Pliny lists its authors indiscriminately with others in Book 1. It is speculative to infer that the audience must have been less well-educated than the supposed readers of, say, the Hippocratic corpus. Moreover, we might observe that the "Democritean" tradition offered its readers a special privilege, a claimed insight, into the real workings of Nature: Nature constructs signs of her intentions for man, and the world itself is a kind of book in a secret language, which can only be read by the truly literate. It was the aspiration to *complete* understanding of Nature, with the book as key metaphor, that "Democritus" and his congeners promised to realise. Why should such an offer have attracted only the half-educated in the Hellenistic world?

2. Astrology as a Hellenistic knowledge-practice

Of "magic" in the Hellenistic world — in the sense of Pierre Bourdieu's objective profanation (1971, 308), the practice of *manteis, baskanoi*, root-cutters and wise folk — we can say that its practice had always existed in numerous forms and that occultism had no direct impact upon that practice except insofar as the scheme of sympathy and antipathy percolated down to practising root-cutters.[34] Hellenistic astrology on the other hand was an entirely new form of knowledge-practice, whose origins are complex and still inscrutable. Use of the heavenly bodies for simple predictions of weather and seasons and as a guide to dates at which farming and other activities should be undertaken was of course very ancient in the Greek world; in the fifth century the parapegmatist Meton had observed the alignment of the summer solstice at Athens because of its significance for meteorological events (Bowen and Goldstein 1988). All this material is generally referred to by the German term *Laienastrologie*. But astrology proper was a radically new and much more sophisticated means of investing the heavens with language.

Its origins lie in the gradual changes that took place in the realm of celestial divination in Achaemenid Babylonia, when the stars came to be conceived as having direct and specific influence upon individual terrestrial objects (trees, plants and stones) and events, such as the configuration of signs on the liver of the sacrificial victim (Oppenheim 1959; Weidner 1967). By the very end of the fifth century BC a new type of personal nativity-omen text begins to appear (two examples of this date are now known). They consist of notations of planetary and stellar positions at the birth of individuals, sometimes named, computed from the astronomical almanacs (Rochberg-Halton 1989, 107). Sachs was surely therefore correct in guessing that the rudimentary origins of Hellenistic personal astrology lie in the Achaemenid period (1967, 19). But the most significant progressive changes in Babylonian celestial divination, and those of greatest importance for Hellenistic astrology, must have occurred in the Seleucid period.[35]

On the other hand, Hellenistic astrology was not a straightforward borrowing of a ready-made Babylonian product. There had been some contact between priestly diviners in Assyria-Babylonia and in Egypt even in the Late Period.[36] But Alexander's conquest evidently made possible a far more intense flow of Babylonian astronomic and astrological lore to the Egyptian temple *astrologoi* than had existed earlier. Several Hellenistic Egyptian texts betray use of Babylonian astronomic and divinatory procedures (e.g. Neugebauer 1949; Hughes 1951), and the earlier group of Graeco-Egyptian astronomical tables is based on Babylonian methods (Jones 1995, 37). It seems, moreover, that the dominant

Greek tradition ascribed its earliest texts to Egypt.[37] At any rate, a vulgate tradition, a fusion of Babylonian and Egyptian ideas, and generally ascribed to "the (ancient) Egyptians", formed in Ptolemaic Egypt at latest by the beginning of the first century BC, and probably earlier.[38] This body of material, translated into the terms of Hellenistic geocentric cosmology (Long 1982, 170; Rochberg-Halton 1989, 106) and assimilated to Greek cultural realities (Konstan, in this volume), in turn formed the basis of the shared technical knowledge presented in the earliest surviving handbooks of astrology, those of Manilius and Dorotheus of Sidon.[39]

It is the technical doctrines of Greek astrology that are usually the focus of academic study. In my present context, however, astrology is important only as a novel means of divination. What was the popular demand for astrological prediction? What claims did astrology make for itself in the Hellenistic market for divination? The following remarks about technical doctrines are intended only to contribute to answering these questions. Where reference to a text is essential, I use Manilius' *Astronomica* exempli gratia, Books 1-2 of which were written between around 9 AD and the death of Augustus; 3-4 after the accession of Tiberius.[40] Manilius' treatise is an example of fundamentalist or "hard" astrology, claiming that the stars "rule by hidden laws" (1.63). Although written in Latin, the poem is entirely dependent upon earlier sources in Greek.

The basic thesis of "hard" astrology is extremely simple. The casting of a horoscope is based on the belief that the zodiac and planets exert different influences, that is physical effluences transmitted by universal sympathy, according to their different positions relative to the native (the subject of the enquiry) (e.g. Sext. Emp. *Math.* 5.4-5). But the grand question is how these influences are to be read. Most systems of divination, from reading tea-leaves or coffee-grounds to the trigrams of the I Ching, consist of a limited (albeit sometimes very large) set of meanings linked to a fixed matrix, crossed by an element of chance. Thus tea-leaves, "makeshift ideograms", are the matrix, the meanings are stored in the memory of the practitioner, chance enters in the outfall of the gesture of emptying the cup. Such a scheme is also the basis of astrology, but the matrix is extremely complicated, while the element of chance is nominally the moment of birth or conception.

Two key steps have to be taken by astrology if it is to turn the heavens into a matrix capable of providing meanings. First, it has to link two quite independent astral phenomena, the zodiac and the planets, which, although their path indeed follows the ecliptic (the sun's route during the year), have no inherent connection with the zodiac. This was done primarily by means of the basic doctrines of the

planetary houses, and of the exaltations and depressions. Second, features of
human life have somehow to be related to the heavenly bodies. To do this, the
astrologers drew a picture of the fixed circle against which the zodiac and planets
appear to an observer to rotate every twenty-four hours. This is the horoscopic
circle. This circle is marked with four cardinal points, the *hôroskopos*, representing
the rising-point at nine o'clock, and then, clock-wise, the mid-heaven (*medium
caelum*, zenith), the setting-point (*occasus*) and the nadir, the "meridian underfoot"
(*imum caelum*). These are the points at which the zodiac and the planets meet,
respectively, the local eastern horizon, the meridian, the western horizon and the
notional nadir (Manilius *Astron.* 2.788-800). The horoscopal circle, a purely
notional diagram, is the crucial astrological device that mediates between the
observed heavens (nature, as it were, albeit of course "divine") and human life
(culture). Thus the cardinal points, mere bearings in the act of observation, acquire
cosmic significance, represented by Manilius as the *compages aeternae*, the
"eternal joints" (as in a piece of carpentry), without which the whole universe —
and by implication human affairs — would whirl apart (2.801-7). The most usual
scheme for inserting human life into the horoscopal circle is the *dôdekatropos*,
the twelve "temples", each occupying 30°, which are set round the "clock-face"
of the horoscopal circle in an anti-clockwise direction from 9 o'clock.[41] These
temples serve in a quite unspecifiable manner to channel the influence of the
heavenly signs and planets as they pass through them towards particular spheres
of human life.[42] From Manilius' language it seems clear that it was the point on
the notional circle occupied by a temple which inspired its association with human
affairs: temple 11, for example, at 11 o'clock, signifies ambition and victory
because it was imagined as aiming for the highest point;[43] temple 9, at one
o'clock, is linked to the sun — evidently displaced from its logical place at
midday by other considerations — and in most schemes (but not Manilius') is
therefore associated with journeys;[44] the "lowest" temple, number 4, at 6 o'clock,
is associated with foundations and darkness, and so Saturn: this temple governs
fathers and the fate of old men.[45] Manilius' alternative, and simpler, techniques
for linking the horoscopal circle with human affairs likewise make clear the rôle
of the horoscopal diagram itself in providing the "metonymic springboard"
required to negotiate this tricky crux between (meaningless) nature and
(interesting) culture. In one scheme, the meridian, the *medium caelum*, is linked
with glory, pre-eminence, popularity, political power; the *occasus* with bringing
things to a conclusion, with marriages and feasts, with death, merrymaking and
religious worship (2.808-40). Another scheme associates not the cardinals but the

segments between them with the four periods of life: and each quadrant likewise with the four ages of man, from infancy to old age (841-55).[46]

Without going into any more detail, and of course the situation is indescribably more complicated than this,[47] we can focus upon three key features of the two earliest surviving astrological treatises, the poems by Manilius and Dorotheus of Sidon, features which we can justifiably claim to have been present also in the now lost Hellenistic material: the tendency towards complexity; the tension between secrecy and the didactic; the stress on the objectivity of the knowledge offered by the stars.

We may roughly distinguish between two functions of complexity, which we might term "extrinsic" and "intrinsic". The first is the "arabesque syndrome", by which I mean the invention of new distinctions by means of which the writer's authority is validated. The discussion of the zodiac at Manilius, *Astron.* 2.150-692 may serve to illustrate this type (cf. Hübner 1982, 453-514).

Manilius offers ten ways of classifying the zodiacal signs. For example, six are "male", six (including Aries) "female"; three are "human", seven "bestial", one both; seven are "single", the rest "double"; some rise *rectis membris*, with their limbs the right way up, others, Taurus, Gemini and Cancer, rise "backwards"; there are three different ways of understanding the opposition "diurnal" ~ "nocturnal" (2.150-222). Finally, there are two criteria unique to Manilius: posture (running, sitting, lying); and disfigurement (e.g. Cancer has no eyes; Sagittarius has only one eye) (244-64). Neither of these is ever mentioned again. We are then given a list of twelve Guardians whom Nature has assigned to each sign, Pallas to Aries, etc. (433-52). "This scheme", he says, "will provide you with an important means of determining the future" — and never mentions it again. At 2.466ff. is to be found the scheme of the *amantia* and the *insidiantia*, the signs which pay court to one another, or not. Again, it never recurs. These distinctions and doctrines are all "arabesques", which have no significant part to play in the main overt purpose of such a treatise, the explanation of how to cast a horoscope, but demonstrate rather the superiority of the writer over others who do not, by implication cannot, deploy such niceties (Barton 1994, 134-42). The tendency towards systematisation of a "vulgate" was continually opposed by the zealous invention of individual variations, personal schemes and doctrines, such as the melothesia of *PMich.* 149 with which we began. Wolfgang Hübner has shown that, despite the high degree of repetition from one astrological source to another, if one compares all the treatises systematically, under the sole rubric of their clas-sification of the zodiacal signs, one finds a bewildering variety of disagreement, mostly very minor and apparently unmotivated (Hübner 1982, 45-299). For example, no two astrological treatises offer exactly the same classification of the signs between terrestrial, aquatic and amphibian (171-73). The writing of a treatise constitutes a tacit, and often enough, as in Manilius *Astron*. 3.1-42, an explicit, claim to personal mastery of the art.

But not all complexity is solely rhetorical, serving to enhance the impression of the writer's originality and knowledge. Some complications, the "intrinsic" type, serve to protect the system as a whole. They permit the over-production of means of generating astrological readings which is such a typical feature of the Graeco-Roman treatises, and surely therefore also of their Hellenistic antecedents. Manilius introduces one of these complications at 2.639-737, namely the zodiacal and planetary *dôdekatemoriai*. The first consists of a method of dividing each zodiacal sign into twelve sub-sections of 2½°, each allocated to one of the signs in reverse order.[48] The planetary dodekatemoria consists of a further subdivision into five of each of these arcs of 2½°, i.e. into units of ½°. Each unit is assigned to one of the five planets excluding Sun and Moon. The structural advantage of such a scheme is that it increases the number of factors to be taken into account by the astrologer in casting a nativity. The zodiacal sign gives one set of possible meanings read off from a prepared scheme of possibilities, e.g. the person born when the Sun is in Taurus is headstrong and bullish. The zodiacal dodekatemoria gives another possible influence, say Pisces, which influences the dominant meaning; and then the planetary dodecatemoria gives yet another possibility of influence, say Mercury. Other examples of "intrinsic" complexity are the "aspects" — the mutual influence of the planets conceived in geometrical relation to one another, one at least of which, the trine aspect, is Babylonian; the thirty-six decans — the segments of the Egyptian celestial circle; the *partes damnandae* — each of the 360° of the zodiac with its own special character; the *dôdekatropos* — the planetary "abodes"; the chronocratores that govern different stages of a person's life. The practical astrologer thus works within a formal paradigm of complete fixity and necessity, in fact with a system that gives him great freedom of manoeuvre in making predictions. But the rhetoric of the treatises dwells exclusively upon the formal paradigm, the "intrinsic" complexity serving to underscore the difficulty of the art.

Second, the tension between secrecy and didacticism. The historical location of astrology within temple contexts both in Babylonia and Egypt[49] gave it originally the status of an esoteric body of learning. The revelatory form of the astrological Hermetica, in which secrets are bestowed upon a "king" or other figure of traditional authority, is appropriate to such an origin (Festugière 1950, 310-12). This secrecy was gradually challenged by the Greek political domination of Mesopotamia and the Nile valley: Berosus' account in his *Babyloniaka* of the "Chaldaean art" is a clear response to this challenge.[50] The transfer of technical astrological lore, by routes which are still wholly unclear, into the contestatory mode of Greek intellectual practice simultaneously increased the rate at which new schemes, extrinsic and intrinsic, could develop and created the demand for a new mode, the didactic, by means of which knowledge of the techniques could be transmitted other than through the laborious apprenticeship modes of the ancient Near-Eastern autocracies (cf. Gabba 1984, 16-18). The tension between the weight of tradition and the pressures of didacticism is evident in the oracular opacity, the despair of Vettius Valens who tried to read him, of one of the earliest writers of an astrological treatise, Critodemus.[51] The very title of the book, *Horasis*, Vision, indicates the vatic mode;[52] yet the citations by Vettius Valens and the surviving epitome (*CCAG* 8.3, 102) show both that he had created or elaborated numerous didactic schemes, of the zodiacal signs, planetary "rulers" and "aspects", climacterics, lengths of life, and so on, and that he stressed his own originality and competence (Boll 1922). In time, as Dorotheus' preface to his Book on "interrogations" (catarchic astrology) suggests, allusion to the "learned men of Babylon and Egypt" became a routine invocation of authority (5.1.3, p. 262 Pingree), but Manilius' metaphoric language of inwardness, depth, penetration and arduous search is evidence of the same ambivalence in slightly different language.[53]

The third key feature of Hellenistic astrological treatises is the claim to precise and infallible knowledge. One of the fragments of Critodemus already reads, "After voyaging over oceans, after traversing great deserts, I was found worthy by the gods of chancing upon a safe haven, the one truly safe, *monês asphalestatês*, haven" (Vett. Val. *Anthol.* 3.12 Kroll = 3.8.3 p. 142.14-16 Pingree). A clear distinction between astronomy and astrology is not to be found before Sextus Empiricus *Math.* 5.1-2 (Hübner 1989, 19). The striking results of Babylonian and Greek astronomy provided the substance of the claim to objective knowledge required by the astrologers if they were to be able to promote their discourse over the traditional forms of divination practised by the ancient state. Cicero explains:

The Chaldaeans ... are considered to have established by protracted observation a science (*scientia*) of the stars, such that it became possible to predict what would happen to each individual, and the destiny each person was born with. (*Div.* 1.2)

Quintus later underscores the tradition of the extreme antiquity of Babylonian astronomical records (1.36). Still more pointed is Manilius' question (4.913-14):

> an minus est sacris rationem ducere signis
> quam pecudum mortes aviumque attendere cantus?[54]

Extispicy and augury, the two props of Roman state divination, are represented as inferior to the scientific knowledge provided by the stars. In the proem, astrology is represented as the high point of human *ratio*, of its capacity to grasp "the innermost nature of the world in its causes", and to see "all that exists anywhere" (1.97-98) (Liuzzi 1990, 26-29). Astrology is above all an empirical science, the result of observations amassed over "long ages", which revealed the *potentia*, the peculiar influence, of each configuration of the stars (1.53-65).[55] And he naturally begins his treatise by summarizing, with Stoic glosses, the structure of the *sphaera* as established by Greek astronomy (1.255-804) (Liuzzi 1990, 32-33). It is precisely the scientific credentials of astrology that recommend its predictions (Flammini 1993). The value of this argument need not detain us here: what is of significance is that the appeal is made in these terms, which presume acknowledgement by Manilius' audience of the high status of Hellenistic astronomy. The appeal is to reason, not to authority or faith; to the idea of a Nature whose order has been written down.

3. Magic and astrology in the market-place

We come finally, and briefly, to consider the place of magic and astrology among the "conventional values" of the Hellenistic world.

My contention has been that our most promising sources of information about magic and astrology in this period are indeed shot through with conventional values, but that these are the values of a culture of bookishness, so that they are of very limited use as sources of information for belief or practice in the Hellenistic world as a whole. (The point certainly also holds for literary representations, such as Theocritus' second *Idyll*, the poem about a girl's attempt to force a faithless lover back to her by magic — suffused as it is by ironic distances between poet and subject, narrator and recipient.)[56] Both discourses are mainly concerned with the authority that their writers can claim in the Hellenistic marketplace of knowledge-practices.

Can we then say nothing of the sense in which magic and astrology may have formed part of the "conventional values" of the Hellenistic world, in the sense understood by the editors in their introduction to the volume? To a limited extent I think we can. My premise is that, just as there were to all intents no thorough-going atheists in antiquity, so hardly anyone was thoroughgoingly sceptical of the possibility of magical effects and astral influences.[57] Moreover, I adapt Evans-Pritchard's notion (1937) of a hierarchy of means, which he deployed for the analysis of Azande divination but which may usefully be applied to magic too — that is, both "magic" and "divination" are really fields of action, covering many different types of practice and practitioner, notionally arranged in a hierarchy of prestige and efficacy. This hierarchy of means has two effects relevant in the present context: on the one hand it helps to prevent scepticism relating to individual incidents (i.e. disconfirmation) from corroding belief in the system as a whole; on the other, by leaving plenty of room for innovation especially in low-level practices, it permits the system to adapt to new circumstances and perceptions.

In the case of magic, we need to distinguish between the horizon of expectation which sustains the mere possibility of magical action, and actual recourse to a magical act or practitioner. Acceptance of the possibility of marvellous events, of which magical action is a small part, was simply an element of the Hellenistic *Lebenswelt*, one of the taken-for-granted background assumptions — eminently a conventional value. Plato, no friend of such claims, conceded: "As to all such matters (the power of incantations) the true facts are hard to learn, nor, if one could learn them, would it be an easy task to convince another" (*Leg.* 11.933a5-7). This commitment starts at the worst case of malign sorcery. As Pliny says, "There is no one who is not afraid of being 'caught' by malevolent curses" (*HN* 28.19, cf. Seneca, *Ben.* 6.35). The commitment extends to the point at which it meets the subject's sense of the absurd, ridiculous or abject, the private stock of images which convey the notion "superstition".[58] Each person deploys a scale of conditions under which appeal to magic or a practitioner might be thinkable. If an individual had a bleeding nose he might try the recipe found in a collection of early mediaeval charms, and say "surgur" into the opposite nostril from that affected (*Additamenta pseudo-Theod.* p. 276.10 Rose). But if it did not work, he would not mind: his commitment to success somewhere higher up the scale of possibilities would not be impaired. Equally, another individual might find such a remedy ridiculous without that attitude extending to a general rejection of the possibility of magical effects — not that such effects could have been clearly defined or delimited by ordinary individuals in the Hellenistic world, since "magic", whatever Greek word we choose as its best equivalent, remained inadequately distinguishable from the wider category of the marvellous, itself a main pillar of the religious *Lebenswelt*.

But, healing magic apart, recourse to a practitioner of one kind or another was more or less problematical, because such a step offered a threat, slight or great, to one's good name and reputation. For recourse to serious magic, that is to a binding spell, is an admission that you cannot manage on your own (cf. Faraone 1991, 20; Winkler 1991, 226). A binding spell is one possible recourse in a restricted number of contexts of social action when all else has failed: many would never take that step, either because they had, though patronage and other social networks, more practical means of leverage; or from "shame", that is, a sense of what belonged to their good name. It is such shame, the refusal to "intimidate the timid", that Plato appeals to (*Leg.* 933b7-c3). For that reason, recourse to serious, especially love and binding (i.e. malign), magic must have been relatively uncommon; and I see no reason to suppose that individuals appealed to such magic more frequently in the Hellenistic period than in the Classical age or (for that matter) any other in Greece right up to the present. There is, at the very least, no documentary evidence for such an assumption: only a small number of curse tablets (*defixiones*) can be dated to the Hellenistic period — indeed, for what it is worth, there are probably more Athenian curse tablets dating from the later fourth century BC than from any other time.[59]

Accusations of malign sorcery are a different matter: there is no necessary relation between the number of magical acts actually performed and the number of accusations. But even so, as far as I know, not a single trial for sorcery is known from the Hellenistic world (as opposed to the Roman Republic). It is generally assumed, on the basis of the apparent absence of such a title from Athenian law, that Hellenistic Greek cities wrote no laws against magical practice as such (Gernet 1951, cxciv n. 2). On the one hand, it seems clear that at Athens, and probably elsewhere, an accusation of death caused by sorcery would generally fall under the rubric of death by poisoning — *pharmakeus*, fem. *pharmakis*, is a common word for a magical practitioner. Accusations of attempted harm by poisoning or sorcery (Plato mentions the placing of maumets at graves or threshholds, *Leg.* 933b1-3) would count as *blabê*, damage, which could of course be to farm livestock as well (cf. Saunders 1991, 318-19). The ambivalence, and especially the psychological orientation, of his entire treatment suggests that Plato is feeling his way. On the other hand, the Twelve Tables at Rome, an Archaic law code, did contain titles against magic: not against magic in general, but against specific acts of sorcery, in particular "stealing" a neighbour's crops — i.e. causing them mysteriously to fail (*XII Tab.* 8.8a = *FIRA*² 1.55). It seems to me by no means impossible that, although in the Greek cities "magic" was not a clear enough category to be sanctioned as such, many Hellenistic law-codes possessed specific rules of this kind. It was the harm caused by magical acts that was to be sanctioned, not magic as such (Reverdin 1945, 237). And Plato certainly implies that in mid-fourth century Athens there were well-known recent cases of farmers who believed that their animals had been bewitched, as well as incidents in which maumets had been found. The difficulty for the court must always have been the issue of proof, the issue with which Plato opens his discussion.

The issue of astrology also needs differentiation. First, the documentary evidence for consultation of astrologers in the Hellenistic period is extremely meagre. The earliest papyrus horoscopes in Greek are for persons born between 50-1 BC (the earliest in fact for 10 BC), and there are only three of them; since the astronomical data listed in the horoscopes are all computed, the nominal date probably only reflects the popularity of astrology a generation later (Jones 1995, 31). The earliest surviving Demotic ostrakon horoscope is for a birth in 38 BC; the earliest archaeological horoscope, for an occasion in 62 BC; the earliest literary horoscope, for a person born in 72 BC. One plausible reason for the absence of early horoscopes on papyrus is that, being at the bottom of the rubbish dumps where they were thrown, they sank below the water table and rotted away: there are very few Hellenistic papyri altogether. On the other hand there is indirect evidence for the success of Hellenistic astrology in the speed with which the authorities at Rome moved against it after its introduction by Manilius of Antioch (Pliny *HN* 35.199). Astrologers were expelled by the praetor peregrinus for the first time in 139 BC (Val. Max. 1.3.3; cf. Livy, *Per.* 54). And slightly earlier, Cato the Elder, who died in 149 BC, mentions the astrologer, *chaldaeus*, in a list of diviners whom a slave bailiff ought not to be permitted to consult (*Agr.* 1.5.4).[60]

But it may be that we should make a relatively sharp distinction for the Hellenistic world between the two main forms of astrology, that is between genethliacal or natal astrology and catarchic astrology or "interrogations". To be sure, genethliacal astrology is the main, often the sole, subject of the surviving treatises, because it was more difficult and involved more skill. But that emphasis may only tell us about the ideal priorities of their authors. It need not tell us what most clients wanted. I suggest that what they wanted, much more often than a natal horoscope, was a prediction of the success of an intended but risky venture, a journey, a law suit or a marriage, about the fate of a prisoner, the identity of a thief. These are the typical problems discussed by Dorotheus in the fifth book of the *Carmen astrologicum*, on catarchic astrology. Analogous to these concerns was the prediction of high-risk outcomes, such as the winners of chariot-races. Moreover, schemes obtained from meteorological phenomena, that went back ultimately to the Babylonian Enuma Anu Enlil series, and were also considered "astrology", provided a form of prediction highly appropriate to the political conditions of the Hellenistic kingdoms and *mutatis mutandis* the later Roman Republic, around which popular opinion could crystallize. That is, I suggest, the spread of astrology was initially the spread of an adjunct to the armoury of low-level, contingent, divinatory means available in the Graeco-Roman world. It was a new means of providing advice — not answers as the modern critics would have it, but advice — on routine daily issues involving risk and uncertainty.

Whereas in Graeco-Roman Egypt astrology was connected mainly with the temple, the art quite evidently lost this institutional context as it spread into the Hellenistic world. It entered into a market relationship to its clients. The low-level practitioners of astrology, that is, the great majority, drew upon the prestige of high-level practitioners, of the writers of treatises, in a word of literacy, astronomy and technical difficulty, to make a niche for themselves in the market place of divinatory means. The success of catarchic astrology presupposes the wide penetration into the urban populations of purely instrumental, anonymous social relationships, the growth of the cash-nexus and no doubt an increase in the number of risk-laden enterprises an individual might undertake. Catarchic astrologers could claim to be all that wise women, ecstatics, diviners, oracle-mongers, reliant upon older informal methods, were not. In fact, we might see catarchic astrology, analogous to the Hellenistic dice oracle, as a thoroughly "modern" phenomenon in the Hellenistic world, and in particular as an early form of that archetypal expression of capitalist rationality, risk-insurance.

The commodity sold, a prediction of whether a given risk is worth running or not, is far from cut-and-dried. The modern critics' charge of irrationality is here, as in the similar case of modern newspaper horoscopes, particularly abstract. An example from Dorotheus will make the point: "If you find the benefics and malefics together in the ascendant or they aspect the ascendant, then know that this action will be middling with a mixture of good and evil in it" (5.2.5, p. 263 Pingree). Catarchic predictions could be negotiated with. They provided a limited frame of reference within which a pragmatic decision of whether to act or not could be made, in a wider context where real risks were often quite imponderable. Both sides, client and practitioner, thus had an interest in maintaining belief in the system. The "intrinsic" complexities of astrology protected both practitioner and client from the threat of disconfirmation.

Catarchic astrology was not only for the majority. The "coronation" horoscope for Antiochus I of Commagene (62 BC) on Nemrud Dağ suggests how kings might use such materials to bolster their legitimacy (Waldmann 1973, 151-52). But what of the social location of genethliacal astrology in the Hellenistic world outside Babylonia? The best guess is that it scarcely existed before the first century BC, and that even then it was mainly for the rich. It surely is telling that the identity of Antiochus' astrologer is unknown, that there are no Hellenistic figures comparable to Ti. Claudius Thrasylus and his son Balbillus, court astrologers to the Julio-Claudians.[61] But for the eminent, or the would-be-eminent, genethliacal astrology had much to offer. They could use it to confirm their exceptional political and social position, or ape such status, by having heaven, through the medium of an astrologer, take a special interest in them. As natives, they could represent themselves as the privileged subjects of a divine drama, men simultaneously destined and free, but also potentially tragic men who could endure the suffering, misfortune and reverse which must some day come.[62]

Saselberg 2, Ilmried
D-85304 Ilmmünster
Germany

Notes

* I would like to thank Troels Engberg-Pedersen and Roger Beck for their critical comments on earlier drafts; Roger Beck and David Konstan kindly checked specific references for me.

1. I have tried to keep to this time-frame in choosing citations, but for this material the "Hellenistic period" used by other contributors, and by for example, J. Barnes et al. 1982, xix, stretching from 300 BC to AD 200, would make at least as much sense.

2. See the (incomplete) lists of authors and texts in Röhr, 1923-24, 56-57 and Festugière 1950, 197. The basic discussions of *ta phusika*, which we may loosely translate as "natural magic", remain Oder 1890, 70-77; Weidlich 1894, 13-35; Hammer-Jensen, 1924; Wellmann 1928 (also 1916; 1924); Festugière 1950, 186-216. Some important reservations concerning Wellmann's assumptions and methods, with regard to his related work on the Physiologus (1930), in Alpers 1984.

3. *PMich* 149, col.6.13-20, tr. Robbins. The papyrus is in a second-century AD hand, though its contents may well be earlier.

4. Cf. the accounts by Galbreath 1971 and Eliade 1976 of the modern occultic revival.

5. See also the remarks of Dale Martin elsewhere in this volume (110-27).

6. Cf. Carey 1992, 6: "Just because we now reject both magic and astrology as irrational is no grounds for assuming they were equated in any way in medieval thinking".

7. *HN* 30.2; cf. Garosi 1976, 18. It is also true that the Zoroastrian pseudepigrapha contain works both on natural magic and on astrology.

8. I include here figures such as Epigenes of Byzantium, Protagoras of Nicaea, Critodemus, Sudines (cf. Hübner 1988), or Seleucus of Seleuceia, some of whom were also in our sense astronomers, e.g. the heliocentric theory of Seleucus. All are to be dated to the third and second centuries BC.

9. Cf. Fraser 1972, 1, 148-519 with notes.

10. "The book is one of the characteristic features of the Hellenistic world" (Pfeiffer 1978, 2, 132).

11. See Momigliano 1975; Kuhrt and Sherwin-White, 1987.

12. = FGrH 263T1 and F1 with commentary; cf. Kuhrt 1987, 545-46.

13. Wellmann's extensive discussion (1938) must, as usual, be used with caution. One main intermediary was probably Sudines (Kroll 1931).

14. Cf. Spoerri 1959, 105-7; W. and H.G. Gundel 1966, 45.

15. Astronomical procedure texts and ephemerides continued to be composed in cuneiform signs on clay tablets long after the alphabetisation of Mesopotamia (Oppenheim 1969, 125). Given the technical difficulties of these texts, Epigenes will have required competent native informants (Bowen and Goldstein 1988, 80).

16. Strab. 16.1.6; Pliny *HN* 6.121-25.

17. Oppenheim's view is cited by Reiner 1985, 592.

18. Democritus: Diog. Laert. 9.34-35 = Diels *Vorsokr.* 68A1, citing the two Hellenistic writers Antisthenes of Rhodes (FGrH 508 F12, second cent. BC) and Demetrius of Magnesia (first cent. BC); Ael. *VH* 4.20 = Diels 68A16; Hippol. *Haer.* 1.13 = Diels 68A40; Suda s.v. = Diels 68A2. Pythagoras: Diog. Laert. 8.3, with the parallel texts listed in Delatte's edition (p.105). It seems probable that the claim goes back at least to Aristoxenus of Tarentum (i.e. mid IVa) (frgs. 12-13 Wehrli). As a pair: Pliny *HN* 30.9; 25.23; cf. Cic. *Tusc.* 4.44; 55; *De Or.* 3.56.

19. Iambl. *Myst.* 8.1, p.195 des Places; the second figure is ascribed to Manetho.

20. Vettius Valens often refers to them as "the king and Petosiris"; in general, see Kroll 1935; Pingree 1974; also Festugière 1950, 88-186; W. & H.G. Gundel 1966, 10-36. The collection of texts ascribed to Nechepso and Petosiris by Rieß (1892) requires thorough revision.

21. The most judicious account, with full references to older literature, is to be found in Fraser 1972, 1, 440-44; a more indulgent one in Kingsley 1995, 325-28, 335-41. It is impossible to compile an agreed collection of Bolus' fragments, since so much depends upon one's judgment about his relation to the rest of the "Democritean" tradition (cf. Sbordone, 1940, xxi-xxix; Schmidt and Stählin 1948, 343; 346-47). The collection in Diels *Vorsokr.* 68 B300 was made under the direct influence of, or even by, Max Wellmann. His earlier collection of 82 fragments of the *Georgika* in 1921, 42-58 simply assumes that all "Democritean" passages on farming derive from Bolus.

22. Giannini speaks of Bolus' "hybrid and will o'the wisp character" (1964, 109).

23. The scholion on Nicander's *Theriaka* 764, calls him *ho Demokriteios*, the follower of Democritus (Diels *Vorsokr.* 68 B300.4). On the other hand, the first of the two Suda entries gives him the epithet *Pythagoreios*, a follower of Pythagoras (Diels *Vorsokr.* 68 B300.1).

24. *Democriti certe Chirocmeta esse constat*, "It is established that the *Chirocmeta* is definitely by Democritus": *HN* 24.160 = Diels *Vorsokr.* 68 B300.2.

25. Callimachus' provision of a Democritus-lexicon in his relevant *pinax* suggests that already he was aware of pseudo-Democritan books (Suda s.v. Kallimachos, ap. Diels *Vorsokr.* 68 A32, cf. Herter 1973, 188). But this must ante-date Bolus (contra Oder 1890, 73-74; Giannini 1964, 109). Pliny says of the supposed *Magika* of Democritus: "they are so deficient in credibility and every propriety that Democritus' admirers claim that these books are forgeries" (*HN* 30.9).

26. Deriving from Kroll 1934, 228.

27. Pliny, in an allusion to a parallel debate over a book by "Pythagoras" that some alleged had been written by Kleemporos, observes: "The very fact that an author of a book has judged it to be worthy of the great man, increases its authority" (*HN* 24.159).

28. The two titles are given as those of two separate books by the first Suda entry (Diels *Vorsokr.* 68 B300.1), cf. Giannini 1964, 109 n. 50. In his edition, Giannini seems in two minds about whether the book actually existed as a separate work (1966, 377 n. 1).

29. See Giannini 1964, 123 n.144 arguing against Ziegler 1949, 1153.36-1154.48; on the date: Ziegler, 1949, 1154.49-59; Giannini 1964, 122; Giannini 1966, 120.

30. *Anon. Rohdei*, ap. Diels *Vorsokr*. 68 B300.7a.

31. For Androtion, see esp. Theophr. *Caus.Pl.* 3.10.3-4 = Jacoby *FGrH* 324 F82; the bibliography is listed by Kingsley 1995, 299 n.34.

32. I differ here from recent emphasis upon the practical character of these writings (Beck 1991, 496-97; Kingsley 1995, 336-43).

33. See esp. Röhr 1923-24, 7-33; for *dunamis* in the Hippocratic writings, Plamböck 1964; also Souilhé 1919.

34. This is not the place to discuss either the relationship between the modern term (whatever it quite means) and possible ancient terms, nor between those ancient terms and actual practices. It will be enough to say that both issues are now under debate, cf. recently Faraone and Obbink (eds.) 1991; Meyer and Mirecki (eds.) 1995.

35. See Neugebauer 1942; Rochberg-Halton 1987, 1988, 1989.

36. The names of three Egyptian dream-interpreters, and three Egyptian scribes, *Musuraja*, appear in a Late Babylonian list of functions at the court in Nineveh (Oppenheim 1969, 100), so that the Babylonian influence on Egyptian omen texts of the XXVI Dynasty is hardly surprising (Parker 1959).

37. This was apparently Manilius' view, *Astron*. 1.40-64; Dorotheus claims to be "king of Egypt" and to be writing for his son Hermes (1.pr.2.; 5.1.1); cf. W. & H.G. Gundel 1966, 10-36 (with Pingree 1968); Barton 1994, 23-29.

38. At the same period the numerical tables (almanacs and ephemerides) required to prepare natal and catarchic horoscopes assimilate specifically Greek astronomical concepts.

39. On the complex issue of Manilius' sources, see in particular Abry 1983; Hübner 1993.

40. Goold 1977, xii; Liuzzi 1990, 11-15.

41. Different versions in Man. *Astron*. 2.856-967 (see fig. 13 in Goold 1977, lix); Paul. *Apoteles*. 14; Firmicus Maternus *Math*. 2.19-20 with P. Monat's notes (Budé).

42. In an obscure passage (2.856-63), Manilius attempts to explain the functioning of the temples more fully. There is a reciprocal relationship between stars and temples: each zodiacal sign and planet seems both to influence any temple it happens to enter, and to receive influences from it.

43. *Palmamque petens victrixque priorum / altius insurgit*, "seeking the prize and rising triumphantly above the earlier (temples)" (2.883-84).

44. *Astron*. 2.905-09; cf. Firm. Mat. *Math*. 2.19.10.

45. *Astron*. 2.929-38. Firmicus does not mention Saturn, but lists *parentes, patrimonium, substantiam, fundamenta, mobilia, et quicquid ad latentes et repositas patrimonii pertinet facultates*, "parents, (heritable) estates, property, substructures, chattels-personal, and anything to do with concealed or stored (i.e. hidden) wealth" (*Math*. 2.19.5).

46. The same scheme appears in the *Liber Hermetis trismegisti* p. 50.5-12 Gundel. Abry has attractively suggested that the two schemes go back to more primitive Hellenistic divisions of the horoscopal circle (1983, 55).

47. Bouché-Leclercq 1899, although in many details out-dated, remains the indispensable exposition of Graeco-Roman astrological doctrines.

48. This is certainly an originally Babylonian scheme (Rochberg-Halton 1988).

49. Oppenheim 1969; Rochberg-Halton 1993; Cumont 1937; Baccani 1989: 67-69; Jones 1995.

50. Schnabel 1923, 20 rightly maintained that Berosus' account of Chaldaean lore formed part of the *Babyloniaka*. Jacoby prints the accounts of Berosos the astrologer under (Pseudo-) Bero(s)os, *FGrH* 680 F15-22b.

51. Generally dated to the late third century BC, but this is a guess based on the list of early astrologers in Firm. Mat. *Math.* 4.proem.5 (2.127 Monat) (W. & H.G. Gundel 1966, 106).
52. Vett. Val. *Anthol.* 3.12 Kroll = 3.8.3, p. 142.12 Pingree; 9 pr. = 9.1.5, p. 316.
53. Note especially the numerous metaphors of the proem, 1.1-117, but also passages such as 2.137-49, where his poem is to be heard not by crowds of men but by the heavens alone. For the language of mysticism still in later astrologers, see Scott 1995, 114.
54. "Is it less valid to see coherent meaning in the stars, which are divine, than to pay attention to sacrificial animals and bird-calls?"
55. It has been suggested that the rôle of accumulating (dissonant) theories or schemes from earlier sources in each treatise is to indicate the antiquity — one might add also the depth, inventiveness and fecundity, all goods of a rhetorical education — of the art (Abry 1983, 52).
56. Goldhill, 1991, 261-72.
57. Cf. Dale Martin in this volume (110-27). For ancient criticism of astrology, Long 1982; Ioppolo 1984. Carey aptly observes of the medieval period: "The principle of celestial influence remained entrenched in the minds of the most 'rational' critics [of astrology]" (1992, 13).
58. Cf. Martin, 110-27 in this volume.
59. Richard Wünsch notoriously dated the bulk of his Attic *defixiones* to the Hellenistic period on the basis of inadequate comparison of the letter forms with those of public inscriptions (1897, 2). Wilhelm argued (1904) on the basis of the names that many of them were more likely to belong to the fourth century BC. The texts themselves have now mostly disappeared; but Ziebarth's later texts (1934) and some others (Faraone 1991, 30 n. 76) serve to support Wilhelm.
60. See also the other evidence collected by Cramer 1954, 44-50.
61. Sudines in the absurd story about Attalus I of Pergamum in Polyaenus *Strat.* 4.20, cf. Frontin. *Str.* 1.11.15, is represented as a hepatoscopist, not a court astrologer.
62. Cf. Achilles Tatius 1.3.2-4, cited by Konstan in this volume, p. 175 n. 39. Eliade attributes an analogous, though by now banal, "parareligious" function to the modern occult: "You admit, consciously or unconsciously, that a grand, though incomprehensible, cosmic drama displays itself and that you are part of it; accordingly, you are not *de trop*" (1976, 61).

Bibliography

Abry, J-H. 1983. "L'Astrologie à Rome: les *Astronomiques* de Manilius", *Pallas* 30, 49-61.

Alpers, K. 1984. "Untersuchungen zum griechischen Physiologus und den Kyraniden", *Vestigia Bibliae* 6, 13-87.

Baccani, D. 1989. "Appunti per oroscopi negli ostraca di Medinet Madi", *AnPap* 1, 67-77.

Barnes, J., Brunschwig, J., Burnyeat, M. & Schofield, M. (eds.) 1982. *Science and Speculation: Studies in Hellenistic theory and practice*. Cambridge/Paris.

Barnes, T.D. (ed.) 1995. *The Sciences in Greco-Roman Society* (Apeiron 27,4). Edmonton.

Barton, T. 1994. *Ancient Astrology*. London/New York.

Beagon, M. 1992. *Roman Nature: the thought of Pliny the Elder*. Oxford.

Beck, R.L. 1991. "Thus spake not Zarathuštra: Zoroastrian pseudepigrapha of the Greco-Roman world", in: Boyce & Grenet, 1991, 491-565.

Bidez, J. & F. Cumont 1938. *Les Mages hellénisés: Zoroastre, Ostanès et Hystaspe d'après la tradition grecque*. Paris.

Bilde, P. 1993. "Jesus and Paul: a Methodological Essay on two Cases of Religious Innovation in the Context of Centre-Periphery Relations", in: Bilde et al. (eds.), 1993, 316-38.

Bilde, P., Engberg-Pedersen, T., Hannestad, L., Zahle, J. & K. Randsborg (eds.) 1993. *Centre and Periphery in the Hellenistic World.* (SHC 4). Aarhus.

Boll, F. 1922. s.v. Kritodamos (4), in: *RE* 11, 1928-30.

Bouché-Leclercq, A. 1899. *L'Astrologie grecque.* Paris.

Bourdieu, P. 1971. "Genèse et structure du champ religieux", *RevFSoc* 12, 295-334.

Bowen, A.C. & B.R. Goldstein 1988. "Meton of Athens and Astronomy in the late fifth century BC", in: E. Leichty et al. (eds.) 1988, 39-81.

Boyce, M. & F. Grenet 1991. *A History of Zoroastrianism, 3: Zoroastrianism under Macedonian and Roman Rule.* (Handbuch der Orientalistik I.8.i.2.2). Leiden.

Burkert, W. 1987. *Ancient Mystery Cults.* Cambridge, Mass./London.

Carey, H.M. 1992. *Courting Disaster: Astrology at the English Court and University in the Later Middle Ages.* Basingstoke.

Cavallo, G. 1983. "Alfabetismo e circolazione del libro", in: Vegetti (ed.) 1983, 166-86.

Cramer, F.H. 1954. *Astrology in Roman Law and Politics.* (MemAPhilSoc 37). Philadelphia.

Cumont, F. 1937. *L'Égypte des astrologues.* Brussels.

Delatte, A. 1938. *Herbarius. Recherches sur le cérémoniel usité chez les anciens pour la cueillette des simples et des plantes magiques* (2nd ed.). (Bibliothèque de la Faculté de Philosophie et Lettres de l'Université de Liége 71). Liège.

Diels, H. 1920. *Antike Technik* (2nd ed.). Berlin.

Dodds, E.R. 1951. *The Greeks and the Irrational* (Sather Classical Lectures 25). Berkeley/Los Angeles.

Eliade, M. 1976. "The Occult and the Modern World", in: Eliade, M., *Occultism, Witchcraft and Cultural Fashions: Essays in Comparative Religions,* 47-68. Chicago.

Evans-Pritchard, E.E. 1937. *Witchcraft, Oracles and Magic among the Azande.* Oxford.

Faraone, C.A. 1991. "The Agonistic Context of Early Greek Binding Spells", in: Faraone & Obbink (eds.) 1991, 3-32.

Faraone, C.A & D. Obbink (eds.) 1991. *Magika Hiera: Ancient Greek Magic and Religion.* New York/Oxford.

Festugière, A-J. 1950. *La révélation d'Hermes Trismégiste, 1: l'astrologie et les sciences occultes* (2nd ed.). Paris.

Flammini, G. 1993. "Manilio e la 'sollertia' nelle storia delle acquisizione tecnico-scientifiche: *Astron.* praef. 66-95", in: D. Liuzzi (ed.) 1993, 185-94.

Fraser, P.M. 1972. *Ptolemaic Alexandria.* Oxford.

Gabba, E. 1984. "Scienza e potere nel mondo ellenistico", in: Giannantoni & Vegetti (eds.) 1984, 13-37.

Galbreath, R. 1971. "The History of Modern Occultism: a Bibliographical Survey", *JPCult* 5, 726-54.

Galter, H.D. (ed.) 1993. *Die Rolle der Astronomie in den Kulturen Mesopotamiens.* (Grazer Morgenländische Studien 3). Graz.

Garosi, R. 1976. "Indagine sulla formazione del concetto di magia nella cultura romana", in: Xella (ed.) 1976, 13-93.

Gernet, L. 1951. "Introduction", in: *Platon, Oeuvres complètes* (Budé) 11, xciv-ccvi. Paris.

Giannantoni, A. & M. Vegetti (eds.) 1984. *La scienza ellenistica. Atti delle 3 Giornate di Studio tenutesi a Pavia, 14-16 Aprile 1982.* (Elenchos 9 [Pavia]).

Giannini, A. 1964. "Studi sulla paradossografia greca, 2: da Callimaco all'età imperiale — la letteratura paradossografica", *Acme* 17, 99-140.

Giannini, A. 1966. *Paradoxographorum graecorum reliquiae.* (Classici greci e latini, sez. Testi e Commenti 3). Milano.

Goldhill, S.D. 1991. *The Poet's Voice: Essays on Poetics and Greek Literature.* Cambridge.

Goold, J.P. (ed., trans.) 1977. *Manilius, Astronomica.* Cambridge, Mass./London.

Gordon, R.L. 1987. "Aelian's Peony: the location of magic in Graeco-Roman tradition", in: *Comparative Criticism: A Yearbook* (E.S. Shaffer ed.) 9, 59-95. Cambridge.

Grafton, A. 1992. *Fälscher und Kritiker: der Betrug in der Wissenschaft* (Kleine Kulturwiss. Bibliothek 32). Berlin. (Original title: *Forgers and Critics: Creativity and Duplicity in Western Scholarship,* Princeton 1990).

Green, P. 1990. *From Alexander to Actium: the Hellenistic Age.* London.

Greenfield, J.C. & M. Sokoloff 1989. "Astrological and related omen texts in Jewish Palestinian Aramaic", *JNES* 48, 201-14.

Gundel, W. & H-G. Gundel 1966. *Astrologumena: die astrologische Literatur in der Antike und ihre Geschichte.* (Sudhoffs Archiv, Beiheft 6). Wiesbaden.

Hammer-Jensen, I. 1924. s.v. Demokritos (Pseudo-Demokrit), in: *RE* Suppl. 4, 219-23.

Harris, W.V. 1989. *Ancient Literacy.* Cambridge, Mass./London.

Herter, H. 1973. s.v. Kallimachos 6, Nachtrag, in: *RE* Suppl. 13, 184-266.

Hübner, W. 1982. *Die Eigenschaften der Tierkreiszeichen in der Antike: ihre Darstellung und Verwendung unter besonderer Berücksichtigung des Manilius.* (Sudhoffs Archiv, Beiheft 22). Wiesbaden.

Hübner, W. 1988. "Zum Planetenfragment des Sudines, P. Genv. inv. 203", *ZPE* 73, 33-42.

Hübner, W. 1989. "Die Begriffe 'Astrologie' und 'Astronomie' in der Antike", *AbhMainz* 1989, 7. Wiesbaden.

Hübner, W. 1993. "Manilio e Teucro di Babilonia in Manilio", in: D. Liuzzi (ed.) 1993, 21-40.

Hughes, G.R. 1951. "A Demotic Astrological Text", *JNES* 10, 256-64.

Ioppolo, A.M. 1984. "L'astrologia nello stoicismo antico", in: Giannantoni & Vegetti (eds.) 1984, 73-91.

Jones, A. 1995. "The Place of Astronomy in Roman Egypt", in: T.D. Barnes (ed.) 1995, 25-51.

Kingsley, P. 1995. *Ancient Philosophy, Mystery, and Magic: Empedocles and Pythagorean Tradition.* Oxford.

Kroll, W. 1931. s.v. Sudines, in: *RE* 4A, 563.

Kroll, W. 1934. "Bolos und Demokritos", *Hermes* 69, 228-32.

Kroll, W. 1935. s.v. Nechepso, in: *RE* 16, 2160-67.

Kuhrt, A. 1987. "Assyrian and Babylonian traditions in classical authors: a critical synthesis", in: Nissen & Renger (eds.) 1987, 539-53.

Kuhrt, A. & S. Sherwin-White (eds.) 1987. *Hellenism in the East: the interaction of Greek and non-Greek civilizations from Syria to central Asia after Alexander.* London.

Laurenti, R. 1985. "La questione Bolo-Democrito", in: *L'atomo fra scienza e letteratura, 12 Giornate filologiche genovesi, 20-1 Febbraio 1984.* (Pubbl. dell'Ist. di filol. class. e med. dell'Univ. di Genova 91), Genova, 75-106.

Leichty, E., Ellis, M. de J. & Gerardi, P. (eds.) 1988. *A Scientific Humanist: Studies in Memory of Abraham Sachs.* (Occasional Publ. of the Samuel Noah Kramer Fund 9). Philadelphia.

Liuzzi, D. 1990. *M. Manilio, Astronomica 1.* Lecce.

Liuzzi, D. (ed.) 1993. *Manilio fra poesia e scienza: Atti del convegno, Lecce 14-16 Maggio 1992.* Lecce/Catalina..

Lloyd, G.E.R. 1979. *Magic, Reason and Experience: Studies in the origins and development of Greek science.* Cambridge.

Lloyd, G.E.R. 1983. *Science, Folklore and Ideology: Studies in the Life Sciences in Ancient Greece*. Cambridge.

Lloyd, G.E.R. 1987. *The Revolutions of Wisdom: Studies in the Claims and Practice of ancient Greek science*. (Sather Classical Lectures 52). Berkeley/Los Angeles.

Long, A.A. 1982. "Astrology: arguments pro and contra", in: J. Barnes et al. (eds.) 1982, 165-92.

McIntosh, C. 1972. *Eliphas Lévi and the French Occult Revival*. London.

Martini, M.C. 1977. *Piante medicamentose e rituali magico-religiosi in Plinio*. (Biblioteca di Cultura 125). Roma.

Meyer, M. & P. Mirecki (eds.) 1995. *Ancient Magic and Ritual Power*. Leiden.

Momigliano, A. 1975. *Alien Wisdom: the limits of Hellenization*. Cambridge.

Müller, C.W. 1965. "Die Heilung 'durch das Gleiche' in den hippokratischen Schriften *De morbo sacro* und *De locis in homine*", *Sudhoffs Archiv f. Geschichte der Medizin u. Naturwissensch.* 49, 225-49.

Neugebauer, O. 1942. "On some astronomical Papyri and related Problems of ancient Geography", *TAPhSoc* n.s. 32, 251-63.

Neugebauer, O. 1949. "The Astronomical Treatise *P. Ryl. 27*", *Det Kongelige Danske Videnskaberskabernes Selskab. Historisk-filosofiske Meddelelser* 32,2. Copenhagen.

Nilsson, M.P. 1961. *Geschichte der griechischen Religion* (2nd ed). (HAW 5.2.2). München.

Nissen, H.J. & J. Renger (eds.) 1987. *Mesopotamien und seine Nachbarn: Politische und kulturelle Wechselbeziehungen im alten Vorderasien vom 4. bis 1. Jahrtausend v. Chr.* (2nd ed.). (Berliner Beiträge zum Vorderen Orient 1). Berlin.

Oder, W. 1890. "Beiträge zur Geschichte der Landwirtschaft bei den Griechen", *RhM* 45, 70-77.

Oder, W. 1910. s.v. Geoponica, in: *RE* 7, 1221-25.

Oppenheim, A.L. 1959. "A new Prayer to the 'Gods of the Night'", *AnalectaBibl* 12, 282-301.

Oppenheim, A.L. 1969. "Divination and celestial observation in the Last Assyrian Empire", *Centaurus* 14, 97-135.

Parker, R.A. 1959. *A Vienna Demotic Papyrus on Eclipse and Lunar Omina*. (Brown Egyptological Studies 2). Providence.

Piccaluga, G. 1987. "La mitizzazione del Vicino Oriente nelle religioni del mondo classico", in: Nissen & Renger (eds.) 1987, 573-612.

Pingree, D. 1968. Review of W. & H.G. Gundel 1966, *Gnomon* 40, 276-80.

Pingree, D. 1974. s.v. Petosiris, *Dictionary of Scientific Biography* 10, 547-49.

Pingree, D. 1987. "Mesopotamian astronomy and astral omens in other civilizations", in: Nissen & Renger (eds.) 1987, 613-31.

Pfeiffer, R. 1978. *Geschichte der klassischen Philologie* (2nd ed.). München.

Plamböck, G. 1964. "Dynamis im Corpus Hippocraticum", *AbhMainz* 1964, 2. Wiesbaden.

Reiner, E. 1985. "The uses of astrology", *JAOS* 105, 589-95.

Reverdin, O. 1945. *La Religion de la cité platonicienne* (École française d'Athènes, Travaux et Mémoires 6). Paris.

Rieß, E. 1892. "Nechepsonis et Petosiridis fragmenta magica", *Philologus Supplb.* 6 (1891-93), 325-94.

Rieß, E. 1894. s.v. Aberglaube, in *RE* 1, 30-93.

Rochberg-Halton, F. 1987. "TCL 6.13: Mixed Traditions in late Babylonian Astrology", *ZDMG* 77, 207-28.

Rochberg-Halton, F. 1988. "Elements of the Babylonian contribution to Hellenistic astrology", *JAOS* 108, 51-62.

Rochberg-Halton, F. 1989. "Babylonian horoscopes and their sources", *Orientalia* 58, 102-23.

Rochberg-Halton, F. 1993. "The Cultural Locus of Astronomy in Late Babylonia", in: Galter (ed.) 1993, 31-45.

Röhr, J. 1923-24. "Der okkulte Kraftbegriff im Altertum", *Philologus Supplb.* 17, 1-95. Leipzig.

Sachs, A. 1967. "La naissance de l'astrologie horoscopique en Babylonie", *Archéologia* (Paris) 15, 13-19.

Saunders, T.J. 1991. *Plato's Penal Code: Tradition, Controversy and Reform in Greek Penology.* Oxford.

Sbordone, F. (ed.) 1940. *Hori Apollinis, Hieroglyphica.* Napoli.

Schmidt, W. & O. Stählin 1948. *Geschichte der griechischen Literatur bis auf die Zeit Justinians* 1.5. (HAW 7.1.5). München.

Schnabel, P. 1923. *Berossos und die babylonisch-hellenistische Literatur.* Leipzig.

Scott, A.B. 1995. "Churches or Books? Sethian Social Organization", *JEarlyCSt* 3, 109-22.

Souilhé, J. 1919. *Étude sur le terme* δύναμις *dans les dialogues du Platon.* Paris.

Spoerri, W. 1959. *Späthellenistische Berichte über Welt, Kultur und Götter.* Basel.

Vegetti, M. (ed.) 1983. *Oralità, scrittura, spettacolo.* Torino.

Waldmann, H. 1973. *Die kommagenischen Kultreformen unter König Mithradates I. Kallinikos und seinem Sohne Antiochos I* (EPRO 34). Leiden.

Weidlich, T. 1894. *Die Sympathie in der antike Literatur.* Stuttgart.

Weidner, E.G. 1967. "Gestirn-Darstellungen auf babylonischen Tontafeln", *AbhWien, phil.-hist. Klasse* 1967.2. Wien.

Wellmann, M. 1916. "Pamphilos", *Hermes* 51, 1-64.

Wellmann, M. 1921. "Die Georgika des Demokritos", *AbhBerlin, phil.-hist. Klasse* 4. Berlin.

Wellmann, M. 1924. "Beiträge zur Quellenanalyse des älteren Plinius", *Hermes* 59, 129-56.

Wellmann, M. 1928. "Die Φυσικά des Bolos-Demokritos und der Magier Anaxilaos aus Larissa, 1", *AbhBerlin, phil.-hist. Klasse* 7. Berlin.

Wellmann, M. 1930. "Der Physiologus: eine religionsgeschichtlich-naturwissenschaftliche Untersuchung", *Philologus Supplb.* 22,1. Leipzig.

Wellmann, M. 1938. "Die Stein- und Gemmenbücher der Antike", *Quellen und Studien zur Geschichte der Naturwissenschaften und der Medizin* 4:4, 86-149.

Wilhelm, A. 1904. "Über die Zeit einiger attischen Fluchtafeln", *ÖJh* 7, 105-26.

Winkler, J.J. 1991. "The Constraints of Eros", in: Faraone & Obbink (eds.) 1991, 214-43.

Wünsch, R. 1897. *Defixionum Tabellae. IG* III, 3, Appendix. Berlin. (Cited here from the reprint, *Inscriptiones Atticae, Supplementum Inscriptionum Atticarum*, 1 [Chicago 1976]).

Xella, P. (ed.) 1976. *Magia: studi di storia delle religioni in memoria di Raffaella Garosi.* Rome.

Ziebarth, E. 1934. "Neue Verfluchungstafeln aus Attika, Boiotien und Euboia", *SBBerlin* 33, 1022-55.

Ziegler, K. 1949. s.v. Paradoxographoi, in: *RE* 18.3, 1137-66.

CONVENTIONAL VALUES OF THE
HELLENISTIC GREEKS:
THE EVIDENCE FROM ASTROLOGY

David Konstan

Although the manual on the interpretation of dreams composed by Artemidorus of Daldis has been mined by several scholars as a source for popular beliefs,[1] little use has been made in this respect of the several astrological treatises that survive from classical antiquity.[2] As evidence for conventional values in the Hellenistic period, the astrological handbooks are of particular utility, since the vogue for such treatises began only after the conquests of Alexander had brought the Greeks into more systematic contact with practices in the East.[3] Earlier, there may have been a vague belief in the efficacy of the planets on human fortune, but nothing like the rigorous science represented in the manuals. The association of birth signs with specific consequences or prescriptions was thus a Hellenistic phenomenon in the Greek-speaking world, and is likely to have been relatively uncontaminated by earlier social expectations and assumptions.

The Greek handbooks may, to be sure, betray some influence of Eastern lore in the assignment of character types and other consequences to celestial patterns, but the world that they portray is in general congruent with contemporary Greek practices and institutions rather than with those of archaic Greece or Babylonia. There is, of course, the danger that treatises composed in the late antique period will reflect beliefs, popular or otherwise, of their own epoch rather than Hellenistic values proper, and the process of sorting out the residue of Hellenistic materials from later strata might have been next to impossible. By good fortune, however, there is now available a version of all five books of the *Carmen astrologicum* by Dorotheus of Sidon, which was composed around the year 50 in the first century AD, comfortably within the geographic and temporal limits for the Hellenistic period adopted by the editors of the present volume.

The poem of Dorotheus survives in an Arabic translation based on a third-century AD Pahlavi version; the Arabic text has recently been edited and provided with a literal translation into English by David Pingree (1976). Pingree has also

collected in an appendix all the Greek fragments of the poem as well as Latin
citations and testimonia. A comparison of these materials with the Arabic makes
it clear that the surviving version is broadly faithful to the original.[4] Thus, it can
generally be relied on to reflect Hellenistic values with reasonable fidelity.[5] It also
corresponds closely enough, in the materials that concern us, to astrological texts
composed slightly later, for example the *Tetrabiblos* of Claudius Ptolemaeus and
the *Anthologiae* of Vettius Valens, both dating to the second century AD, as well
as to the Latin *Astronomica* of Manilius, which is more or less contemporary with
Dorotheus' poem.[6] Even though, as Pingree writes, "Dorotheus asserts that he
drew his teachings from Babylonian and Egyptian sources, it is nevertheless
obvious that he owes all his teachings to the learning of the so-called Hellenistic
epoch, and not to earlier learning".[7] Occasional interpolations of later materials,
for example two insertions ascribed to Vettius Valens, are easily isolated.

In comparison with Ptolemy's handbook, not to say Manilius' versified treatise,
Dorotheus' poem has a further virtue for the discovery of popular values and
beliefs. Ancient astrology was conceived of as a science, and its theorists
developed complex and highly precise rules and measurements by which to draw
inferences from the stars concerning the human condition. Such calculations take
up a great deal of space in the more technical treatises such as those of Ptolemy
and Manilius.[8] Dorotheus, however, writes in a highly practical vein. His object
is to provide instructions to the novice astrologer (the book is addresssed to his
son) on how to take readings and offer predictions to the individuals and families
who consulted (and presumably paid) the professionals. Dorotheus is interested
precisely in what one is to tell the petitioner: "If you find Mars in quartile to the
Sun on the left side, then say that his father will die before his mother so that she
will become a widow" (1.15.2).[9] Thus, his book is all the more useful as a guide
to what people of his time wanted to know: their anxieties and hopes for the
future, what counted as success or failure, the rôles in life they might expect to
occupy, the comportment they regarded as admirable or the reverse, the actions
they commended, the personalities or characters they held in contempt.

There is no reason, moreover, to think that these expectations were characteristic
only of the highest strata in Hellenistic society. Dorotheus provides responses
concerning the possibilities and dangers that confront slaves as well as free people,
women as well as men, the poor and the rich alike. His text thus appears to be
a broad compendium of popular Hellenistic values, fears and aspirations. Indeed,
in the very limits of the subjects he sees fit to comment on one may gain insight
into the central preoccupations of people in his time.[10]

One of Dorotheus' basic principles in the interpretation of heavenly signs is metaphor or analogy. Thus, Sagittarius implies disease among horses, Leo among lions, etc. (1.1.6). Venus tends to involve matters of love, Jupiter of power, while Mercury suggests trickery, intelligence, and speech.[11] Dorotheus exploits an interpretive grid or rather grids, with possibilities of multiple intersections among the celestial symbols.[12] This method has consequences for the nature of Dorotheus' prognostications: some signs automatically predict good luck, for example, while others predict bad. Thus, that Dorotheus, in his treatment of runaway slaves in Book 5, anticipates a fair degree of success for the fugitives does not necessarily mean that he is sympathetic toward their plight. But an overview of the kinds of questions Dorotheus treats may serve as a map of the immediate concerns of those who consulted astrologers.

Books 1-4 focus on natal signs, while Book 5 concerns the signs under which an activity is undertaken (5.1). Books on commencements or *katarkhai* are not usual among surviving astrological treatises, and Dorotheus' is the earliest exemplar.[13] I shall review summarily the major categories, as I perceive them, in this last book before examining in greater detail materials from Books 1 and 2. Book 5, then, begins with questions concerning *Property*, including building a house (6) or demolishing one (7); renting property (8); buying and selling (9) in general and more specifically the buying of land (10), slaves (11),[14] and animals (12); the freeing of slaves (13); and, as a codicil, it would seem, chapters on asking for favours (14) and writing a letter (15).

Next comes the subject of *Marriage* (16). The fate of the couple's property is a central concern (5.16.13). The nativities of both partners may indicate mutual love (5.16.28), and may do so also in the case of two men or two women who form a friendship (5.16.29); it is of interest that love in marriage is analogous to friendly relations among same-sex partners. Dorotheus further treats the separation of couples (17), and whether the return of the woman to her husband's house bodes well or ill. This is followed by a brief section (18) on extracting a child from a woman's womb, which appears to be an appendix to the chapters on marriage.

The third general subject is *Business*, beginning with partnerships (18), which is something of a sequel to the section on marriage. This is followed by a discussion of debt (20); travel, including departure from home (21) and return (22) — topics closely related to the issue of trade; propitious and unpropitious signs for building or buying a ship (23);[15] "commencing to build a ship" (24); and launching it (25).[16] A codicil to this section concerns the arrival of a letter (26).

Fourth is *Personal welfare*, beginning with "Bondage and chains" (27): "If a man is bound because of the anger of kings or the anger of a man against his slaves, then look at the Moon at that hour" (5.27.1). The equivalence of the two structures of dependency — of an ordinary person upon a potentate and of a slave upon his master — is of interest, for it suggests that free people were in certain respects imagined to be as vulnerable to arbitrary treatment as slaves, an equation decidedly Hellenistic as opposed to attitudes characteristic of the classical democratic polis.[17] Imprisonment leads naturally (cf. ch. 28) to the topic of sickness (29, 31).

The fifth subject is *Loss of property*, beginning with a chapter on prospects for property in general (32), followed by cases tried before a judge (33) — who wins, who loses, and especially the question of the honesty of the judge.[18] A short chapter on exile (34) is perhaps a codicil to that on judgments. Theft (35) follows naturally upon judgments: a long chapter deals with whether stolen objects will be found, where they may be hidden, and who has received the stolen goods — the "fence" is an important figure in burglaries. There is a good deal on the condition and nature of the stolen property (5.35.44); I imagine that the latter theme served to test the astrologer's power, as in the prediction that it is "something worked in fire or in a kiln" (5.35.50).[19] There is also a lengthy discussion of the nature of the thief: "If the indicator of the characteristic[s] of the thief is Jupiter, then the thief will be white, fat, great in his eyes", etc. (5.35.86); Saturn indicates a repulsive face, black colour, small eyes, pallor,[20] hairy limbs, etc. (5.35.87). This kind of thing was, I imagine, safe material for the astrologer, who could intrigue his audience with details of the thief's constitution such as higher joints "more ample than his lower" (5.35.100), "bluish-black eyes" (5.35.103), and one leg larger and longer than the other (5.35.106). Still under the theme of loss of property comes the runaway slave (36), a topic akin to that of theft (cf. 5.36.51). Signs indicate whether escape is habitual in the slave (5.36.6), the direction of his flight (5.36.8-15), the cause of his flight, and the likelihood of recapture: a certain combination of the Moon and Venus shows, e.g., that the runaway "will not be caught, and if he is caught and sent back to his master, then he will be content with him" (5.36.22). Various other fates are predicted for the refugee as well, for example, drowning, crucifixion, and burning alive (5.36.35, 42, 43).

Sixth and last is *Sickness and death*, beginning with the exorcism of haunting spirits (37), which is followed by the kindred subject of medicine, including topics such as diarrhoea (38), surgery or cupping (39), infections of the eyes (40), and general prognosis (41). The attention to digestion and eye problems suggests the importance of such disorders. Book 5 concludes with a penultimate chapter on wills (42), followed by a final discussion (43), rather oddly placed, on the times at which to buy and sell at a fair price.

Such are the commencements, and Dorotheus' treatment reflects certain primary concerns: bondage and illness, loss of property, trade and debt, adjudication of quarrels, marriage and death. People wanted to know their chances of survival and success in a world of risk but relative stability: business, establishment of a family, and medical treatment were the major undertakings that required consultation with an astrologer.

I turn now to the books on nativities, and more particularly to the first two books (Books 3 and 4 are rather more technical). Book 1 concerns the upbringing and condition of the native, that is, the person whose birth signs are read, and first of all Dorotheus discusses whether the native will have "a good upbringing" or none at all (1.7.1). "If the Moon is as I told you and is in its own triplicity and the benefics aspect the malefics from trine, he is not ruined but he is brought up in another house than his parents' because he is expelled and is brought up in the house of strangers, and sometimes he will be a slave and will be employed and will be miserable" (1.7.14). Exposure or expulsion of children is a major preoccupation.

Signs also indicate social status, in particular whether the native is a slave or free (1.10): "If you find the Moon when the nativity is nocturnal in the seventh or fourth sign in the aspect of the malefics, judge for him destitution and slavery and difficulty in livelihood" (1.10.14). Other signs predict slavery (1.10.19, 20, 27, 29, etc.); still others promise manumission (1.10.26, 34, 39, etc.) or freedom throughout life (1.10.30). Another chapter (11) is devoted to "how many will own the native if he is a slave".

Inheritance is a major concern (1.12.17-20), and thus the condition of the parents is relevant: certain signs indicate that "all the property of his father and his mother will be squandered" (1.12.31); the father may also "desire his expulsion and his ousting from the house" (1.12.34). Thus, specific chapters are dedicated to the lots of the father and mother (13-14); status and property are the main topics (e.g., 1.14.7), as well as the parents' divorce (1.14.8-16). Another section concerns the death of the parents (15); yet another, inheritance of their property (16) — both the father's and the mother's.

There follow chapters on the number of children the mother will bear before and after the native (17), the number of brothers (18), their fortunes (19), the love or enmity between them (20), and related matters such as whether some brothers are in fact sons of concubines (1.21.9). Other signs indicate absence of brothers, or that those who are born "will not survive or will be enemies" (1.21.31); but "If you find the lot of fortune and the lot of brothers together, then he will benefit from his brothers and, if they die, he will inherit their properties" (1.21.36).

In family affairs, the question of property is always present, and in the following chapters (22-27), Dorotheus turns naturally to the topic of the native's fortune, which includes his wealth, health, and property. A few sample charts illustrate fortunes such as being "praised with the praise of kings and nobles and wealthy men" (1.24.7), great eminence and wealth (1.24.11), poverty (1.24.13-14), slavery (1.24.19), recognition from "nobles and mighty people" (1.26.23), high station or the reverse (1.26.24, 25), loss of property (1.26.27, 31, 33), etc. Status and property are closely related: "If you find Saturn with the Moon in one of the cardines, then, even if he is the son of a king, it indicates his fall from fortune and property" (1.27.1; cf. 1.27.16). Wealth and patronage are connected (1.27.17-18); enmities are dangerous, especially within the family (1.27.37-40).

The second book of Dorotheus treats marriage and children. A bad sign indicates that one "will never marry" or will have a "marriage with slave girls or whores or old women who are disgraced or those young in years, or he is a leaser of whores; we have seen someone in [a nativity] like this who leased his wife, and he was disgraced in this" (2.1.3; cf. 2.16.11, 2.18.7). The shameful behaviour of the wife is a cause of considerable consternation: "If you find Venus cadent [and] Mars and Jupiter aspecting it by day while the lords of its triplicity are in midheaven, then they indicate that the wife will be a whore, well known in the mouths of the majority of men, because Jupiter indicates fame in the city, but this [native] will attain disgrace from its [Venus'] badness" (2.1.7). Contrariwise, "If Jupiter is with Venus, then predict that he will have intercourse with a praiseworthy woman" (2.1.11); other signs indicate that the wife will be of low class, a foreigner or pauper, or else a singer or dancer (2.1.14-15). A woman's lot may predict "women who will marry [several] men in succession and will play the whore with men" (2.3.3), or else that she will marry a relative (2.3.4); if she is a slave, the same sign indicates that she will marry her master (2.3.5).

One may be tempted to see here an anxiety over the chastity of wives comparable to that in modern Mediterranean communities as described by various anthropologists and sometimes projected back to Greek and Roman society.[21] But I am not convinced that Dorotheus' account reveals a society predicated on shame and honour in domestic life based on the reputation of female relations. For example, Dorotheus notes: "If Venus is with Mercury and Mars, then this indicates that he will be one who will have no stability in marriage, but he will rejoice in this woman one time, in that woman another time. If with this they are in midheaven and Venus is in midheaven while Mars and Mercury aspect [it], then this native will be one of those men who befriend women. If he is one [for] whom [the planets] aspecting Venus are eastern, then this will occur publicly" (2.3.15-17). Dorotheus in the next sentence returns to the woman's debauchery. There seems to be an equivalence here between men's and women's sexual behaviour. The perspective remains that of the man, but the issue is not so much shameful conduct in and of itself as its effect on marriage and the household; corrupt behaviour on the part of either spouse puts the condition and reputation of the house at risk.

Not marrying at all is thus equivalent to marriage with a bad woman: neither leads to a sound estate and inheritance. So too, marriage with a slave or stranger bodes ill, quite independently of the character of the woman. Consider the following: "If Venus is in the cardine under the earth, it indicates the death of the native's woman and of his child ... If the cardine under the earth is a tropical sign, especially Cancer or Capricorn, then this is bad and worse because the native will be desirous of intercourse with disgraced women or whores in public, and debt will always come upon him because of this" (2.4.11-12). Women's infidelity is coupled with barrenness as twin consequences of a single celestial pattern (2.4.14). Marriage with widows is a problem because they may be past childbearing (2.4.15). Signs that indicate marriage to a sister or near relative involve the prospect of children as well (2.4.17-18). The estate and inheritance are always central to Dorotheus' concerns.

Marriage with relatives leads to the possibility of intercourse in prohibited or suspicious degrees, as with a man's own daughter or older sister or maternal aunt (2.4.20); from this Dorotheus passes easily to a man's marriage with "a woman in whom he will take pleasure, but, however that is, the loss of his property will come upon him because of the woman, but if the native is female, then the woman is a Lesbian" (2.4.21).[22] The question of a woman's sexual comportment, which responds to the position of Venus and other combinations of planets and stars, is simply one more factor in a successful marriage, along with longevity of the spouses, production of children, status of the partners, wantonness or multiple marriages of the husband, etc., all relating to the stability of the family rather than centering on the question of honour as such. Dorotheus follows this discussion with a chapter on the number of times a man or woman will marry (5): "If you find Venus cadent from midheaven, say [that there is] little constancy toward women in men, and say similarly in the woman with respect to their husbands if you find Mars in the seventh" (2.5.3); so too, death of a man's women is associated with a lack of constancy in the man, and a related sign indicates "for women the death of their husbands" (2.6.6-7). The symmetry is apparent (cf. also 2.5.12, 15).

The section on marriage concludes with a treatment of homoeroticism (7). "If Venus is in the house of Mercury and Mercury is in a bad place, then the native will not love women, but his pleasure will be in boys" (2.7.2). Comparably, "If Venus is in the cardine of the West in opposition and the Moon is in the ascendent, then, if the native is female, it indicates that she will be a Lesbian, desirous of women, and if the native is a male, he will be desirous of males" (2.7.6). The parallelism between the sexes is striking. Now, as is well known, Greek homoeroticism was asymmetrical: the distinction between the active and receptive partners was qualitative.[23] Dorotheus reflects this attitude as well: under certain signs involving Venus and Saturn, "the native will be effeminate [and] will be one of those in whom one does [something] like what one does in women" (2.7.9); Venus may also indicate that "the native will be effeminate, weak in his joints and strength, and one will do in him the act of women" (2.7.10; cf. 2.26.15). Again, certain signs indicate of a woman that "she will be a Lesbian", while the corresponding conjunction in a masculine sign indicates for males that "they will not do to women as they ought to" (2.7.12) Finally, certain combinations indicate that "the woman will be notorious for adultery" (2.7.15); there follows immediately: "If you find, in the nativity of females, the two luminaries in masculine signs and Venus in a masculine sign, in the cardines, then this native, if it is a female, is one of those [women] who do in women the act of men" (2.7.16; cf. 2.26.15). The chapter concludes with a further sign indicating that women "will have much intercourse with men and a great number of men will have intercourse with them" (2.7.17).

Women's eroticism is thus analogous to that of men in being asymmetrical: the dominant female who adopts the part of the male corresponds to the male who assumes the rôle of a woman in intercourse. Lesbians in the male rôle are further associated, by juxtaposition, with a hyperactive sexuality. I am not sure of the extent to which pre-Hellenistic sources analogize sexual relations between women to the asymmetrical model of masculine pederasty: to my mind, the poems of Sappho, for example, do not indicate a necessary difference in rôle between lover and beloved.[24] Here, however, the parallelism is clear: males and females are alike in that a desire for one of the same sex is associated with a reversal of customary gender rôles.

The handbook of Dorotheus may also shed light on a question that has excited considerable controversy recently in the area of ancient sexuality. While some scholars have argued that the ancient Greeks did not regard sexual preference as a fixed characteristic constitutive of a person's identity — these are the so-called constructionists — others have maintained that catamites, at all events, and the tribad or dominant female were recognized as distinct types or natures; they were not perceived simply as optional styles of behaviour, like a preference for meat versus fish, for example.[25] On the surface of it, at least, the idea that sexual preference is indicated by the stars at a person's nativity would seem to suggest that homoeroticism, and in particular the rôles of catamite and tribad, are innate and inalterable. Dorotheus' text may thus be seen as support for the anti-constructionist interpretation of sexual codes in classical antiquity. Dorotheus, we may note, is consistent with Manilius (e.g. 5.140-56) and Claudius Ptolemy (3.14.171-73; 4.5.188) in this respect.[26]

But perhaps the issue is not so neatly resolved. Indeed, the problem may lead to questions that lie at the very heart of the practice of astrology and the view of life on which it rests. For, as we have seen, the planets and constellations indicate not just sexual style but also such matters as wealth and poverty, number of children, success in marriage or business, health and sickness, slavery or freedom, one's profession, personal continence, traits of character — a whole range of consequences, most of which we would not necessarily classify as aspects of a person's identity or inborn characteristics that mark one's inner nature. It is we — or at all events I — who have raised the issue of identity in connection with sexuality, as opposed to the other traits or properties treated by Dorotheus. After all, homoerotic behaviour is discussed by Dorotheus as a codicil to his treatment of marriage, representing, it would appear, the case in which marriage will not be contracted (and, consequently, in which there will be no children or heirs); it does not seem to be a subject of special interest to Dorotheus in its own right.

When the heavens indicate that a man will be prosperous and then lose his wealth, in the kind of complex story that Dorotheus sometimes spins from his celestial observations, it does not obviously mean that wealth or poverty are attributes of the individual. All that can be said is that the stars indicate how things will turn out. So too, they indicate that certain people will turn out to have conventional sexual preferences while others will be different. Dorotheus informs us, of course, that a man who plays the rôle of a woman in sex is a type worth noting, just as it is of interest — vital interest, indeed — whether a person will turn out to be free or enslaved. Astrology does not fix natures as slave or free, fertile or childless, active or passive in sex; it tells what will occur and what people will do.

Following the discussion of marriage (the text notes the transition explicitly at this point, thus subsuming the treatment of sexuality under marriage) comes, naturally enough, the matter of children (8-13). It is good to have many children: "If Saturn is with it [sc. the sign of few children], then it indicates that he will be sterile or will have few children or will be grieved with an intense grief on account of [his] children" (2.10.11; cf. 2.10.16). Parents are evidently interested as well in the number of male and female children they will have (2.12.1-3, 2.13.1-4), but there is no great stress on this topic, which is handled parenthetically in the discussion of numbers of children generally. Death and expulsion of children are both treated as examples of misfortune (2.12.4, 2.13.4). Adoption may compensate for the loss of children (2.14.2).

The rest of Book 2 deals with the effects of planets in various positions, and so constitutes a miscellany of predictions, e.g. support from kings and nobility (2.14.7) or service in the courts of kings (2.14.12), and leadership, whether of men, in business, in commerce, or of armies (2.14.14). Mars aspecting Venus from trine indicates horsemanship and love of women, apparently regarded as two forms of mounting (2.14.18). There is also discussion of sickliness (2.15.4) and loss of inherited property (2.15.5) — these two misfortunes are often associated (e.g. 2.15.6, 12, 13, 23, 29; 2.18.2, 2.19.3, etc.); generosity (2.15.20); effeminacy or, alternatively, marriage with "slave girls or disgraced women" or debauchery among whores (2.15.25) — note again the connection between sexual license and the rôle of the catamite; greed (2.15.28); skill in crafts (2.15.33); shamelessness (2.15.37); stammering (2.16.12); self-reliance (2.16.20); stewardship for kings (2.18.1); leader of the community or city, or position of judge (2.19.1); learning in law or a position as secretary for potentates (2.19.8); death of brothers (2.21.5); career as teacher (2.27.6), under Mercury, of course, or as magician or thief (2.27.10), or overseer for kings (2.29.3; cf. 2.30.2); intercourse with one's brothers' wives or one's mother or, for women, with mothers' or sisters' husbands (2.33.10); love of wine and a swollen liver (4.1.71); poor hearing (4.1.73); eye problems (4.1.91, 111); suicide (4.1.164); being a midget (4.1.135). An unusual number of predictions involve being bitten by lions (2.16.5, 16; 2.22.5; 4.1.68; 4.1.150-51, etc.), generally as a consequence of Leo's influence.

The world of Dorotheus may be indicated in part by what it excludes: there is little of civic life, apart from the possibility of being a judge or finding oneself involved in a court process; most often, political advancement takes the form of being intimate with kings or grandees.[27] No predictions in the Arabic version deal with a military career, whether in a royal army or as a mercenary; however, Dorotheus himself certainly treated the subject of soldiering (Appendix II D [p. 432] in Pingree's edition), perhaps at some length — a salutary reminder of our faulty knowledge of the original. Nothing of athletics or the arts here: the one mention of poetry as an occupation concerns a debauched man who evidently composes seductive lyrics (2.19.27). Little too about natural disasters such as storms and floods that might do damage to agriculture; the contrast with the treatise on prognostication from thunderbolts attributed to Nigidius Figulus in the first century BC is in this respect striking.[28] Life revolves rather around inheritance, marriage, children, business (especially connected with seafaring), wealth and poverty. Concerns rarely extend beyond the nuclear family to more distant kin, fellow citizens, or friends (but see Appendix II E, F [pp. 432-34] in Pingree's edition for indications that friendship may have played a larger rôle in Dorotheus' original text); everything centres upon the patrimonial estate. Marriage is a mutual matter, and sexual excess or romantic involvement play little part except for their potential effect on the stability of the household; the emphasis is on constancy rather than on the "true love" that is so pervasive a preoccupation in modern horoscopes (and in Hellenistic literature, for example Apollonius of Rhodes and Theocritus). Trade or commerce may take one far from home, but the hope is to return again to the familial domain as soon as possible.

One vignette, more detailed than most in Dorotheus but indicative of the values he represents, runs: "If Mars aspects Mercury from opposition, then he will have little shame [but will be] a master of lies and books or bewitchment and injury, and his livelihood will be from this, and he will have little property, but his wife will be good, and he will not cease being surety and giving guarantees for it, but he will run away from the discharge of [his] trust, and he will submit it to the judges and to argument, and fear will come to him and dread of [his] superiors, and he will depart for places in a land other than his own, especially if Mercury is in Saturn's term or in its own term and house" (2.16.25).

The relative absence of interest in farming or stock-breeding suggests that Dorotheus may have had in mind primarily an urban audience for his astrological poem. In light of the importance Dorotheus accords to travel and shipping, one might be tempted to associate his composition more particularly with the area of Sidon, from which Dorotheus himself hailed, and the perennial involvement of the Phoenicians with commerce and the sea.[29] Such finely tuned inferences from the work as we have it are risky, however. Dorotheus' poem will have respected not only the actual interests of his contemporaries but also literary conventions and the tastes of a cultivated public, although its substantial influence on later handbooks may indicate that in its choice of topics it held appeal for a more general audience too.

The nature of the astrological art is no doubt in part responsible for the patterns that Dorotheus elicits from the heavens, as we have seen: planets have their particular associations, and in various combinations augur well or ill. Nevertheless, the overall themes, and the focus on private or familial life generally, seem characteristic of Hellenistic concerns, like those reflected by New Comedy, for example, in contrast to the topics of civic governance or war and peace broached by Aristophanes.[30] In dream manuals and other accounts of the interpretation of dreams, too, it appears that Hellenistic and later sources tended to dwell on domestic prospects, as opposed to examples of dream interpretations dating back to the time of the classical city-state in which there is a wider preoccupation with the values and activities of the community.[31] Such materials do not in themselves indicate that there was a decline in political commitment in the Hellenistic world. Rather, they suggest that new literary forms, such as astrological manuals, and the practices they subtended entered into the construction of a readership and clientele defined in part by a set of interests centred on personal life and fortunes. Astrology was the locus of a discourse that intersected with others, private and public, in Hellenistic Greece. It is of course important to determine which strata and segments of Greek society were engaged most actively with such procedures. Although the literary level and themes of Dorotheus' handbook suggest an educated, municipal, and perhaps commercially minded audience, however, it is hazardous to infer from the text the social profile of his constituency.

There remains the question of what a belief in astrology itself signifies for the values of Hellenistic Greeks. What does it mean for ordinary people to consult professional interpreters of horoscopes in the hopes of learning something of their future? What does it mean to believe that so much of what occurs in a lifetime is predetermined by the pattern of the planets and constellations? It would be easy, but also facile, to associate the Hellenistic interest in astrology with the rôle of magic, mystery religions, and the almost divine power of kings and princes — remote, inscrutable, implacable — over local life, and thus to take astrology as a symptom of insecurity and powerlessness in the face of forces beyond individual control.[32] A preoccupation with prognostication may arise under very various conditions, as the recent vogue of fortune-telling, astrology, and related practices in the United States and elsewhere indicates. What is more, a good case can be made that astrology reflected an interest in scientific precision rather than a need for reassuring superstition, and in this respect was a symptom of social confidence rather than the reverse.[33] Astrology refined and rendered mathematically rigorous rough prognostive techniques such as the reading of livers and omens, and had something of the appeal of, say, scientific weather forecasting today.[34]

Apart from the desire to know the future, however, the conviction that the events of one's life are determined by impersonal configurations in the heavens, rather than by human effort or desert, suggests a vision of the world that is based more on the blind action of fortune than on individual responsibility and reward of merit.[35] Such a view accords with the emphasis on *tuchê* that is to be found in Hellenistic documents, including inscriptions: more and more, chance is elevated to the position of a major deity.[36] The subordination of ethics and character to destiny is reflected, perhaps, in the collocation of personal traits such as generosity or greed with afflictions such as sickness or death, whether of oneself or of near relatives, in the predictions: how one behaves is as much a matter of fate as what happens to one in the world.[37] The contrast that is so clear in the Hellenistic philosophical schools between what is *par' hêmin* or *eph' hêmin*, that is, in one's own power, and what is beyond one's control appears to be suspended or abolished in the astrological tradition.[38] All is equally written in the stars — even our personal strengths and weaknesses; the most we can do is to be prepared for events when they arrive. In implying that only this minimal control is granted us over our destinies, the astrologers would seem to be at one with the dream interpreters, for it was a commonplace that the only advantage to be derived from prognostic dreams was a capacity to endure with tranquillity what will befall one.[39]

The Stoics too, of course, believed in the efficacy of the stars over human affairs, or rather in the interdependency of all of nature, celestial and terrestrial.[40] Anna Maria Ioppolo observes that "no Stoic could accept a strict predetermination of human destiny by means of the stars, because this would have meant the abolition of moral responsibility".[41] But perhaps, despite their emphasis on virtue, the rôle of individual control and responsibility had in fact contracted in Stoic belief to a very small domain of ethical freedom that resided more in understanding the interrelations among the totality of things than in effecting changes in one's own circumstances.

Or else the power of the stars was understood to be, in the end, obscure and contingent, susceptible to alteration for hidden reasons.[42] Astrology might thus be compatible with an abiding conviction in the virtue of hard work, decent behaviour, and love for one's family. These values are everywhere in evidence in Dorotheus' text as the substratum of his prognoses, the standard against which consequences are judged to be good or bad. The model life, if the stars permit it, is one of a stable marriage, abundance of children, good relations within and outside the family, and material prosperity — in a word, a conventional life, with just the right degree of deference to ideals of justice and moderation to permit a comfortable sense that prosperity, if one enjoys it, is one's due, while adversity, should it happen, is a thing beyond our control, to be endured as the will of heaven.

Department of Classics
Brown University
Providence, RI 02912
USA

Notes

1. E.g. Foucault 1984, 16-50; Price 1986; Winkler 1989a; MacAlister 1995. Bowersock 1994, 77-98 (esp. 80-87) has faulted Foucault, Winkler and MacAlister for taking the dreams reported by Artemidorus as typical rather than extraordinary and pertaining to an élite genre of predictive interpretation. As a witness to conventional values, however, the content of the dreams is of less interest than the content of the predictions, and it is to this latter category that the interpretations in the astrological writers correspond.

2. Exceptions are MacMullen 1971; Liviabella Furiani 1978; cf. also Tester 1987, 79-81; Barton 1994, 30.

3. See Cumont 1912, 30-32; Neugebauer 1962, 102-3; Long 1982, 166; Tester 1987, 19; Martin (this volume) init.; Gordon (this volume) section 2 init. Montanari Caldini 1973 notes that the Latin translation attributed to Germanicus (1st century AD) of Aratus' poem on the constellations (ca. 280 BC) introduces astrological motifs absent in the original.

4. Tester 1978, 434-35; but the caution of Saliba 1978, 110 is well taken: "the spirit of the text rather than the letter is what is preserved in the final product", i.e. the Arabic version that survives. My own sense is that our text of Dorotheus is closer to the prose paraphrases in Hephaestio (5th century) than to the actual verses of Dorotheus' poem that he quotes now and again in the course of his exposition. But when did the paraphrase tradition begin? David Pingree has indicated in a personal communication to me (25 January 1995) his belief that "the prose paraphrases in Hephaestio are his own"; on the basis of additional researches now in progress, however, he is persuaded that "the Pahlavi version antedated Hephaestio by at least a century and a half; but the Arabic version of it *to some extent* may have been influenced by later Greek authors who studied Dorotheus and explained and expanded much of his poetry. All of this, however, still requires a lot of work to sustain or disprove". Ole Thomsen suggested to me (oral communication) that the prose summaries or *diêgêseis* of Callimachus' poems (e.g. the *Iambi*) are perhaps analogous to the paraphrases of Dorotheus' poem, which, like the poems of Callimachus, is written in a learned Alexandrian style; cf. also Stegemann 1942, 336-37 on the transmission of the prose paraphrases.

5. Cf. Tester 1978, 437.

6. Dorotheus' poem had a great influence on later treatises; cf. Hübner 1988.

7. Pingree 1976, xi.

8. Cf. MacMullen 1971, 105.

9. Cf. Tester 1987, 168. An addressee is a standard element in classical didactic poetry and may serve various narrative functions (see Clay, Mitsis and Schiesaro 1994); cf. also Barton 1994, 82-83 on the initiatory rhetoric associated with astrological treatises. It is best not to forget that Dorotheus' original composition was in the tradition of elevated Alexandrian verse, and may not have been intended to serve in the first instance as a practical guide, any more than Aratus' *Phainomena* was designed primarily as a handbook for sailors or

Nicander's poem on snake-bites as a medical text; cf. Stegemann 1942, 346-47 on the language and style of Dorotheus' poem. Some Alexandrian writers, however, e.g. Eratosthenes, evidently did employ poetry as a vehicle for serious scientific treatises (Blomqvist 1992, 56).

10. The contrast, for example, with the themes emphasized by Firmicus Maternus is noticeable; for the latter, see the summary in MacMullen 1971, 111-16. Barton 1994, 93 and Gordon (this volume) section 3 suggest that catarchic astrology, dealing with the appropriate days on which to commence an activity, may have been especially accessible to a poor clientele, while geneathlic astrology was for the rich only.

11. Cf. 5.30 for explicit associations between Venus and marriage, Mercury and trade, Mars and war, Jupiter and kings.

12. See Gordon (this volume) section 2 for an indication of the complex and sometimes purely ornamental methods of calculation generated by the astrological writers; on the "grammar" of quasi-scientific interpretive systems, see Martin (this volume).

13. Cf. Tester 1987, 89.

14. For example: "If the Moon is in Aries, it indicates that this slave will be a runaway and will not get used to [his] station and will be incompatible with his master" (5.11.1), whereas "If the Moon is in Taurus, then the slave which is bought will be a worker, patient, strong, obedient, sticking to the work of a slave with his whole self, a humble man" (5.11.2). While it is clear that Dorotheus sees in docile slaves good fortune for the petitioner, he does not moralize. The condition of freedom or slavery is labile and it may happen that a slave is the one to consult the astrologer.

15. This is best done "in a sign whose nature is moist, one of the watery signs" (5.23.2).

16. For example: "If the Moon is in Gemini [in] eight degrees of it, then it indicates that what is in this ship will reach [its destination] and there will be profit from it, but lingering and slowness will occur in its return and its departure" (5.25.3).

17. One may also note that arbitrary anger rather than wrong-doing is the cause of imprisonment.

18. For example: "If Saturn is in the cardine, midheaven, it indicates that, because of their injustice in judging, shame and misery and loathing will reach the judges" (5.33.9). With other signs, "the defendent will be deprived of his wish by injustice and false testimony" (5.33.13; cf. 5.33.20 on bribes and favouritism, as well as 5.33.22-23 on the judge's sympathy for the defendent). Dorotheus looks also to the possibility of reconciliation, and to causes of arguments among family members — as always, restricted to parents, spouses, children and siblings (5.33.35-41).

19. Cf. Lucian *Alexander* 21; Hippolytus *Haer.* 4.28.1-2, 4.34 with commentary in Ganschinietz 1913, 31-33, 38-40, 43-45; I am grateful to Richard Gordon for providing me with these references.

20. I presume that white and black in these examples refer to hair colour.

21. See for example, Cohen 1991, 54-69; contra, in the case of Rome, Treggiari 1991, 313, who ascribes the development of the double standard characteristic of a shame-and-honour culture to Moslem influence.

22. Cf. 2.26.19, where effeminacy in a man is associated with marrying a whore.

23. Cf. Housman 1903, 393 n.1: "Between *philopaidia* and *philogunia* the Romans saw no incongruity at all, but they did see incongruity between *to paskhein* and *to dran*"; Winkler 1989b, 70: "The calculus of correctness operated not on the sameness/difference of the genders but on the dominance/submission of the persons involved"; Halperin 1990, 30: "sex in classical Athens ... effectively divides, classifies, and distributes its participants into distinct and radically opposed categories".

24. See Konstan 1995, 58; Greene 1994, 54 maintains that in Sappho fragment 94 each woman "is to be both lover and beloved, active participants in a reciprocity of desire — both of them active, desiring subjects". Lardinois 1994, 79 argues forcefully (against Parker 1993) that "Sappho talked about young, adolescent women in her poetry", and suggests that Sappho was "an instructor of young women's choruses" (80). Even if her addressees were young, it is not clear to me that in Sappho's poetry (or indeed in fifth-century Athenian literature) the opposition between dominant and passive female in a homoerotic relationship was perceived as parallel to male pederasty.

25. On constructionism, see Halperin 1990; Sinfield 1994, 14-19; opposed: Richlin 1993; Boswell 1990.

26. It is curious that the only texts (apart from the *Glossaria*) cited by LSJ for the word *tribas* are astrological: Manetho, Ptolemy's *Tetrabiblos*, and Vettius Valens. Incidentally, LSJ's gloss on *hetairistria* in Plato's *Symposium* 191E "= *tribas*" thus seems particularly tendentious, especially in light of the fact that Aristophanes' allegory draws no distinction in function between the two halves of the original female (or, for that matter, of the original male).

27. Contrast the importance of the imperial court in the astrological treatise of Vettius Valens.

28. Cf. Swoboda 1964, 30-35; Liuzzi 1983, 84-87; for Nigidius' methods in adapting Etruscan lore, see Weinstock 1950, 48.

29. Stegemann 1942, 332 suggests that Dorotheus may in fact have come from Syria; cf. Stegemann 1940, 14-15.

30. Cf. Konstan 1995, 4. The restricted themes of Menandrean comedy may, however, be understood as an artistic choice rather than a historical limitation (Zagagi 1995, 95), and one must be wary of inferring from such sources a general disengagement from civic politics throughout the Hellenistic world.

31. See MacAlister 1996, "Introduction".

32. Discussion in Tester 1987, 17; Gordon (this volume) init. Gordon (this volume) section 3 notes that more curse tablets seem datable to the late fourth century BC than to any other period.

33. Cf. Neugebauer 1962, 171: "Compared with the background of religion, magic and mysticism, the fundamental doctrines of astrology are pure science". Barton 1994, 15-17 argues that the inclusion of astrology alongside medicine as a branch of knowledge in antiquity destabilizes the polarity between science and pseudoscience; she is thus sceptical of the search for precursors to modern scientific practices and discourses, and invites attention rather to the question of how forms of knowledge achieve authority in a given social context. Cf. also Martin (this volume) init. on the absence of a structured opposition between "natural" and "supernatural" in the classical understanding of *phusis*.

34. On the conception of prognostication as a *tekhnê* in the classical period, see, for example, [Aeschylus] *Prometheus Bound* 484-99; Gordon (this volume) section 3 suggests that catarchic astrology is rational insofar as it helps the petitioner to make a decision in otherwise uncertain conditions.

35. Richard L. Gordon has remarked (oral communication) that nativities may indeed suggest necessity, but *katarkhai* on the contrary offer the freedom to choose an auspicious occasion for a commencement; Gordon sees the two practices as distinct in their social character.

36. See the discussion by Sfameni Gasparro (this volume).

37. See, e.g., 1.21.27-28; cf. Cicero *De divinatione* 2.89 on the mixture of habits, mind, body, action, fortune and experience in astrological predictions; Long 1982, 177.

38. Cf. Ioppolo 1984, 91: "All the efforts of the Stoics were thus addressed to distinguishing physical from moral determinism, as their astrological doctrine also confirms".

39. Cf. Achilles Tatius 1.3.2-4: "Often the celestial powers delight to whisper to us at night about what the future holds — not that we may contrive a defence to forestall it (for no one can rise above fate) but that we may bear it more lightly when it comes" (trans. Winkler 1989c, 178); Artemidorus *Onirocritica* 1.2.

40. But see Long 1982, 167-72 for the view that classical Stoicism may have had little interest in astrology per se as a means of divination.

41. Ioppolo 1984, 89; she adds: "It is thus clear that when we speak of astrology in ancient Stoicism, we are referring to a weak sense, if we mean by this the fact that the Stoics regarded the stars only as signs and not as causes of human destiny"; cf. Denyer 1985 on the Stoic interpretation of divination as a form of communication or signs rather than natural science.

42. See Claudius Ptolemy's defence of astrology in *Tetrabiblos* 1.1-3; Long 1982, 181-83; Barton 1994, 69; cf. Barton 1994, 79 and Gordon (this volume) section 2 fin. on the flexibility of astrological procedures, which offer the practitioner a wide range of choices.

Bibliography

Barnes, J., Brunschwig, J., Burnyeat, M. & Schofield, M. (eds.) 1982. *Science and Speculation: Studies in Hellenistic Theory and Practice*. Cambridge.

Barton, Tamsyn S. 1994. *Power and Knowledge: Astrology, Physiognomics, and Medicine under the Roman Empire*. Ann Arbor.

Bilde, P., Engberg-Pedersen, T., Hannestad, L. & Zahle, J. (eds.) 1992. *Ethnicity in Hellenistic Egypt* (SHC 3). Aarhus.

Blomqvist, J. 1992. "Alexandrian Science: the Case of Eratosthenes", in: Bilde et al. (eds.) 1992, 53-73.

Boswell, J. 1990. "Concepts, Experience, Sexuality", *Differences* 2.1, 67-87.

Bowersock, G.W. 1994. *Fiction as History: Nero to Julian*. Berkeley/Los Angeles.

Bradley, K. 1994. *Slavery and Society at Rome*. Cambridge.

Clay, J.S, Mitsis, P. & Schiesaro, A. (eds.) 1994. *Mega nepios: il ruolo del destinatario nell'epos didascalico*. (Materiali e Discussioni 31).

Cohen, D. 1991. *Law, Sexuality and Society: The Enforcement of Morals in Classical Antiquity*. Cambridge.

Cumont, F. 1912. *Astrology and Religion among the Greeks and Romans*. New York.

Denyer, N. 1985. "The Case Against Divination: An Examination of Cicero's De divinatione", *PCPhS* N.S. 31, 1-10.

Foucault, M. 1984. *Histoire de la sexualité*, vol. 3, *Le souci de soi*. Paris.

Ganschinietz, R. 1913. *Hippolytus' Kapitel gegen die Magier: Ref. haer. IV.28-42*. Leipzig.

Giannantoni G. & Vegetti, M. (eds.) 1984. *La scienza ellenistica*. Napoli.

Greene, E. 1994. "Apostrophe and Women's Erotics in the Poetry of Sappho", *TAPhA* 124, 41-56.

Halperin, D.M. 1990. *One Hundred Years of Homosexuality and Other Essays on Greek Love*. New York.

Housman, A.E. 1903. Review of S.G. Owen, *A. Persi Flacci et D Iuni Iuvenalis Saturae*, *ClR* 17, 392-94.

Hübner, W. 1988. "Nachtrag zum Planetenfragment des Sudines P. Gen. inv. 203 (vgl. ZPE 73, 1988, 33ff.)", *ZPE* 74, 109-10.

Ioppolo, A. M. 1984. "L'astrologia nello stoicismo antico", in: Giannantoni & Vegetti (eds.) 1984, 73-91.

Konstan, D. 1995. *Greek Comedy and Ideology*. Oxford.

Lardinois, A. 1994. "Subject and Circumstance in Sappho's Poetry", *TAPhA* 124, 57-84.

Liuzzi, D. (trans.) 1983. *Nigidio Figulo "astrologo e mago": Testimonianze e frammenti*. Lecce.

Liviabella Furiani, P. 1978. "La Donna nella 'Tetrabiblos' di Claudio Tolomeo", *GiorItFil* n.s. 9, 310-21.

Long, A.A. 1982. "Astrology: Arguments Pro and Contra", in: Barnes, Brunschwig, Burnyeat & Schofield (eds.) 1982, 165-92.

MacAlister, S. 1996. *Dreams and Suicides: The Greek Novel in Antiquity and the Byzantine Empire*. London.

MacMullen, R. 1971. "Social History in Astrology", *AncSoc* 2, 105-16.

Montanari Caldini, R. 1973. "L'astrologia nei *Prognostica* di Germanico", *StItFilCl* n.s. 45, 137-204.

Neugebauer, O. 1962. *The Exact Sciences in Antiquity* (2nd ed.). New York.

Olyan, S.M. 1994. "'And with a Male You Shall Not Lie the Lying Down of a Woman': On the Meaning and Significance of Leviticus 18:22 and 20:13", *JHistSex* 5, 179-206.

Parker, H.N. 1993. "Sappho Schoolmistress", *TAPhA* 123, 309-51.

Pingree, D. (ed.) 1976. *Dorotheus Sidonius Carmen astrologicum*. Stuttgart.

Price, S.R.F. 1986. "The Future of Dreams: From Freud to Artemidorus", *PastPres* 113, 3-37.

Reardon, B.P. (ed.) 1989. *Collected Ancient Greek Novels*. Berkeley/Los Angeles.

Richlin, A. 1993. "Not Before Homosexuality: The Materiality of the *Cinaedus* and the Roman Law against Love between Men", *JHistSex* 3, 523-73.

Saliba, G. 1978. Review of Pingree 1976, in: *Isis* 69, 109-10.

Sinfield, A. 1994. *Cultural Politics — Queer Reading*. Philadelphia.

Stegemann, V. 1940. *Fragmente des Dorotheos von Sidon*. Heidelberg.

Stegemann, V. 1942. "Dorotheus von Sidon: Ein Bericht über die Rekonstruktionsmöglichkeiten seines astrologischen Werkes", *RhM* 91, 326-49.

Swoboda, A. (ed.) 1964 (orig. 1889). *P. Nigidii Figuli Operum Reliquiae*. Amsterdam.

Tester, S.J. 1978. Review of Pingree 1976, *Erasmus* 30, 434-38.

Tester, S.J. 1987. *A History of Western Astrology*. Woodbridge, Suffolk.

Treggiari, S. 1991. *Roman Marriage: Iusti Coniuges from the Time of Cicero to the Time of Ulpian*. Oxford.

Weinstock, S. 1950. "C. Fonteius Capito and the *Libri Tagetici*", *BSR* n.s. 5, 44-49.

Winkler, J.J. 1989a. "Unnatural Acts: Erotic Protocols in Artemidorus' *Dream Analysis*", in: Winkler, 1989b, 17-44.

Winkler, J.J. 1989b. *The Constraints of Desire: Essays in the Anthropology of Sex and Gender in Ancient Greece*. New York.

Winkler, J.J. (trans.) 1989c. "Achilles Tatius: *Leucippe and Clitophon*", in: Reardon (ed.) 1989, 170-284.

Zagagi, N. 1995. *The Comedy of Menander: Convention, Variation and Originality*. Bloomington.

A PROFESSOR AND HIS SLAVE:
CONVENTIONS AND VALUES IN THE
LIFE OF AESOP

Tomas Hägg

The text I propose to investigate in search of Hellenistic conventional values is one that almost never appears in the source indices of scholarly works on the Hellenistic period: the anonymous *Life of Aesop*.[1] There are several reasons for this: the subliterate genre to which the text seems to belong, its composite character, the difficulties in dating it (or its composite parts), and the fact that the *editio princeps* of the earliest version we possess was issued as late as 1952.[2] The *Life of Aesop* — alias the *Aesop Romance* — has simply not belonged to the established corpus of ancient texts to which historians and others turn for information (and certainly not in regard to the Hellenistic period). It is indicative of the state of things that Keith Hopkins, in a stimulating article of 1993, could claim that he is the first to use this text — the biography of a slave — to illuminate ancient slavery (Hopkins 1993, 3).[3]

I shall therefore start with a presentation of the text and a fairly detailed discussion of its date and composition, seeking to justify its inclusion among the few literary witnesses to Hellenistic popular thought.

The version I shall deal with is transmitted in one medieval manuscript only, a codex of the 10th century labelled G after its original location in the monastery of Grottaferrata, and now preserved in the Pierpont Morgan Library, New York (MS 397). It was first published by Ben Edwin Perry in 1952 (Perry 1952), and is since 1990 available in a new critical edition by Manolis Papathomopoulos.[4] Perry's text was translated by Lloyd W. Daly (Daly 1961); I quote from his translation, with occasional minor modifications intended partly to adapt it to the new critical text.

Before the Greek text of G was published, the *Life of Aesop* had for a century been available in a shortened, less colourful version of late antique or early medieval origin, transmitted in several manuscripts and styled W after its first editor, Anton Westermann (1845). And long before that it had been known in a derivative Byzantine version, conventionally ascribed to Maximos Planudes (13th cent.),[5] printed as early as circa 1479. In addition, there are now a fair number of papyrus fragments,[6] testifying to the Life's considerable popularity in antiquity, in various versions. The oldest papyrus, the *Berolinensis* 11628, dates in the late second or early third century AD, thus constituting the most solid *terminus ante quem* for the composition of the Life.[7]

   The story begins with a vivid and concrete description of the main character (1):

The fabulist Aesop, the great benefactor of mankind, was by chance a slave but by origin a Phrygian from Amorion in Phrygia, of exceedingly loathsome aspect, decayed, potbellied, misshapen of head, snub-nosed, saddle-backed, swarthy, dwarfish, bandy-legged, short-armed, squint-eyed, liver-lipped — a pure mistake of nature. In addition to this he had a defect more serious than his unsightliness in being speechless, for he was dumb and could not talk.

After this description,[8] we are immediately brought *in medias res*. Aesop, it appears, is the slave of an unnamed master on a farm somewhere in Asia Minor. Already the first scene shows his inventiveness: in spite of his dumbness, he manages to escape from an intrigue staged by malicious fellow slaves. He also manages to help a woman who has lost her way; she turns out to be a priestess of Isis, and as a reward the goddess herself relieves Aesop of his dumbness and persuades the Muses to confer on him "the power to devise stories and the ability to conceive and elaborate tales in Greek" (7). Aesop's newly acquired capacity to speak turns out to be a mixed blessing to fellow slaves and master alike, so he is promptly handed over to a slave dealer and brought to Ephesus to be sold.

   Unable to sell the ugly slave in Ephesus, the slave dealer crosses over to Samos, where Aesop is sold to the philosopher Xanthus. A substantial part of the Life (20-91) is then taken up by the description of the relationship between Xanthus and his new slave; in fact, the title of the whole work in MS. G is: "The Book of Xanthus the Philosopher and Aesop his Slave, on the Career of Aesop" (*Biblos Xanthou philosophou kai Aisôpou doulou autou peri anastrophês Aisôpou*). *Anastrophê*, by the way, is perhaps better rendered as "way of life" than by Daly's "career": it is the moral side of Aesop's life, his "behaviour" (*Wandel*), that is in focus. Anyway, in a series of lively and humorous scenes, the slave's dealings with his master, his master's wife and his master's students are described. As Niklas Holzberg has recently shown (Holzberg 1992a),[9] the structuring of this part of the Life is more elaborate than was earlier supposed. It is not just a string of anecdotes — as Hopkins (1993, 11f.) still thinks — but a deliberate literary composition. Different kinds of Aesopic *logoi* are used in the different parts of the story, and each series is arranged so as to achieve an effect of *Steigerung*.

After an expository section (20-33), the action begins. Aesop first (34-64) plays a number of practical jokes on Xanthus, trying to teach the professor to use words exactly. So, if the master orders: "Pick up the oil flask and the towels, and let's go to the bath!" (38), the slave does exactly that, but no more — and having arrived in the bath Xanthus discovers to his astonishment and anger that there is no oil in the flask. Again and again the same pattern is repeated, with more and more serious consequences; but Xanthus never gets the opportunity he longs for to punish his slave. Aesop is the better sophist of the two and always provides a watertight defence for his actions.

At last, Xanthus has learnt his lesson and Aesop achieves his first goal, to be treated as a thinking person. He is now given tasks to accomplish, rather than orders to obey. The next group of scenes (65-91) shows how Aesop, with a typical combination of intelligence and sophistic quibbling, manages to rescue his master from various difficulties, saving his property, his reputation, even his life. His constant aim now is to gain his freedom as a reward for his services to his master; but each time Xanthus goes back on his word. At last, it is the Samian people's assembly that enforces Aesop's emancipation, after he has helped them interpret an omen that had defied Xanthus's own attempts.

Thus a new stage in Aesop's career begins (92-100): he acts as a political counsellor to Samos in its dealings with King Croesus of Lydia. Aesop himself visits Croesus and succeeds in preventing a war beteen Lydia and Samos. In this section, as well as in the Delphi section at the end of the Life, the author has recourse to a third type of Aesopic *logos*, namely, the fable. Instead of letting his hero give direct advice or instruction, he presents him telling fables to achieve his purpose. On Samos — in contrast to Delphi — he is successful in this activity and spends many years there as a respected man.

Aesop then decides to make a lecture-tour around the world, and finally arrives in Babylon. He wins a reputation for wisdom there too and becomes a counsellor to King Lycorus. Since he is childless, he adopts a young man to make him "the heir to his own wisdom" (103). The adopted son, however, brings false accusations against Aesop, who is condemned to death. But he is spared and hidden away by a disloyal servant of the king, and is later rehabilitated and employed by the king for an important mission to King Nectanebo of Egypt. Again showing his resourcefulness and cleverness, he outwits the Egyptians and returns to Babylon in triumph. This whole Babylon-Memphis section of the work (101-23) is closely modelled on the Assyrian *Book of Ahiqar*, a work which circulated in a variety of languages (the earliest version surviving is in Aramaic); Ahiqar as a wise man was already known to the Greeks in the classical period (see Haslam 1986, 150f., with further refs.).

From Babylon Aesop travels to Delphi, where he meets his fate (124-42). Addressing the people of Delphi, he offends them by claiming that they are all descendants of slaves, namely, of prisoners of war sent to Apollo by victors as a tenth of their spoils. The officials of Delphi, afraid that Aesop will destroy the city's reputation on his continued travels, have a golden cup placed in his luggage and then accuse him of having stolen it from the temple. He is put in prison, and this time all his telling of fables cannot save him. He is sentenced to death for sacrilege, is dragged off from the shrine of the Muses where he has taken refuge, and finally throws himself off the cliff.

The composite character of this text is obvious, and has been stressed, often indeed exaggerated. But there is also a unity, as shown by Holzberg: the hand of an author, rather than just a compiler, may be perceived. Leitmotifs can be found all through the work, and there is, as we have seen, an artistic structuring of the narrative that prevents it from being just a random collection of episodes. But at what date did this anonymous author put his stamp on the *Life of Aesop*? And in what sense — or in what parts — may the work be described and used as a Hellenistic work?

The date commonly ascribed to the archetype of the surviving versions of the Life is the first century AD. The arguments were brought forward by Ben Edwin Perry in 1936; nothing of importance seems to have been added to them since, nor have their validity been seriously questioned. But Perry's cautious conclusion in his first major study was the following: "the most that one may say with certainty is that the *Life of Aesop*, in the oldest form that we know it (i.e. in G), must have been composed, or rewritten, at some time between 100 BC and 200 AD" (Perry 1936, 26). The *terminus ante quem* is the Berlin papyrus fragment dated in the late second or early third century; at the other end, the numerous Latin words and the appearance of Isis in the story are said to exclude a date before the first century BC. Perry himself in 1936 favoured a date in the second century AD, rather in the early than in the later part of that century. In 1952, however, because he was convinced there must have been an intermediate copy between the archetype and the Berlin papyrus, he opted for the first century AD.[10] In later writings, he constantly refers to the Life as a first-century text, presumably composed in Egypt; and so do practically all others, mostly without any specific comments of their own.[11] Only Francisco Adrados favours an earlier date, reaffirming his view as late as 1993: "And I still think that the prototype of recensions G and W, pace Perry, is from the Hellenistic epoch".[12]

What we learn from this retrospect is that the conventional dating "first century AD" is just a convenient shorthand for "first century BC *or* first century AD *or* second century AD". For all we know, then, the surviving Life may well have been composed in late Hellenistic times; but it may also be post-Hadrianic. It may fall as a whole well within the stricter definition of "the Hellenistic period" suggested by the convenors of the conference on which the present book is based, namely from Alexander to Augustus; or it may as a whole belong outside even their more liberal chronological framework of Alexander to Hadrian.

Now, we do not necessarily have to deal with the Life *as a whole*, nor would that actually be desirable. Few will believe that our late Hellenistic or early imperial author created his work relying only on oral sources and his own imagination: there will already have existed a biographical tradition codified in one or several written Lives, which he could use as a framework for the inclusion of other legendary material as well as inventions of his own. And for some of the constituent parts of his work it is possible to discern the approximate date, or at least some *termini ante* or *post quos*.

It was once fashionable to speak of a *Volksbuch* on Aesop which circulated in Ionic prose already in the sixth century BC. Chambry, Perry, Adrados, West and others have effectively dispensed with that notion.[13] But Martin West, to whom we owe the most lucid and closely argued discussion of the early stages of the *Life of Aesop*, makes a good case for the existence of a written Life as early as the middle of the fifth century BC (West 1984, 116-28).[14] The key passage is a brief reference in Aristophanes (*Av.* 471f.): "You are ignorant and incurious, and *have never explored Aesop* (*oud' Aisôpon pepatêkas*), who used to tell that the lark existed before everything else" (trans. West 1984, 121). The Greek word which West translates with "explore", is *pateô*, which, as he shows, can hardly refer to anything other than reading. If we combine this fact with various other references in Aristophanes and Herodotus and some further testimonia,[15] it appears that there probably existed in the fifth century BC a written book containing various fables of Aesop, set in a biographical framework. In that book, Aesop's servitude is already located in Samos, and a man named Xanthos or Xanthes appears (though a certain Iadmon is mentioned as Aesop's master). Its author was probably a Samian, or used Samian sources. The book certainly also included the story of Aesop's violent death in Delphi, perhaps the oldest part of the Aesop legend, evidently modelled on the old *pharmakos* ritual, the killing (or expulsion) of the ugly scapegoat (Wiechers 1961, 31-42; Adrados 1979b, 105-8).[16] It is possible that certain elements of the introductory part of the surviving Life as well were prefigured in the fifth-century book, since there may be traces of the *pharmakos* rite there too.[17]

The next potential Life of Aesop we know of is the *Aesopica* (*Aisôpeia*) of Demetrius of Phalerum, composed in the late fourth century BC. Perry argues that this was not just a collection of fables, but that it also included, "by way of introduction ... , some account of Aesop personally and a few anecdotes about his clever actions".[18] Demetrius' work, Perry maintains, "must have been a principal source-book ... for the author of the *Vita*" (Perry 1966, 287 n. 2). He specifically mentions the breadbasket episode narrated in ch. 18-19 of the surviving Life as probably taken over from Demetrius.[19] It is not unlikely that Perry is right about the nature of the *Aesopica*; but, as he himself admits, it cannot be proved.[20]

Another early source for our *Life of Aesop* has already been mentioned: the Assyrian *Book of Ahiqar*, which was adapted to fit in between Aesop's inter-ference in Samian-Lydian politics and his fatal visit to Delphi. Aesop assumes the rôle of the wise Ahiqar, the King of Babylon is identified as Lycorus[21] and the King of Egypt appears as Nectanebo; but the general intrigue and the display of conventional wisdom are common to both. It should be noted, however, that the content of Aesop's hortatory speech to his adopted son is quite different from that of Ahiqar's corresponding speeches in the surviving versions (Haslam 1986, 152-55). Yet the fact that the precepts are almost wholly irrelevant to their context indicates that Aesop's speech was not invented by the author of the Life, but taken over more or less *en bloc* from some unknown source, whether another version of the *Book of Ahiqar* or some Greek ethical treatise.[22] Whatever their source — and it is not inconceivable that it was Hellenistic Greek — these precepts obviously represent a kind of conservative morality quite alien to the spirit of the rest of the Life (cf. Oettinger 1992, 21f.).

We can now see that, for our purposes, some parts at least of the present *Life of Aesop* should be set aside, or treated with extra caution, because they originate in substance before the Hellenistic period. This is true, first and foremost, for the Babylon-Memphis section, which is the most palpable *Fremdkörper* in the Life.[23] It also goes for the Delphi part, though it is obvious that much younger material has been added there to the original framework. Aesop's telling of fables in this part is probably part of an old narrative, but we cannot be sure that it contained all or the same fables as the surviving Life.[24]

It is true that Samos as the locality of Aesop's servitude and also a person named Xanthus belong, like Delphi, to the traditional, pre-Hellenistic story. Perhaps the contrast between the clever slave and his stupid master was already worked out at that early stage. But the episodes actually narrated in this part of the Life to illustrate that contrast are almost certainly not of classical origin. Some assorted indications of a post-classical date may briefly be mentioned. Most importantly, much of intrigue and characterization is similar to New Comedy, as demonstrated by Holzberg (1992a, 47-63, 72). The direction of the influence cannot be in doubt: it must have flowed from Comedy to Life.[25] There are traces of popular Cynic philosophy, especially in the rude behaviour of Aesop himself towards his master and mistress. In fact, some of the episodes told about Aesop are very similar to anecdotes told about Diogenes of Sinope.[26] The figure of Socrates, too, lies behind some traits in the characterization of Aesop; and his dealings with the sophists, as described by Plato, have perhaps influenced the description of Aesop's discussions with the professor and his students.[27] The emphasis on Aesop's deformed body, not only in the initial description, recalls Hellenistic art and its obsession with human deformity.[28]

These observations, though of different weight and clarity, together establish the late fourth century BC as a *terminus post quem* for the Xanthus part of the Life. We may now view the matter from the other side. There are reasons to believe that the surviving Life was composed in Egypt, although the case is not quite as clear as Perry maintains.[29] The adaptation of the Ahiqar material to fit the context appears to have been made in Egypt.[30] The rôle of Isis as the leader of the Muses suggests Egyptian religious syncretism.[31] The large Xanthus part, on the other hand, seems to be free of specifically Egyptian traits and may thus have been taken over by the author from a Hellenistic source without substantial modifications or additions.[32]

The same is possibly true for the Samos-Lydia part; at least, there are no references to a connection between Aesop and Croesus before the fourth century.[33] Holzberg (1992a, 64, 66f.), however, suggests that the narrative of this part of Aesop's career was deliberately structured so as to make it a counterpart to the Babylon-Memphis part, in turn closely modelled on the story of Ahiqar. It may then, in its developed form, be the creation of the author of the Life himself.

To sum up, following the order of the present text of the Life: The introductory part is a mixture of old (*pharmakos* rite) and new (Isis); the Xanthus part, which takes up half the text, is probably Hellenistic in substance; the Samos-Lydia part may be mostly a new invention; the Babylon-Memphis part has an old oriental model; the Delphi part is again a mixture of old and new.

Thus, for an investigation with the present aim, it seems wisest to concentrate on the Xanthus part, which may well go back on a separate Hellenistic work under the title "The Book of Xanthus the Philosopher and Aesop his Slave", the first part of the title transmitted in G (cf. above); for a whole life, this is a curious title, even with the addition "on Aesop's Way of Life".[34] The most reasonable explanation is that this title was originally attached to a work which covered precisely Aesop's life as a slave on Samos, and that it was mechanically taken over when that story was extended to form the surviving *Life of Aesop* (which actually covers his life, except for childhood/youth).[35] No doubt there are both pre-Hellenistic or post-Hellenistic elements in the Xanthus part as well; but we may be fairly confident, I believe, that in the main it mirrors values and beliefs current in the Hellenistic period. But current where, or with whom?

This brings us to the problem of genre, readership and tendency. To a large extent, these are questions which have to be addressed after the analysis of the values propagated by the text. The identification of these values should help situate the work, rather than the reverse. But some indications of earlier efforts to define its nature may be given at this point.

Michael Haslam's (1980, 54) characterization of the *Life of Aesop* as a "quasi-biographical specimen[s] of folk-literature" well represents the *communis opinio*. Perry, as usual, provides the most articulate characterization of the work and the most specific definition of its cultural context. Inevitably, by being so explicit he also reveals the risks one takes in using the label "folk-literature" in relation to antiquity.

The *Life of Aesop* belongs to a species of ancient folk-literature of which very little has survived. Like the fabulous history of Alexander, it is a naïve, popular, and anonymous book, composed for the entertainment and edification of the common people rather than for educated men, and making little or no pretense to historical accuracy or literary elegance ...

But unlike the romance of Alexander, the biography of Aesop is concerned with a cultural, not a military hero, and in this respect it is almost without parallel among the ancient Greek texts that have come down to us. ...

[The *Life of Aesop*] gives us the portrait of a wise man as seen through the eyes of the poor in spirit, at the same time enlivened by a spontaneous and vigorous, if somewhat homely, wit ...

... for us the *Life of Aesop* is interesting not for such artistic value as it may possess — though that too, I suspect, has been unduly disparaged — but because it is one of the few genuinely popular books that have come down from ancient times.[36]

In another place, Perry speaks of "Aesop as the exponent of the common man's wit and wisdom in the form of fable-lore, in conflict with the aristocratic Apollo as leader of the Muses and the patron of Greek poetry and art on the intellectual plane of fashion" (Perry 1962b, 633). The authentic biographical tradition concerning Aesop ends already with Demetrius of Phalerum, Perry explains; from now on, it is a matter of "framing Aesop in the (fanciful) history of ideas and cultural values" (Perry 1962a, 334, repeated 1965, xlii). Francisco Adrados (1979b, 102) adds: Aesop of the Life "is a man of the people who triumphs over cities and kings and confronts the powerful Delphic priesthood. He is a person who acts in opposition to the conventional values ..."

This all, at first sight, looks promising for our purpose. But what, exactly, is "a genuinely popular book" of antiquity? Considering how small the proportion of genuinely literate people was even among the Greeks of the late Hellenistic period, one may wonder who the prospective readers of such a product were, and who the author.[37] Are uneducated writers possible at all among the Hellenistic Greeks? Is this really a book of the people and for the people, or is it something that only masquerades as such?

Perry's characterization provoked doubts immediately in some of the reviews of his two books. He exaggerated, some felt, the popular character of the language of G: some vulgarisms should rather be ascribed to the Byzantine tradition of the text (Hausrath 1937, 771; Dölger 1953);[38] on the other hand, the text was said to contain more elements characteristic of a studied rhetorical style than Perry would admit (Adrados 1953, 324f.). The anti-intellectualist — or, more specifically, anti-Apollinian — tendency was considered overstated by some (Rose 1953; Blake 1954, 80-82). And Keith Hopkins (1993, 11 n. 15) now finds Perry's "assumptions about the sophisticated tastes of the educated in the Roman world and the reading capacity of the common people ... questionable". But, on the whole, there seems to have been little opposition to the description of the *Life of Aesop* as a genuine piece of folk-literature, as the quotation from Haslam shows.

I shall return to these questions at the end of my paper. Now it is high time to turn to the analysis proper of the conventional values which our text may mirror or propagate. I shall analyse its picture of two social groups, the slaves (as represented by Aesop and his fellow slaves) and the intellectuals (the professor and his students), and also its representation of gender rôles (the professor's wife in relation to her husband and to their slave).

First, the slaves. As will have become evident, my approach is different from that of Keith Hopkins in his recent article "Novel Evidence for Roman Slavery", though we happen to use the same source. His purpose, like mine, is "not to squeeze fiction for facts, but to interpret fiction as a mirror of Roman [in my case, Hellenistic] thinking and feeling" (Hopkins 1993, 4 n. 3). But Hopkins chooses to ignore the composite character of the work — the "multiple sites, origins and fantasies" (Hopkins 1993, 11 n. 14) from which it stems — and seems to regard its very anonymity and popularity as a kind of guarantee for its general trustworthiness as a witness to Roman slavery:

The multiple versions and surviving copies of the *Life of Aesop* ... indicate its forgotten popularity, and dramatically increase its utility for us; what we have is not a single author's idiosyncratic vision, but a collective, composite work incorporating many different stories told about slaves ... Its survival in Egypt and the occasional adaptation of the text to Egyptian conditions should not mislead us into thinking that it relates primarily to Egypt, any more than its being written first in Greek should make us think that it related primarily to Greek slavery. In my view, the *Life of Aesop* is a generic work, related generally, but not specifically, to slavery in the whole Roman world.[39]

This is, to put it mildly, an optimistic point of view. The notion of a "collective" work brings us back to the old romantic myth of the "folk-book", which modern literary research has exposed.[40] My analytical approach, in contrast, by focussing on a relatively uniform and apparently non-Egyptian part of the Life, permits us to operate within a more limited chronological and ethnic framework: Hellenistic Greek rather than generally "Roman".[41] And my concern, of course, is not with slavery generally, but, in particular, with people's attitude towards slaves.

Aesop himself is no doubt an atypical slave. But this does not mean that the Life necessarily depicts an atypical condition for a slave. On the contrary, the point of the story is often that his surroundings — his owner, his owner's friends, his fellow slaves — treat him as if he were an ordinary slave, with surprising and comical effects. Aesop constantly encounters people's conventional attitudes toward a house slave, and each time he has to assert his otherness. So let us look at these conventional attitudes.

The first confrontation between Xanthus and Aesop takes place in the Samian agora, where Aesop and two other slaves are put up for sale (20-27). The most important quality in a slave, it becomes clear, is his outward appearance. Aesop's two fellow slaves on this occasion are a teacher (*grammatikos*) and a harpist (*psaltês*), and the slave dealer has brought them precisely to Samos because there should be a demand for intellectual slaves there, considering all the students Xanthus's celebrated school of philosophy attracts. Still, when it comes to having them sold at a good price, the slave dealer exerts himself in dressing them up beautifully and in hiding the young teacher's only physical defect, his thin legs. Aesop's deformity, in contrast, cannot be hidden, and the slave dealer consequently does not expect to get him sold at all. Xanthus, the philosopher, at first totally embraces this conventional estimate of a slave's worth, praising before his students the slave dealer for his commercial genius: he has put the two young and handsome slaves up for sale together with the ugly one, to emphasize their beauty.

When the beautiful slaves turn out to be too expensive for Xanthus, and his students suggest that he should buy Aesop instead, Xanthus still clings to appearance only, protesting that his wife at all events would not tolerate an ugly slave. By chance a conversation begins between Aesop, the students and Xanthus, and Aesop's wit and cleverness are demonstrated in full; and so Xanthus is persuaded to buy the ugly slave after all. He gets him at cost price, 75 denarii, whereas the *grammatikos* would have cost him 3000. It is Aesop himself, not the philosopher, who formulates the moral of the whole scene, by using a parable (26):

Aesop:	Don't look at my appearance (*to eidos*), but examine my soul.
Xanthus:	What is appearance?
Aesop:	It's like what often happens when we go to a wine shop to buy wine. The jars we see are ugly, but the wine tastes good.[42]

One might compare Alcibiades in Plato's *Symposium* (215a-b) who likens Socrates to a Silenus statue hiding the effigy of a god. Aesop, like Socrates, is ugly in appearance, but appearance deceives. True value is to be found inside the person, even inside a slave. Thus, Socratic insight is used in the *Life of Aesop* to expose a conventional assumption which even a celebrated philosopher like Xanthus is shown to share.

Outer appearance as the popular index of a slave's value continues to be illustrated in the narrative: the tax collectors remit the sales tax out of pity for the buyer (27), Xanthus's wife on seeing the new slave threatens to leave the house (31), the gardener refuses to believe that one so ugly can read (37), and the people of Samos at first refuse to listen to his interpretation of an omen for the same reason (87). Yet, both Xanthus and his wife quickly come to appreciate and make use of Aesop's cleverness. There is now, in the next series of episodes, another conventional attitude towards slaves that is again and again unwittingly demonstrated by Xanthus, to his own detriment.

In the episode with the empty oil flask (38) referred to above, Xanthus makes the mistake of not simply ordering his slave to accompany him to the bath, but of specifying what things he should bring: the oil flask and the towels. Aesop takes his revenge by not bringing what the master has not specified, namely, the oil. This, I presume, is an authentic representation of a normal attitude towards slaves, to treat and address them as infants, as people totally devoid of experience, ambition, and initiative of their own.[43] A slave is by definition an unthinking creature, he has to be programmed to perform even daily tasks. Aesop has already shown that he is a thinking being, but still Xanthus automatically assumes the conventional attitude towards him.

Xanthus, of course, fails to catch the point and changes his behaviour in the wrong direction. He takes pains to specify his orders in still greater detail, but always happens to leave some gap which allows Aesop to act in absurd ways, while taking his master literally and obeying his words rather than his intent. The authentic glimpse in the flask episode thus gives way to caricature and literary exaggeration in the following episodes. Not until the game has developed in absurdum does Xanthus finally learn his lesson and starts treating Aesop as a thinking human being, rather than as a slave.

A couple of other typical attitudes towards slaves are much emphasized throughout the narrative. Aesop's master, the philosopher, is always looking for an opportunity to beat him; but his philosophical disposition mostly prevents him from doing so, since he must have a rational cause for punishment, not only an emotional one. Aesop's mistress, on the other hand, comes to regard Aesop, in spite of his ugliness, as an attractive sexual partner, and after watching him masturbating one morning, forces him to satisfy her desires to the extreme (75). These are topics we recognize from comedy, the beating syndrome from (Roman) New Comedy, the sexual potency of slaves especially from Aristophanes (cf. Goins 1989, 28f.); and there is a combination of both in Herodas's Mime 5, "The Jealous Mistress".[44] Does that mean that they are literary conventions rather than mirroring authentic behaviour?

Probably they are both. Their topicalization no doubt reflects the literary conventions of comedy, but there is some reality to which the topoi correspond that is common to the classical and Hellenistic periods. As always in the interpretation of literary sources, we have to consider the condensation typical of the medium: the frequency with which the heroes of the ideal novels are shipwrecked or slaves are beaten in New Comedy is of course "unrealistic", but the events in themselves are taken from real life. No doubt, as documentary sources demonstrate, many households could boast of well functioning relation-ships between masters and slaves.[45] Still, literature shows us, in artistic articulation and enlargement, the tensions that were also there.

So, Keith Hopkins (1993, 14f., 22f.) is probably right in interpreting the topos of the virile slave who tempts and seduces his mistress as the expression of a constant underlying fear in slave masters that such things could happen. Inevitably, male domestic slaves would sometimes be left alone with the mistress in the house, they would follow her to the bath, etc. Slaves of both sexes were in fact witness to the most private life of their master and mistress, being ever-present in the house, in the bed-chamber, even in the toilet, attending "with a towel and a pitcher of water", as the *Life of Aesop* demonstrates (67). No weakness could be concealed.[46] Such a system can function psychologically only on the assumption that the slave is an inanimate object, like a piece of furniture, or perhaps an animal. But however much the master tried to regard his slave as of another order, as non-human, as a *thing*, the anxiety would always be there that he was in fact his equal or even superior, a human being with intelligence and attractiveness, his rival rather than his tool.

The beating topos, in turn, testifies to the persistent and enforced tendency to regard the slave as, precisely, a tool. When a tool does not function the way it is supposed to, a reaction of irrational anger lies close at hand, a wish to throw it away or destroy it. Hopkins (1993, 18) aptly compares this response, in a slightly different context, with the modern consumer's "frustration or fury at not being able to understand or follow the instructions which accompany a self-assembly kit for a piece of household equipment". Rational behaviour towards a slave is something unnatural and out-of-place, since by definition the slave himself is not a rational being. The irony in the case of Xanthus, the philosopher, is that he cannot overcome his professional commitment to reason, and thus only exceptionally (58; 77) has the satisfaction of actually laying hands on his slave. He is constantly frustrated, lacking the slave-owner's normal outlet for his aggressions.

We turn now to gender rôles. To a large extent, the *Life of Aesop* gives voice to a blatant misogyny. We have already seen the depiction of Xanthus's wife as lecherous and unfaithful. She is also described as quarrelsome and wasteful. Aesop himself, in his conversations with Xanthus and his wife, eloquently represents the misogynistic viewpoint. But these traits again have the character of literary convention derived from Old Comedy and other Greek literature, and they are anyway too common and stereotyped to be of major interest. What deserves greater attention is the attitude of Xanthus himself towards his wife.

Now, on a closer look, Xanthus is not quite the unsympathetic or ridiculous character that his rôle vis-à-vis Aesop, the hero, has made most critics assume. Despite his many stupid acts and utterances, he is also described as a rather decent man, even with a touch of self-irony (28; 40). He is, of course, inferior to Aesop in intelligence and wit, but no doubt a reflective person — and an unusually humane slave owner. His wife even rebukes him for being a *doulokoitês*, a "slave-lover" (49). Aesop's chief complaint with Xanthus is not that he treats him badly — then he would simply run away (26) — but that he refuses to set him free, in spite of the outstanding services Aesop performs for him. True, Xanthus

again and again goes back on his promises to free Aesop (74; 79; 80; 90) — but
the conventional attitude towards slaves obviously allows him to do so without
breaking any moral code or feeling any kind of remorse; and Aesop knows he
has nobody to appeal to, no "right" that is his. His emotional response may be
revenge (74W, implemented in 75W), but he soon returns to his rational tactic
of performing services.

In his relationship to his wife, Xanthus differs markedly from the misogyny
which is so characteristic of other males in the story: of Aesop, in the first place
(32; 49; 50), but also of Xanthus's students (24) and of a countryman who is
accidentally brought into the action (64). Officially, it is true, Xanthus teaches
that one "should not listen to a woman" (*mê peithesthai gunaiki),* as his students
are eager to point out (24W). And when there is risk that his wife will leave him,
he tries to give the impression that it is the dowry he is afraid of losing (29). But
behind this façade the author permits us to see small glimpses of Xanthus's
personal affection for his wife. The first comes when Xanthus has just brought
home his new slave and presents him to his wife. She finds Aesop repulsive and
says she will leave the house. Xanthus wants Aesop to use his verbal skills to
prevent this, but Aesop just comes out with (31):

Aesop:	Well, let her go her way and be damned.
Xanthus:	Shut up, you trash. Don't you realize that I love her more than my life (*philô autên huper emauton*)?
Aesop:	You love the woman (*phileis to gunaion*)?
Xanthus:	I certainly do.
Aesop:	You want her to stay?
Xanthus:	I do, you contemptible fool.

This declaration of love only meets with contempt in Aesop. His diagnosis is
ready: his master *gunaikokrateitai,* he is ruled by his wife, he is "hen-pecked"
(31, also 29) — the typical male comment in such a situation. Later in the
narrative, it is mentioned incidentally that Xanthus saves a special pig for the
celebration of his wife's birthday (42). And when Xanthus himself is invited to
a party by one of his students, he takes extra portions of each course that is served
and has Aesop put them in a basket. He says (44): "Then take them to her who
cares for me (*têi eunoousêi*)." Xanthus's charming periphrasis for "wife", *hê
eunoousa,* becomes the point of departure for one of Aesop's sophistic tricks
against him. He brings the food home and shows it to Xanthus's wife, who
naturally assumes that it is meant for her (45):

Xanthus's wife: Did your master send this to me?
Aesop: No.
Xanthus's wife: And to whom did he send it?
Aesop: To her who cares for him (*têi eunoousêi*).
Xanthus's wife: And who cares for him (*autôi eunoei*), you runaway?
Aesop: Just wait a little, and you'll see who cares for him.

So he brings the house dog who devours the food, and Aesop returns to Xanthus to report that his command has been executed. Xanthus's wife, for her part, decides again to leave their house (46): "For when he prefers (*proekrinen*) the bitch to me, how can I live with (*sunoikêsô*) him any longer?" Here we catch a rare glimpse of the reciprocy in this marriage:[47] to the wife, too, it is evidently a question of more than a formal economic arrangement.

Unsuspectingly, Xanthus returns home from the party in his best mood, only to find his wife totally unresponsive (49):

[He] went to the bedroom, where he began to talk sweet talk (*kolakeuein*) to his wife and shower her with kisses (*kataphilein*). But she turned her back on Xanthus and said: "Don't come near me, you slave-lover (*doulokoita*), or rather you dog-lover (*kunokoita*). Give me back my dowry."

So she again assumes the conventional Xanthippe rôle. She moves home to her parents, and Aesop can triumphantly demonstrate to Xanthus that "the one who cares for you" is *not* synonymous with "wife" (50).

There is reason, I think, to emphasize these unexpected expressions of love and affection between Xanthus and his wife. They do not conform to the literary-conventional rôles played by the philosopher and his wife, and they are not necessary for the plot (as romantic love is in the ideal Greek novel). They are therefore all the more worth attention as potential testimony to actual gender rôles among Hellenistic Greeks. For there is no sign, as far as I can see, that they are meant to contribute to characterizing Xanthus as a ridiculous or stupid person; they are rather part of the the set of traits which make him, for all his snobbery and dumbness, a surprisingly sympathetic character.

It should also be noted that there is no mention of Xanthus having any sexual aspirations for or relations with the young female slaves of the household (30: *paidiskaria, korasia*), corresponding to his wife's dreams of a handsome new slave (32-33) or her subsequent affair with Aesop (75). In the symposia, he sometimes drinks too much, as Aesop observes (68), but there is no hint at sexual orgies with harp players or dancers, as in other anecdotes of philosophers' way of life:[48] no,

Xanthus, as we have seen, simply goes home to his wife, hoping to find her responsive to his drunken advances (49).

We shall now turn to the third and last set of values, those concerned with intellectuals and the philosophical life, and the way these were viewed from outside, perhaps from below. One might say that the Xanthus part of the *Life of Aesop* bridges the gap between, on the one side, the caricatures of classical sophists provided, in their different ways, by Aristophanes[49] and Plato, and, on the other, Lucian's satirical works portraying philosophers of the imperial period and such anecdotes as are collected by Diogenes Laertius, Athenaeus and others.[50]

Xanthus, it is emphasized in the Life, was a distinguished philosopher who had studied in Athens "under philosophers, rhetoricians, and philologists (*grammatikois*)" (36) and now attracted to his island many students from Greece and Asia Minor (20). We may perhaps venture to compare Xanthus's imagined position on Samos with that of Posidonius on Rhodes. In that way, we will be able to see in a popular mirror the activities and reputation of such Hellenistic philosophers, whom we are otherwise accustomed to regard with the admiring eyes of a Cicero. What impression did they and their students make on their non-intellectual fellow citizens? Were learning and a philosophical way of life met with sympathy and respect? If not, what particular aspects of their pursuits did arouse resentment or ridicule?

To judge from the *Life of Aesop*, there was little understanding among ordinary people of the more central tenets of the Hellenistic schools of philosophy. Xanthus, we are shown, resorts to philosophical jargon simply to avoid giving straight answers to common people's questions, as when the gardener asks why weeds grow up much quicker than the plants that he waters and to which he gives all kinds of attention (35):

When Xanthus heard this philosophical question (*zêtêma*) and couldn't, on the spur of the moment, think of an answer to it, he said: "All things are subject to the stewardship of divine providence (*panta têi theiai pronoiai dioikeitai*)".

Aesop, as usual, sees right through him and begins to laugh. Xanthus gets angry, but has to put up with the retort (36): "If you talk nonsense (*mêden legêis*), you'll have to expect to be jeered at". Xanthus weakly objects: "Things that are at the disposal of the divine order of nature are not subject to inquiry by philosophers (*ta gar hupo theias phuseôs dioikoumena hupo philosophôn zêteisthai ou dunatai*)", whereupon Aesop, the slave, solves the problem to the gardener's full satisfaction (37).[51]

Once only does Aesop allude with something like respect to formal education and philosophy, namely, when he rebukes Xanthus for forgetting precisely these values in his attempt to commit suicide (85):

"Master, where is your philosophy? Where is your boasted education (*to tês paideias phruagma*)? Where is your doctrine of self-control (*to tês enkrateias dogma*)? Come now, master, are you in such an ill-considered and cowardly rush to die that you would throw away the pleasure of life (*to hêdu zên*) by hanging yourself? Think it over (*metanoêson*), master."

Otherwise, of course, the point steadily driven home is that the slave Aesop, without any formal education but with his inborn intelligence, defeats the philosopher and his students in every test and discussion. This is innate in the comic genre and essential to the plot; and it may be that an utterance like the one just quoted better indicates what common people would actually expect from those with a philosophical education: a greater capability to deal with crises in life, to let reason prevail over emotions.

This is, in fact, visible also in the way Xanthus is depicted earlier in the narrative. We have already seen how his philosophical disposition hinders him from finding a physical outlet for his aggression against his clever slave. Another character trait should probably also be seen in connection with his profession: he is ostentatiously economical. He is obviously rich — in addition to Aesop, he owns a number of slave girls (30) as well as (at least) enough male slaves to carry his wife around in a litter (22).[52] Still, when he hears the price of the two attractive slaves put up for sale together with Aesop, the *grammatikos* and the *psaltês*, he at once looses interest, saying to his students (24W): "it's a principle (*dogma*) with me not to buy high-priced slaves but to be served by cheap ones". On another occasion, he invites his friends to lunch with the following words (39):

"Gentlemen, will you share my simple fare (*eutelôs aristêsai*)? There will be lentil (*phakon*). We ought to judge our friends by their good will (*têi prothumiai*) and not by the elegance of their food. On occasion the humblest dishes afford a more genial pleasure than more pretentious ones if the host serves them with a gracious welcome (*met' eunoias protrepetai*)."

The lunch turns out to be even more frugal than the host had intended, since Aesop chooses to take Xanthus at his word and cooks only one lentil! So frugality as such comes under a bright comical light through this practical joke; but the pompous way in which the philosopher announces his intention of serving good will (*prothumia, eunoia*) rather than good food has already shown us that an outside onlooker would hardly accept that greed is paraded as philosophical moderation. We may assume that among common people it was considered perverse not to display and enjoy one's wealth (cf. Petronius's Trimalchio, with satire from the reverse viewpoint), and that there was little understanding for purely ethical restraints on consumption.

The philosophical debates and discourses that we are invited to listen to in the Life are of course caricatures in both form and content. The formal traits that are ridiculed are easiest to come to terms with. We have already seen something of Xanthus's pompous style in his invitation to lunch. But another example will more clearly display the kind of inflated intellectual discourse that people obviously reacted against. Xanthus arrives with his students *(scholastikoi)* in the slave market and discovers Aesop placed between the two handsome young slaves. He exclaims (23):

Xanthus:	Bravo! Well done, by Hera! An acute and philosophical, indeed a marvellously, a perfectly experienced man!
The students :	What are you praising, professor (*kathêgêta*)? What is worthy of your admiration? Let us in on it, too. Don't begrudge us a share of the beautiful (*metaschein tou kalou*).
Xanthus:	Gentlemen and scholars (*andres philologoi*), you must not think that philosophy consists only in what can be put in words, but also in acts. Indeed, unspoken philosophy (*hê sigômenê philosophia*) often surpasses beyond expectation that which is expressed in words. You can observe this in the case of dancers, how by the movement of their hands they surpass that which is communicated by many words. Just as philosophy can very well consist in acts, in the same way this display too expresses an unspoken philosophy. You see, this man had two handsome slaves and one ugly. He put the ugly one between the handsome ones in order that his ugliness should make their beauty noticeable, for if the ugliness were not set in contrast to that which is superior to it, the appearance of the handsome ones would not have been put to the test.
The students:	You are marvellous, professor. How fine of you to perceive so clearly his purpose!

This excellent parody of academic vices needs little comment. The stuffy atmosphere of the classroom is well captured, with the students flattering their professor and the professor delighting in his own instruction and in the admiration he earns. A question which might have been answered in a few simple words is taken as a pretext for the delivery of a small lecture on spoken and silent philosophy, only marginally relevant to the topic. When the real answer comes, it is drowned in fine words and empty philosophemes. And the author has already shown us how ordinary customers at the sale *actually* reacted to the display: contrary to the philosopher's theory, they turned their backs on all three slaves, because "that one spoils their appearance, too!" (21).

What we have been presented with is, no doubt, a lifelike picture of how people in general would regard the groups of students, with their professor in the middle, whom they would encounter in the streets and stoas, and parts of whose conversation they could sometimes overhear.

If the parody of philosophical form and pretence is clear enough, the actual contents of some of the discussions between Xanthus, his students and Aesop are more difficult to come to grips with. What is the relation here between fiction and reality? There are topics like: "What circumstance will produce great consternation among men?" (47), "Why is it that a sheep being led to the slaughter doesn't make a sound, but a pig squeals loudly?" (48), "Why is it that when we defecate, we often look down at our own droppings?" (67), or, as in the very first discussion between Aesop and Xanthus, why does the philosopher urinate while walking along instead of taking "a little time off for the physical necessities?" (28). There is little of what is discussed in the Xanthus part of the Life that comes closer to philosophy than these topics.

Is this really the kind of topic that people imagined intellectuals as discussing? Or is the choice of topics on the author's part perhaps merely a way of placing the pretentious form of the discussions more in focus through the contrast between an academic form and a trivial or low subject? The comic effect of the contrast between form and content may be exemplified by the conclusion of the urination debate (28):

Xanthus:	I urinated as I walked along (*peripatôn ourêsa*) to avoid three unpleasant consequences.
Aesop:	What are they?
Xanthus:	The heat of the earth, the acrid smell of the urine, and the burning of the sun.
Aesop:	How's that?
Xanthus:	You see that the sun is directly overhead (*mesouranei*) and has scorched the earth with its heat, and when I stand still to urinate, the hot ground burns my feet, the acrid smell of the urine invades my nostrils and blocks my outlets (*ekroas*),[53] and the sun burns my head. It was because I wanted to avoid these three consequences that I urinated as I walked along.
Aesop:	You've convinced me. Well invented (*sophôs epenoêsas*). Walk on.

On the other hand, the choice of topic, while naturally a caricature, is perhaps not so far from what people actually thought philosophers or sophists might discuss in all seriousness. One may compare the kind of topics we know were given for exercise to the students in the imperial schools of rhetoric and which prominent sophists excelled in too — Dio's encomium of a parrot and Lucian's of a fly, etc. (cf. Anderson 1993, 171-99). The writing and performance of such *adoxa* will have looked as ridiculous to a contemporary outsider, who could not appreciate the professional virtuosity displayed, as it does to many of us today.[54]

In the case of the conversations about urination and excretion, the obvious affinity with topics occurring in Old Comedy must be taken into account as well. As in comedy, these discussions will also have been included and elaborated for the simple reason that they were supposed to have an immediate appeal to the intended audience.[55]

This leads us to the last consideration: What kind of audience is the *Life of Aesop* addressing? Are we entitled to characterize it as a specimen of popular literature? If it mirrors attitudes and values of the Hellenistic Greeks, at what level of society are they? My attempt to answer these questions must obviously be provisional — these are complex matters, and we lack much of the comparative material that would permit one to formulate conclusions with any degree of confidence.

First, the author. I am still referring, in the first place, to the Xanthus part of the Life, considering it as a unity in two respects: as an autonomous, probably Hellenistic work incorporated, more or less unaltered, into the extant Life, and as a structured whole rather than a collection of anecdotes. Whoever put this together must have been a man of some education. The parodies of intellectual rhetoric must have been composed by someone with a formal schooling. We should not let the instances of vulgar vocabulary and vulgar topics mislead us into assuming that the author too was "vulgar", in the sense that he belonged to the lower strata of society. Such a person could not have written the intellectual parts, supposing he could write at all, while an educated man of course could use vulgarisms if it happened to suit his purpose. In addition, we may note that some of the vulgar words in the Life, like some of the topics, may have a literary pedigree, deriving from Aristophanes and other Attic comedians,[56] while others may simply reflect contemporary daily language.

Thus, the author cannot, as far as I can see, be used to justify the label "popular literature" for the work. Given the restriction of literacy to the very highest levels of Hellenistic society,[57] it would indeed be strange if he could be. But his intended audience, or part of it, may well be a different matter.

Just as many of Aristophanes's jokes will have had a special appeal to the more simple-minded among his Athenian audience, it seems likely that our story, with its simple jokes, its daily-life situations, and not least its insistent mockery of intellectuals and their pretensions, was primarily directed to a popular audience. This does not preclude, of course, that intellectual readers too might have enjoyed the story and the jokes. But we should note, for instance, that the caricature of the philosophical life it provides is not distinct enough, as far as I can judge, to allow us to identify what particular philosophical sect the author is ridiculing.[58] It is not the kind of refined satire that would have appealed to people with a more intimate knowledge of the different schools of Hellenistic philosophy, and which has survived in other anecdotal material (cf. Decleva Caizzi 1993).

On the other hand, the fact that the hero of the story is a slave should not lead us to believe that the author had slaves, in particular, in mind as his audience. This is not a revolutionary text, in my opinion, any more than Greek and Roman New Comedy is. There is, no doubt, an element of inversion of the normal social order involved, but that is another matter. Thus, I disagree with Keith Hopkins (1993, 19) who writes:

What is so remarkable surely about this story, designed I must stress to be read in a slave society (and perhaps even, as often happened, designed to be read aloud by a slave reader to his listening master and family), is that we are asked and expected in a slave society to side with the slave against the master.

Now, I have no quarrel with the imagined scene itself: such reading aloud within the household, whether by master or slave, is probably how we should envisage much of the consumption of the entertainment literatures of Hellenistic and Roman times (cf. Hägg 1994, 58). But this text does not expect us to "side with the slave against the master". Aesop is a totally atypical slave. There is no loyalty described between him and his fellow-slaves; quite the contrary.[59] The proper resolution of the tension underlying the story is not that slaves in general are to be more respected or given power, but that Aesop, the fabulist, should be set free — be relieved from the servitude which is entirely unfitting for his genius.

The values and attitudes, then, which the story of "Xanthus the Philosopher and Aesop his Slave" demonstrates or implies, are to my mind likely to have been common among people in the Greek Hellenistic world. There is indeed nothing very surprising in the values as such, as we have seen; but that, after all, presumably lies in the very nature of "conventional values". The importance of this work, in our context, is that it gives us a contemporary confirmation of constants and developments which, with our better knowledge of the fourth century BC and of the early imperial period, we might well conjecture for the Hellenistic age, but for which we to a large extent lack the documentation.

Department of Greek, Latin and Egyptology
University of Bergen
Sydnesplassen 7
N-5007 Bergen
Norway

Notes

1. The paper on which the present article is based was first read in the Petronian Society, Munich Section; I wish to thank Niklas Holzberg and the other participants in the discussion for valuable criticism. The final version also profited from comments of the participants in the Conventional Values conference at Rungstedgaard; the more specific of these debts are acknowledged in the notes. Finally, I thank David Konstan for correcting my English and contributing insightful comments on the subject matter as well.

2. For a succinct and up-to-date presentation of the text and the *Stand der Forschung*, see Holzberg 1993, 84-93; for an extensive bibliography, see Beschorner and Holzberg 1992. Holzberg, having analysed the narrative structure, ends by remarking that the social and moral message of the text still remains to be investigated: "Denn Textanalyse, die nach der geistigen Aussage und dem Zeitbezug von Literatur fragt, gibt es im Bereich der Erforschung des Äsop-Romans noch nicht..." (Holzberg 1993, 93). I hope the present contribution may be regarded as a beginning.

3. Hopkins 1993, 11 n. 14 notes that there is "mercifully little written in modern times about the *Life of Aesop*", but still seems to have missed some of the more important contributions, which makes his handling of the text as a source somewhat shaky. E.g., quoting (12 n. 15) from ch. 109, he seems unaware of the background provided by the Oriental *Life of Ahiqar*, and consequently finds Aesop "the surprising mouthpiece of almost conventional wisdom". Cf. also below, n. 22 and n. 41. My observation that the *Life of Aesop* still remains outside the conventional canon of Classical literature is now confirmed by its conspicuous omission in Paul Zanker's brilliant study of "the image of the intellectual in Antiquity" (Zanker 1995).

4. I quote from the second corrected edition (Papathomopoulos 1991). Papathomopoulos's edition corrects a number of Perry's mistakes, but it is still far from being the definitive critical edition of this manuscript; cf. the reviews by Haslam 1992, Adrados 1993 and Dijk 1994b.

5. The ascription, though questioned by some (cf. Hausrath 1937, 774-76), is upheld by Perry 1936, 217-28; 1965, xvii; but cf. Dölger 1953, 375.

6. Among them, notably *POxy*. 3331 + 3720, published with important commentary by Haslam 1980 and 1986.

7. On the text of the papyri, see Perry (1936, 39-70), and, for later additions, Haslam 1980 and 1986.

8. There is a remarkably similar description of the slave Pseudolus in Plaut. *Pseud.* 1218-20. (I owe this reference to Ole Thomsen.) In the comedy, the description has a dramatic function, which it lacks in the Life.

9. Cf. the review by Dijk 1994a.

10. Perry 1952, 5 n. 16. In the table (22) the date is specified as between *c*. 30 BC and AD 100. However, this specific-looking date, quoted e.g. by Papathomopoulos 1991, 22, is no more than a translation into figures of Perry's ascription of the *Life* to a writer living in Roman Egypt.

11. But cf. Shipp 1983, 96: "The manuscript [sc. G] has many koine features that agree with Perry's dating [sc. in the first century AD]." Hopkins 1993, 11 n. 14 finds the date "plausible", but (rightly) suspects that "it involves simply working back from the earliest known papyrus fragment". The potentially most promising way of dating the prototype of G and W would be through an analysis of the language; but the most detailed study so far of this kind, Hostetter 1955, is inconclusive, ending (p. 129) by declaring the "unclassical forms and constructions" in G "in accord with Hellenistic literary usage", evidently defining "Hellenistic" very widely (including, i.e., "early church literature"). Cf. also Adrados 1981,

326, recognizing, with reference to Kindstrand 1976, 25-49, "Cynic" language and style in the *Vita Aesopi*.

12. Adrados 1993, 664. Cf. Adrados 1979a, 664, and 1979b, 112 n. 16. A thorough and circumspect investigation of the Life's language and style is evidently a desideratum.
13. Bibliographical refs. in Beschorner and Holzberg 1992b, 173. Cf. also Nøjgaard 1964, 469-70 and La Penna 1962, 282-84.
14. Adrados 1979b discusses some of the same material, though in a more unfocussed manner and with less convincing conclusions.
15. The testimonia are collected in Perry 1952, 211-29 and interpreted in Perry 1965, xxxv-xlvi.
16. On this rite, cf. Burkert 1985, 82-84.
17. Cf. Adrados 1979b, 107f.: the role played by figs in the first episode.
18. Argued in Perry 1962a; the quotation is from Perry 1966, 286 n. 2.
19. Perry 1966, 286f. n. 2. However, his reference to Hor. *Sat.* 1.1.46-49, to support the existence of a biographical introduction in Demetrius' work, begs the question: "Horace could not have read the story about Aesop in the *Vita* as we have it, because that book was not yet written in his time, before 31 BC".
20. Perry's theory is conditionally approved by Adrados 1979a, 665.
21. *Lykoros* is the form of the name in the Berlin and Oxyrhynchus papyri and should be preferred to the trivialized *Lykourgos* of the manuscript tradition; see Haslam 1986, 149 n. 2, 164.
22. Haslam 1986, 154f. points to similarities with the precepts of the Seven Wise Men in the collection attributed to Sosiades. Oettinger 1992, 20-22 traces a connection with a North Syrian type of *Weisheitssprüche*, subjected to occasional *Entorientalisierung*.
23. Holzberg 1992a, 65-69 demonstrates how the Ahiqar story is structurally integrated in the Life, but does not deny its role as *Vorlage*.
24. See Merkle 1992 with refs. to earlier discussion.
25. It should be noted that Alexis, the poet of Middle and New Comedy, wrote a piece called *Aesop*. The only fragment (Ath. 10.38.431d-f; test. 33 in Perry 1952, 223; fr. 9 PCG), however, quotes a conversation between Aesop and Solon, a topic *not* included in the *Life*.
26. Cf. Rose 1953, La Penna 1962, 306-9, Adrados 1978; 1979b, 112 n. 16; 1981, 326-28 and the judicious discussion in Jedrkiewicz 1989, 116-27.
27. Cf. Compton 1990, Jedrkiewicz 1989, 111-15 and Schauer and Merkle 1992.
28. Although there is an Attic cup of the mid fifth century which depicts a dwarfish Aesop (cf. Zanker 1995, 33f., 348), the literary testimonia of the classical period do not emphasize his ugliness or deformity the way the Life does. Wiechers 1961, 32, however, connects Aesop's ugliness with the *pharmakos* figure. La Penna 1962, 280f. likewise prefers to locate Aesop's deformity among the oldest material in the Aesop legend.
29. The arguments of La Penna 1962, 268-73 against an Egyptian origin deserve consideration. La Penna himself, referring to the textual variants in *Vita Aesopi* 141, tentatively suggests that version G was composed for people in Syria and Palestine, version W for Sicily.
30. See Perry 1952, 4-10 and Haslam 1986, 150. La Penna 1962, 271, however, rightly points to the curious fact that the role which King Nectanebo plays here is less glorious than one would have believed from a nationalistic Egyptian writer (cf. his role in the *Alexander Romance*).
31. For Isis *Mousanagôgos*, see *POxy.* 1380.62 (2nd cent. AD), and cf. Plut. *De Is. et Os.* 3.352b. But, of course, the cult of Isis was widespread by the end of the Hellenistic period.
32. Minor points of language and terminology may of course have been changed in the redactional process. For instance, Hopkins 1993, 15 n. 22, and 25 points to the term

stratêgos employed in ch. 65 for a "local district magistrate", "a term used in this sense as far as I know only in Egypt under Greek and Roman rule".

33. Cf. Perry 1962a, 313 n. 27, 332-34 who thinks the bringing together of Aesop and Croesus is "a dramatic literary invention of the fourth century", further propagated by Demetrius in his *Aesopica*. Cf. the comedy of Alexis (4th/3rd cent. BC; above, n. 25) which makes Aesop meet Solon.

34. There is also the possibility (as David Konstan points out to me) that the whole title is original, then with *anastrophê* used in its earlier sense "reversal", which would fit well with the Xanthus part of the Life, culminating with Aesop's emancipation. The sense "way of life" is attested from Polybius onwards (LSJ s.v. II.3), and will anyway be how the title was understood in the Imperial period (cf. the New Testament usage).

35. The subscription of G, on the other hand, is formulated as if we had read a full biography: *Aisôpou genna, anatrophê, prokopê kai apobiôsis*. In Rec. W, two of the best manuscripts (followed by Perry in his text) have the title *Bios Aisôpou tou philosophou*, and the others, too, display various phrases containing *bios* and/or *diêgêsis* (see Perry 1952, 81, 133).

36. Perry 1936, 1f.; cf. Perry 1952, 3f.

37. Cf. Harris 1989, 116-47 for a low estimate of Hellenistic literacy in general, and esp. p. 126 touching on our question (but not mentioning the *Life of Aesop*): "Any assumption that the intellectually less demanding genres of Hellenistic literature aimed at, or reached, a truly popular audience of readers should be resisted. The papyri show conclusively that popular literature did not exist in any ordinary sense of that expression ..." Cf. also p. 227-28 and my comments in Hägg 1994.

38. Hostetter 1955, a dissertation supervised by Perry, reaffirms the latter's view.

39. Hopkins 1993, 11. Hopkins (6 n. 6) also remarks: "I use the term 'Roman slavery' rather crudely to refer to slavery in the Roman empire, without implying either uniformity or consistency — just as one might use the term 'bread' to cover bread in France, England, Russia and the USA, in spite of the known variations". Very well; but as soon as one proceeds from basic definition to actual description, one has to choose what bread to describe.

40. Jack Winkler 1991, 279, too, in his chapter on the *Life of Aesop*, calls it a "genuine folk-book", envisaging a kind of collective authorship. It is important, I think, to distinguish between, on the one hand, the various anecdotes and other legendary material circulating through the centuries about a figure like Aesop, and, on the other, the existence of a written story based on such material. The former stage is "collective" in the sense that many people tell and develop these anecdotes, each with his own selection and adaptation; but as soon as it comes to collecting them in a book with a continuous story, the choice and framework are due to one person, and the designation "folk-book" misleading.

41. The fact that Aesop is a slave only in the first 90 chapters saves Hopkins from more serious consequences of his unitarian view. But on p. 25 he declares that "the murder of the scapegoat", i.e. the execution of Aesop in Delphi (132-42), "reflects ... the endemic hostility to the clever slave in Roman society". Aesop's death, however, is one of the really ancient elements of the legend, already known to Herodotus (2.134). Cf. also above, n. 3.

42. Aesop again elaborates this topic in ch. 88.

43. The same attitude, as Hopkins 1993, 19 n. 31 notes, is witnessed by Plut. *De garr.* 18.511d-e.

44. There is ample comparative material in Headlam's notes to Herod. 5. (David Konstan kindly turned my attention to this text).

45. I owe this point to Sarah Pomeroy.

46. See now also Hunter 1994, 70-95 (Ch. 3, "Slaves in the Household: Was Privacy Possible?"), with illustrative material both from Classical literary and archaeological sources and from records of the plantation households of the American South.

47. Cf. also her acute description (in a negative context) of her husband's character in the beginning of ch. 31.

48. See, e.g., Alciphron 3.19, on the behaviour of the Epicurean and the Cynic, quoted in Decleva Caizzi 1993, 303f.

49. On the function of intellectuals in Aristophanes's plays, see the illuminating discussion in Zimmermann 1993.

50. For an interpretation of these anecdotes, see Decleva Caizzi 1993. The original and thought-provoking introductory parts of her article (303-7), sketching a programmme for the investigation of contemporary popular views of Hellenistic philosophers, are not persued further in the rest of her article, which is a more historically orientated study of Zeno.

51. On this scene, cf. La Penna 1962a, 302f., who sees in Aesop's solution (37) the victory of science over a philosophical-religious attempt at explanation (Xanthus's Providence).

52. Pointed out by Hopkins 1993, 17 n. 26.

53. Adopting Papathomopoulos's plausible conjecture for *akoas* (G). Perry deletes the whole phrase.

54. I owe this point to Johnny Christensen.

55. On "scatological humour" in Attic comedy, see Henderson 1975, 187-203.

56. Cf. Hostetter 1955, 124f., who, however, prefers to regard these words as belonging to the "vernacular" in both classical and Hellenistic times and surfacing in works like comedy and the *Life of Aesop*, while they were taboo in most other literature.

57. Cf. the references above, n. 37.

58. Rather, there seems to be a mixture of the various special vocabularies and other characteristics of the schools: Platonism (26 *to eidos*, 35 *pronoia*, 23 *metaschein tou kalou* and *hê sigômenê philosophia*), Stoicism (36 *ta ... hupo theias phuseôs dioikoumena*, 85 *enkrateia*), Epicureanism (85 *to hêdu zên*). The discourse on "peripatetic" urination may parody Aristotle and other scientific writings (Hippocrates?), the obsession with excrement and other bodily functions may be modelled on Cynicism (on Aesop himself as a Cynic type, see the references above, n. 26). These are only scattered observations, and the topic evidently needs a closer study.

59. The clearest instances of a failure of loyalty are in the initial part of the *Life* (2-19), i.e., outside my selected part of the story, but inside that of Hopkins. Note that the other slaves mostly operate *as a group*, against Aesop.

Bibliography

Adrados, F.R. 1953. Review of Perry 1952, *Gnomon* 25, 323-28.

Adrados, F.R. 1978. "Elementos cinicos en las 'Vidas' de Esopo y Secundo y en el 'Diálogo' de Alejandro y los gimnosofistas", in: S.J. Bilbao, *Homenaje a Eleuterio Elorduy, S.J.*, 309-28.

Adrados, F.R. 1979a. *Historia de la fábula greco-latina, 1: Introducción y de los origines a la edad helenística*. Madrid.

Adrados, F.R. 1979b. "The 'Life of Aesop' and the Origins of Novel in Antiquity", *QuadUrbin* 30, 93-112.

Adrados, F.R. 1981. "Sociolingüística y griego antiguo", *RevEspLing* 11, 311-29.

Adrados, F.R. 1993. Review of Papathomopoulos 1990, *Gnomon* 65, 660-64.

Adrados, F.R. & Reverdin, O. (eds.) 1984. *La Fable*. (EntrHardt 30). Vandoeuvres.

Anderson, G. 1993. *The Second Sophistic: A Cultural Phenomenon in the Roman Empire*. London/New York.

Beschorner, A. & Holzberg, N. 1992. "A Bibliography of the Aesop Romance", in: Holzberg (ed.) 1992b, 165-87.

Blake, W.E. 1954. Review of Perry 1952, *AJPh* 75, 79-84.

Bremer, J.M. & Handley, E.W. (eds.) 1993. *Aristophane*. (EntrHardt 38). Vandoeuvres.

Bulloch, A., Gruen, E.S., Long, A.A. & Stewart, A. (eds.) 1993. *Images and Ideologies: Self-Definition in the Hellenistic World*. Berkeley/Los Angeles.

Burkert, W. 1985. *Greek Religion: Archaic and Classical*. Trans. by J. Raffan. Oxford.

Compton, T. 1990. "The Trial of the Satirist: Poetic *Vitae* (Aesop, Archilochus, Homer) as Background for Plato's *Apology*", *AJPh* 111, 330-47.

Daly, L.W. (ed.) 1961. *Aesop Without Morals: The Famous Fables, and a Life of Aesop*. New York/London.

Decleva Caizzi, F. 1993. "The Porch and the Garden: Early Hellenistic Images of the Philosophical Life", in: Bulloch, Gruen, Long & Stewart (eds.) 1993, 303-29.

Dijk, G.-J. van 1994a. Review of Holzberg 1992b, *Mnemosyne* 47, 384-89.

Dijk, G.-J. van 1994b. Review of Papathomopoulos 1990, *Mnemosyne* 47, 550-55.

Dölger, F. 1953. Review of Perry 1952, *ByzZ* 46, 373-78.

Eriksen, R. (ed.) 1994. *Contexts of Pre-Novel Narrative: The European Tradition*. Berlin/New York.

Goins, S.E. 1989. "The Influence of Old Comedy on the *Vita Aesopis* (sic)", *ClW* 83, 28-30.

Hägg, T. 1994. "Orality, Literacy, and the 'Readership' of the Early Greek Novel", in: Eriksen (ed.) 1994, 47-81.

Harris, W.V. 1989. *Ancient Literacy*. Cambridge, Mass./London.

Haslam, M.W. 1980. "3331. *Life of Aesop*", in: R.A. Coles & M.W. Haslam (eds.) *The Oxyrhynchus Papyri*, vol. 47, London, 53-56.

Haslam, M.W. 1986. "3720. *Life of Aesop* (Addendum to 3331)", in: M.W. Haslam (ed.) *The Oxyrhynchus Papyri*, vol. 53, London, 149-72.

Haslam, M.W. 1992. Review of Papathomopoulos 1990, *ClR* 42, 188-89.

Hausrath, A. 1937. Review of Perry 1936, *PhilWoch* 57, 770-77.

Henderson, J. 1975 *The Maculate Muse: Obscene Language in Attic Comedy*. New Haven/London.

Holzberg, N. 1992a. "Der Äsop-Roman. Eine strukturanalytische Interpretation", in: Holzberg (ed.) 1992b, 33-75.

Holzberg, N. (ed.) 1992b. *Der Äsop-Roman. Motivgeschichte und Erzählstruktur*. Tübingen.

Holzberg, N. 1993. *Die antike Fabel. Eine Einführung*. Darmstadt.

Hopkins, K. 1993. "Novel Evidence for Roman Slavery", *PastPres* 138, 3-27.

Hostetter, W.H. 1955. "A Linguistic Study of the Vulgar Greek Life of Aesop". Diss. University of Illinois. Urbana.

Hunter, V.J. 1994. *Policing Athens: Social Control in the Attic Lawsuits, 420-320 B.C.* Princeton.

Jedrkiewicz, S. 1989. *Sapere e paradosso nell'antichità: Esopo e la favola*. (Filologia e critica 60). Rome.

Kindstrand, J.F. 1976. *Bion of Borysthenes: A Collection of the Fragments with Introduction and Commentary*. (Acta Universitatis Upsaliensis. Studia Graeca Upsaliensia 11). Uppsala.

La Penna, A. 1962. "Il romanzo di Esopo", *Athenaeum* 40, 264-314.

Merkle, S. 1992. "Die Fabel von Frosch und Maus. Zur Funktion der *logoi* im Delphi-Teil des Äsop-Romans", in: Holzberg (ed.) 1992b, 110-27.

Nøjgaard, M. 1964. *La fable antique*, vol. 1: *La fable grecque avant Phèdre*. Copenhagen.

Oettinger, N. 1992. "Achikars Weisheitssprüche im Licht älterer Fabeldichtung", in: Holzberg (ed.) 1992b, 3-22.

Papathomopoulos, M. (ed.) 1990. *Ho bios tou Aisôpou. Hê parallagê G. Kritikê ekdosê me eisagôgê kai metaphrasê*. Ioannina.

Papathomopoulos, M. (ed.) 1991. *Ho bios tou Aisôpou. Hê parallagê G. Kritikê ekdosê me eisagôgê kai metaphrasê* (2nd ed). Ioannina.

Perry, B.E. 1936. *Studies in the Text History of the Life and Fables of Aesop*. (Philological Monographs published by the American Philological Association 7). Haverford, Pa. (Repr. Chico, Cal. 1981).

Perry, B.E. 1952. *Aesopica: A Series of Texts Relating to Aesop or Ascribed to him or Closely Connected with the Literary Tradition that Bears his Name*. Urbana. (Repr. New York 1980).

Perry, B.E. 1962a. "Demetrius of Phalerum and the Aesopic Fables", *TAPhA* 93, 287-346.

Perry, B.E. 1962b. Review of Wiechers 1961, *Gnomon* 34, 620-22.

Perry, B.E. (ed.) 1965. *Babrius and Phaedrus Newly Edited and Translated into English, together with an Historical Introduction and a Comprehensive Survey of Greek and Latin Fables in the Aesopic Tradition*, The Loeb Classical Library, vol. 436. London/Cambridge, Mass.

Perry, B.E. 1966. "Some Addenda to the Life of Aesop", *ByzZ* 59, 285-304.

Rose, H.J. 1953. Review of Perry 1952, *ClR* 67, 154-55.

Schauer, M. & Merkle, S. 1992. "Äsop und Sokrates", in: Holzberg (ed.) 1992b, 85-96.

Shipp, G.P. 1983. "Notes on the Language of *Vita Aesopi* G", *Antichthon* 17, 96-106.

West, M.L. 1984. "The Ascription of Fables to Aesop in Archaic and Classical Greece", in: Adrados & Reverdin (eds.) 1984, 105-36.

Wiechers, A. 1961. *Aesop in Delphi*. (Beiträge zur klassischen Philologie 2). Meisenheim.

Winkler, J.J. 1991. *Auctor & Actor: A Narratological Reading of Apuleius's Golden Ass*. Berkeley.

Zanker, P. 1995. *The Mask of Socrates: The Image of the Intellectual in Antiquity*. Trans. A. Shapiro. (Sather Classical Lectures 59). Berkeley.

Zimmermann, B. 1993. "Aristophanes und die Intellektuellen", in: Bremer & Handley (eds.) 1993, 255-86.

FAMILY VALUES:
THE USES OF THE PAST

Sarah B. Pomeroy

Is there a history of the Greek family?[1] Since history studies change over time, we must ask whether there were changes in the family from the classical to the Hellenistic period? Were new family shapes and structures, values and behaviour introduced in response to the changing world? The principal historiographic question I shall pose is whether a synchronic or a diachronic approach is most appropriate to the study of the Greek family.

Interest in the family is not a new phenomenon in ancient history. Most historians in the past have believed that the family did change over large periods of time, though they did not discuss relatively minor historical transitions such as that from the classical to the Hellenistic period. Beginning in the 1860s J.J. Bachofen, Numa Denis Fustel de Coulanges, John McLennan, Friedrich Engels,[2] and others, attempted to trace the history of human family patterns. The existence of matriarchy and promiscuous intercourse preceding patriarchy and the monogamous family was postulated. Like Herodotus, who sometimes wrote about non-Greeks (such as Amazons) whom he could not possibly have seen himself, some nineteenth century historians were not adverse to using "armchair" anthropology in their speculations about the development of the family. This sort of historicism, starting with prehistory, is no longer considered either fashionable or enlightening, and the works of the nineteenth century have been properly relegated to the category of social philosophy rather than history.

The belief in historical change, however, is still a valid model and provides the structure for the most useful general study of the Greek family published in the twentieth century: W.K. Lacey's *The Family in Classical Greece* (1968). Lacey discusses families in the archaic and classical periods but, as he once told me, he avoided the Hellenistic because he found it "too confusing". Since I was trained as a papyrologist, I've never hesitated to discuss the Hellenistic world. Nevertheless, as I was writing this paper and using evidence other than Greek papyri from Egypt, I began to appreciate Professor Lacey's caution. For the study of the Hellenistic family there are many primary sources, but they are disparate and incommensurate, and defy generalization.

Most scholars who have written about the Greek family in the last decade have preferred a synchronic approach. Mark Golden, in *Children and Childhood in Classical Athens* (1990), argues against the notion of historical change in the classical Athenian family, and consequently organizes his evidence and his book not chronologically, but by family rôle and relationship. Similarly, Virginia Hunter, in *Policing Athens. Social Control in the Attic Lawsuits* (1994), employs a synchronic approach to her study of the Athenian family and society. Citing continuities in laws and practices concerning adoption, Lene Rubinstein[3] also argues that the fourth century was not a period of transition. Although Golden, Hunter, and Rubinstein use evidence from *New Comedy*, none of them explores the changes that Macedonian domination imposed on the Greek world in the private sphere; all discuss only the classical period in detail. This time frame, I believe, is the principal reason for their rejection of the developmental perspective and their emphasis on continuity. Classicists are among the most conservative of historians. As we see, it has taken nearly half a century for ancient historians to fully accept the theory of *La longue durée*. Only by avoiding the Hellenistic period, however, have they been able to cling to the Braudelian historical model.

In contrast to Golden, Hunter, and Rubinstein, I believe that a chronological framework is more often appropriate for the study of the Greek family than a synchronic, topical approach, and I am using this framework for the book I have just completed on the family in classical and Hellenistic Greece.[4] Of course, when the primary sources are few, or derive from a limited historical period, as is the case for many individual families, it is difficult to demonstrate change over time. Changes in social structures often come about slowly and may or may not coincide with political events. For example, as I shall emphasize in this paper, major population upheavals following war and migration do affect family relationships. Widows and grass widows (or abandoned wives) are created; in some cities young men are decimated, in others their numbers increase. For Greeks in Ptolemaic Egypt infanticide vanished, but bigamy, intermarriage between Greeks and non-Greeks, and brother-sister marriage entered the historical record. There was a major change in the relationship between *oikos* and *polis*. In the classical period, the family regularly mediated between the individual and the political group. Citizens had become members of the Athenian *polis* not as individuals; rather, they first had to be accepted as members of a family. In contrast, in the Hellenistic period some states were not reluctant to grant citizenship to individuals whose parents had not also been citizens. In an endeavour to recruit new citizens, states such as Miletus and Ilion ignored family membership, legitimacy, and, gender. Except among the ruling élite, descent was less important than it had formerly been. The *oikos* idea with its perpetuation protected by such legal devices as the *epiklêrate* was not transported to new territories such as Egypt. In other words, the Aristotelian formulation that the *oikos* precedes the *polis* is no longer generally applicable in the Hellenistic period.[5]

The first body of evidence we will examine in some detail consists of funerary foundations.[6] The *polis* provided the model for the administrative structures of funerary foundations for private families. Beginning in the late fourth century, some wealthy people established foundations to institutionalize offerings to dead members of their family, attempting to ensure their own future care as well. Funds were contributed to make certain that proper attention would be paid to the memory of the dead and to support the maintenance of their tombs. As an additional bulwark against the ravages of mortality and the migration of kinsmen to distant parts of the cosmopolis, the founders of such cults had their endowments publicized and recorded in elaborate detail in inscriptions that have endured.

Although only the wealthy could create such cults and they were neither common nor found in all parts of the Greek world, we shall examine them briefly here because they show both the perpetuation of traditional beliefs regarding death, the family, and society, and adaptation to the new circumstances of the Hellenistic period. The evidence for the funerary foundations is not Athenian: all the inscriptions were found in areas of the Eastern Aegean. Whereas Athenian practices concerning the dead emphasize the involvement of close kin, these Hellenistic, non-Athenian versions were necessarily less exclusionary.

A microhistory of Epicteta of Thera is sufficient to demonstrate some of the changes in the Greek family in the Hellenistic period.[7] Epicteta established her foundation between 210 and 195 in honour of the Muses, her husband, her two deceased sons, and herself. The founders of such cults could not boast of heroic ancestors like those celebrated by Pindar, whom art had immortalized. Nevertheless, Epicteta's family constructed a lineage for themselves. Four members of the family were designated as "heroes", an example of hyperbole, euphemism, and wishful thinking. Excerpts from her testament follow:

... Epicteta daughter of Grinnus, sane and in her right mind, devised by will the following ... I leave [this will] according to the instruction given to me by my husband Phoinix, who had the Mouseion built for our deceased son Cratesilochus, and had the reliefs and the statues of himself and Cratesilochus and the heroic monuments brought there, and had asked me to finish the construction of the Mouseion ...

I leave the Mouseion and the holy precinct of the heroic monuments to my daughter Epiteleia, in order that she, having inherited the proceeds of my other estates as well, will pay every year in the month of Eleusinius 210 dr. to the association of the men's club, which I have formed from the kinsmen ...

My daughter's son Andragoras shall hold the priesthood of the Muses and the Heroes, but if something shall happen to him, always the eldest from the family of Epiteleia ...

The names of the relatives I have assembled are written below:

Hypereides son of Thrasyleon; Antisthenes son of Isocles, by adoption son of Grinnus; Aristodamus son of Isocles; Timesius son of Praxiteles; Evagoras son of Procleidas; Procleidas son of Evagoras; Cartidamas son of Procleidas; Hagnosthenes son of Cartidamas; Procleidas son of Alcimedon; Bolacrates son of Aglosthenes; Archinicus son of Gorgopas; Startophus son of Bolocrates; Gorgopas son of Archinicus; Gorgopas son of Erchestratus; Gorgopas son of Cartidamas; Agathostratus son of Cratesilochus; Mollis son of Polymedes; Cartidamas and Cratesilochus and Dion and Dorocleidas, sons of Agathostratus; Himertus son of Himerophon; Critus son of Teisanor; Polynicus and Evagoras, sons of Soteles. Also their wives, living together with them, shall be admitted and their children, the female children as long as they are under their father's guardianship, the male as well when they are of age, and their issue under the same conditions. Also the heiresses and their husbands living together with them shall be admitted and their children according to the same rules as written above. Also my namesake Epicteta shall be admitted; and my daughter Epiteleia; and the daughters of Gorgopas, Mnaso and Ainesippa; and the daughters of Thrasyleon, Basilodika and Telesippa; and Callidica, daughter of Isocles; and their husbands, living together with them. Also Aristarchus' daughter Epiteleia shall be admitted, and the children of all these.[8]

As we see, Epicteta's immediate family was small and her natural expectation that one of her sons, at least, would look after her in her old age was unfulfilled. Her daughter, Epiteleia, was her only surviving child: she employs her son-in-law Hypereides as *kurios* for the transaction. Like other women in the Hellenistic period,[9] she is in charge of a substantial fortune. She probably had become wealthy through both dowry and inheritance. *Oliganthrôpia* (i.e. a "lack of men") is evident in two generations of Epicteta's family. She had no brothers, for her father Grinnus had adopted a certain Antisthenes, son of Isocles (lines 81-82, 108). Epicteta's own sons had died: Cratesilochus predeceased his father Phoinix, and Andragoras died two years after his father. Epiteleia was her mother's sole heir. Perhaps because her daughter's children were legally members of another family, and Epicteta's had died out, she felt she needed to create inducements to secure their future ministrations. Her daughter's family was destined to inherit her fortune. Nevertheless, it would be natural to have been concerned lest after her death they might wish to put the funds to other uses. No reasons for worry are, however, apparent. Epiteleia's ties to her mother's family are evident in that her son Andragoras bears the same name as her deceased brother. Although he was an only son, he was not named for a member of his father's family. As priest of the cult of the dead, Andragoras would fulfill the duty of an actual descendant of Epicteta and Phoinix, even if he had not been legally adopted.

Despite the fact that only the female members of her nuclear family survive, Epicteta designated males as the original participants of her foundation. The title is first announced as "the association of the men's club" (lines 22-23). This preference is understandable in the general context of Greek patriarchal tradition. The foundation's institutions are adopted from political administration, and, of course, only men were versed in government. Furthermore, practical reasons dictated the preference for males. As a result of patrilocal marriage Epicteta's female relatives may have lived far from the site of the cult, and have had obligations to their husband's families that would prevent them from carrying out the duties assigned to members of the foundation. Thus, the participation of female children is limited to the period when they are under their father's guardianship (lines 95-96). But Epicteta has second thoughts, more practical ones. She admits on equal terms: wives of the original members, and, as we have mentioned, their daughters who are still under their father's guardianship; as well as descendants of the original members; and *epikleroi* with their husbands and offspring. Finally she admits eight women with their husbands and children, including her own daughter, two sisters of her son-in-law, and three additional women who are daughters or sisters of other members of the group. Epicteta drafted into her family foundation people with whom she had no kinship ties recognized by law or terminology. A large number of participants are only relatives of relatives. Using them she constructed for herself a family with as many lateral branches as any we might find in classical Athens. Even so, the entire group consists of 25 named males and only eight named females. This list of names indicates that demographic and historical forces shaped the structure and composition of both the nuclear and extended family. These, in turn, affected the financial status of women such as Epicteta. Yet she attempted to create an institution where mostly male kin would care for the family tomb as they had done three hundred years earlier in the classical period.

Such foundations would encourage and institutionalize family reunions. They were particularly valuable in the Hellenistic period when the family network was likely to have been small. Some male members of the immediate family were doubtless permanently separated from their kinsmen because they had become mercenaries or had emigrated. Some families who had emigrated had no distant male relatives, and, as seems to have been the case in Epicteta's family, the rate of family extinction may have been accelerated by female infanticide. Thus, parenthetically, it is impossible to draw a simple conclusion concerning the status of women. Female infanticide is a symptom of the low status of women. On the other hand, the Hellenistic period offers plenty of evidence for the improvement of women's financial and legal status, with women like Epicteta and her daughter Epiteleia managing a large amount of money, expecting, apparently, an obligatory nod from the male guardians whom they select. Specific laws governing women's guardianship in Hellenistic Thera are not known. According to the rules of the *anchisteia* in Athens,[10] Epicteta's guardian should have been her adopted brother. In no legal system that is known was a mother-in-law part of her son-in-law's *anchisteia*, nor was there any necessity that he serve as her guardian. In other words, a widow like Epicteta who had no close male relatives was free to select as her guardian any man whom she found congenial.

Like Epicteta, a certain Diomedon who endowed a funerary foundation in honour of Heracles Diomedonteius in the third to second century BC in Cos seems to have had a dearth of kinsmen, at least in the neighbourhood.[11] The inscription is admittedly fragmentary. Though kinsmen are mentioned in general, the only person named is his slave Libys. Diomedon directs that commemorative activities be carried out by his slave, Libys, and his slave's children, all of whom he frees.[12] The arrangements for Libys and his children are made at the very beginning of the inscription, preceding and following a brief general sentence giving instructions for Diomedon's descendants. Perhaps Diomedon did not yet have children, or they had emigrated elsewhere. He shows more concern for Libys than for his relatives. It may be that there were no laws or customs similar to those at Athens that obliged him to give preference to relatives in the disposition of his property and affections. Polybius (20.6.5-6) states that in Boeotia in 192, childless men did not bequeath their property to their relatives, as had been customary previously, but instead left their property to their friends to be used in common for feasting and drinking. Even many who had relatives gave the major portion of their property to their eating clubs. Polybius reports this symptom of family disintegration with disapproval. The evidence of funerary foundations is consistent with Polybius' report. Even those who have kinsmen seem to consider them unreliable. Their ministrations are no longer assumed to be natural, nor are they imposed by law: rather they must be bribed. From the preceding survey, we might deduce that the family was of less value in the Hellenistic period than it had been formerly, but the trend is far from monolineal. Nostalgia complicates the picture.

Nostalgia is a symptom of historical change, and of the general belief that the change has been for the worse. This idealisation of the past is characteristic of many Hellenistic artists and intellectuals who found inspiration among their dead ancestors. A case in point is Demosthenes' nephew, Demochares II. Like his uncle, Demochares pursued both a literary and political career, and his son Laches II was also active in politics.[13] Demochares II, born to Laches I and Demosthenes' sister probably between 355 and 350, was a soldier, administrator, politician, diplomat, orator, and historian. Demosthenes had no sons and his daughter predeceased him, but his nephew was his spiritual heir. Demochares wrote over twenty books of *Histories* about his own time.[14] Cicero (*Brut.* 286, cf. *De Or.* 2.95) identified Demochares as his uncle's literary heir when he declared that the *Histories* belonged more to the genre of rhetoric than history. Demochares' ideals and policies in support of the independent democracy of Athens and in opposition to Macedonian domination were similar to his uncle's. Demochares' embassies to Lysimachus and Antipater, around 286, were more successful than Demosthenes' journey to Philip II had been, for he returned to Athens having obtained gifts from Lysimachus worth 130 talents.[15] Despite Demochares' encounters with the Macedonians and the advent of the Hellenistic period, we see in his behaviour an attempt to perpetuate the classical democratic traditions for which his family had become famous.

Similarly, for some Hellenistic artists family tradition was a source of pride and profit. Families that had enjoyed economic success reproduced themselves in each generation without distinguishing classical from Hellenistic: the same names and the same artistic styles occur.[16] For example, it is not always possible to determine to which Praxiteles, son of Cephisodotus, a particular sculpture should be attributed. Sometimes people deliberately created a fictitious genealogy. Although they were not related to the famous bearers of the name, they assumed it or bestowed it upon their children, expecting to enjoy the fame and fortune of the earlier homonymous practitioner. Homonymous artists were rampant. The same phenomenon occurs among the Hellenistic physicians who use the name "Hippocrates" probably without being descended from earlier physicians of that name.

Feelings of nostalgia for family traditions were not confined to the élite. At both Sparta and Athens nostalgia for a so-called "ancestral constitution" arose. As far as the family was concerned, such nostalgia was expressed in a reverence for legislation attributed to Lycurgus and Solon. New laws were also promulgated and purported to be revivals of archaic legislation. Thus, the past was recreated and invented as was expedient, and the historical testimony to change over time was blurred.

The Peripatetics were especially active in this conservative movement, for they specialized in antiquarian research. Aristotle and his followers collected the constitutions of various Greek cities. They failed to consider that some laws could have been promulgated and published, but never obeyed or effected. Perhaps such considerations were irrelevant to Demetrius of Phalerum when he seized the opportunity to govern Athens. Demetrius had studied with Theophrastus. Like Demochares he was a historian: thus it was natural for him to look to the past. Demetrius was also a politician who exploited the past as propaganda for his reforms. Instituting measures affecting the conduct of private life, Demetrius attempted to make them more acceptable by claiming he was reviving Solonian legislation.

According to Cicero, Demetrius outlawed the use of large decorated gravestones that had drawn attention to burials of the wealthy. Such tombstones were found in the archaic period, but had gone out of fashion during the first three quarters of the fifth century.[17] Whether these changes in commemoration were the result of legislation or artistic fashion is uncertain. Although we know of no specific legislation curbing the use of such monuments until the enactments of Demetrius, and we have only Cicero's testimony that he was reviving earlier laws, Demetrius' legislation is consistent with the sumptuary intention of other laws attributed to Solon. At any rate, Ruschenbusch includes Demetrius' legislation in his compilation of Solon's laws.[18]

Demetrius also created a board of *gunaikonomoi* ("regulators of women").[19] Aristotle (*Pol.* 1322b37-1323a3) had approved of such magistrates. At Athens their duties included control over women's participation in funerals and festivals. Some fragments of *New Comedy* constitute the earliest evidence for *gunaikonomoi* at Athens, though they appear earlier in inscriptions at other Greek cities such as Thasos and Gambreum dated to 340 or later, where they are instructed to prevent excessive lamentation. Evidently, women, doubtless many of whom were widows, were considered likely to overindulge in disorderly expressions of grief. Plutarch and others had attributed sumptuary restrictions governing women and funerals to Solon. In this case Demetrius was actually reinstating Solon's restrictions.

These retrogressive social notions were not confined to the old Greek cities. Peripatetic philosophers including Demetrius advised Ptolemy I concerning the design of the administrative structures of his new state.[20] We surmise that Ptolemy, upon becoming sovereign of Egypt, would have wanted to know about the population of his adoptive country, and consulted Demetrius who had recent experience in organizing such a survey at Athens.

Demetrius had classified the inhabitants of Attica according to political status: citizens, metics, and slaves. Because the resulting total number of citizens is so small, scholars have deduced that only adult males were included. In Egypt, women definitely were counted because they were liable for the salt tax, and the inhabitants were classified into more categories than had been used at Athens. There is no doubt that the categories and their sequence were inspired by traditional Greek patterns of thought concerning gender hierarchy and ideology. These ideas are encapsulated in Peripatetic writings about family structure. According to Aristotle (*Pol.* 1253a19-20), the state is composed of individual *oikoi* or households. Each household is governed by a single ruler: the male rules over the female, the child, and the slave. The father is superior to the mother. Dominance and subordination are biologically determined and therefore inevitable. The form of the Ptolemaic census, which is a vertical list, imposes a patriarchal hierarchy with a chain of being starting at the top with a male head of the household, descending through his wife, children, and slaves, sometimes down to animals. For example:

> Antigonos, son of Kottion
> Nikaia (or Nike), his wife
> Ptolemy, his son
> Theophilos, his son
> [.]llw, his peasant
> Taias (?), his sister; total 6, of which 4 (men)
>   (*P. Lille dem.* III 99, col. iii, lines 16-21)

> Eupolemos, son of Nikon
> Eiren[e], his wife
> Herakl[eitos], his son
> Nik[aia] (or Nik[e]), his wife
> Polem[on], his son
> Nauplion (?), his wife
> Philoxenos, his son; total 7, of which 3 (men)[21]
> sheep: 170; lambs: 25; calves(?): 1
> pigs: 10
>   (*P. Lille dem.* III 99, col. iv, lines 6-14, 230-228 BC)

Except for the placement of siblings and children, this order is almost invariable. As in Aristotle's description, the family relationships reported are those between the male head and the other individuals in the household, but they are not reciprocal. Thus, a woman may be identified as a "wife", or a "mother", and a younger man as a "son", but the head of household is not also termed a "husband" or a "father". The focus is on the male who is considered the head of the house. This emphasis is a constant feature of population lists in the Ptolemaic period.

Aristotle (*Pol.* 1253b5-13) states that one man who heads the household plays three rôles: husband, father, and master of slaves. In the classical polis and in

Ptolemaic Egypt he might play the second and third rôle in relationship to several people. Marriage in the old Greek cities was regularly monogamous. In Ptolemaic Egypt, in contrast, a man might play the rôle of husband simultaneously more than once. The lists give a few examples of bigamy and one of trigamy. There is no distinction here between Greek and Demotic papyri. Some examples of bigamy occur in *P. Sorbonne* inv. no. 331, fr. 2 (col. i, lines 44-45, fr. 6, col.i, lines 106-7, fr. 10, lines 144-45, fr. 12, col. i, lines 175-76, fr. 13. col. ii, lines 166a-67) where two women, both identified as "wife" (*gunê*), appear together. In *P. Lille démotique* III 101 (col. iv, lines 30-33) a soldier has two wives and a "nurse". This group perhaps constitutes trigamy. The possibility of bigamy is the reason for the monogyny clause in marriage contracts, for example in *P. Elephantine* 1 (lines 8-9) of 311, where it is written that "it shall not be lawful for Heraclides to bring home another woman for himself in such a way as to inflict contumely on Demetria, nor to beget children by another woman", and in *P. Tebtunis* I 104 (lines 18-21), of 92 BC where it is stated: "It shall not be lawful for Philiscus to bring home for himself another wife in addition to Apollonia, nor to maintain a female concubine, nor a little boyfriend, nor to beget children by another woman while Apollonia is alive, nor to dwell in another house over which Apollonia has no rights". Such husbands could have emulated some of the Ptolemaic kings and their Macedonian predecessors. Ptolemy I, Ptolemy VIII, Philip II of Macedon, and Alexander the Great also were not monogamous. Polygyny was not limited to the Macedonian monarchs. In Susa in 324 Alexander had celebrated mass marriages of his troops with native women (Arrian 7.4.4-8). More than ten thousand of his men married Asian women. Many had children by them (Arrian 7.10.3). These women were lawful wives, not concubines. According to Arrian (7.12.2) when Alexander sent his veterans back to Macedonia he told his men that if they had children by Asian wives, they should leave them in Asia so as not to make trouble in Macedonia between foreigners and children of foreign wives and the children and mothers they had left at home. This change from strict monogamy to permissible bigamy constitutes a major change in the paradigm of the Greek family from the classical to the Hellenistic period.

According to traditional Greek ideals, a woman's principal function was not production, but reproduction. Therefore, within a family a woman is much more useful as a wife than as a daughter, and a widow is completely useless. For example, in *Corpus Papyrorum Raineri* XIII, a collection of tax documents from the third century, twenty-four people are recorded as *huios*, but only two as *thugatêr*.[22] Although so few women are identified as thugatêr, some two hundred are listed as *gunê*.[23] Few women are identified as *thugatêr*, but some two hundred are listed as *gunê*. Moreover, wives are usually listed without patronymics, only by a proper name, followed by *gunê*. A few wives have no personal identity at all: they are nameless, and appear generically as *gunê*.[24] When her husband dies, the wife loses her position and sometimes her proper name as well: she is sent from second place on the list to the bottom where she may be recorded simply as *mêtêr*.[25] What better way than anonymity to implement the advice Pericles had given to widows that "the best women are those who are known neither for praise nor blame".[26] In addition, for a widow to remain at the head of a list after her husband died, appearing to exercise authority over her sons, would have been abnormal. Aristotle (*Pol.* 1269b24-1270a15) had declared that states in which women ruled men were badly governed. Of course, Ptolemaic queens began to assume the prerogatives of kings and eventually Cleopatra VII governed Egypt. The census reports, however, predate this transition to female rule. In the reports only in the few all-female households of mother and daughter does a woman appear at the top of a list.[27]

The Ptolemies and their advisor Demetrius were faced with a family structure in Egypt that was different from that of classical Greece. Herodotus (2.35) had, in fact, described the sexual division of labour in Egypt as exactly the opposite to that in Greece. Examination of the private documents from Ptolemaic Egypt suggests that in many cases the androcentric hierarchical *oikos* model based on the nuclear family was imposed by the Greek authorities and reflected only in official documents. They reveal that some of the inhabitants, at least, behaved differently, and had a different view of the family from that recorded in the government's records. Lived reality was different and often contradicted the official picture. Families that include married siblings living in the same household, women who are active in the economy, and dominant widows, in particular, do not conform to the model. Nevertheless, the design of the census reflects traditional Greek priorities and values. Furthermore, a papyrus of 280-250 mentions a *gunaikonomos*.[28] This probably refers to a magistrate in Alexandria, and constitutes another example of Demetrius' influence. What other advice could one have expected from a historian? Like Demetrius and Ptolemy I, historians generally look back, not forward, or forward only in the expectation that history will repeat itself.

The loosening of restrictions on widows was an unforeseen result of the demographic changes beginning in the fourth century and continuing in the Hellenistic period. Women like Epicteta and many Spartans (see below), were sole heirs to substantial fortunes. Not only were there few, or in Epicteta's case, no men in their nuclear families, but probably as a result of emigration, there were few close male relatives in the extended family.

Widows and women described as *"mêtêr"* appear frequently in the population lists from Ptolemaic Egypt. In fact, the latter are so numerous that they are often designated by an abbreviation or a ligature (*"h"*). Legal and demographic considerations indicate that these women are widows rather than divorcées.

Lists of Greeks who were inscribed as new citizens at Miletus and Ilion at the end of the third and in the second century BC show some organizational and demographic features similar to those in the papyri.[29] At Ilion one hundred and fifty one males and eighty females are registered. The proportion of women who emigrated to Ilion with their adult sons is remarkably high. There are twenty-three mothers with adult sons, both with and without additional members of the son's family. These unmarried mothers whose names are preceded by the pronoun *mêtêr* are probably widows whose sons are their *kurioi*. In addition, the Ilion inscription lists eight unaccompanied, apparently unrelated, widows as a group, preceded by the rubric *Chêrai* ("widows").[30] The group is inscribed at the very end of the set of family inscriptions, preceding a list of single men. At Miletus also, the names of single women, some with children, are inscribed. They are part of extended family groups. A mother of two sons is accompanied by her own father and mother, and another mother is accompanied by her adult son and his wife.[31] These women are probably widows. Single men, even families as emigrants, are a feature of Greek history traceable back to the archaic period. Emigrant widows without kinsmen are a new feature of the Hellenistic period, and symptomatic of both dislocation in the traditional family and the loosening of family bonds on respectable women.

At Sparta as well, old values were exploited in an attempt to solve new problems. The revolutionary kings Agis IV and Cleomenes III claimed to be restoring the Lycurgan polity. They were faced with vast inequalities in the distribution of wealth among Spartans, where women, especially members of the royal family, owned two-fifths of the public land and the major portion of private land (Arist. *Pol.* 1270a23-4, Plut. *Agis* 7.3-4). They had gained this property through dowry and inheritance. Agis's mother Agesistrata and grandmother Archidamia, both widows, were the richest of all Spartans, including men and women. Heiresses and wealthy widows were sought in marriage. For example, Agiatis, who had inherited the great wealth of her father Gylippus, was married first to Agis IV, and when widowed she was married to Cleomenes III (Plut. *Cleom.* 1.2). The programmes of Agis and Cleomenes were multi-faceted, but the *sine qua non* was a redistribution of land. Women agreed to contribute property for redistribution, but, as in the past, they do not seem to have been affected by other reforms. Agis and Cleomenes also succeeded for a time in reviving the educational system known as the agoge.[32] Agis himself set an example by wearing the old-fashioned short cloak and living a life of austerity (Plut. *Agis* 4.14) and Cleomenes followed suit (Plut. *Cleom.* 13). The *sussitia* were revived. The Hellenistic period was a time when dining clubs were popular; thus the communal messes were not anachronistic. In another tribute to the past, Plutarch (*Cleom.* 18.4) ascribed Cleomenes' military successes to the revival of the ancient virtues of courage and obedience.

Stoic influence was a factor in the Spartan revolution.[33] Sphaerus, a follower of Cleanthes, went to Sparta and lectured the youths and ephebes (Plut. *Cleom.* 2). He wrote *"Peri Basileias"* (*"On Kingship"*) for Agis or Cleomenes, and also wrote two other treatises dealing with Sparta: *"Peri Lakonikes Politeias"* (*"On the Spartan Constitution"*), and *"Peri Lukourgou kai Sokratous"* (*"On Lycurgus and Socrates"*).[34] But these ethical reforms were limited to men. There is no evidence that after the redistribution of land, the Hellenistic revolutionaries attempted to create a utopian "communal family" that would include women. It is quite possible that the so-called "Sayings of Spartan Women" attributed to Plutarch, and purported to be quotations from brave and patriotic women of archaic and classical Sparta, were actually invented during this period. Thus, in attempting to revive "the good old days" they recreated the same problems that, according to Aristotle (*Pol.* 1270a1), had allowed women to be "ungoverned" (*anesis*), and had eventually been responsible for the failure of the original Lycurgan polity.

In conclusion, the picture of the Hellenistic Greek family that emerges is not one of a simple linear progression, but is complicated by nostalgia, by the influence of historians who were politically conservative, and by the exploitation of the past as propaganda.

Hunter College and the Graduate School
City University of New York
285 Central Park West
New York, NY 10024
USA

Notes

1. This paper is presented here essentially as delivered at Rungstedgaard on 26 January 1995. For a more detailed discussion of the topics covered see my *Families in Classical and Hellenistic Greece.* Oxford 1997.
2. See, e.g. Bachofen 1861, Fustel de Coulanges 1980 (1864), McLennan 1865, and Engels 1884.

3. 1993, esp. 7-10, 15, 82.
4. Note 1, above.
5. Arist. *Pol.* 1252b15-18, and see further Pomeroy 1994b.
6. See further Laum 1914, vol. 1, 9, and Bruck 1926, 271-76.
7. Michel 1001 = *IJG* II pp. 77-94, no. 24, and see now Wittenburg 1990. References below will be to Wittenburg's text.
8. Lines 2-107, excerpted, trans. adapted from Wittenburg 1990, 159-61.
9. See further Pomeroy 1989, Ch. 5.
10. See further Harrison 1968, 143-49, et passim.
11. *IJG* II, 24B, pp. 94-102. Cf. Epicurus, who died in 270 leaving no direct descendants, and who directed his heirs to make an annual deduction from his estate to pay for offerings to his father, mother, brothers, and himself (Diog. Laert. 10.16-18).
12. *IJG* II, 24B, pp. 94-102, Face A, lines 3-6.
13. See further Plut. *Demetr.* 24.11-12; Swoboda 1901; Swoboda 1925; and Blass 1993, 304-9.
14. Athen. 6.253b-d, *FGrH* ii 75, and see further Susemihl 1891, vol. 1, 552-58.
15. Ps.-Plut. *Mor.* 851f. Shear 1978, 82, n. 225, identifies this Antipater not as the son of Cassander, but as "the Etesian", the nephew who was in exile at Lysimachus' court.
16. See further Pomeroy 1993.
17. See recently Kovacsovics 1990, 73-87. Mikalson 1984, 223-24, argues that the production of grave stelai was resumed ca. 425/424, as compensation for prior maltreatment of the dead during the plague years. Pemberton 1989 suggests that the *dexiôsis* motif was introduced at this time and indicates reconciliation. See further Houby-Nielsen, this volume.
18. The following list is assembled from the testimony in Ps.-Demos. 43.62 = Ruschenbusch 1966, F 109; Cic. *Leg.* 2.63-4 = Ruschenbusch F 72a, from Demetrius of Phalerum, F 135 (Wehrli) = Jacoby, *FGrH* 228 F 9; Plut. *Sol.* 21.5 = Ruschenbusch F 72c.
19. Philochorus, *FGrH* 328 F 65, Timocles Fr. 34 (Kassel-Austin) = Athen. 7.245b-c, Plaut. *Aul.* 498-502.
20. See further Pomeroy 1994a.
21. One person with a male name is a boy, not a man.
22. P. 276 s.v. *thugatêr* and *huios*.
23. Ibid, p. 276 s.v. *gunê* and *thugatêr*.
24. See e.g. *CPR* XIII 12, col. ii, lines 78, 84, 89.
25. E.g. *CPR* XIII, passim, and *P. Petr.* III 59 c, recto col. ii, line 8, col. iii, line 13, d, line 18.
26. Thuc. 2.45.2.
27. E.g. *P. Sorb.* inv. 331 fr. 6, col. ii, lines 85-86.
28. *P. Hibeh* II 196 = *SB* VI 9559; see further Bingen 1957.
29. For the inscriptions: Rehm 1914; Günther 1988; and Frisch 1975, no. 64 — Hellenistic.
30. Frisch 1975, no. 64, lines 58-59.
31. Rehm 1914, 34 i, lines 5-8, and Günther 1988, 301, no. 3, lines 8-9.
32. Plut. *Cleom.* 11.18. See further Fuks 1962a and 1962b.
33. The extent of this influence is debatable. For the view that it was minimal see most recently Green 1994; for the opposite view see Erskine 1990.
34. Diog. Laert. 7.177, for the fragments von Arnim, *SVF* 1.620-630, pp. 139-42. See further Jacoby, *FGrH* 585, and most recently, Erskine 1990, esp. 123-49, who, however, does not indicate whether women are included in his discussion of Spartan "citizens".

Bibliography

Bachofen, J.J. 1861. *Das Mutterrecht*. Stuttgart.

Bingen, J. 1957. "Le papyrus du gyneconome", *ChronEg* 32, 337-39.

Blass, F. 1893. *Die Attische Beredsamkeit* (2nd ed.). Vol. 3. Leipzig.

Bruck, B. 1926. *Totenteil und Seelgerat im griechischen Recht* (Münchener Beiträge zur Papyrusforschung und antiken Rechtsgeschichte 9). München.

Bülow-Jacobsen, A. (ed.) 1994. *Proceedings of the 20th International Congress of Papyrologists*. Copenhagen, 23-29 August 1992. Copenhagen.

Cohen, J.D. Shaye (ed.) 1993. *The Jewish Family in Antiquity* (Brown Judaic Studies). Atlanta.

Engels, F. 1884. *Der Ursprung der Familie des Privateigentums und des Staates*. Zürich.

Erskine, A. 1990. *The Hellenistic Stoa*. Ithaca, N.Y.

Frisch, P. 1975. *Die Inschriften von Ilion*. Bonn.

Fuks, A. 1962a. "Agis, Cleomenes and Equality", *ClPh* 57, 161-66, (= Stern, M. & Amit, M. (eds.) *Social Coflict in Ancient Greece*. Jerusalem/Leiden, 1984, 250-55).

Fuks, A. 1962b. "Patterns and types of social-economic revolution in Greece from the fourth to the second century B.C.", *AncSoc* 5 (1962), 51-81 (= Stern, M. & Amit, M. (eds.) *Social Conflict in Ancient Greece*. Jerusalem/Leiden, 1984, 9-39).

Fustel de Coulanges, N.D. 1980 [1864]. *The Ancient City* (Eng. trans. from *La cité antique*). Baltimore/London.

Golden, M. 1990. *Children and Childhood in Classical Athens*. Baltimore.

Green, P. 1994. "Philosophers, Kings, and Democracy, or How Political Was the Stoa", *AncPhil* 14, 147-56.

Günther, Wolfgang 1988. "Milesische Bürgerrechts-und Proxenieverleihungen der hellenistischen Zeit", *Chiron* 18, 383-419.

Harrison, A.R.W. 1968. *The Law of Athens*. Vol. 1. Oxford.

Houby-Nielsen, S. "Grave Gifts, Women, and Conventional Values in Hellenistic Athens", this volume.

Hunter, V. 1994. *Policing Athens. Social Control in the Attic Lawsuits*. Princeton.

Kovacsovics, W.K. 1990. *Die Eckterrasse an der Graberstrasse des Kerameikos. Kerameikos* XIV. Berlin.

Lacey, W.K. 1968. *The Family in Classical Greece*. Ithaca/London.

Laum, B. 1914. *Stiftungen in der griechischen und römischen Antike. Ein Beitrag zur antiken Kulturgeschichte*. Leipzig/Berlin.

McLennan, J. 1865. *Primitive Marriage*. Edinburgh.

Mikalson, J.D. 1984. "Religion and the Plague in Athens, 431-423 B.C.", in: Rigsby, 1984, 217-25.

Pemberton, E.G. 1989. "The Dexiosis on Attic Gravestones", *MedArch* 2, 45-50.

Pomeroy, S.B. 1989. *Women in Hellenistic Egypt from Alexander to Cleopatra* (with a new foreword and addenda). Detroit.

Pomeroy, S.B. 1993. "Some Greek Families: Production and Reproduction", in: Cohen (ed.) 1993, 155-63.

Pomeroy, S.B. 1994a. "Family History in Ptolemaic Egypt", in: Bülow-Jacobsen (ed.) 1994, 593-97.

Pomeroy, S.B. 1994b. *Xenophon, Oeconomicus: A Social and Historical Commentary*. Oxford.

Pomeroy, S.B. 1997. *Families in Classical and Hellenistic Greece*. Oxford.

Rehm, A. 1914. *Das Delphinion in Milet. Die Inschriften. Milet* I.3. Berlin.

Rigsby, K.J. (ed.) 1984. *Studies Presented to Sterling Dow* (GRBM 10). Durham, N.C.

Rubinstein, Lene 1993. *Adoption in iv. Century Athens*. Copenhagen.

Ruschenbusch, E. 1966. *Solonos Nomoi: Die Fragmente des solonischen Gesetzeswerkes mit einer Text- und Überlieferungsgeschichte*. (Historia Einzelschriften 9). Wiesbaden.

Shear, T. Leslie, Jr. 1978. *Kallias of Sphettos and the Revolt of Athens in 286 B.C.* (Hesperia, Suppl. 17). Princeton.

Susemihl, F. 1891. *Geschichte der griechischen Literatur in der Alexandrinerzeit.* Leipzig.

Swoboda, H. 1901. s.v. Demochares 6, in: *RE* 4, 2863-67.

Swoboda, H. 1925. s.vv. Laches 6 and 7, in: *RE* 12, 339.

Wittenburg, A. 1990. *Il testamento di Epikteta.* Trieste.

GRAVE GIFTS, WOMEN, AND CONVENTIONAL VALUES IN HELLENISTIC ATHENS[1]

Sanne Houby-Nielsen

> Whoever lost her husband lost her respect
> and whoever lost her mother lost her conversation
> and whoever lost her brother lost her wings
> and whoever lost her sister lost her walks
> and whoever lost small children lost her heart
> (Mother's lament from Gortinia,
> after Holst-Warhaft 1995, 50)

Introduction

Grave gifts in antiquity constitute an invaluable source material in any attempt to ascertain conventional values — the values of a "silent group" of people. In Athens several thousand burials dating from the early Iron Age to early Roman times are known, many of which contain grave gifts. The character of these burials (degree of elaboration, consumption of wealth, character of rituals) provides an insight into religious beliefs and into varying socio-economic hierachical structures, as well as into concepts of age and gender. In fact, burials constitute by far the most extensive source material relating to Iron Age and early Archaic Athenian society available to us today.[2] What has so far not been realized is that burial customs also provide us with a unique source for studying material remains stemming from a complex ritual undertaken especially by women, no doubt one of the most silent groups of people in antiquity. For many years scholars seem to have implicitly regarded women as those responsible for the deposition of grave goods, at least in the historical periods.[3] However, it has not been realized that this material constitutes a rather direct source on women's history in contradiction to, for instance, stage plays and most vase paintings, which often form the basis for reconstructions of the lives of women in ancient Greece. In the following I therefore hope to show that the study of Classical-Hellenistic grave gifts can afford us a most vivid glimpse of ancient female values and modes of expression. I will argue that in the choice of grave gifts, the active participation of women in the creation of a new urban lifestyle or ideology is demonstrated, an ideology which came to dominate most parts of the Mediterranean and was to last well into the Roman era, and one which demanded both new female and male ideals that in some sense form the first true origin of modern gender rôles in the Western world. It will furthermore hopefully be apparent how the "language" of grave gifts "below ground" sometimes conflicts with the values celebrated above ground on the Classical figure-decorated grave reliefs and makes the latter appear strangely old-fashioned. In this way, the study of grave gifts may help explain why a large-scale production of Classical figure-decorated grave reliefs was not resumed soon after Demetrius of Phalerum had been expelled from Athens in 307. Moreover, this tension between values expressed "below ground" and the values celebrated and applauded for a rather more public audience "above ground" certainly demonstrates how grave gifts form a parallel mode of expression to the well-known women's laments at death and burial in ancient as well as modern, rural Greece. These laments apparently constituted a social protest of such threatening dimensions that first the Classical city-state and later the Byzantine church attempted to control them by legislation and by channelling the need for them into more acceptable media (tragedies, public funeral orations, and certain church rituals) (Alexiou 1974; Holst-Warhaft 1995).

I have reached the conclusions outlined here very gradually. Therefore, in accordance with the course of my research, the paper starts with an analysis of Classical-Hellenistic burials containing grave gifts, and here concentrates on burials with mirrors and strigils. It then proceeds to a more contextual study of the meaning of the mirror and strigil before conclusions are drawn.

It remains to be said that the present article is an abridged version of a longer account[4] which attempts to give a socio-cultural explanation for the disappearance of Attic figure-decorated grave reliefs around 300 and return of production on a rather limited scale in Late Hellenistic times.

An introductory survey of strigils and mirrors in funerary contexts

It is a well-known and often stated fact that in the Hellenistic period, i.e. after around 300 BC,[5] strigils and mirrors were very often deposited as grave gifts in Greece, mirrors supposedly for women and strigils for men (Knigge and Willemsen 1966, 46; Kurtz and Boardman 1971, 165; Pemberton 1985, 273). In spite of these statements, inconsistencies to this pattern were also noted (Kurtz & Boardman 1971, 209), and later J.-P. Thuillier has pointed to evidence from Italy which contradicts the widespread concept of the strigil as solely indicating a male grave (Thuillier 1989). And most recently E. Kotera-Feyer has drawn attention to several excavators' reports of male graves containing mirrors and female ones containing strigils in Italy, Cyprus, Northern Greece and the Peloponnese.[6]

A closer study of the contexts of the Athenian mirror and/or strigil-containing graves shows that the above-mentioned "facts" certainly need adjustment and that the popularity of the mirror and strigil as grave gifts in Athens must be looked at in a broader social context.[7]

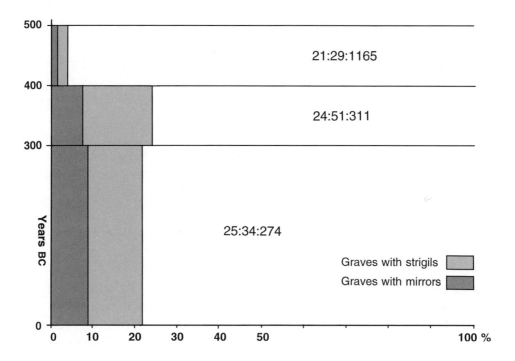

Fig. 1. The frequency of mirror- and strigil-containing burials in Athens.

Firstly, in Fig. 1, I have attempted to give a more precise impression of just *how much* the practice of depositing strigils and mirrors increases over time in Athens. And, as seen from this figure, there is an impressive increase from 2.4% to 24% burials containing one or both of these objects *not* around 300 but already around the year 400, and the same frequency characterizes burials dated to the "Hellenistic" period.[8] Secondly, as we shall see, several grave contexts as well as sex-determined skeletons show that after the end of the fifth century strigils were given not only to men, but also to women, and conversely mirrors may be given to men. In fact one of the characteristics of the fourth century and Hellenistic period is that strigils are increasingly found in grave contexts which have a "female" touch and refer to beautification, bathing and hygiene. For this reason strigils and mirrors are not infrequently found in the same grave. At the same time, the mirror "changes" context, since it becomes detached from its former narrow connection with bridal equipment in favour of purely hygienic equipment. This is indeed an interesting development, since the mirror and the strigil function as two totally separate attributes in the iconography on Archaic and Classical tombstones, as I will return to. And it is certainly of interest that a similar development may be traced in the depositional pattern of strigils and mirrors in sanctuaries, as I will describe below.

The remarkable increase in the practice of depositing strigils and mirrors in Athenian burials since around 400 as well as the gradual absorption of the strigils into a sphere of pure hygiene and beautification has, as mentioned, to be seen in a wider Mediterranean perspective. For, especially since the fourth century, the strigil and mirror also become popular grave gifts and funerary symbols in the rest of Greece, and in several other parts of the Mediterranean, especially Italy, and they appear in Thracian graves and in burials in Roman provinces.[9] Especially in Italy, there are indications that since the fourth century the strigil was connected more and more with hygiene than with athletics (Kotera-Feyer 1993, 118). The power and durability of these objects as symbols may be illustrated by the so-called "Pictish stones" from Scotland dating between the second and ninth century AD. Here mirror and comb function together as a symbol which turns a sign for a male name into a female one, and the source of inspiration for the mirror-comb motif must without doubt be sought in the neighbouring Roman provinces (Samson 1992).[10] Finally, it is noteworthy that strigil and mirror graves represent most of the social hierachical scale both in Athens as well as in the Mediterranean in general. They are thus found in cemeteries ranging from "poor" to "rich", and they are even found in the "princely" tombs at Vergina. Accordingly, the strigils are made of metals ranging from iron, over bronze, silver and gilded iron or bronze, sometimes richly inlaid (Kotera-Feyer 1993, 89-90, 118, 148).[11]

Even though the change in attitude towards the mirror and the strigil as symbolic objects noted in Athens forms part of a general Mediterranean phenomenon with far-reaching effects in time and space of the kind just described, one should be cautious in applying the same more specific significance to or specific explanation for this change to the various Mediterranean and Western European cultures. My own explanation for the symbolic value of the strigil and mirror in Athenian fourth century and Hellenistic burials is therefore imbedded in Athenian cultural history.

Mirrors and strigils: some general remarks

In daily life men may have used mirrors for various purposes. For instance, late sources mention the use of mirrors by professionel barbers (Lucian *Ind.* 29; Plut. *Mor.* 42B). Other sources underline how the mirror is used very differently by men and women. We are thus told that Socrates recommended that his students use a mirror to criticize their character (rather than looks). A similar story is told about Demosthenes and about a father when advising his son on how to use his mother's mirror (Apul. *Apol.* 415, 421; Phaedr. 3 fab. 8).

A passage by Aristophanes has been taken to indicate that women used strigils to shave their legs (Ar. *Thesm.* 556), and Theocritus' poem *Epithalamy of Helen* (hymn 18) may suggest that women used a strigil to cleanse their bodies after athletic training. An Attic vase painting showing Atalante in a stadium with a strigil (Paris, Louvre CA 2259; *ARV* 795, 100; Boardman 1991, fig. 369) and a little Hellenistic bronze statuette of a girl dressed in a runner skirt and holding a strigil in her raised hand points in the same direction (Scanlon 1988). In Olynthus, a strigil was found in the kitchen section of a house. This is readily explicable, since kitchen and bathroom were often connected, no doubt because the water was heated in the kitchen.[12]

It is, however, risky to attempt to reconstruct the *actual* day-to-day function of these objects on the grounds of funerary rituals and cult, and mirrors and strigils are mostly found in contexts such as graves and sanctuaries. These two contexts by no means reflect daily life directly. Rather, "distorted" perceptions of gender rôles, age and status, family relations, etc., are expressed by means of grave gifts and votives. Even the handling of objects in profane contexts may not reflect reality, but rather, for instance "wishful thinking" (for instance expensive furniture purchased for borrowed money; the photo of a beloved son above the piano, though he has not shown up for years, etc.). (For burials as symbolic, see Morris 1992.) The power of the strigil and mirror as symbolic objects finds a forceful expression verging on fetishism in the deliberate destruction of these items that can sometimes be observed. For instance, a burnt mirror was found in one of the Kerameikos graves (*Ker.* VII.1, 247), and in Gela strigils may be pierced by nails (*NSc* 14, 1932, 35-36, fig. 6a; Kurtz and Boardman 1971, 216, fig. 44). In Myrina in Minor Asia strigils were perhaps deliberately broken before being deposited in burials (See Kotera-Feyer 1993, 114, nn. 14-15, for further references). For these reasons it is purely the symbolic value of the strigil and mirror — in Athenian society — which I seek to encompass in the following sections. For this purpose a brief survey of the various contexts in which the strigil and mirror are used as symbols is worthwhile.

The strigil and the mirror as symbols of gender rôles

"Official" funerary rituals: tombstones, offering-trenches

Tombstones had of course many functions. One of these was to provide passers-by
with an image of the deceased member(s) of a certain *oikos* and thereby a picture
of the *oikos* as such. The imagery of Attic Archaic and Classical tombstones is
very repetitive, as are the virtues referred to in the epitaphs. Time and again
certain gender rôles are stressed: for instance the good, the brave, the wise *oikos*-
man and the dutiful, child-bearing wife. Many aspects of a citizen's lifestyle, such
as his rôle as a symposiast or his profession, almost never entered the imagery
of the tombstones, even though these aspects in other contexts were fully accepted
as part of citizen identity (compare Schmitt Pantel 1992 and Berger 1970). The
same may be said of the tombstone imagery of women. All depending on
economic status, women no doubt often left their houses. Well-to-do women with
slaves to do the housework went out frequently to attend or minister at weddings,
funerals, or religious functions, to take their children to play with neighbouring
children or to accompany them to festivals and gymnastic competitions, to visit
neighbours or take care of relatives.[13] And women belonging to less prosperous
households, apart from fulfilling tasks of the just described nature, would leave
the house for various purposes such as work in the fields, fetching water, shopping
and selling in the marketplace (Just 1991, 105-25; Scheidel 1995). Perhaps for
these reasons, agricultural implements may be found in sanctuaries serving a
female clientele in particular (Kron 1992). Again female reality of this kind is
never hinted at in Attic Classical tombstone-imagery, a circumstance which does
not necessarily indicate that the commemorated women belonged solely to a well-
to-do class (where the confinement of the citizen's female relatives to the house
was a matter of prestige), since Attic tombstones need not only have been
affordable for wealthy people (Nielsen et al. 1989; for a contrary opinion, see
Schmaltz 1983, 136; compare also Clairmont 1993, intr. vol. 66). Rather, it is a
question of tradition of imagery within a certain "genre", the tombstone. And on
tombstones, men are warriors, wise men and ephebes, while women are shown
as belonging to a rich *oikos*, as modest and anything but provocative, and seated
indoors, and this is a "genre" in which women are often shown as mothers (see
recently Hoffmann 1993, 163-65). On late fourth century reliefs, women's dress
may become extremely transparent — but their whole appearance (seated indoors,
often veiled and not looking directly at the viewer) outweighs any provocation
which may be inherent in this depiction. The imagery of women assures the
passers-by that the *oikos*-man to whom the woman belongs has his house under
control, and that his children are legitimate.

The strigil and mirror constitute important attributes in the tombstone depictions of the just discussed gender rôles. A principal rule concerning the strigil is that it is always a male attribute, never a female one (Clairmont 1993, index: "strigil", lists 65 tombstones with men (perhaps boys) holding a strigil). The same is true for white-ground lekythoi, which may be discussed in connection with tombstones, since they were often placed above the grave, for instance on the steps of a tombstone (as often depicted on the lekythoi themselves), and the few known monumental white-ground lekythoi may even have replaced tombstones (Kurtz 1975, 69). In this context the strigil almost exclusively signals the young man and the palaestra. It thus functions as a reference to the *ephebeia*-world as a whole consisting not only of athletics, but also of lectures, writing practice and military exercise (Cassimatis 1991, 35; Lissarraque 1992, 201-2). On Attic tombstones dating to the fourth century, however, there is some tendency to employ the strigil as an attribute of the elderly man, thereby signalling the bath rather than athletics.[14]

Just as the strigil belongs exclusively to the male world on tombstones and marker vases, the mirror solely belongs to the female world, in fact specifically the young woman.[15] Often the woman is seated and holds the mirror in front of her, staring thoughtfully at her own reflection. This depiction is closely related to scenes showing the toilet of the bride on Attic vase painting (Sutton 1981, 203, especially W68, W69). And it is exactly the same scene, which we find in wedding preparations in Attic tragedy, as in *Medea*, where the mirror plays a significant rôle in the gruesome death of the bride Glauke (Rehm 1994, 103). Thus the mirror appears to constitute an important attribute in the celebration of the married woman or bride on tombstones. Moreover, very dramatic funerary rituals connected with offering-trenches and offering-places near the grave celebrated much the same virtues as the tombstones. For bridal vases (loutrophoroi, lebetes gamikoi, powder pyxides) with representations of the bride and her mirror (which could be taken as equivalent of concepts such as "bride", "married woman") and weapons (which could be taken as equivalent to concepts such as "warrior") were sometimes destroyed in these trenches.[16] And the very drama, noise and smell of fire involved in this ritual is likely to have attracted notice from — and thus have been intended for — a larger audience (such as neighbours) than merely the burying *oikos*.

Painted pottery used at weddings and symposia
In Attic vase painting men may carry mirrors and women may hold strigils. Nevertheless, a principal rule is that when the mirror becomes "male" and the

strigil "female", we are moving into a field of sexual provocation and seductiveness. Thus, the mirror may be connected with various concepts of women. The interdependency of motives depicting "respectable" and "non-respectable" women often makes it difficult to decide whether real social types (for instance "the married woman", "the *hetaira*", etc.) are shown, or rather different male concepts pertaining to women (for instance notions of lecherous or innocent women).[17]

The mirror is standard equipment in scenes showing the bridal bath or wedding-preparation in general. Here several women may be shown preparing the bridal bath and carrying special bridal vases (loutrophoroi or lebetes gamikoi) or handing perfume vases (e.g. alabastra) to a seated bride who holds a mirror in front of her. A half-open door leading to the bedroom may also be shown (see most recently Oakley and Sinos 1993, 16, 18, 23, 36, 41). On a black-figure pyxis, a scene of this type has been reduced and shows only girls making a bed above which hangs a mirror (Oakley and Sinos 1993, fig. 104 [Warsaw, Nat. Mus. 142319]). From the 430s the bride may even be shown naked at her bath. Thus a pyxis in New York (1972.118.148) shows a crouching bride, her hands raised to her head to wash her hair while Eros pours water over her from a hydria. An object which is probably a mirror hangs near her (Sabetai 1993, 193; Oakley and Sinos 1993, 15-16, figs. 20-21).

A very different concept of women is inherent in scenes showing a "sitting woman" holding a mirror (or other objects), who is confronted by a man, or several men, offering her a purse of money or an alabastron as a gift, again eventually showing a half-open door leading to a bedroom.[18] Though certainly not a depiction of a bride, the connection with bridal scenes is clear. And the bridal bed in wedding scenes in fact resembles banqueting couches in symposia scenes, the main difference being that on the former a blanket may hang down and a mirror may hang on the wall above the bed (Oakley and Sinos 1993, 36). In late fifth and fourth century red-figure pottery, the mirror has become intimately connected with renderings of Aphrodite and women who are beautifying themselves and surrounded by Erotes (Schefold 1930; Burn 1987, 26-44). And Eros and Aphrodite have on the whole become very popular figures since the middle of the fifth century. It is noteworthy that Eros is never shown in scenes showing love-making, but only in scenes of more discreet meetings between the two sexes (Sutton 1981, 74; Burn 1987, 32). In fact the *symposium* vases which carried the majority of known love-making scenes cease to be produced in the fifth century. For this reason the mirror becomes more and more tied up with an iconography which stresses a discreet eroticism (Sutton 1981, 74).

On a very few fifth century vases a man is depicted as holding a mirror, apparently presenting it as a gift to a woman (Sutton 1981, 336, G 104 [ARV 814.2], G 149 [ARV 1077.3], G 151 [ARV 1116.38]). The scene is dubious, but should probably be seen in the light of other scenes of gift-giving, which mostly carry the notion of "courtship" and thus an invitation to sex, as mentioned above (Sutton 1981, 337). In this connection one might be allowed to make a short detour to Italy and mention a red-figure crater painted by a painter trained in South Italian vase painting tradition, and dating to the first quarter of the fourth century (Lady Lever Art Gallery, Port Sunlight [LL 5045]; for this vase, see Robertson 1992).[19] For on its rear side three youths in mantles are depicted, the one in the centre holding a mirror. As Martin Robertson states (Robertson 1992), this motif — probably Attic or South Italian in origin — suggests an erotic scene (*eromenos* between rival *erastai*), and the mirror is apparently used as an attribute to underline the eroticism of a young male.

When studying depictions of the strigil on Attic vase painting, one notices that by far the majority of the strigil depictions relate to the ephebe and the palaestra and therefore do not deviate much from the meaning of the strigil on tombstones. One recalls the scenes showing an ephebe holding a strigil, or scenes in which the strigil is hanging on the wall behind a symposiast and refers to his status as an ephebe, or scenes where it simply floats in the air in order to designate that the scene takes place in a palaestra (Bérard and Durand 1989, 33). This use of the strigil as a symbol referring to the ephebeia seems to have been copied by South Italian painters (Cassimatis 1991). However, for the present article it is especially interesting, that on a small group of red-figure vases the shapes of which were meant for wine consumption (crater, stamnos, cup), we suddenly meet women holding a strigil. Similar scenes are found on a red-figure neck-amphora, the shape of which could be for transport of finer wine, but also on pelikai, which were probably for storing oil. Apart from one cup showing Atalante in a stadium (Paris, Louvre CA 2259; *ARV* 795, 100; Boardman 1991, fig. 369), the scenes in question are bathing scenes. Most often several naked women are grouped around a high-stemmed washbasin using the strigil to scrape their bodies (or the strigil is hanging in the background) (pl. 8).[20] When only one naked woman is shown engaged in a similar activity, this is probably a reduced scene of the former variant (Syracuse no. 20.065 (pelike); *CV* Italia XVII Siracusa I, III.1 pl. 7). The fact that several naked women are often shown washing together prevents us from interpreting the scene as a traditional bridal bath. There does, however, exist a strong connection between these washing scenes and scenes showing one naked woman at a laver (Sabetai 1993, 193) — but without a strigil. And it is a popular topic on miniature hydriai (for perfume) painted by the Washing Painter. Washing scenes of the latter kind may indeed carry nuptial overtones, as their very vase shape also suggests, but as mentioned, these washing women do not hold a strigil (Sabetai 1993, 191-99, esp. 194). It seems that scenes of the strigil-using bathing women are much more closely related to a tradition rooted in Archaic vase painting for using the naked bathing woman as an erotic motif on sympotic vases (especially drinking-cups) (Sutton 1981, 46; Pomeroy 1975, 143; Williams 1983, 99; Durand and Lissarrague 1980, esp. 98-99). Apart from their wine-related shapes, the presence of *komos*-scenes and scenes of women holding *olisboi* on the back of some of the vases with strigil-using women supports this impression (for instance the back of the pelike in Syracuse: Deubner 1936, 342 fig. 5). On a Boeotian crater from the end of the fifth century, women and Eros hold strigils (de Montpellier 831-1-110; Ginouvès 1962, pl. XXIX.97). It seems therefore that the strigil in the hands of women is meant to add to the intimacy of the scene, giving the (male) spectator the feeling of peeping into the private secrets of women's toilet. Perhaps a reflection of this situation is to be found in one of Plautus' plays dating to around 200. For Plautus let one of his *hetairai* in his comedy *Pseudolus* be called Xystilis, a name which Plautus perhaps took over from a Greek drama and which is likely to be derived from *xystos*. The *xystos* was the special room in the palaestra used for oiling one's body, and thus the connection strigil-*hetaira* could again be at hand (Plaut. *Pseud.* 210; Thomsen 1987, n. 188).[21] It is no doubt associations such as these (intimate toilet as preparation for sex) which prevented the strigil from entering the iconography of Attic tombstones as a female attribute.

In summary we may conclude that there existed a tradition in Attic vase painting for using the mirror both in depictions of sexual restraint and in depictions of sexual seduction. Regarding the strigil, this could both associate with the young man or boy (including all the possible homosexual references inherent in such motives) and with the bath of the older man, as well as with female sexual invitation. Contrary, however, to this tradition, the strigil and the mirror never alluded directly to sexual seduction on tombstones and marker vases, just as pottery showing an invitation to extra-marital sex, or the performance of sexual acts (for instance symposiastic motives), were seen never to form part of the (rather public) ritual of the funerary offering-trenches.

Women and the deposition of grave gifts

Bearing in mind the restricted and almost "moralistic" repertoire of depictions on tombstones in which the strigil and the mirror function as two absolutely separate attributes with very different associational references, it is most interesting to discover that this is not at all so "below ground". For throughout the fourth century, when most of the Attic Classical figure-decorated tombstones were produced, the strigil and the mirror are often deposited together in the same grave, and on the whole, grave contexts containing strigils become increasingly similar to grave contexts containing mirrors. In other words, the conventional values expressed through the depositional pattern of grave gifts oppose the ones celebrated on tombstones. This circumstance becomes even more intriguing when the fact that women were probably responsible for the selection of grave gifts is taken into consideration. At least I hope the following survey of evidence for this view will appear convincing.

Evidence of all sorts (for instance ancient literary sources, iconography, terracottas, and modern anthropological studies in rural Greece) abounds for the great rôle played by women in funerary rituals as composers and performers of laments, as mourners, and as caretakers of the corpse (washing and dressing) from Mycenaean times to the present in Greece.[22] However, scholars, as far as I know, have not dealt explicitly with the problem of who actually deposited the gifts which we find in burials. On the other hand, they often point to Attic white-ground lekythoi for women's rôle as bringers of gifts *to* the grave and general caretaking of the grave in the Classical period, and here they often seem to imply that the gifts which women are seen carrying to the grave are the same as those found in the graves (Kurtz and Boardman 1971, 103-4; Kurtz 1988, 147; Rehm 1994, 28, 33; Lissarrague 1992, 169-70; Garland 1985, 108). A standard motif on white-ground lekythoi is women carrying vases in baskets towards a tombstone near which the deceased is shown. There are, however, some inconsistencies between the vase types carried by these women and actual vase types found in graves, and it is somewhat uncertain how literally these scenes should be interpreted. For instance exaleiptra are very commonly represented as gifts on the lekythoi, but are only very rarely found in graves (Kurtz-Boardman 1971, 103; Houby-Nielsen 1995, 152).

On a recently published black-figure skyphos sherd in the Herbert Cahn collection, a row of women carrying aryballoi, alabastra and bowls with eggs is shown (Kreuzer 1992, no. 125). Eggs play a well-known rôle in funerary cult (Meuli 1946, 191 n. 4; Boardman 1955, 54 n. 22; Garland 1985, 10, 70, 113, 158 with references), and a few graves in Kerameikos contained terracotta eggs (Vierneisel 1964, 448, fig. 34; *Ker.* VII.1, 96 no. 275). In addition, eggs are common on omphalos bowls which often form part of funerary scenes in South Italian vase painting, and actual omphalos bowls with terracotta eggs are sometimes found in South Italian tombs (Trendall and Cambitoglou 1978, 126 no. 227, to mention one example; Hornbostel 1980, 213 no. 122). Therefore, the row of women on the skyphos sherd could very well be shown as carrying gifts to be deposited in a grave. However, as with the scenes on white-ground lekythoi, the scene may also show us a post-funeral ritual. Still, funerary scenes of this kind do underline the very important rôle which women possessed as keepers of the grave and bringers of gifts to it, and make it highly likely that women also chose and placed the gifts inside it.

Another indicator for the connection "women and choice of grave gifts" in ancient Athens is constituted by ancient Greek ideas of pollution. Birth and death were two occasions which the ancient Greeks believed especially to cause natural pollution. And on both occasions women were the main caretakers who dealt with purifying devices or had to conform to regulatory rules in order to minimize the risk of pollution, or were a risk for men to become polluted. Thus, women who had just conceived were believed to be polluted for 40 days and were denied access to sanctuaries, as were men for a certain number of days after they had had intercourse with a woman. And as soon as a member of a household passed away, the whole house became polluted, and women of the household appear to have been especially responsible for the purifying rituals concerning the corpse. They washed, anointed and dressed the corpse as preparation for the lying-in state (Parker 1983, 33-35). To this day in certain areas of rural Greece, all important death rites are performed exclusively by women. For instance, irrespective of who pays for the burial of a deceased husband, his wife decides the details surrounding the laying-out of his corpse and the quantity and quality of the funeral meal, and she even plays a decisive rôle in the choice of grave monument, just as she is responsible for the daily care of the grave and for the washing and anointment of the exhumed bones. When a widow dies, it is a female relative, often a daughter-in-law, who takes care of her burial (Danforth and Tsiaras 1982, 48-69, 119-22).

Natural pollution and women are therefore intimately connected. From Aristophanes we know that lekythoi (probably containing some kind of perfumed oil) were held suitable to place at the bedside of the corpse and that it was common practice to place a water jar at the entrance of a house of a recently deceased person as part of the purifying rituals, and it is implied in the play that these tasks were women's tasks (*Eccl.* 1030). This brings us to the mass of lekythoi in fifth century Kerameikos burials. Here they constitute 70% of grave gifts for adults and were often deposited in large numbers per burial (Houby-Nielsen 1995, table 7), and were very often placed evenly around the body of the deceased. U. Knigge therefore rightly regarded the lekythoi found in the burials as being the same

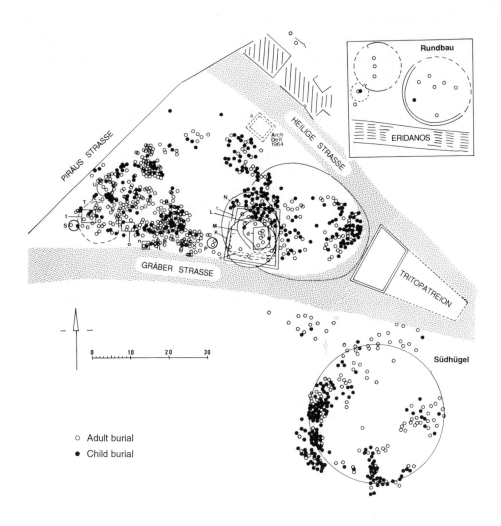

Fig. 2. Map of Kerameikos showing the distribution of adult and child burials in the fifth century BC. *(After Houby-Nielsen 1995, fig. 7).*

lekythoi that were used at the *prothesis* to minimize pollution (*Ker.* IX, 15 with references; see also Kurtz and Boardman 1971, 207-9). This idea gains even more weight when a practice which a fifth century law from Iulis on Keos alludes to is considered. According to this, there existed a practice of sweeping the house after the *prothesis* had taken place and of bringing this dirt and other remains from the *prothesis*-rituals to the grave (Parker 1983, 35-36). Viewed from this angle, the lekythoi are polluted remains stemming from the lying-in-state for which reason they had to be dealt with and placed in the burials by women.

In Hellenistic Athens the practice of depositing oil containers continues, though now in the shape of the so-called unguentaria or tear-flasks rather than lekythoi. The continuity of this practice suggests continuity of its intended function (purification). Means of purification easily overlap with superstitious beliefs which are not difficult to connect with women either. And in this field another characteristic practice in Hellenistic Athens probably belongs — the deposition of nails in burials.[23] Nails are common not only in Athenian burials, but — like mirrors and strigils — in other parts of Greece, as well as in other Mediterranean countries, such as Libya (Dent et al. 1976-1977, 207, tomb A, C 6 and C 18 and C 15). Sometimes they may stem from a wooden coffin or bier (Schlörb-Vierneisel 1966, 78), but in other cases there is no immediate explanation for their occurrence in the burials or offering-places (Schlörb-Vierneisel 1966, 81). And as mentioned earlier on, there existed a ritual of "killing" objects by piercing them with nails (Kurtz and Boardman 1971, 217), and one recalls the late antique dolls pierced with nails found in Egypt (see most recently Beyer 1995, 83, fig. 4). In a Hellenistic burial in Aetolia, nails had been placed around the head of the body (*ARep* 1993/94, 23: Naupaktos). The most likely explanation for this practice is to be sought after in the field of superstition, for instance as an attempt to kill spirits of the dead. On analogy to modern rural Greece, this could also point to female involvement in burial practice.

Nevertheless, the most decisive evidence for women's rôle in the deposition of grave gifts stems from the burials themselves. A good starting example comes from outside Athens. It is a Hellenistic burial in Patras of a woman lying in the supine position with arms at her side (pl. 9). Here a mirror has been placed on her lower body covering her womb and vagina, forcefully demonstrating the distance between the world of grave gifts and the world of tombstone imagery. Considering the importance women attached to the mirror as a votive gift in sancturies concerned with childbirth, marriage, fertility and lovemaking — as I will come back to later on — the underlying significance of this position of the mirror is likely to be sought after in the world of female reality.

By far the most conclusive evidence, however, stem from child burials in Athens, especially in the fifth century. When studying these, part of the world of female reality becomes indeed very palpable. For never in the history of Athens have so many babies and small children been buried in complex and careful ways (making them archaeologically visible) as in this century (fig. 2 and pl. 10). Babies and children were equipped with a repertoire of grave gifts which was not only much more varied than the types of grave gifts chosen for adults, but also clearly expressed the age at which the child died or the status which the child did not live to experience. These grave gifts had been selected with great thoughtfulness, and were often very carefully arranged around the vase containing the dead child (pl. 11) (Houby-Nielsen 1995, 149-54). The responsibility for the arrangement of these burials must surely be sought among the various groups of women who had the daily contact with babies and small children. It is true that fathers were responsible for their children's needs. In particular a father had to provide the wherewithal for the child's (especially a son's) education, and he would introduce the child (son) to the various forms of social and cultural life in Athens (horse races, gymnastic contests, etc.) (Alexandrakis 1988, 79-101). It is also true that children did not legally belong to their mothers, but to their fathers, and fathers had the legal right to decide whether or not the newborn child should be raised (Pomeroy 1983, 207-8). Nevertheless, from the time the child was born till around the age of 6-7 years, it was primarily in the hands of women in daily life. This is not only recommended by philosophers, but also speeches in courts, mythology, tragedies and material evidence (terracottas of *kourotrophoi*, imagery of women with children in vase painting and on tombstones, etc.) point to women, whether wet-nurses, dry-nurses, slave-girls, mothers, aunts or grandmothers, as the main caretakers of babies and small children (Alexandrakis 1988, 79-101; Siurla-Theodoridou 1989, 256-63, 366-70; Garland 1990, 106-21). For this reason there is hardly any doubt that women — unspecific as the term "women" is — were responsible for the arrangement of baby and small child burials.

The evidence from vase painting, the Patras burial, the carefully arranged baby and small child burials, the various modes of dealing with pollution and the evils of the dead person combined with anthropological studies in modern, rural Greece all point towards women as being responsible for the deposition of grave goods. It is therefore time to study more closely what women may have expressed when they deposited grave gifts, such as the strigil and the mirror.

Burial contexts consistent with tombstone imagery

In the fifth century we find some instances where the strigil has been deposited together with grave gifts which clearly refer to childhood and youth, for instance astragals, various terracotta figurines and balls (App. 1, group V). The burial of Eupheros in Kerameikos is especially interesting, since the age and sex of the deceased has been determined as being of a boy about 15 years old and his grave gifts and tombstone are preserved. The grave gifts consist of vases for drinking and pouring (a kantharos and an oinochoe), several white-ground lekythoi, a needle, a terracotta figurine (a monkey), an astragal, and two strigils placed at his left arm. And his tombstone shows a young boy holding a strigil (in his right hand) (Schlörb-Vierneisel 1964, pl. 51.1). In this way the burial of Eupheros is a striking example of accordance between tombstone imagery, choice of grave gifts and age and sex of the deceased. The other burials in this group deviate slightly from the strigil imagery on tombstones, since the lengths of the coffins suggest burials of small children and not young men (*Ker*. VII.1, no. 350; Schlörb-Vierneisel 1966, 56/hS 164, 91/hS 97 [offering-place, but probably belonging to a child], 148/HS 45). A similar pattern is found in Corinth and Olynthus (App. 1, group V). Nevertheless, when women furnished baby sons with a strigil, it may have been in an attempt to express a status the children did not live to experience, for instance ephebe, as a material expression of "untimely death" so to speak.

Mirrors often occur in adult burials dating to the fifth and fourth century, which also contain powder-pyxis, pyxis of the lekanis type[24] and perhaps exaleiptron, apart from a variety of other toilet items (tweezers, spatula, soap, and shell) and drinking- and eating-vases (App. 2, group II). Often such a combination of grave gifts is interpreted as alluding to the toilet of the bride, the reason being that mirrors, pyxides and exaleiptra constitute important attributes in vase painting showing bridal scenes, and wedding symbolism in general is intimately connected with the funerary sphere (see recently Rehm 1994). Unfortunately, only few female skeletal investigations support this theory. A few fifth- and fourth-century mirror-contexts of the just described kind also contained a spindle whorl (App. 2, group III), or they contained a terracotta feeder (for feeding babies) and astragals apart from mirror, pyxides, make-up, etc. (App. 2, group IV). Moreover, all of these burials were inhumations of non-children, and when the sex had been determined, it was female.

Taken together, these types of funerary contexts do suggest that important aspects of female life are expressed, such as wedding, work at the loom, and the care of infants. The numerous fifth-century child burials support this impression. For from around 510 till around 425 child burials suddenly constitute 50% of all burials in Kerameikos (compare fig. 2), as well as in most other grave fields in Attica, against about 30% in sixth-century Kerameikos (Morris 1987, Appendix A1, 218-221; Houby-Nielsen 1995, 135, Tables 1-2). As I have argued elsewhere (Houby-Nielsen 1995, 148-55), this notable will on the part of women to invest baby and child burials with complex burial rites (consisting of amphorai and larnakes as coffins, and many grave gifts which make them archaeologically detectable) certainly implies that women stress their rôle as mothers (of legitimate children). Alongside the "warrior", the "mother" was the most celebrated gender rôle in Classical Athens (Loraux 1981; Vedder 1983; for some reservation against this view, see Demand 1994, 121-40).

On the whole then, it seems that in the fifth- and fourth-century women in some cases expressed a gender ideology, which i.e. concentrates on the "ephebe", the "bride", the "housewife", and the "mother" and in this way comes close to the ideology exhibited on tombstones and dramatized in the rituals of the offering-trenches.

Summing up we note that *some* mirror and strigil contexts dating to the fifth and fourth century correspond to official gender imagery in Classical Athens. But, as will be apparent in the following section, the majority of strigil and mirror contexts do not.

Burial contexts inconsistent with tombstone imagery

To begin with I would like to draw attention to a puzzling Hellenistic burial in Kerameikos (App. 1, group VII). It belonged to a man about 42 years-old, who was equipped with a strigil, but also a loom-weight. Two more Hellenistic burials of men contained loom-weights (*Ker.* XIV, 122/Me 34, 118/Me 33 and a loom-weight was also found in the fill of a male grave 30/Eck 58). These burials strongly contradict the imagery of Attic Classical tombstones, which take a special delight in referring to the dutiful woman as working at the loom by showing wool baskets, or they depict her with a distaff. Classical tombstones certainly never connect men with this task (see Clairmont 1993, vol. VI. general index "distaff", "kalathos"). Perhaps the loom-weights, when deposited in male graves, are meant to recall the profession of the deceased. In Kerameikos a house has been excavated, the architecture of which and small finds point to a house of *hetairai*, and the find of more than 100 loom-weights testifies to cloth production (Knigge 1980, 256-65; Knigge 1981, 385-93; Knigge 1983, 209-21; Knigge 1984, 27-35; Knigge 1987, 481-84). This weaving mill is perhaps to be identified with the *sunoikia* mentioned by Isaeus (6.20-22), which was owned by a man called Euktemon and run by a prostitute.

When weaving-equipment is found in women's graves it is likely to denote domestic production or in a more abstract way, dutifulness and the like.

Another Hellenistic strigil-burial of an adult person, the skeleton of which has not been sex-determined, contained a thimble and a knife, and a couple of other burials of adults, likewise not sex-determined, contained a needle in addition to a strigil (App. 1, group IX). Again, we are perhaps faced with a reference to a textile profession. If these burials are correctly interpreted, they correspond nicely with a tendency in Hellenistic times to indicate various social functions of the deceased on funerary columns in the shape of pictures of for instance a temple key, a comic mask, a plough (on a funerary column commemorating a woman) and a sickle (Conze 1911-22 vol. 4, 6).

Another noteworthy burial dates to the fourth century and contained grave gifts which would without doubt have caused the burial to be classed as female, had the skeleton not been sex-determined. For the skeleton was that of a young man, probably the actor Makareus. Apart from a variety of objects not commented upon here, this young man was buried together with a mirror, a marble pyxis, two red-figure pyxides and two lekanides — all items which are intimately connected with the female toilet in vase painting, and especially scenes showing the preparation of the bride. Among the other objects we find two shells, and, as we shall see below, shells form part of toilet equipment. This example of a deposition of powder pyxides in a male grave forcefully outdates T.L. Shear's and S.R. Robert's observations from 1936 and 1978 respectively, that pyxides have been found only in women's graves (Shear 1936, 314; Roberts 1978, 178). Obviously, a very female repertoire of grave gifts was chosen here to express Makareus' rôle as an actor, somebody moving back and forth between a male and a female world. However, Makareus' rôle as an actor is hardly the sole explanation for his female grave furnishings. His grave gifts are also the result of a time phenomenon. For a male grave in Cyprus dating to the end of the fourth century also contained a mirror (Kotera-Feyer 1993, 77 n.18). And as the previously mentioned curious strigil burials indicated, the fourth century is a period when also the strigil begins to change symbolic value. For as we shall see below, strigil contexts tend to become more and more identical with mirror contexts in the fourth century and the Hellenistic period in Attica. A similar development is detectable in Corinth and Olynthus (see App. 1, groups II-III), and as mentioned earlier on, isolated cases are reported from various parts of Central and Northern Greece, the Peloponnese (Kotera-Feyer 1993, 75-108) and Crete (Pologiorgi 1991). In addition to these cases, a burial in Argos dating to the fourth century ought to be mentioned, since it contained a pyxis, plemochoe, loom-weight, various other vases and two strigils (Bruneau 1970, 530, T.3). The underlying explanation for both the curious male mirror-contexts and the feminized strigil-contexts is best described by looking more closely at burials with strigils.

In the Classical and Hellenistic period the majority of burials containing a strigil gives a rather neutral impression in terms of gender, the strigil itself being the most gender-"laden" item (App. 1, group I-II). One grave was marked by a panathenaic vase and therefore probably commemorated a victorious athlete (Willemsen 1977, 128). Nevertheless, in the few cases where we possess more secure information regarding the sex and age of the deceased, it is certainly interesting to note that mature and elderly men as well as mature women were equipped with strigils.[25] Also a burial of a fallen warrior along with other possible warrior burials, and a burial of an envoy from Corfu contained strigils. And again the status of these deceased persons suggests men of mature age (Gebauer 1938, 615; Knigge 1972, esp. 607 fig. 26; compare also App. 1, group VIII). Apparently we are therefore faced with a tendency to emphasize the bath rather than athletics and the palaestra (or the world of the young ephebe) when depositing grave gifts. In that case, such a wish corresponds well with the tendency to depict elderly men with strigils on fourth-century tombstones, mentioned earlier on. On the other hand, the strigil as a grave gift for a mature woman conflicts not only with Attic tombstone imagery, which never combines women with strigils, but even with scenes of women holding strigils in vase painting, since these women are invariably depicted as young. Of course the strigil may have been given to the woman at a young age, and it may therefore simply represent a personal item which the woman had become especially attached to. However, it is the fact that the strigil on the whole becomes such a common grave gift in the fourth century and the Hellenistic period (compare fig. 1) which shows that the *act* of depositing strigils in burials carried a new significance. And whatever this significance is, it sometimes conflicts with tombstone imagery.

Another very frequent type of burial context is even more surprising. Thus, already in the later part of the fifth century one comes across a couple of curious adult (judged by the length of the tombs) burials, which apart from lekythoi or pyxides, contain bridal vases — and a strigil (App. 1, group IVA). Moreover, in the fourth century a strigil and two feeding cups had been deposited in an adult burial, hereby possibly combining the strigil with items which referred to a mother rôle (App. 1, group IVB). Surely, one would have expected a mirror in these burials, not a strigil. These burials are no less surprising when it is considered that the strigil was never allowed to enter the sphere of the bride and certainly not imagery of "the mother" either in vase painting or on tombstones. Besides these curious burials, we are also faced with a large group of burials containing what we would normally term female toilet requisites (pyxides, mirrors, soap, razor blade, shell, jewellery) (App. 1, group III, and compare group VI). The presence of pyxides and mirrors again gives associations to the bridal toilet.

However, the appearance of a strigil in these burials is new and breaks completely with the imagery of wedding-preparation. Together with the just discussed burials with strigil and vases for perfumed oil (App. 1, group I-II), it is strigil contexts of this kind which especially characterize the fourth century and the

Hellenistic period in Attica as well as other parts of Greece (App. 1, group III).[26]

Unfortunately, we possess little information regarding the age and sex of the buried persons belonging to this group. A couple of burials (with beads and strigils) belong to men, according to the appurtenant tombstones (*Ker.* XIV, 109/Me 27 and 110/Me 26). On the other hand, the aforementioned burial (*Ker.* XIV, 116/Me 39; App. 1, group II) of a mature woman with a strigil verifies the connection "women-strigils" in funerary ritual.

All in all, we may therefore conclude that the strigil contexts in question could be ascribed to men as well as to women. In male burials, the strigil is likely to refer to hygiene and bath, as already argued. However, in female burials the presence of a strigil together with items traditionally regarded as referring to the bridal bath (pyxis, mirror, lebes gamikos, loutrophoros) suggests a new concept of the wedding and thus of the bride and married woman. This accords well with evidence of child burials in the Hellenistic period. For in this period women appear not to stress their rôle as mothers in the way they did in the fifth century through child burials. Instead women seem in general to cease to bury babies and children with as much material goods as earlier. At least, recognizable child burials of the Hellenistic period are very rarely reported. The evidence from Kerameikos is not conclusive, but suggestive. Lack of interest in the early excavations for the Hellenistic period makes it difficult to interpret burial customs from this period. It ought to be noted, though, that in the most coherently excavated part of the Kerameikos from this period (an area north of the Street of Tombs) only 19 fourth-century burials belonged to children, as against 111 adult burials. And from the third century stem 200 adult burials but only 3 child burials. Naturally, a child necropolis may be expected to lie somewhere apart from the burials of adults (as for instance is the case in the fifth century), and underneath the Ay. Triadha church, part of a big cemetery has been excavated consisting of 13 child burials, as against 46 adult burials.[27] Still, it is curious that (to my knowledge) no Hellenistic child necropolis has yet been reported from Athens, and it should not be forgotten that disinterest in formal burial of small children is known from previous periods (Proto-Geometric, Middle Geometric and Proto-Attic) (Morris 1987, esp. 93-96).

The fact that natural shells are frequently found in fourth-century and Hellenistic Attic burials with strigil, mirror and other toilet equipment deserves attention (pl. 13) (see App. 1, group III and app. 2, group II, IV). Natural shells are also reported from various other cemeteries in Greece and in Italy dating to the same period (Papapostolou 1982; see also Ridgway 1996, 349 "conchiglie"). On the so-called "Aberdeen" reliefs from Sparta, recently interpreted as related to the Spartan cult of Demeter and thus a cult predominantly attended by women, various items are shown which refer to female toilet (Walker 1989). We observe a shell (imitation or natural), unguentaria, sponge, comb, cosmetic box, pestle and mortar (for grinding cosmetics), spatula, sandals, loin cloth (for menstruation), various other objects not related to the toilet (distaff, spindle, torch, bowl, needles) — and a strigil and mirror — in other words, much the same combination of artefacts as in Hellenistic tombs in Athens. The women named on the reliefs clearly belong to the upper class of Roman Sparta. Whether or not the items depicted on the reliefs commemorate the grooming of a cult statue, the grooming of the priestesses in charge of the cult, or recall ritual purification of the participants before entering the temenos, the reliefs give us an impression of a rich repertoire of female toilet equipment, of which strigil, mirror and shells form a part.

In the already mentioned woman's grave in Patras (Papapostolou 1982) dating to the early Hellenistic period, an elaborate and rich equipment for body care was found together with jewellery. Apart from a strigil, this burial contained a mirror, a pair of sandals, golden earrings in the shape of erotes, other gold jewellery, a silver comb — and two silver shells (pl. 12), that is a collection of objects very close to the toilet equipment on the Aberdeen reliefs, but also to the more plain toilet equipment in Athenian burials where no silver shells were deposited, but as we saw, natural shells (pl. 13). The Patras burial has been interpreted as the burial of a bride or young girl, who died too young to experience marriage, owing to the presence of sandals, which are known to have been a common bride gift, and to the presence of mock jewellery with representations of Hermes (Papapostolou 1982, 337). This may be so, although the similarity of its grave gifts to the Aberdeen reliefs and simple Athenian burials could also simply suggest a rich girl with a rich toilet equipment. Finds of Iron Age model terracotta boots in Attic burials of sub-adult women have also been interpreted as marriage boots given to girls who died before marriage with reference to Hesychius' nymphides, and on analogy with these burials a similar pair of Iron Age model boots found in Isthmia has been interpreted as a female dedication (Morgan 1994, 120-21 with references to the discussion of the Iron Age model boots from Attica, nn. 41-42). A pair of rather plain leather sandals was also found in a fourth-century grave in the Kerameikos at the feet of the skeleton. The person, assumed to be a woman, was not, however, buried with any other outstanding items (black lekythos and unguentarium) suggesting wedding symbolism (*Ker*. XIV, 46, 44/Eck 53; Kovacsovics 1984). If the Patras-burial is that of a young bride, it tells us that contrary to Archaic and Classical wedding symbolism "above" and "below" ground, the strigil is now "allowed" to enter the sphere of wedding symbolism, and — as already mentioned — this testifies to a different concept of the bride and the wedding. Indeed, strigils from Italy carrying a dedicatory inscription to a bride confirm the connection between wedding and strigil (Thuillier 1989 mentions work on this subject by F.-H. Pairault).

All in all, the choice of grave gifts, uneven as this kind of evidence may be, leaves an impression of a changed attitude to certain gender rôles such as "mother", "bride", "married woman", "ephebe" and "mature man" in some of those funerary rituals for which women are likely to have been responsible.

Mirrors and strigils as grave gifts. A female expression of new male and female ideals

The appearance of new types of strigil and mirror burials (esp. App. 1, group II-III, VI and App. 2, group 5) in the last quarter of the fifth century, and their popularity in the fourth century and Hellenistic times have to be seen in the light of a wave of changes in conventional values in fourth-century and Hellenistic Athens.

Throughout most of the fifth century it had been fashionable to display wealth by making large donations to liturgies, games, etc., in order to demonstrate a democratic spirit. Conversely, the fourth century and Hellenistic period was marked by private comsumption of wealth, where personal extravagance became a status symbol (see recently Morris 1992/93, 1994). Investments were no longer made in temple-buildings except for small *naiskoi* and the repair of older temples (I have gained this impression from a survey of Travlos 1971 and Travlos 1988 with references). A good example of the kind of sacred investments which were made in Hellenistic times is a small *naiskos* in Trapouria built on a very high podium to create a dramatic effect (Lauter 1980). On the other hand, the first political buildings appear in the fourth century (Hansen and Fischer-Hansen 1994), and what is of special interest here, private houses became more spacious and equipped with a separate bathroom. In addition, the number of baths open to the public increased significantly from the last quarter of the fifth century. In Athens several such baths are known dating from the fifth to the first century (Nielsen 1990, 6 n. 7) one of which with a room full of soap, dating to a period preceding 404/3, was situated in Kerameikos (Gebauer and Johannes 1936; Gebauer 1940, 327). It is also well-known in architectural history that the bathing sections of the palaestra began to expand at the expense of the sporting facilities to such a degree that the two terms balaneion and gymnasium became interchangeable (Yegül 1992, 23). Thus the growing interest in the hot bath at the end of the fifth century —

though at first met with contempt and suspicion by several philosophers[28] — was
to develop into a most conspicuous bathing culture throughout the Roman empire,
causing Rome to house 856 baths and Constantinople more than 150 by the end
of the fourth century AD. Bathing had become a lifestyle and part of a national
identity (Yegül 1992, 4-5).

On this background it appears as if the Late Classical and Hellenistic strigil
and mirror burials in a narrow sense were meant to recall bath, body care and
beautification, but in a wider sense signalled luxury, leisure, and responsiveness
to a new time spirit. In particular the deposition of strigils and other items for
hygiene and beautification in female burials defined the woman as an attractive
woman who had time to care for her appearance. In this way, women can be seen
to have played an active part in the shaping of new gender rôles and conventional
values. Probably the choice of strigils as grave gifts for women even indicates
that women now stepped out of their homes and visited the public baths. At least
the frequent use of the strigil as a grave gift for a woman from the beginning of
the fourth century deserves a place in the discussion of whether or not women
other than prostitutes frequented the public baths in Late Classical times, for
instance at different hours of the day than men (for this discussion, see Ginouvès
1962, 220-23). And it should not be forgotten that in Hellenistic times public baths
did develop two sections, one for men and one for women (Nielsen 1990, 7-8).

The Classical-Hellenistic burials, most of which are of a rather plain nature
and must have belonged to a very broad sector of the Attic population, also force
us to reconsider the common scholarly notion that it was the new powerful and
influential position of Hellenistic queens which changed the relationship between
men and women in general and not a change which originated in the "silent
groups" of people.

In referring to female eroticism, leisure, and thus wealthiness, the Attic fourth-
century and Hellenistic female grave contexts also express a spirit which is often
displayed on late Hellenistic grave reliefs from outside Attica. For instance, it has
recently been shown that while depictions of men on tombstones from Smyrna
stuck closely to Late Classical models in an attempt to present them as adhering
to traditionel behavioural norms of the Classical *polis*, the imagery of women
totally breaks with Classical ideals. Apparently this happened in an attempt to
present the married woman both as virtuous and as possessing an erotic charm
(Zanker 1993). Thus, women are invariably enveloped in large all-covering himatia
and standing in the so-called *pudicitia* pose, a pose which express modesty and
restraint. But the drapery strongly underlines the curves of the woman's body,
moreover she may smile discreetly and she is depicted amidst a great variety of

toilet items, sun hat and fan and always a slave girl, all of which define the deceased woman as voluptuous, rich and attractive. Occasionally the woman appears in the company of children, but in sharp contrast to women on Classical Attic tombstones, she does not pay the slightest attention to her children, but leaves them to nurses to take care of.

A new relationship between the sexes and new concepts of eroticism
The similarity in choice of grave gifts (items for hygiene and bath) for men and women, beginning in the fourth century and being especially characteristic of the Hellenistic period, is very remarkable. It corresponds to the striking lack of sex differentiation of Attic Hellenistic tombstones, the majority of which were rather plain funerary columns with just a name inscription. Hereby burial customs break a thousand year-old tradition for sex-specific grave gifts and grave markers and thus attest to important changes in attitude to the relationship between the two sexes. This similarity in burial customs between men and women may confirm scholarly theories of a new intimacy between the sexes in the Late Classical period and Hellenistic times. Thus, scholars have for a long time pointed to various written sources which indicate a tension between the two sexes in Athens at the end of the fifth century and early fourth century, but also suggest a new kind of intimacy between man and wife, which among other things rests on a more egalitarian intellectual education. In describing this development, scholars referred especially to Euripides' *Medea* and *Alkestis*, a dialogue termed *Aspasia* written down by Aeschines of Sphettus, to Menander's plays, to various philosophical schools playing with the idea of equality between men and women, to the elegy for the beloved Lyde by the poet Antimachus of Colophon, and to the powerful position of Hellenistic queens (Ferguson 1911, 71-78; Vatin 1970; Pomeroy 1975, 120-48; Pomeroy 1984, 3-41; Neumer-Pfau 1982, 16-35; Gehrke 1990, 73-75). C. Schneider even spoke of "the emancipation of women" as an established phenomenon in fifth- to fourth-century Athens, which he took to have formed the roots of "the discovery of the woman" in Hellenistic times. Unfortunately, Schneider also appears to regard the Hellenistic period as a period where — in Schneider's words — "a true nature of women" had the chance to break loose, a nature which he exemplifies by murderous Macedonian and Seleucid queens, described as demonic, wild and destructive (Schneider 1967, 78-94).

Studies in the cult of Aphrodite seem to fall in line with theories of a new kind of marital relationsship and theories of a new type of female ideal which differentiated less strictly between the accepted behaviour of *hetairai* and that of married women in the Hellenistic period. Already in the Late Classical period, Aphrodite became an increasingly popular figure on marriage vases, and since the third century Aphrodite became more prominent as patron goddess of the civic marriage than Hera (Götte 1957, 60-61; Vatin 1970, 53-55). In Hellenistic times Aphrodite had turned into an embodiment of beauty and marital love and was used in this sense as a prototype for statues of Hellenistic queens (Neumer-Pfau 1982, 55-60).

Late Classical and Hellenistic burial customs in Athens seem to reflect this change in the status of Aphrodite. As mentioned earlier on, natural (or even silver) shells are not uncommon in Late Classical and Hellenistic burials in Greece and Italy, where they formed part of elaborate hygiene and beautification equipment. The appearance of shells in Attic burials and elsewhere coincides with the appearance of terracottas in the Greek world in the late fourth century showing Aphrodite naked in an open mussel shell (pl. 14). The sudden interest in this subject may be related to the existence of a myth about the birth of Aphrodite from a shell, though it is only known from late antique sources (LIMC II. group 1.B). It is therefore possible that the deposition of shells in burials together with items for beautification — and on the whole the general popularity of the shell motif in Hellenistic jewellery and other items related with personal embellishment found in Greece and Italy[29] — reflects the new status of Aphrodite as an tutelary goddess for the married woman and the bride. In Roman times sarcophagi were sometimes decorated with scenes of Nereids bringing mussel shells along with other toilet items to a wedding (Zahlhaas 1975, 537). A fragment of a fourth-century terracotta showing a crouching Aphrodite found near the Tritopatreion in Kerameikos (Trumpf-Lyritzaki 1969, 127, pl. 31), points more directly to a connection between Aphrodite and funerary rituals in Athens (for an eschatological character of Aphrodite, see Trumpf-Lyritzaki 1969, 127).

In such a period of change of older, traditional concepts of women, where women define themselves as fulfilling the ideals of both Hera and Aphrodite through a funerary symbolism which centres on "the bathing and vain woman", we can hardly say with certainty that erotic art was made solely for men and hetairai as is often thought. This is especially true for the general interest among Greek artists since the end of the fifth century in subjects such as "bathing women" or "naked women occupied with their toilet". Vase painters, terracotta makers and sculptors delighted in the female naked body and used her toilet or bath as an excuse to depict her naked. The various Hellenistic statue types of the more or less naked Aphrodite, all of which go back to a few Late Classical statue types showing Aphrodite naked at her bath or at her toilet, form part of this interest (Neumer-Pfau 1982, 2). In fact the "bathing woman" becomes an established literary theme in Hellenistic times (Ginouvès 1962, 112, 164-73), as

Callimachus' hymn *The Bath of Pallas* exemplifies (Callim. *Lav.Pall.* (hymn 5) 17-22). The funerary ideology which women expressed through choice of grave gifts should warn us not to interpret statues of naked women, such as Praxiteles' Cnidian Aphrodite, to have been made only in order to stimulate a male audience's sexual fantasy, as has recently been suggested (Osborne 1994). Regarding the latter, it is true that Aphrodite's pudica-gesture can be taken to imply a (male) intruder and that a couple of anecdotes (Plin. *NH* 36.20-1; Pseudo-Lucian *Amores* 11-16) describe male visitors' sexual incitement when confronted with Praxiteles' statue and even attempt at intercourse. However, Pliny is himself rather doubtful as to the authenticity of these stories, of which there obviously existed many and which functioned as popular custodial tales (*NH* 7.127; Isager 1991, 153). Thus, the Cnidian Aphrodite was not the only statue to provoke stories of attempts at statue-rape, since Pliny tells a similar anecdote about an Eros made by Praxiteles (Plin. *NH* 36.22; Brüschweiler-Mooser 1973, 108-9; Isager 1991, 154). In fact Neumer-Pfau has already pointed to the probability of an exemplary nature of the Cnidian Aphrodite (flirting, provocative, playing with her bashfulness) intended especially for women (an important group of worshippers in the sanctuary) to learn from, for which reason the statue was made very realistic in order to make it easier for women to identify with Aphrodite (Neumer-Pfau 1982, 171-72). The very point of Pliny's anecdote is also to exemplify the realism of Praxiteles' work (Isager 1991, 154). Perhaps we may even have to extend this line of reasoning to the owners in antiquity of Greek Late Classical mirrors decorated with naked women or with scenes of sexual intercourse (for examples of these mirrors: Boardman and La Rocca 1975, 134-35; Cameron 1979, 53, also looks for new interpretations as to the identity of the owners).

The mirror and strigil as votive gifts

At this point it is worth considering briefly the use of the strigil and the mirror as votive gifts. Strigils have been found in sanctuaries which functioned as centres for athletic competitions (Olympia, Nemea, Isthmia (Kotera Feyer 1993, 84, 100, nn. 4, 7-9 with references), Delphi).[30] The dedication of strigils in Asclepius sanctuaries (Aleshire 1989), in Eleusis and Dodona and the Kabirion sanctuary is not surprising either (Kotera-Feyer 1993, 84, nn. 5-6 with references). However, strigils have also been found in sanctuaries in Attica of a more female character (Athena on the Acropolis of Athens, Artemis Brauronia),[31] and in the Peloponnese and Perachora: Hera Limnaia, Athena Alea in Tegea (Kotera-Feyer 1993, 100, n. 3), Argive Heraion (Waldstein 1892, 299), but unfortunately it is impossible to say much more about these dedications.

Turning to the mirror, a clearer tendency can be followed. For the use of the mirror as votive gift undergoes an interesting development which in some way parallels its development as a grave gift. In those cases where mirrors carry dedicatory inscriptions, the dedicators are women.[32] In Archaic and Classical times mirrors are especially dedicated to Artemis, Athena and Hera, that is to goddesses who take care of marriage and the birth of children, in more exceptional cases to Apollo and Zeus (Simon 1986, 221). In Attica the connection Artemis — mirror is especially strong, since many mirrors were dedicated to Artemis in Brauron. In the so-called Tomb of Iphigenia in Brauron, and in the Artemis Brauronia sanctuary itself, more than a dozen mirrors were found, one of which carried a fine dedicatory inscription from a girl (*Ergon* 1956, 27; *Ergon* 1957, 21; *Ergon* 1961, 28 fig. 28, 32; *BCH* 86, 1962, 679 fig. 11). In the "temple inventories" which registered votives for Artemis Brauronia, a group of 119 mirrors is mentioned (Linders 1972, 27, *IG* 112 1516 and 1522 line 30). It is noteworthy that apart from the Kotilion sanctuary near Bassai, which is either for Artemis or Aphrodite and received mirrors as gifts (Simon 1986, 221), there is no evidence for mirror dedications to Aphrodite in Archaic and Classical times.

This changes in Hellenistic times. Now mirrors were dedicated not only to Asclepius (Aleshire 1989, 44), but also to Aphrodite. For according to Callimachus the mirror became the exclusive gift of Aphrodite and was considered an unsuitable gift for Athena (Callim. *Lav.Pall.* (Hymn 5) 17-22; *Anth.Pal.* 6.1.18-20, 210-11; see also Simon 1986, 221-22). It has been suggested that this circumstance reflects a different attitude to dedication practices, in which offerings became more neatly associated with the receiving gods (Simon 1986, 221). However, it is more likely that Aphrodite's new central rôle as patron goddess for marriage mentioned earlier on and the general change in female gender rôles over time made the mirror a proper gift to Aphrodite.

Grave gifts, tombstones and new conventional values

From the last quarter of the fifth century, grave contexts increasingly referred to an idle, luxurious lifestyle for both men and women. In doing so, they fully adhere to new conventional values and especially to a changed perception of women in Late Classical and Hellenistic Athens. In a wider sense, the grave gifts formed part of a new urban ideology which came to characterize most of the Hellenistic world and created a kind of cultural koinê. For even though cities were submitted to highly different political systems, civic lifestyle centred around common institutions such as gymnasia and the *ephebeia*, along with religious festivals which furthered a feeling of cultural unity (Gauthier 1993, esp. 225-28). Public baths certainly also belong in this range of important public, culturally unifying institutions. They eventually developed into thermae which spread all over the Roman empire and saw to it that everyone, irrespective of sex, skin-colour or religion could have a hot bath. Of course, each area interpreted and developed these institutions independently, as their varying architectonic expressions manifest, and one should certainly be wary of speaking of a "Hellenization" process, owing to all the imperialist implications this term embodies (Alcock 1994). Nevertheless, there existed common conventional values, general as they may be, which among other things caused people even in the remotest Roman provinces to deposit toilet equipment in tombs, which included the strigil and the mirror. In Smyrna, artists of the Late Hellenistic period grasped the new tunes and created a completely new imagery of women on tombstones, and even in Athens we occasionally meet references to the new spirit on Roman funerary columns in the shape of small reliefs showing a seated woman holding a fan. Therefore the popularity of Hellenistic-Roman funerary columns at the expense of traditional Classical funerary art should not be seen as "decline", a term which has often been connected with the Hellenistic period, but more as a response to a general trend towards personal ostentation rather than to ostentatious burial custom as was the case in previous centuries. The equal use of funerary columns for both men and women must certainly also be seen as a reponse to the development described above, where the gap in status between man and woman had become narrowed.

Viewed in relation to this sweeping survey of a new urban lifestyle, fourth-century Classical tombstones appear strangely old-fashioned in their continuous effort to stress traditional civic values and female ideals which were on their way out. Only in a few instances, such as in depictions of old men with strigils or of women dressed in diaphanous drapery, do we perceive a spirit of contemporary society also met with in the choice of grave gifts. With this background, I would not find it at all surprising if the production of Classical figure-decorated grave reliefs turns out to cease, owing more to profound changes in the conventional values of Athenians than to a law against funerary ostentation.[33]

The Royal Museum of Fine Arts
The Royal Cast Collection
Toldbodgade 40
DK-1253 Copenhagen K
Denmark

Appendix 1: Strigil burial contexts

For pyxis types, see excursus on p. 254.

	Group I. *Strigil alone or together with a few different items:* One or two vases for drinking, eating or pouring, or an amphora, or a coin(s), or wreath of gold-plated leaves or nails or a pair of sandals, or a bronze or iron boss.	**Group II.** *Strigil + oil container and/or sometimes drinking- and/or eating-vases.* A: Strigil + lekythos and/or alabastron or unguentarium = a basic composition. B: IIA + various drinking- and/or eating-vases. C: Strigil + vases for drinking and/or eating and pouring, and for cooking. Sometimes also objects such as nails, coin, egg, lamp, askos, strigil cleaner, kalathos, glass buttons or fragments of gold plate.	**Group III.** *Body care and embellishment.* IIIA: Group I, IIA or IIB + pyxis (lekanis-type) and/or powder-pyxis and/or **mirror** and/or jewellery and/or soap and/or razor blade and/or shell and/or beads IIIB: Strigil + kothon. Sometimes also buttons, phiale, loom-weight, feeding-cup, amphoriskos, diadem of gold-plate, mock coin, nails, bier-ring and lead object, knife, ivory plate, ivory handle.
Athens **5th cent.**	AA 1938, 615; Ker. VII.1: 431, 521; AD 27, 32-35: XXX; AD 23, 43-48: II. XIV (5th cent. ?); AD 29, 120: IX.	IIA and IIB: AM 1966: 81/hS 173; AM 1976: 10/VEck 7; AA 1984, 58; Ker. VII.1: 78, 262, 282, 362, 482, 610, 630; Ker. IX: 100, 128; AA 1972, GS 2; AM 1977: 128, 137; AE 1958: no. 20?; AD 27, 32-35: XCV; AD 27, 142, XIX; AD 29, 120: IX ; AD 30, 23.	IIIA: AD 27, 32-35: XXXI (lekanis-type); AD 25, 79-84: XXXVIII-XXIX (lekanis-type ?, pyxis); AD 25, 87: II (pyxis).
4th cent.	AM 1966: 183/hS 28; AD 28, 26-27: II; AD 40, 31 no. 17.	IIA and IIB: AE 1958 nr. 4; AM 1966: 111/hS 69, 146/hS 3,187/hS 10; Ker. XIV: 23/Eck 14, 30/Eck 58, 31/Eck 57, 92/DP 10, 111/ Me 25, 114/Me 35, 115/Me 57, 116/Me 39; AD 27, 32-35: I, LXI, LXIX, LXXXIV, LXXXV; AD 32, 23: II and III; AAA 1973, 277-88: V; AD 28, 26-27: I; AD 42, 23: 13; AD 39, 11-14: K36.	IIIA: Ker. XIV: 20/Eck 78 (soap), 91/DP 8 (pyxis), 109/Me 27 (8 terracotta beads), 110/Me 26 (1 eye pearl); AM 1966: 144/hS 196 (10 gold-plated terracotta rosettes. from jewellery?), 176/hS 34 (shell, loom-weight).

1st-3rd cent.	*Ker.* XIV: 105/DP 5, 175/Me 64 (ring: belonging to the strigil?); *Ker.* IX: 384 (wreath of gold-plated leaves), 404; *AD* 42, 24-25: 5 (gold plate); *AD* 35, 50: I (2 iron rings, from the two strigils?)	IIA and IIB: *AM* 1966: 202/hS 4; *Ker.* XIV: 78/Eck 4, 72/Eck 8, 128/Me 37; *AD* 27, 32-35: XXIII; *AD* 24, 67: I; *AD* 23, 43-48: XII; *AD* 27, 93: XXXIX; *AD* 34, 33-37: 4; *AD* 29, 112: XXII; *AD* 32, 23: I (gold plate); *AD* 32, 25: 2; *AD* 34, 20 no. 20:11 *Ker.* IX: 356, 376, 377, E99, E115.	IIIA: *AD* 29, 95 (pyxis); *AD* 29, 112: XIX (pyxis); *AD* 34, 33-37: K2 (pyxis); *AD* 25: V (**mirror**, razor blade); *AD* 27, 109-13: IX (**mirror**); *AD* 27, 93: XXXVIII (**mirror?**); *AD* 34, 33-34: 17 (rings - jewellery?); *Ker.* IX: 385 (bronze ring), E109 (arm-ring); *AD* 42, 23 no. 27 (gold finger-ring).
Olynthus **5th cent.**	*Olynthus* XI: 348: 2, 4, 8, 364:4, 5, 7, 17, 25, 350:6, 382, 396		IIIB: *Olynthus* XI: 348:3 (kothon), 350 (kothon), 364:20 (kothon).
4th cent.	*Olynthus* XI: 11, 21, 110, 172, 182, 229, 244, 311, 372, 419, 426, 448, 586.	IIA: *Olynthus* XI: 33, 413, 568.	*Olynthus* XI: 71 (bronze finger-ring), 226 (lekanis-type), 248 (bracelet), 257 (**mirror**), 264 (pyxis), finger-ring, (loom-weight).
Corinth **5th cent.**	*Corinth* XIII: 493, 438.	IIC: (Strigil + the common composition in North Cemetery: "oinochoe and skyphos" + sometimes other vase-types for drinking and eating and various other items) *Corinth* XIII: 277, 283, 322, 342, 344, 351, 359, 369-70, 386, 397, 401, 403, 407, 410-12, 423, 428.	
4th cent.		IIC: *Corinth* XIII: 442-43, 446-47, 458-60, 481.	
1st-3rd cent.		IIB and IIC: *Corinth* XIII: 492; *Hesp.* 54, 1985: 1969-6, 1976-3, 1976-2.	IIIA: *Corinth* XII: 494 (powder-pyxis), 495 (feeding-cup, powder-pyxis)

(Strigil contexts, continued)	**Group IV**. *Wedding and mother-rôle.* IVA: Group I or II or III + lebes gamikos and/or loutrophoros. IVB: I or II or III + feeding-cup (adult grave). Sometimes also phiale or plate or coin.	**Group V**. *Childhood.* Strigil + astragals and/or terracottas and/or balls and/or small lekanis and/or small vases for drinking and eating. Sometimes also amphoriskos, phiale, needle and egg, coin, iron knife.	**Group VI.** *Childhood and body care and beautification.* Group V (among child associated objects also a bronze rattle) + **mirror** and/or soap or bracelet.
Athens **5th cent.**	IVA: AD 25, 84-87: XXXIII; AE 1958 no. 20.	Ker. VII.1: 275, 350; AM 1964: Eupheros; AM 1966: 56/hS 164, 91/hS 97; AD 29, 120: 1.	
4th cent.	IVB: AD 42, 23: 4.	AM 1966: 148/hS 45.	AM 1966: 158/hS 87 (**mirror**); Ker. XIV: 11/Eck 75 (soap).
1st-3rd cent.			
Olynthus **5th cent.**		Olynthus XI: 576.	
4th cent.		Olynthus XI: 91, 109, 145, 153, 280, 302, 401, 411, 422.	Olynthus XI: 266 (bracelet).
Corinth **5th cent.**		Corinth XIII: 349, 404, 405, 424.	
4th cent.		Olynthus XI: 453.	
1st-3rd cent.			

	Group VII. *Strigil + loom-weight.* I or II + loom-weight(s)	Group VIII. *Strigil + warrior equipment.* Group I or II + weapon. Sometimes also an ostrich egg.	Group IX. *Strigil + sewing equipment.* Group I or IIA + a thimble or a needle. (Sometimes also a knife).
Athens 5th cent.			
4th cent.		AD 27, 68.	AM 1966, 123/hS 122; AD 23, 43-48: IV (pin or needle?); AD 42, 23: 10 (pins or needles?)
1st-3rd cent.	Ker. XIV: 68/Eck 37.	Ker. IX: E84 (lance?).	Ker. XIV: 105/DP 5.
Olynthus 5th cent.		Olynthus XI: 364: 21.	
4th cent.	Olynthus XI: 227.		
Corinth 5th cent.		Corinth XIII: 262, 366-67, 357, 415.	
4th cent.		Corinth XIII: 409.	
1st-3rd cent.			

Appendix 2: Mirror contexts

For pyxis types, see excursus on p. 254.

	Group I. *Mirror alone or together with lekythos and/or alabastron and/or unguentarium and/or glass bottles.* Sometimes also nail, bone-tube, phiale, kantharos, plate, amphora, kalpis, mock coin.	Group II. *Beautification and body care (related with bridal bath).* Group I + exaleiptron or Group I + powder pyxis and/or lekanis and perhaps shell + spatula + tweezers + soap. Sometimes also lamp, knife, ivory handle, rosettes, small rings, spoon, button, omphalos, phiale, chytra, needle, balls, vases for drinking, eating and pouring.	Group III. *Wedding and housework.* Group II + spindle whorl.
5th cent.	*AM* 1966, 49/hS 85; *Ker.* VII.1, 247; *AD* 39: K20; *AD* 24, 73; *AD* 32, 22-23; *AD* 27, 127; *AD* 25; 79-84: XXII; *AD* 23, 89:XVI (mirror?); *AD* 29, 120: VIII.	*Hesp.* 1963, A; *AE* 1968, 18:11, 111:99; *Ker.* VII.1, 242, 541; *Ker.* IX, 188; *AD* 38, 112: XXXIII; *AD* 27, 32-35: LIV; *AD* 33, 24: T2; *AD* 25, 79-84: XXXVIII.	*Hesp.* 1963, B.
4th cent.	*AM* 1966, 164/hS 18, *Ker.* IX, 360; *Ker.* XIV, 96/DP 6, 106/Me 55, 127/Me 28, 174/Me 63; *AD* 29, 120: T.XIX; *AD* 28, 26-27: T.III; *AD* 34, 33-37: K6; *AD* 39, 11-14: K29.	*AM* 1966, 126/50; 157/hS 80; *AE* 1968, 16 no. 11; *AD* 29, T.XXIII; *AD* 23, 43-48: XXV; *AD* 29, 128: T.X; *AD* 27, 109-113: XVIII; *AD* 34, 33-37, K4: *AA* 1978, 56 no. 37; *Ker.* XIV, 24/Eck 64,* 46/Eck 54 (tiny rings).	*Ker.* XIV, 22/Eck 69.
3rd-1st cent.	*Hesp.* 1963, T; *Ker.* IX, 369, 371, 395, E 95A, E 110; *AD* 22, 54-56, TIII; *AD* 23, 43-48, TX; *AD* 27, 93: TXXXVIII (kalpis); *AD* 27, 109-13: TXI; *AD* 31, 39-40: T.7; *AD* 28, 74-76: TII; *AD* 25, 79-84: TXXIII.	*AM* 1977, 134 (also shell).	

* See commentary on p. 255 for this grave

	Group IV. *Bride and/or mother-rôle?* Group II + feeder + astragals (in **adult** grave) or group II + astragals (in **adult** grave). Sometimes also skyphos, make-up, shell, bronze handle, bronze wheel.	**Group V.** *Body care and beautification (with no traditional connection to the bridal bath).* Group I + strigil and/or tweezers and/or razor blade and/or jewellery. Sometimes also knife, mock coin, diadem of gold-plate foliage, phiale, astragals.
5th cent.	*Hesp.* 1963, D; *AD* 39, 11-14, K56.	
4th cent.	*Ker.* XIV, 8/Eck 72.	*AM* 1966, 158/hS 87; *Ker.* XIV, 16/Eck 66, 88/DP 14.
1st-3rd cent.		*Ker.*IX, 388 (**strigil?** rings); *AD* 27, 109-13: TIX (**strigil**); *AD* 34, 33-37: T20 (bronze-chain, diadem of gold-plated foliage; *AD* 42, 24-25: T3 (golden earrings, diadem of gold-plated foliage), T.7 (gold earrings, rings); *AD* 25, 75-76: T.I (beads, rings, gold ear-rings, razor blade). T.V (**strigil**, razor blade).

Appendix 3

Fig. 1 is based on the burials published in: Charitonidis 1958; Boulter 1963; Schlörb-Vierneisel 1964; Vierneisel 1964; Schlörb-Vierneisel 1966; Knigge 1966; Knigge and Willemsen 1966; Knigge 1972; Knigge and Freytag gen. Löringhoff 1974; Knigge and Freytag gen. Löringhoff 1975; Knigge 1976; Freytag gen. Löringhoff 1976; Kübler 1976; Willemsen 1977; Knigge, Stichel and Woyski 1978; Knigge 1980a; Knigge 1980b; Knigge 1981; Knigge 1983; Knigge 1984; Knigge, Freytag gen. Löringhoff, Kovacsovics and Stichel 1984; Knigge 1987; Kovacsovics 1990.

  In addition to these publications, those cemeteries and graves which are preliminarily published in the *Archaiologikon Deltion* and *Archaiologika analekta eks Athinon* between 1960 and 1994 were integrated.

Excursus: Pyxis

When placing graves with strigil and/or mirror and "pyxis" in the various groups of the appendices, I have kept in mind that the term "pyxis" covers several different vase shapes which appear in different burial contexts pointing to rather different purposes. From a survey of the burials containing a "pyxis" listed below, I have gained the impression that "pyxides" (with a bowl-shaped body) in child burials were meant as containers for food, since they are extremely common in child burials together with vases for drinking and eating, and since pyxides with a cylindrical body, which in vase-painting are associated with the female toilet, only rarely occur in child burials. The same conclusion is reached by U. Knigge (*Ker.* IX, 55). The same seems to apply for "pyxides" (with a bowl-shaped body) in offering-places of the fourth century BC, since they solely appear together with vases for drinking and eating. However, "pyxides" (with bowl-shaped bodies) occur much more rarely in burials of adults, and when they occur, they are often found together with items for body care — such as mirrors, strigils and pyxides with a cylindrical body — and may even contain make-up powder. For this reason I believe that pyxides with a bowl-shaped body in adult burials with strigils and mirrors are likely to refer to body care, along with the strigil and the mirror, rather than being meant as containers for food.

  Regarding the following list of burials: When pyxides have a cylindrical body, I mention this in brackets and refer to *Agora* XII, pp.173-78 for their parallels. If nothing else is stated, the pyxis has a bowl-shaped body and is variously called "Deckelpyxis", "Henkellose Deckelpyxis", "Einhenklige Deckelpyxis", "Deckelschale", or "Lekanis". Regarding *Kerameikos* VII.1 the vases of which were still unpublished when the present article was written, I have presumed that when K. Kübler mentions "Deckelschüssel" and "Deckelpyxis", the pyxis in question has a bowl-shaped body, since "pyxides" called by these terms are mostly characteristic of infant and child burials. Furthermore, when Kübler refers to a "Pyxis", I have presumed it is a "true" pyxis with cylindrical body, since K. Kübler mentions this type as being characteristic of female graves (*Ker.* VII.1, p. 194).

Burials with "pyxides"

5th cent. Kerameikos:

Infant and child burials: *Ker.* VII.1: 2, 38, 44, 52, 57 ("rotfigurige Pyxis"), 61-62, 66-68, 74, 76, 105, 111, 116, 124, 132, 135, 137, 155-56, 165, 184, 187, 191, 210, 232, 245, 249, 251, 253, 261 ("Pyxis mit weisser Schminke und schwarzen, blättrigen Resten ... Unterteil einer zweiten Tonpyxis, darin zwei weiche, im Bruch weissliche kleine, kegelförmige Gegenstände"), 350, 353, 375, 383, 440, 477, 489, 512, 553, 566-67, 599, 618 ("schwarze Pyxis"); *Ker.* IX: 9, 13, 16-17, 34, 45, 64, 66, 69, 77, 89, 92, 102, 132, 146 (cylindrical body), 152, 154, 168, 174, 188, 198-99, 203, 213, 217, 222, 229, 236, 261, 263, 267, 283, 288, 293 (besides a lekanis also a lid of a pyxis), 297, 301-2, E3 (cylindrical body) (child?), E11, E12 (child ?), E13, E16, E21 (child ?), E24 (child ?), E37,

E52 (child ?), E56 (child ?), E58, E59, E61 (child ?), E66 (child ?), E67, E70, E73 (child ?), E75 (child?), Pr1, Pr2, Pr6, Pr11 (child ?), Pr13; *AM* 1964: Lissos-grave (cylindrical body); *AM* 1966: 41/hS 144, 46/hS 165, 44/hS 185, 52/hS 201, 82/hS 143, 99/hS 108.

Adult burials: *AM* 1966: 77/hS 118 (cremation) (cylindrical body), 102/hS 51 (cremation) (cylindrical body); *Ker.* VII.1: 130, 273 (cremation), 276, 300 (cremation), 324 ("rotfigurige Pyxis"), 386 (cremation), 443 (cremation), 541 (cremation) ("rotfigurige Pyxis"); *Ker.* IX: 151 (cylindrical body).

Age insecure: *Ker.* VII.1: 528 ("zwei schwarze Pyxiden ... In einer der Pyxiden ein Stück grünlicher, fettiger Masse"), 593 ("Alabasterpyxis gefüllt mit Astragalen").

Offering-trench: *AA* 1964: p. 432-34, figs. 21, 24 (besides a lekanis, also pyxides with cylindrical body).

4th cent. Kerameikos:
Infant and child burials: *AM* 1966: 107/hS 167, 135/hS 39, 171/hS 199; *Ker.* IX: 351.

Adult burials: *AM* 1966: 126/hS 50, 151/hS 33, 157/hS 80 (pyxis with flaring body), 170/hS 200 (cylindrical body); *Ker.* XIV: 8/Eck 72 (two pyxides with cylindrical body), 22/? (two pyxides with cylindrical body), 24/Eck 64 (observe: two bowl-shaped pyxides with make-up; three pyxides with cylindrical body, one of which is of marble), 135/Me 59 (cylindrical body).

Offering-places: *AM* 1966: 105/hS 146, 108/hS 166, 109/hS 84, 114/hS 52, 136/hS 39, 138/hS 374 (besides lekanis also pyxis with cylindrical body), 160/hS 83; *Ker.* XIV: 4, 17, 18, 21, 25/Eck 85, 28/Eck 19, 35/Eck 84.

Hellenistic Kerameikos:
Young person: *Ker.* XIV: 103/DP 3 (cylindrical body).
Adult: *Ker.*IX, 363 (cylindrical body).

Notes

1. I wish to thank most cordially the "Hellenism Initiative" and the Danish Research Council for the Humanities for providing me with a grant which made it possible for me to work with a most fascinating and neglected period in the history of Athens, the result of which is the present article and Houby-Nielsen (in press). And I would like to warmly thank Sarah Pomeroy for encouragement and criticism, and Rudolf Stichel for information regarding unpublished Hellenistic burials in the Kerameikos. I am much obliged to Signe and Jacob Isager for their help and comments regarding my use of ancient written sources. Also, I am grateful to Anders Andrén, Ole Thomsen, and Tobias Fischer-Hansen for having directed my attention to valuable references and to the editors Lise Hannestad and Troels Engberg-Pedersen for their criticism of my original lecture and later my manuscript. Last but not least, I am grateful to Peter Crabb for having revised my English.
2. See for instance, D'Onofrio 1982; Morris 1987; Morris 1992; Whitley 1991; Strömberg 1993; Houby-Nielsen 1995.

3. I have not found any references to scholars who specifically deal with this problem, but see p. 230 for references to scholars who seem indirectly to have regarded women to be the responsible group.

4. Houby-Nielsen (in press).

5. From now on all dates are BC unless otherwise stated.

6. Kotera-Feyer 1993; and Francesca R. Serra Ridgway has published a Hellenistic burial in Tarquinia which apart from various items related with hygiene also contained a mirror and a strigil (Ridgway 1996, T. 65).

7. Kotera-Feyer 1993, 95-99, deals with strigil finds from Attica. She does not, however, include the finds reported in the *Archaiologikon Deltion*, and the significant increase in the deposition of strigils is not mentioned, just as it was not the aim of her chapter to analyse the strigil finds from a broader social point of view.

8. See Appendices 1 and 3 for the calculation of this increase.

9. For Greece and the Mediterranean, see Kotera-Feyer 1993, 75-146; a rich girl-burial in Germany may serve as an example of popularity of the mirror as a grave gift in the Roman provinces, Goethert 1990.

10. I thank Anders Andrén for this reference.

11. For a very fine and richly inlaid strigil found in a Roman public bath in Wales, see Boon 1980.

12. *Olynthus* VIII, 117-18, pls. 39, 99, house AVII2, room a; for the connection kitchen and bathroom, see Ginouvés 1962, 177 n. 7, who refers to *Olynthus* VII, 200 and XII, 369-97 and *Hesperia* 22, 1953, 199 and *Hesperia* 23, 1954, 328-46.

13. Pomeroy 1975, 71-73, 75-84; Alexandrakis 1988, 83; especially Just 1991, 105-25 and Scheidel 1995 conveys a picture of rather less confinement for women than did Flacelière 1965, 55, for example.

14. Clairmont 1993, vol. 6, general index "strigil": of 65 tombstones dating to the 4th century and showing a man holding a strigil, 12 are depicted as elderly men.

15. For the woman with mirror depicted as young on tombstones, see Clairmont 1993, intr. vol. 26; for the mirror and strigil as symbols of respectively male and female gender roles, Lissarraque 1992, 201-2; regarding the mirror as "an emblem of femininity in art", see Sutton 1981, 337.

16. Vierneisel 1964, 435 fig. 24 and 455 fig. 42; Schlörb-Vierneisel 1966, 72 no. 138; Knigge 1975, 126, nos. 13-14; Stichel 1984, 56-61; Houby-Nielsen 1992; Houby-Nielsen (1997).

17. See Meyer 1988 for the interpretation of the various types of "sitting women" as different male wishful concepts of women; also Sutton 1981, 821, warns that in some scenes of gift giving involving "sitting women", "there may be an element of fantasy that should not be overlooked"; also Sabetai 1993, 191-94 for an overlap between scenes of washing hetairai and washing brides.

18. See Sutton 1981, "Gift giving", esp. scenes involving sitting women p. 284 and p. 290 for an interpretation of the mirror as a gift to purchase a woman's affection; see also Meyer 1988, 106, for the motif "sitting woman holding a mirror" who interprets the mirror not as a gift but as an attribute in a depiction of an abstraction of a female character.

19. I am indebted to Tobias Fischer-Hansen for drawing my attention to this article.

20. Sutton 1981, 334 n. 136 with references: Bari, Mus.civ. 4979, *ARV* 236.4, 1638 (column crater); Palermo, *ARV* 565.39, 1656 (neck amphora); Boston inv. 95.21, *ARV* 1052.19, 1680 (stamnos), see also *BMusFA* 37, 1939, fig. 10; Vienna inv. 2166, *ARV* 1111.1, *Para* 452, Ginouvès 1962, pl. XVIII.53 (column crater); *Para* 349.29 bis (column crater); Naples inv. 3030, *ARV* 500.31 (pelike); 521.4 (shape not stated); *Para* 421 (shape not stated).

21. I am most grateful to Ole Thomsen for furnishing these references.

22. Alexiou 1974, esp. 4-23 and esp. n. 107; Pomeroy 1975, esp. 44; Danforth and Tsiaras 1982; Garland 1985, 24, 43-45; Caraveli 1986; Siurla-Theodoridou 1989, 41-42, 104-17, 213-14; Just 1991, esp. 110; Shapiro 1991; Holst-Warhaft 1995.

23. The following list does not claim to be complete: *AD* 23, B1, 1968, 92: T.XVI; *AD* 25, B1, 1970, 75-76: T.II, T.V, 82: T. XXII, XXIII; *AD* 29, B1, 1973-74, 113: T. XXII, 122: T.VIII, 131: T. X; *AD* 28, B1, 1973, 26-27: T. II; *AD* 30, B1, 1975, 29: T.I; *AD* 31, B1, 1976, 39: T.7; *AD* 32, B1, 1977, 23 (Odos Monastiriou and Alikarnassou): T.II, T.III; *AD* 34, B1, 1979, 23: no. 27, 35: T.20, T.22; *AD* 42, B1, 1987, 25: T.3; Schlörb-Vierneisel 1966, 144/hS 196, 146/hS 3; *Ker.* XIV, 17/Eck 56 (offering place), 35/Eck 84 (offering place), 60/Eck 39 (offering place), 159/Me 20 (offering place), 20/Eck 78, 22/ Eck 69, 35/Eck 84, 46/Eck 54, 55/Eck 46, 59/Eck 45, 68/Eck 37, 106/Me 55, 113/Me 38 (from wooden coffin), 118/Me 33, 128/Me 37, 145/Me 5 (from wooden coffin), 156/Me 2; *Ker.* IX, E84, E86, E103.

24. For the bowl-shaped lekanis as forming part of a toilet set when found in adult graves, see Excursus.

25. *Ker.* XIV, 23/Eck 14 (28 year-old man), 30/Eck 58 (50 year-old man), 111/Me 35 (42 year-old man), 116/Me 39 (40 year-old woman), 128/Me 37 (37 year-old man), 68/Eck 37 (42 year-old man).

26. Note especially a grave in Northern Greece in which a strigil was found together with a mirror, combs, shoes, pyxis, needle and clothes (Kotera-Feyer 1993, 84 n. 8 with references).

27. For the area north of the Street of Tombs, see Schlörb-Vierneisel 1966 and Knigge 1966. I thank Dr. Stichel most warmly for providing me with the number of child burials from his excavation adjoining this area and for the information regarding the Roman necropolis below the Ay. Triadha church.

28. For references, see Nielsen 1990, 7 n. 14; Yegül 1992, 6-7.

29. Compare the elaborate Hellenistic silver box in the shape of a cockleshell found in Taranto, (De Juliis 1989, pl. CXXIX, 462-63).

30. *Fouilles de Delphes* V, 108 nos. 544, 544 bis, fig. 370 bis; four golden strigils dedicated by Sybarites: Theopompus ap. Ath. XIII 605, B, C; see Rouse 1902, 281.

31. *CIA* 117-75, ii 642-738; Rouse 1902, 395 (not mentioned by Kotera-Feyer 1993); *CIA* ii 751ff.; Rouse 1902, 397.

32. Lazzarini 1976, 170, mentions six examples of mirrors with female dedicatory inscriptions from six different sanctuaries.

33. And if Clairmont's dating system is accepted, the production of tombstones peaks in the second quarter of the 4th century and then declines.

Bibliography

Alcock, S.E. 1994. "Breaking up the Hellenistic world: survey and society", in: Morris (ed.) 1994, 171-90.

Alcock, S.E. & Osborne, R. (eds.) 1994. *Placing the Gods. Sanctuaries and Sacred Space in Ancient Greece*. Oxford.

Aleshire, S. 1989. *The Athenian Asklepieion. The People, their Dedications, and the Inventories*. Amsterdam.

Alexandrakis, D.S. 1988. *The Education of Children from Birth to the Age of Fourteen in Classical Athens (500-300 B.C.)*. Ph.D. dissertation. Ann Arbor.

Alexiou, M. 1974. *The Ritual Lament in Greek Tradition*. London.

Atalay, E. & Voutiras, E. 1979. "Ein Späthellenistisches Grabrelief aus Phokaia", *AA*, 58-67.

Bérard, C. & Durand, J.L. 1989. "Intering the Image", in: Bérard et al. 1989, 23-38.

Bérard, C., Bron, C., Durand, J.-L., Frontisi-Ducroux, F., Lissarrague, F., Schnapp, A. & Vernant, J.-P. (eds.) 1989. *A City of Images. Iconography and Society in Ancient Greece.* Princeton.

Berger, E. 1970. *Das Basler Artzrelief. Studien zum Griechischen Grab- und votivrelief um 500 v. Chr. und zur vorhippokratischen Medizin.* Basel.

Beyer, J.M. 1995. "Big Brother is Watching You. Marie Theres Fögen untersucht die Spätantike Wissenskontrolle", *AntW* 26:2, 82-84.

Boardman, J. 1955. "Painted Funerary Plaques and some remarks on Prothesis", *BSA* 50, 51-66.

Boardman, J. 1991. *Athenian Red Figure Vases. The Archaic Period.* London.

Boardman, J. & E. La Rocca 1975. *Eros in Greece.* New York.

Boegehold, A.L. & Scafuro, A.C. (eds.) 1994. *Athenian Identity and Civic Ideology.* Baltimore/London.

Bonfante, L. 1989. "Nudity as a Costume", *AJA* 93, 543-70.

Bookidis, N. 1990. "Ritual Dining in the Sanctuary of Demeter and Kore at Corinth: Some Observations", in: Murray (ed.) 1990, 86-94.

Bookidis, N. 1993. "Ritual dining at Corinth", in: Marinatos & Hägg (eds.) 1993, 45-61.

Boon, G.C. 1980. "A Richly Inlaid Strigil from the Fortress Baths, Caerleon", *AntJ* 60, 333-37.

Boulter, G.C. 1963. "Graves in Lenormant Street, Athens", *Hesperia* 32, 113-37.

Breitenstein, N. 1941. *Danish National Museum. Department of Oriental, and Classical Antiquities. Catalogue of Terracottas. Cypriote, Greek, Etrusco-Italian and Roman.* Copenhagen.

Bruneau, Ph. 1970. "Tombes d'Argos", *BCH* 94, 437-531.

Brüschweiler-Mooser, V.L. 1973. *Ausgewählte Künstleranekdoten. Eine Quellenuntersuchung.* Zürich.

Bulloch, A., Gruen, E.S., Long, A.A. & Stewart, A. (eds.) 1993. *Images and Ideologies. Self-definition in the Hellenistic World.* Berkeley/Los Angeles/London.

Burn, L. 1987. *The Meidias Painter.* Oxford.

Cameron, A. & Kuhrt, A. (eds.) 1983. *Images of Women in Antiquity.* Detroit.

Cameron, F. 1979. *Greek Bronze Hand-Mirrors in South Italy with Special Reference to Calabria.* (BAR, IntSer 58). Oxford.

Caraveli, A. 1986. "The Bitter Wounding: The Lament as Social Protest in Rural Greece", in: Dubisch (ed.) 1986, 169-94.

Cassimatis, H. 1991. "Les autels dans la ceramique italiote dans les civilisations méditerranéennes de l'antiquité", in: Étienne & le Dinahet (eds.) 1991, 33-43.

Charitonidis, S.I. 1958. "Anaskaphi klassikon taphon para tin plateian Syntagmatos", *AD* (1961), 1-152.

Clairmont, C.W. 1993. *Classical Attic Tombstones*, intr. vol., vols. 1-6. Kilchberg.

Conze, A. 1893-1922. *Die attischen Grabreliefs.* Berlin.

Coulson, W. & Kyrieleis, H. (eds.) 1992. *Proceedings of an International Symposion on the Olympic Games, 5-9 September 1988.* Athens.

Danforth, L.M. & Tsiaras, A. 1982. *The Death Rituals of Rural Greece.* Princeton.

De Juliis, E.M. (ed.) 1989. *Gli ori di Taranto in età ellenistica.* Milano.

Demand, N. 1994. *Birth, Death, and Motherhood in Classical Greece.* London.

Dent, J.S., Lloyd, J.A. & Riley, J.A. 1976-1977. "Some Hellenistic and Early Roman Tombs from Bengazi", *LibAnt* 13-14, 131-213.

Deubner, L. 1936. "Zu den Thesmophoria und anderen Attischen Festen", *AA*, 335-43.

D'Onofrio, A.M. 1982. "Korai e kouroi funerari Attici", *AnnAStorAnt* 4, 135-70.

Dubisch, J. (ed.) 1986. *Gender and Power in Rural Greece.* Princeton.

Durand J.L. & Lissarrague, F. 1980. "Un lieu d'image? L'espace du loutérion", *Hephaistos* 2, 89-106.

Étienne, R. & le Dinahet, M.-Th. (eds.) 1991. *L'espace sacrificiel*. Paris.

Ferguson, W.S. 1911. *Hellenistic Athens. An Historical Essay*. London.

Flacelière, E.R. 1965. *Daily Life in Greece at the Time of Pericles*. London.

Freytag gen. Löringhoff, B. von 1976. "Archaische und Klassische Grabfunde auf dem Hang nördlich der 'Eckterrasse' im Kerameikos", *AM* 91, 31-61.

Garland, R. 1985. *The Greek Way of Death*. London.

Garland, R. 1990. *The Greek Way of Life from Conception to Old Age*. London.

Gauthier, P. 1993. "Les cités héllenistiques", in: Hansen (ed.) 1993, 211-31.

Gebauer, K. 1938. "Ausgrabungen im Kerameikos II", *AA*, 608-16.

Gebauer, K. 1940. "Ausgrabungen im Kerameikos", *AA*, 310-62.

Gebauer, K. & H. Johannes 1936. "Ausgrabungen im Kerameikos", *AA*, 207-14.

Gehrke, H.J. 1990. *Geschichte des Hellenismus*. München.

Ginouvès, R. 1962. *Balaneutiké. Recherches sur le bain dans l'antiquité grecque*. Paris.

Goethert, K. 1990. "Ein reiches Mädchengrab der augusteischen Zeit aus Elchweiler, Kreis Birkenfeld", *TrZ* 53, 241-80.

Götte, E. 1957. *Frauengemachbilder in der Vasenmalerei des fünften Jahrhunderts*. München.

Hansen, M.H. (ed.) 1993. *The Ancient Greek City-State*. (Acts of the Copenhagen Polis Centre 1). Copenhagen.

Hansen, M.H. & Fischer-Hansen, T. 1994. "Monumental Political Architecture in Archaic and Classical Greek *Poleis*. Evidence and Historical Significance", in: Whitehead (ed.) 1994, 23-90.

Hoffmann, G. 1988. "La jeune fille et la mort: quelques stèles à épigramme", *AnnAStorAnt* 10, 73-82.

Hoffmann, G. 1993. "Portrait de groupe avec dame. Etude sociologique des monuments", in: Clairmont 1993, intr. vol., 160-79.

Holst-Warhaft, G. 1995. *Dangerous Voices. Women's Laments and Greek Literature*. London/New York.

Hornbostel, W. (ed.) 1980. *Aus Gräbern und Heiligtümern. Die Antikensammlung Walter Kropatscheck*. Mainz.

Houby-Nielsen, S. 1992. "Interaction between Chieftains and Citizens? 7th Cent. B.C. Burial Customs in Athens", *ActaHyp* 4, 343-74.

Houby-Nielsen, S. 1995. "'Burial Language in Archaic and Classical Kerameikos", *Proceedings of the Danish Institute at Athens* 1, 129-91.

Houby-Nielsen, S. (1997) "The Role of Burial Customs in Late 8th and 7th Cent. B.C. Kerameikos", in: Hägg (ed.) (to appear in 1997).

Houby-Nielsen, S. (in press). "Revival of Archaic Funerary Practices in Hellenistic and Roman Kerameikos", *Proceedings of the Danish Institute at Athens* 2.

Hägg, R. (ed.) (in print), "The Role of Religion in the Early Greek Polis". Third International Seminar on Ancient Greek Cult. Swedish Institute at Athens 16-18 October 1992.

Isager, J. 1991. *Pliny on Art and Society*. Odense/London.

Just, R. 1991. *Women in Athenian Law and Life*. London/New York.

Knigge, U. 1966. "II. Gräber hS 205-230", *AM* 81, 112-35.

Knigge, U. 1972. "Untersuchungen bei den Gesandtstelen im Kerameikos zu Athen", *AA* 1972, 584-629.

Knigge, U. 1975. "Aison, der Meidiasmaler? Zu einer rotfigurigen oinochoe aus dem Kerameikos", *AM* 90, 123-43.

Knigge, U. 1976. *Südhügel. Kerameikos. Ergebnisse der Ausgrabungen* IX. Berlin.

Knigge, U. 1980a. "Der Rundbau am Eridanos. Mit Beiträgen von B. Bohen und W. Koenigs", in: Koenigs et al. 1980, 57-98.

Knigge, U. 1980b. "Kerameikos. Tätigkeitsbericht 1978", *AA*, 256-65.

Knigge, U. 1981. "Kerameikos. Tätigkeitsbericht 1979", *AA*, 385-93.

Knigge, U. 1983. "Kerameikos. Tätigkeitsbericht 1981", *AA*, 209-21.

Knigge, U. 1984. "Kerameikos. Tätigkeitsbericht 1982", *AA*, 27-35.

Knigge, U. 1987. "Ausgrabungen im Kerameikos 1983-1985", *AA*, 481-84.

Knigge, U. & Freytag gen. Löringhoff , B. von 1974. "Die Ausgrabungen im Kerameikos. Tätigkeitsbericht 1973/74", *AA*, 181-98.

Knigge, U. & Freytag gen. Löringhoff, B. von 1975. "Kerameikos. Tätigkeitsbericht 1973/74", *AA*, 456-68.

Knigge, U., Freytag gen. Löringhoff, B. von, Kovacsovics, W. & Stichel, R.H.W. 1984. "Kerameikos. Tätigheitsbericht 1982", *AA*, 27-61.

Knigge, U., Stichel, R.H.W. & Woyski, K. von 1978. "Kerameikos. Tätigkeitsbericht 1975/76", *AA*, 44-67.

Knigge, U. & Willemsen, F. 1966. "Die Ausgrabungen im Kerameikos 1963. 2. Die Höhe östlich des Querweges", *AD* 19, B1, (1964), 42-46.

Koenigs, W., Knigge, U. & Mallwitz, A. 1980. *Rundbauten im Kerameikos. Kerameikos. Ergebnisse der Ausgrabungen* XII. Berlin.

Kotera-Feyer, E. 1993. *Die Strigilis.* (Europäische Hochschulschriften Reihe 38 Archäologie). Frankfurt.

Kovacsovics, W.K. 1984. "Ein Sandalenfund aus dem Kerameikos", *AM* 99, 265-74.

Kovacsovics, W. 1990. *Die Eckterrasse im Grabbezirk des Kerameikos. Kerameikos. Ergebnisse der Ausgrabungen* XIV. Berlin.

Kreuzer, B. 1992. *Frühe Zeichner 1500-500 v.Chr. Ägyptische, Griechische und Etruskische Vasenfragmente der Sammlung H.A. Cahn*, ed. by V.M. Strocka. Basel Waldkirch.

Kron, U. 1992. "Frauenfeste in Demeterheiligtümern: Das Thesmophorion von Bitalemi. Eine archäologische Fallstudie", *AA*, 611-50.

Kurtz, D. 1975. *Athenian White Lekythoi.* Oxford.

Kurtz, D. 1988. "Mistress and Maid", *AnnAStorAnt* 10, 141-49.

Kurtz, D. & Boardman, J. 1971. *Greek Burial Customs.* London.

Kübler, K. 1976. *Die Nekropole der Mitte des 6. bis Ende des 5. Jhs. Kerameikos. Ergebnisse der Ausgrabungen* VII. T.1. Berlin.

Lazzarini, M.L. 1976. *Le formule delle dediche votive nella Grecia arcaica.* (MemLinc Ser. 8. 19,2). Roma.

Lauter, H. 1980. "Ein ländliches Heiligtum hellenistischer Zeit in Trapouria /Attika", *AA*, 242-55.

Lind, H. 1988. "Ein Hetärenhaus am Heiligen Tor? Der Athener Bau Z und die bei Isaios (6, 20f.) erwähnte Synoikia Euktemons", *MusHelv* 45, 158-69.

Linders, T. 1972. *Studies in the Treasure Records of Artemis Brauronia found in Athens.* Stockholm.

Lissarrague, F. 1992. "Figures of Women", in: Schmitt Pantel (ed.) 1992, 139-229.

Loraux, N. 1981. "Le lit, la guerre", *L'Homme* 21(1), 37-67.

Marinatos, N. & Hägg, R. (eds.) 1995. *Greek Sanctuaries. New Approaches.* London/New York.

Meuli, K. 1946. "Griechische Opferbräuche", in: *Phyllobolia für P. von der Mühll.* Basel.

Meyer, M. 1988. "Männer mit Geld", *JdI* 103, 1988, 87-125.

Morgan, C. 1994. "The Evolution of a Sacral 'Landscape': Isthmia, Perachora, and the Early Corinthian State", in: Alcock and Osborne (eds.) 1994, 105-42.

Morris, I. 1987. *Burial and Ancient Society. The Rise of the Greek City-State.* Cambridge.

Morris, I. 1992. *Death-ritual and Social Structure in Classical Antiquity.* Cambridge.

Morris, I. 1992/93. "Law, Culture and Funerary Art in Athens 600-300 B.C.", *Hephaistos* 11/12, 35-51.

Morris, I. 1994. "Everyman's grave", in: Boegehold & Scafuro (eds.) 1994, 67-101.

Morris, I. (ed.) 1994. *Classical Greece. Ancient Histories and Modern Archaeologies.* Cambridge.

Murray, O. (ed.) 1990. *Sympotica. A Symposium on the* Symposion. Oxford.

Neumer-Pfau, W. 1982. *Studien zur Ikonographie und Gesellschaftlichen Funktion hellenistischer Aphrodite-Statuen.* Bonn.

Nielsen, I. 1990. *Thermae et Balnea. The Architecture and Cultural History of Roman Baths.* Aarhus.

Nielsen, T.H. et al. 1989. "Athenian Grave Monuments and Social Class", *GRBS* 30, 411-20.

Oakley, J.H. & R. Sinos 1993. *The Wedding in Ancient Athens.* London.

Osborne, R. 1994. "Looking on — Greek Style. Does the Sculpted Girl Speak to Women too", in: Morris (ed.) 1994, 81-96.

Papapostolou, I.A. 1982. "Ellenistikoi taphoi tis Patras I", *AD* 32, A, 1977, 281-343.

Parker, R. 1983. *Miasma. Pollution and Purification in Early Greek Religion.* Oxford.

Pemberton, E.G. 1985. "Ten Hellenistic Graves in Ancient Corinth", *Hesperia*, 54, 271-307.

Pologiorgi, M. 1991. "Apo to klasiko kai ellenistiko nekrotapheio tis Kydonias", *AD* 40 A, 1985, 162-77.

Pomeroy, S.B. 1975. *Goddesses, Whores, Wives, and Slaves. Women in Classical Antiquity.* New York.

Pomeroy, S.B. 1983. "Infanticide in Hellenistic Greece", in: Cameron & Kuhrt (eds.) 1983, 207-22.

Pomeroy, S.B. 1984. *Women in Hellenistic Egypt. From Alexander to Cleopatra.* New York.

Raschke, W.J. (ed.) 1988. *The Archaeology of the Olympics and Other Festivals in Antiquity.* London.

Rehm, R. 1994. *Marriage to Death. The Conflation of Wedding and Funerary Rituals in Greek Tragedy.* Princeton.

Ridgway, F.R.S. 1996. *I corredi del Fondo Scataglini a Tarquinia* I. Milano.

Roberts, S.R. 1978. *The Attic Pyxis.* Chicago.

Robertson, M. 1992. "A Red-Figure Krater: South Italian or Etruscan", *OJA* 1 179-85.

Rouse, W.H.D. 1902. *Greek Votive Offerings. An Essay in History of Greek Religion.* Cambridge.

Sabetai, V. 1993. *The Washing Painter. A Contribution to the Wedding and Genre Iconography in the Second Half of the Fifth Century B.C.* Cincinnati.

Samson, R. 1992. "The Reinterpretation of the Pictish Symbols", *JBrArchAss* 145, 29-65.

Scanlon, T.F. 1988. "Virgineum Gymnasium. Spartan Females and Early Greek Athletics", in: Raschke (ed.) 1988, 185-216.

Schefold, K. 1930. *Kertscher Vasen.* Berlin.

Scheidel, W. 1995. "The Most Silent Women of Greece and Rome: Rural Labour and Women's Life in the Ancient World (I)", *GaR* 42:2, 202-17.

Schlörb-Vierneisel, B. 1964. "Zwei klassische Kindergräber im Kerameikos", *AM* 79, 85-104.

Schlörb-Vierneisel, B. 1966. "Eridanos-Nekropole I. Gräber und Opferstellen hS 1-204", *AM* 81, 4-111.

Schmalz, B. 1983. *Griechische Grabreliefs.* Darmstadt.

Schmitt Pantel, P. 1992. *La cité au banquet. Histoire des repas publics dans les cités grecques.* Rome.

Schmitt Pantel, P. (ed.) 1992. *A History of Women in the West I. From Ancient Goddesses to Christian Saints.* Cambridge, Mass./London.

Schneider, C. 1967. *Kulturgeschichte des Hellenismus.* München.

Shapiro, A. 1991. "The Iconography of Mourning in Athenian Art", *AJA* 95, 629-56.

Shear, T.L. 1936. "Psimythion", in: *Classical Studies Presented to Edward Capps on his 70th Birthday*, Princeton, 314-17.

Simon, C. 1986. *The Archaic Votive Offerings and Cults of Ionia*. Berkeley/Los Angeles.

Siurla-Theodoridou, V. 1989. *Die Familie in der Griechischen Kunst und Literatur des 8. und 6. Jahrhunderts v. Chr*. München.

Snodgrass, A.M. 1971. *The Dark Age of Greece. An Archaeological Survey of the Eleventh to the Eight Centuries B.C.* Edinburgh.

Stichel, R.H.W. 1984. "Grabung im Bezirk des Dionysios von Kollytos", *AA*, 56-61.

Strömberg, A. 1993. *Male of Female? A Methodological Study of Grave Gifts as Sexindicators in Iron Age Burials from Athens*. Jonsered.

Sutton, R.F. 1981. *Interaction between Men and Women Portrayed on Attic Red-Figure Pottery*. Ann Arbor.

Thomsen, O. 1987. *Pseudolus. Tosproget udgave med noter og kommentarer*. Aarhus.

Thuillier, J.-P. 1989. "Les strigiles de l'Italie antique", *RA*, 339-42.

Travlos, J. 1971. *Bildlexikon zur Topographie des antiken Athens*. Tübingen.

Travlos, J. 1988. *Bildlexikon zur Topographie des antiken Attikas*. Tübingen.

Trendall, A.D. & Cambitoglou, A. 1978. *The Red-Figured Vases of Apulia* I. *Early and Middle Apulian*. Oxford.

Trumpf-Lyritzaki, M. 1969. *Griechische Figuren-Vasen des Reichen Stils und der späte Klassik*. Bonn.

Vatin, C. 1970. *Recherches sur le mariage et la condition de la femme mariée à l'époque hellénistique*. Paris.

Vedder, U. 1988. "Frauentod — Kriegertod im Spiegel der attischen Grabkunst des 4. Jhr. v. Chr.", *AM* 103, 161-91.

Vierneisel, K. 1964. "Die Ausgrabungen im Kerameikos", *AA*, 420-67.

Waldstein, C. 1892. *Excavations of the American School of Athens at Heraion of Argos*. London.

Walker, S. 1989. "Two Spartan Women and the Eleusinion", in: Walker & Cameron (eds.) 1989, 130-41.

Walker, S. & A. Cameron (eds.) 1989. *The Greek Renaissance in the Roman Empire*. (BICS suppl. 55). London.

Whitehead, D. (ed.) 1994. *From Political Architecture to Stephanus Byzantius. Sources for the Ancient Greek Polis*. (Historia Einzelschriften 87). Stuttgart.

Whitley, A.J.M. 1993. *Style and Society in Dark Age Greece. The Changing Face of a Pre-literate Society 1100-700 B.C.* Cambridge.

Willemsen, F. 1977. "Zu den Lakedaimoniergräbern im Kerameikos", *AM* 92, 117-57.

Williams, D. 1983. "Women on Athenian Vases: Problems of Interpretation", in: Cameron & Kuhrt (eds.) 1983, 92-106.

Yegül, F. 1992. *Bath and Bathing in Classical Antiquity*. New York.

Zahlhaas, G. 1975. "Über die Auswirkungen der weiblichen Schönheit Römisches Toilettegerät", *Gymnasium* 82, 527-44.

Zanker, P. 1993. "The Hellenistic Grave *Stelai* from Smyrna: Identity and Self-image in the Polis", in: Bulloch et al. (eds.) 1993, 212-30.

CONVENTIONAL VALUES IN THE HELLENISTIC WORLD: MASCULINITY

Halvor Moxnes

Introduction

What was "masculinity" in the Hellenistic age? In what ways does the Hellenistic age differ from the classical Greek period with its heroes and warriors epitomising the masculine ideal? This is not a question that has been much discussed. Given the vast amount of material that needs to be taken into account to give a full answer, this study can obviously only give an example of such an inquiry into some of the transformations that took place. We shall focus on two authors from the early imperial period, Dio Chrysostom and Plutarch who are chosen to complement each other. They were not only from the same period, but also from similar social and cultural backgrounds. Both were Greek intellectuals well at home in the Roman world; both had good connections in Rome and advocated concord between Greeks and Romans. As moralists they were more conventional than highly original thinkers. Thus, they are particularly useful for a study of conventional values towards the end of the Hellenistic period. They wrote in a situation in which Greek values had to be adapted to the new social and political order brought about by the expansion of the Roman empire.

This study attempts to read some texts by Dio Chrysostom and Plutarch from the perspective of what they say about "masculinity". This is a perspective that I as a reader choose to apply to the texts, from a modern interest. Dio and Plutarch of course did not phrase the issue in that way. They addressed citizens of Greek cities in the Eastern part of the Roman empire in late first and early second century AD. They were concerned about the rôles and the responsibilities of these citizens, who were adult, free men. From our perspective it is therefore possible to study their advice about rôles and responsibilities as part of a discussion of male identity.

But what do we mean by "male identity"? Gender rôles belong to the assumed, unspoken values of a society, that which is taken for granted. It is mostly when they change or are threatened that they become a part of public discourse. A pre-condition for a study of masculinity in texts from a distant period is a reflection on the way in which we carry our own gender identities and cultural presupposi-tions with us. It is always from some particular perspective that we look at masculinity in a period that is different from our own. And the cultural picture in Western Europe and Northern America now seems to be one of uncertainty, ambiguity and ambivalence when it comes to presentations of masculinity.

In recent decades the so-called "modern", Western societies in particular have experienced considerable changes in gender rôles as well as in conceptions of gender. An indication of these changes is the popularity of gender studies that have become important not only within social sciences but in the humanities as well. It all started with women studies, now well established in most Western universities. The study of masculinity, or men's studies, have only recently started to make an impact (Brod 1987). It is a sign of maturity in scholarly approach that a broader field now emerges where those two areas are combined to gender studies with a focus on interrelations between the two.

With their methodological discussions these studies have also influenced research on historical societies and ancient texts. The same is true of anthro-pological studies focusing on gender rôles. Particularly helpful for studies of the Hellenistic world are works in Mediterranean anthropology with its special focus on honour and shame (Gilmore 1987, Moxnes 1993). Critics of the attempt to establish the Mediterranean as an area with distinct cultural characteristics have questioned this emphasis on honour and shame as typically Mediterranean values and argue that they are much more universal. This criticism has led to renewed reflection and a useful refining of the general hypothesis. It is true that honour and shame are important social values in many premodern societies far beyond the Mediterranean. The most characteristic aspect of honour and shame in the Mediterranean, however, appears to be the association of these concepts with gender rôles and sexuality. It is this aspect that makes works on contemporary Mediterranean societies relevant for a study of masculinity in ancient texts from the same area.

In his introduction to a number of studies that discusses the challenges to Mediterranean studies of honour and shame, David G. Gilmore (1987, 2-21) portrays manhood in the Circum-Mediterranean under four aspects: (1) manhood as a public virtue, (2) sex and marriage, (3) man's rôle as provider, and (4) man as protector and his need for autonomy. It is with the two first aspects and their interrelationship that we are concerned in this study.

Gilmore (1987, 90-103) suggests that there is a basic uncertainty among Mediterranean men about their masculine rôle. What is often regarded as a traditional, self-conscious "macho-image" of the Mediterranean man is in reality much more uncertain and wrought with ambiguities. The masculine rôle is not something "given", it always has to be defined vis-à-vis the feminine. Due to the uncertainty of masculinity, men are always under pressure not to appear to be feminine, for instance in "speech, dress, comportment or affect". The sexual aspect appears typically in the competition between men over women, in a triangular relationship that has homoerotic overtones. A man whose wife has a relationship with another man is "shamed", that is, he is put in a passive position, which is that of a woman. Symbolically he is made feminine, as if he was made subject to an homosexual assault. Thus, male dishonour "implies more than loss of social prestige, it also implies loss of male social identity, of masculinity" (Gilmore 1987, 11). It is this combination of aspects that is intriguing: an ideal manhood that makes men's real lives a continuous test, a masculinity that is based on strength to protect one's honour, but at the same time is constantly under suspicion of weakness, identified with femininity.

Gilmore has pointed to a fundamental uncertainty about the relations between the masculine and the feminine when it comes to definitions of manhood and a man's honour. In another study of the Mediterranean circumference Michael A. Marcus (1987) has given an historical perspective on the difficulty of describing manhood and male honour in a general sense. Marcus studied the Ghiyata tribe in Eastern Morocco and changes in the social and economic conditions that occurred with the arrival of the French colonial rule in the 1920s. Before that, in a period with a weak central government, many tribes could lead a semi-autonomous existence based on military strength and intertribal feuds. This fostered a strong warrior ethos, in which "symbols of independence, force and the active defence of honour were attributes of the ideal male" (1987, 53). But since not all tribesmen had horses and were warriors, honour was restricted and did not inhere in all of them.

The arrival of a strong colonial power put an end to autonomy and feuding, forced the tribal élite to submit to French authority, and changed the economic conditions of the tribe. These changes also affected their sense of "honour". When the conditions that had made their warrior ethos possible were changed, they were left with the question: "How, then, may Ghiyata prove themselves real men in their altered social circumstances?" (1987, 56). Marcus suggests that "honour" is an ambivalent moral conception, dependent upon the social sphere. Since honour through feuding was no longer possible, he found that the Ghiyata had to reorient themselves, and see how honour could be obtained in their new circumstances:

Ghiyata today see virtue as bound up more with such exemplary, individual, and "pacifist" conducts as equity and probity (*nishan*) in one's dealings, showing hospitality and generosity without *apparent* ulterior motive (to say that one "gives bread" is a common compliment), not "enlarging" oneself or envying the good fortune of others, keeping one's word (*kilma*), and the like (1987, 57).

These ideals are drawn from Islam, and as with the honour of the feuding period, they are considered to be possessed only by an elect few.

With their studies, Gilmore, Marcus and others have given helpful perspectives and questions that can fruitfully be addressed also to ancient texts. And it is to these that we shall now turn.

Dio Chrysostom, Plutarch and masculinity in a period of change

Dio Chrysostom and Plutarch were in many ways conventional in their philosophical reflections and addressed matters of practical, moral interest. We shall therefore expect that their ideas of masculinity will reflect social conventions. But there is always the question of whose social conventions: are they "general", that is, shared by both high and low class, or do they belong to particular groups, for instance all free men or only the élite? Moreover, we sense in the writings of Dio and Plutarch a growing uncertainty about the rôle of the male citizen. It could no longer be taken for granted. The issues relating to an ideology of masculinity could not be solved simply by referring to established conventions. A discussion was needed.

Can we find any external reasons for this uneasiness about the masculine rôle? There has been much discussion on the effects upon social relations and personal identity of the political changes that the Greek *polis* underwent in the Hellenistic period. It has been argued that the loss of political autonomy had consequences for the rôle and self-understanding of the male citizens as well. In particular, it has been suggested that the loss of independence and thereby the loss of security that the city represented led to a rise in individualism.

This picture may be too simplistic. M. Foucault (1986), among others, has argued that the political changes did not so much lead to a decline of the cities as to a change in the exercise of power. When the Romans established their hegemony over the Greek cities, the civic institutions were preserved. The Romans even continued the practice of the Hellenistic rulers of declaring the "freedom" and the "autonomy" of Greek cities that were under their authority. These declarations did not have a specific legal bearing, they represented a form of "polite language" that expressed cordial relations between the Roman senate or the emperor and the Greek cities under their rule (Gruen 1984, 132-57).

The political changes that occurred did not so much lead to a rapid growth of individualism as to "an alteration in the technologies of self-formation" (Martin 1994, 124). Foucault (1986) has stated convincingly that when power was wielded by the emperor and his representatives, this affected the ways in which the citizens of the Greek cities played their rôle. Their position and status was no longer primarily defined by competition with their peers within an agonistic city society, but by their position vis-à-vis external powers. Thus, they had to establish a new relationship to their own status, to their obligations and thereby also to the formation of their identity. Consequently, we may ask what happened to the old ideals of masculinity when one of their most characteristic aspects, agonistic competition, was made obsolete?

Many of the *Orations* of Dio Chrysostom speak to this situation. As a political and moral philosopher and orator, Dio exhorted Greek cities to rule themselves in a proper way under Roman rule. His own personal history was a vivid illustration of the new situation for the élite in these cities. Dio belonged to a leading family in his hometown Prusa in Bithynia in the province of Asia and he had as a philosopher secured the patronage of several Roman emperors, although he fell out of favour with Domitian and was exiled for a period. In his *Orations,* mostly addressed to various Greek cities in the Eastern part of the empire, he describes a situation in which the old "hero" ideals of competition, strength, warfare, so important to the old Greek cities, had become outdated due to the new political situation. And Dio found that the attempts by men of the city élite to continue to live according to these ideals, in the form of seeking honour for themselves, in competition for positions and prestige, were becoming increasingly destructive (Moxnes 1994, 205-13). Such competition destroyed the character of the individual, as well as that of the community and it created strife and dissension in the city body. Moreover, it threatened to destroy the rest of political independence and self-government since internal conflicts gave the Romans an excuse to come in to take direct control to restore order.

As an orator Dio spoke directly to the character of his addressees. The purpose of many of his speeches was to bring about a change in their understanding of what their tasks were and what it meant to be citizens involved in city affairs. Since "citizens" meant free men of the city, these texts are a primary source of Dio's view of masculinity as a public virtue.

Masculinity as a public virtue

In his address to the Rhodians (*Or.* 31) Dio explicitly contrasts the rôle of his audience with that of their ancestors, and sets up two different kinds of ideals for the male citizen. The purpose of his exhortation is that the city shall not be found doing anything "unworthy of itself or alien to the general decorum of its public life" (*Or.* 31.157). The goal is that they shall show themselves to be heirs to the ancient Greeks, like the Athenians and Spartans and thereby take first place among the Greeks of their own day. But they must not think that this comes automatically to them, even if they seem to think they can make that claim: "for it is only among those Hellenes who still live and are sensible of the difference between honour and dishonour (*timê* and *adoxia*) that it is possible to be first" (*Or.* 31.159).

But honour and shame are not timeless values that carry the same meaning at all times and in all places. We see here how Dio is involved in a reinterpretation of the meaning of honour adapted to new circumstances. In order to show themselves to be true heirs of the ancient Greeks, and to behave in an honourable way, different qualities are required of Dio's addressees than of Greek citizens in an earlier period. The ancestors of the Rhodians lived in an independent city, thus their virtues were different:

For whereas they had many other ways in which to display their virtues — in assuming the leadership over the others, in lending succour to the victims of injustice, in gaining allies, founding cities, winning wars — for you it is not possible to do any of these things (*Or.* 31.161).

Here Dio presents the old warrior, fighting virtues that represented the honour of classical Greece in the days of independent cities (Adkins 1960, 153-70). In contrast to that, Dio portrays the situation of his addressees as one that requires much more peaceful virtues:

But there is left for you, I think, the privilege of assuming the leadership over yourselves, in administering your city, of honouring and supporting by your cheers a distinguished man in a manner unlike that of the majority, of deliberating in council, of sitting in judgement, of offering sacrifice to the gods, and of holding high festival — in all these matters it is possible for you to show yourselves better than the rest of the world (*Or.* 31.162).

This represents the tasks that were left after the city-states came under Rome's authority and no longer could enter into alliances or fight wars. When he made this speech, Dio was a loyal client of the emperor. Consequently, he shows an acceptance of these political changes and addresses the requirements of the social and political situation as he sees it. Thus, there is a conscious shift away from the old hero and warrior ideal as something of the past, towards the new ideal: "leadership over yourselves (*to heautôn proestanai*)". Dio upholds the importance of the institutions of the city and argues for civic virtues. It is clear that he has in mind the leaders of the community, not the majority of the citizen body. He comes across as arguing as a "responsible" citizen, addressing other citizens who belong to the élite and who claim to carry responsibility for the city. Thus, it is the rôle of a "city gentleman" that is here described (Gleason 1990, 393).

The contrast in male identity is not only one between "ancient" virtues and such that were valid in a new situation. The new situation that the male élite in Greek cities faced was one with several options. In an address to the citizens of his own hometown Prusa (*Or.* 44.10), Dio encourages them to trust in the virtues that they themselves possess. He develops this at great length and lists not only the virtues associated with city life, especially the keeping of peace and harmony, in contrast to disunity, but also those of "daily" life, like taking care of one's body and soul, and rearing children.

To concentrate upon what they as citizens can themselves do is preferable to another course of action: to seek privileges and honours from the emperor or his representatives. Dio uses here the technical terminology of *eleutheria* ("freedom") not about political independence, but about a certain recognition that could be granted a city by the emperor (*Or.* 31.106, 112). This was a privilege that Prusa probably did not obtain. But he speaks of it as "so called freedom" (*tên legomenên eleutherian*) compared to "true freedom" (*tên de alêthên eleutherian*) that they could themselves gain if they ran their own affairs in a worthy manner (*Or.* 44.12). This advice may have sounded hypocritical coming from somebody who was himself the client of several emperors. Maybe this advice was also self-serving, a way for Dio to rebuff expectations that he should act as a broker between the emperor and the city to procure privileges. But it was more than that, it was part of Dio's effort to keep civic responsibility in the forefront of male virtues and to maintain a sense of self-sufficiency and independence among the élites of Greek cities.

Plutarch, Dio's contemporary and a member of the city élite in a small town near Delphi in Greece, shared many of the same concerns. He was particularly worried that members of the city aristocracy might seek a career in Rome and in the Roman administration and leave the responsibility for their own home city. He was also, like Dio, very much concerned with the problem of factions and urged harmony in the city. His treatises on *Precepts of Statecraft*, addressed to Sardis, were written at about the same time as Dio addressed many of the cities in the Greek East with a similar message. C.P. Jones points out how they use a stock of common arguments:

These were no longer the days of ancient Greece; power belonged to others, before whom the Eastern cities were as children. Greeks who struggled for mastery over one another were scrambling for trifles and bringing disgrace upon themselves. It was better to acquiesce in the peace that Roman power had established throughout the world (Jones 1971, 118).

However, it was not just the temptations of Rome and advantages in going into Roman service that threatened the civic spirit that Dio wanted to encourage. There are also other developments that he finds alien or, at the very least, not helpful for his purpose. In his address to the Alexandrians (*Or.* 32) Dio contrasts the praise bestowed on men for "good discipline, gentleness, concord, civic order, etc". with praise for material wealth, especially as gained by commerce, that is "arrivals and departures of vessels, and superiority in size of population, in merchandise and ships". These matters, Dio says, are fit for praise in the case of a fair, a harbour and a marketplace, but not in a city! That is, a city is something more than a marketplace. It has civic institutions and it has citizens from whom a certain character is required.

Dio may here be reflecting traditional negative views on commerce as an activity not suited for a free man, or criticizing the growth of commercial activity and a new group of economic "entrepreneurs". He makes a conscious attempt to link the identity of the individual to the city as a community that had to reorient itself compared to its former historical rôle. Dio did not want the community to become totally dependent upon the emperor and favours from him, thus, a certain independence was needed. But this independence could not be built primarily on economic progress. Instead, Dio is arguing for the need of a "civic spirit". This concern for the city aims at bringing fame to the city throughout the Hellenistic world, but now in a peaceful competition, based on the citizens and their concord and harmony as well as on their worthy behaviour. Dio's praise of concord and worthy and quiet behaviour was not a praise of abstract virtues. His arguments for concord in the city correspond to a typical pattern, it is used by the élite to make the larger population accept their rule. Likewise in Dio's description a worthy behaviour is that displayed by the élite and which sets them apart from "the majority". Just as the ancient ideals of honour through war and fights belonged to the warrior or hero, the new ideals of honourable civic behaviour were not for everybody, they were for the male élite.

Body and character

The "leadership over oneself" that Dio encouraged was not primarily an inner quality. It was played out in the public city life in the undertaking of responsibility for civic institutions. This public life was indeed public, in terms of everybody being in view. It was carried out where men walked around in the city, where they were visible and exposed to judgment and evaluation at all times —not merely their words, but their total appearance, the way they walked, their posture, etc., were watched. Dio mentions this as a reason why they are admired by others:

That indeed is the reason why you are admired for such characteristics as I shall mention — and they are regarded by all the world as no trifling matters — your gait, the way you trim your hair, that no one struts pompously through your city streets, but that even foreigners sojourning here are forced by your conventional manners to walk sedately; ... for all these customs you are admired, you are loved, more than by your harbours, your fortifications, your shipyards are you honoured by that strain in your customs which is antique and Hellenic (*Or.* 31.162-63).

Why are hairstyles and a sedate manner of walking more worthy of admiration than the city's fortifications and harbours? And why were these traits in particular pointed out as customs that were "antique and Hellenic?" Whereas in the first part of this section of his speech, Dio seems to be arguing and exhorting, here he is pointing out to his audience something which they already do and that is met with general admiration. It is taken for granted that this behaviour is admirable and that it sets them apart from non-Hellenic cities, so that the visitor who comes to Rhodes "recognises instantly on disembarking, even if he happens to be of barbarian race, that he has not come to some city of Syria or Cilicia" (*Or.* 31.163). What are the presuppositions behind this passage, the "silent assumptions" that Dio can take for granted?

It is a common presupposition in the Mediterranean world, and elsewhere as well, that one can judge the character of a person from his or her bodily characteristics and movements. In many societies this is developed into an art of observation, and there were even handbooks for this in antiquity (Gleason 1990). There were special traits to look for in order to find out if a person was trustworthy or not; for instance staring blue eyes were a bad sign. One area of particular interest in physiognomy was how to detect gender deviance. The author of one of these handbooks, Polemo, was a contemporary of Dio and Plutarch and a citizen of Smyrna in Asia Minor (Jones 1971, 118). He belonged to the same group of influential philosophers with contacts to emperors and consuls. He also shared the same political views, and encouraged his co-citizens in Smyrna to settle their disputes within the city, so that the Romans did not have to interfere. Polemo developed a system of "decoding" the signs of gender deviance, and thereby he gives information about the construction of gender systems. It is based on the presupposition that there exist masculine and feminine "types", and that these types do not necessarily correspond to anatomical sex (Gleason 1990, 390-93).

Polemo gives descriptions of walk, posture, etc., that identify characteristics used to judge a man: "You should know that a certain amplitude in a man's stride signifies trustworthiness, sincerity, liberality and a high-minded nature free from anger. Such men come off successfully in their encounters with kings" (Gleason 1990, 392). On the basis of this description it is easy to recognise that Dio in his statement to the Rhodians refers to well known standards for masculine behaviour. Likewise, in his speech to the Alexandrians Dio uses the same standards of measurement: "walking is a universal and uncomplicated activity, but while one man's gait reveals his composure and the attention he gives to his conduct, another's reveals his inner disorder and lack of self-restraint" (*Or.* 32.54). Plutarch gives a similar description when he explains how Pericles changed his personal habits when he entered politics: "Pericles also changed his personal habits of life, so that he walked slowly, spoke gently, always showed a composed countenance, kept his hand under his cloak, and trod only one path" (*Praecepta gerendae reipublicae* 800 C).

We are here dealing with cultural norms of masculinity that are common in many societies. From a man's walk it is possible to judge his character and thereby also whether he is fit for responsible positions in the city. Deviations from the norm reveal a character that is unstable and thus not to be trusted. It is because the "outside" reveals the "inside" that Dio can argue that a behaviour that corresponds to traditional and conventional norms among the male élite is more admirable than harbours and fortifications. In one sense these may be regarded as mere "external" factors. But Dio's argument can also be seen as a way for an old élite to keep its superiority in the face of growing competition. Another aspect of the same argument is that Dio makes this behaviour into a mark of group identity. The function of a sedate walk as a cultural norm is strengthened and made into a mark that separated Greeks from the non-Greek, the barbarians: it made foreigners recognise that they had arrived in a Greek city and not a city of Syria or Cilicia.

The masculine ideal as boundary
In Dio's speech to the Alexandrians (*Or.* 32) exhortations to behave with composure and balance is stated in terms of "behaving like a man". But this however

turns out to be a masculine ideal that not all men can attain. Dio speaks to the Alexandrian audience gathered in the theatre and exhorts them to change their behaviour, and not to behave like musicians and jesters — people held in low esteem. The point that he wants to make is political and concerned with the ability of the Alexandrians to rule themselves. He contends that the Romans had to come in to establish direct rule, not because they revolted, but because they were untrustworthy, given to "piping" and "dancing" (*Or.* 32.51, 71). Their city is full of music and play, and their behaviour is similar, they are not serious (*Or.* 32.4).

Thus, Dio challenges them to behave in a serious manner, and it is from the outset of his speech introduced as a challenge to be true men. He starts by telling them an anecdote, warning them not to repeat the mistake of the Athenians:

when Apollo said that, if they wished to have good men as citizens, they should put that which was best into the ears of the boys, they pierced one of the ears of each and inserted a bit of gold, not understanding what the god intended. In fact such an ornament was suitable rather for girls and for sons of Lydians and Phrygians, whereas for sons of Greeks, ... nothing else was suitable but education and reason (*paideia kai logos*), for it is natural that those who get these blessings should prove to be good men (*andres agathoi*) and saviours of the state (*Or.* 32.3).

Masculine behaviour is identified with the Greeks, while the feminine is identified not only with girls, but also with Lydians and Phrygians, that is, with non-Greek people. This is in line with a Greek tendency to regard barbarians as savages or effeminates (Jones 1971, 124-25). The contrast between masculine and feminine runs through this speech, and the masculine ideal is represented by the free man. To return to the spectators in the theatre, Dio concedes that even among "better people there are those who need some diversion and amusement in life, but they should take it with decorum and as befits free men (*anthrôpoi eleutheroi*)" (*Or.* 32.46). He contrasts them with the entertainers of Alexandria, of whom he has a very negative view, and he says that they "fight not for anything that is real or important, but for an enjoyment that is fleeting, a fancy that has no substance".

This contrast is finally put into the vocabulary of "manly" or "unmanly" and "honour and shame": "so great is the misfortune of these poor wretches, that they regard as manly (*anandreion*) what is most unmanly of all (*anandrôtaton*), and as dignified *(semnos)* what is most shameful *(to aischiston)*" (*Or.* 32.49). He continues with a statement that reveals some of the hidden assumptions about masculinity in his text: "For in the one case it is the death of a bad man (but a man), in the other of a (slave) in hard luck". The contrast that this translation tries to bear out by adding "but a man", is that between a "bad man" and somebody who is like a slave, that is, wanting in manhood or unworthy of being a man. The first man might have achieved something noble had he not encountered such an evil spirit, but the other shows with his total behaviour that he is no real man: "shouting and frenzy caused by an ill-starred voice and a wicked nod of the head ..." (*Or.* 32.49). The underlying assumption in Dio's judgment of the contrast between a "bad man" and somebody who was not a man at all, appears to be similar to the one M. Herzfeld found in his fieldwork among Cretans: there was less focus attached to "being a good man" than to "being *good at* being a man" (Gilmore 1987, 16).

When Dio returns from his digression about the "bad man", he extols the character of the "noble soul" and the virtues for which he is willing to die: "justice and virtue and ancestral rights and laws and a good king" (*Or.* 32.50). The contrast to that is the "low-born outcast" who has no real male virtues.

It is difficult to attribute a real local flavour to Dio's criticism of the Alexandrians; he draws on a common stock of ideals and their opposites. It is interesting to note, however, that from Alexandria a few decades earlier, we actually have a discussion of similar virtues that also turns around the concept of "masculinity". That is in the treatise *De Iosepho* by the Jewish writer Philo of Alexandria. Philo gives an allegorical exposition of the offices that provide food for Pharaoh: a chief baker, a chief butler and a chief cook. It is possibly the knowledge of the use of eunuchs at the court that provided Philo with this image of the emasculated man, when he says: "all are eunuchs, since the lover of pleasure is barren of all the necessities, temperance, modesty, self-restraint, justice and every virtue" (*Ios.* 153). Thus, the "lover of pleasure" (*philêdonos*) is described as "emasculated", he does not possess the truly "manly virtues".

In what sense are the characteristic elements of masculinity in Dio's discussion truly conventional? Several of them are part of stock language from handbooks, which proves that they were widespread, but Gleason's remark that it is the rôle of a "city gentleman" that Dio describes points towards a specific function of his ideals of masculinity. They are substitutes for the old heroic ideals associated with warfare with other city-states. War was no longer possible or desirable, but the spirit of competition was still alive. Dio's ideals appear to speak to a need for the Greek cities to maintain their special status also within the Roman empire, to distinguish themselves from cities in other provinces, like Syria and Cilicia, but now with the peaceful means of "proper" behaviour. In this respect Dio's ideals serve as a common characteristics that distinguishes the city as a totality from the barbarians. But this proper behaviour that reflected character strengths was also a means of making distinctions within the city. There is an obvious élitist perspective to Dio's presentations of an orderly walk, measured movements and restricted emotions. With these descriptions he defines "masculinity" as a social rôle that distinguishes the male élite from the "city rabble". It is a masculinity that is carefully cultivated by and for the few.

Masculinity and sexuality

So far we have been concerned with masculinity as a public virtue. But how is this rôle related to the other important area of masculine identity, sexuality and marriage? It should be noted at the outset that we do not presuppose a clear cut division between "public" and "private" rôles. In the literature from the classical period there are many examples that the way in which a man handled his sexual affairs was an important political issue; it was understood to reveal basic character traits that determined his behaviour has a citizen (Winkler 1990). This remains the case in the Hellenistic period as well, but the balance of the argument shifts more towards the question of the relation between two individuals.

The male rôle in sexuality and marriage is central to all discussions of masculinity. This is where gender rôles are most explicitly played out and where the moral discussion about what it is to be a man generates most heat. Gender is a symbolic category, and therefore it carries strong moral overtones. Feminist and masculine characteristics do not correspond to female and male sex, they exist in an overlapping continuum. However, there is a tendency in cultures to distinguish and to polarise gender rôles (Gilmore 1990, 22-23). As a result of this condition, in almost all cultures we find the notion that "manhood is a critical threshold that boys must pass through testing". Furthermore, those who are found wanting in this test, often played out on the public scene, have their gender identity questioned with epithets like "effete", "unmanly", "effeminate", "emasculated", etc. Different from criticism of women, who may be accused of being a "bad woman", it is men's very right to their gender identity that is threatened (Gilmore 1990, 11).

The Hellenistic configuration of gender rôles and sexuality is illustrated by Plutarch's discussion of two types of relationships, that between a man and woman in marriage, and that between an adult man and a young boy, that is, a youth in the ambiguous period between child and adult. This latter form of relationship, which was often idealised in the classical period and that coexisted with marriage, was looked upon with more scepticism in the Hellenistic period. Plutarch as well as Dio were sceptical of this sort of relationship, but for what reasons?

The treatise *On Love* (*Amatorius*) in the Moralia presents Plutarch's views in a discussion of the advantage of marriage compared to a pederast relationship.

This is a treatise that abounds with commonplaces. It also shows Plutarch's great skill as an author. It has a novel-like setting, the discussion of love is placed in the setting of a story about a young man from Thespiae who is carried off into marriage by a rich widow. The discussions of the dialogue are held between two parties, Pisias and Anthemion, who both were in love with the boy, and their "advocates" Protogones and Daphneus, with Plutarch acting as a mediator. The first section of the dialogue centres on what is best, a pederast relationship or marriage. The second part focuses on whether Eros is a god, and what his powers are, and the last part advances arguments for marriage. Plutarch comes out as a strong defender of marriage.

"Masculine love" versus pederasty

When Plutarch argues for the power of Eros, however, he turns to "masculine love" as his main examples (*Amat.* 759E). The power of Eros is compared with that of other gods, particularly that of Ares, the god of battle. Eros is said to be stronger than Ares even in that area: "A man filled with Love has no need of Ares to fight his enemies; if he has his own god with him, he is 'ready to cross fire and sea, the air itself', on behalf of his friend, wherever the friend may bid him" (*Amat.* 760D). In order to prove his point, Plutarch adduces several examples, all of them from the classical period and most of them lauding relationships between men.

The first example is the story of how Cleomachus of Pharsalia died when he helped the Chalcidians in their battle against the Eritreans. Cleomachus, who was said to possess great courage, and who thus fulfilled the heroic masculine ideal, gained extra courage from his young lover. This young man is described in a supportive rôle, like a wife: he watches the battle, and before the battle, he embraces Cleomachus and puts his helmet on him. Cleomachus is successful in securing victory, but is himself killed. The importance of the support of love through this pederast relationship for Cleomachus' heroic efforts is recognised by the Chalcidians. Plutarch adds to the description of the battle that "formerly they had frowned on pederasty, but now they accepted it more than others did" (*Amat.* 761A).

Other examples elaborate on how male relationships belong within a heroic, warrior-like setting and how love between hoplites makes them better fighters. Plutarch sees a close correspondence between warlike attitudes among people like the Spartans and their attraction to love. Most of the examples are male love for other males, and Plutarch lists among the "great heroes of old" Achilles and Epaminondas as well as Heracles (*Amat.* 761D -E). In this way, love and courage are combined, we might say "naturally", in the masculine ideal of the heroic warrior of old. In contrast, women are not associated with fight and the god Ares, but Plutarch uses the example of the woman Alcestis to show the extraordinary power of Eros. Eros can give even women courage beyond what belongs to their nature, so that they can gain male characteristics: "if Love possesses them, it leads them to acts of courage beyond the bounds of nature (*para phusin*) even to die" (*Amat.* 761E).

This shows how Plutarch can use examples of an "old morality". These stories of war and fighting represent the very type of masculine honour that no longer had any place in city life, but they continued to play a rôle as examples for human relations. In these narratives love is the initiator and supporter of human courage. The prime example is the erastes who is loved by his eromenos, a relationship that is also called "friendship" (*philia*) and found among soldier lovers. Thus, the ideal is not only that of the young boy who supports his lover in an heroic fight, but also of two soldiers who through love encourage one another.

In his discussion of Eros in the second part of the treatise, Plutarch has gone back to ancient Greece and the warrior ideal for his examples of love between men. These examples stand in partial contrast to his views in the first section, in which he discusses pederast love versus marriage. Here he combines positions from the classical period, found in Plato, with more traditional, "un-philosophical" views. We shall now look at this part of the treatise focusing on Plutarch's picture of the young boy, Bacchon. He is at the centre of the argument between the two parties and is put in an awkward position as the coveted prize of both an adult man and a woman. What is the masculine rôle that is envisaged for him? How can he preserve his honour as a man?

The arguments in defence of pederasty focus mostly on the rôle of the adult man, the erastes. Pisias, the would-be lover of Bacchon, and his friend, Protogenes, hold the Platonic position. Marriage with a woman is well and good in order to produce children, but true love is not possible with women. Eros expresses itself in the attachment of an adult man to a young soul, i.e. a young man, and through friendship (*philia*) brings him to virtue (*aretê*) (*Amat.* 750C, 751A). It is this man who represents the masculine ideal, whereas the man who loves women is presented as lacking in masculinity. The argument centres around the difference between what is normal, viz. a moderate desire for women with a view to procreation, and an excessive desire, one that gets out of control and becomes too powerful. The excessive desire for women has for its gain only pleasure (*hêdonê*) and is genuinely unmasculine, and it is a mistake to apply to this the name of "love" (*Amat.* 750). Protogenes describes the excessive love of women as "lax and housebound", it lives in the "bosoms and beds of women". This type of love seeks a "soft life" (*malkatha*), its pleasure is devoid of manliness (*anandros*) and of friendship and inspiration. Thus, it is really shameful for a man to be possessed by it.

The important word in this argument appears to be that of "friendship" (*philia*). That is the only relationship fitting for a free man, while relationships that only include pleasure is unworthy of a free man (*aneleutheros*). Therefore, it is not proper for a free man to make love to a slave boy: "such a love is mere copulation like the love of women" (*Amat.* 751A-B). "Love" of slaves and of women are paralleled, because none of them can be based on friendship, which is a mutual relationship that is reserved for free men. This Platonic position is well summed up by D.M. Halperin who remarks that "the notion that sexual desire aims not at physical gratification but at moral and intellectual self-expression, at the release of the lover's own creative energies, is one to which Plato remains deeply committed" (Halperin 1990, 276). This implies that the relationship between the adult male and his young beloved is not understood in the traditional sense as "active" versus "passive". Rather, the friendship character of the relationship and its goal in *aretê* removes exploitation and allows for reciprocity and mutuality (Halperin 1990, 269).

How does Plutarch respond to this argument that is coming from a Platonic tradition? His counter argument is not so much philosophical as practical and conventional. Russell (1972, 92) says that Plutarch is here "pleading an anti-Platonic, almost anti-philosophical cause, once again he is on the side of the ordinary, human morality of Greece". He undercuts the Platonic image of the philosopher as lover who through a chaste friendship wants to educate the young boy in virtue. Plutarch achieves this by means of popular ridicule: the lofty philosopher is accused of nurturing a strong erotic desire for the young boy. Moreover, Plutarch responds from the position of a traditional hierarchical view of sexuality, which was found in Athens at the time of Plato and which is well known in traditional societies in the Mediterranean even today (Delaney 1987, 35-48). This view is based not on mutuality, but on an "ethic of sexual domination" on the side of the adult male in his relations with women and male youths alike. There is a clear division of rôles into "active, dominant" and "passive, dominated" (Halperin 1990, 270-71). Within this system of aggressive sexual rule, a young boy who was in the process of becoming a free male citizen was seen as being in great danger in a relationship with an adult man. The expression for this aggression was "*hubris*", it indicated that men went beyond their boundaries. By doing so in sexual matters they inflicted shame on women whom they seduced as well as upon their husbands. In a description of the unnatural vices typically found in cities, Dio Chrysostom concludes his examples of *hubris* with that of a man who was not satisfied with seducing women and who proceeded to exploit young men (*Or.* 7.149-52).

It is such objections from the point of view of sexual and social hierarchy that Plutarch introduces through Daphneus, a critic of pederasty (*Amat.* 751C-D). In this view there is no honourable way out for a youth in such a relationship. If he was exposed to sexual assault by force, it meant that he was treated like a slave and would lose his honour. If he consented too eagerly, it was a sign of weakness and effeminacy on his part, the implications being that he accepted the passive rôle that was "natural" for a woman, but unnatural for a man.

It is from a similar common sense view that Plutarch in the last section of this treatise contrasts the union between husband and wife with the condemnable "union" between two men (*Amat.* 768E). This passage is a rehearsal of conventional views of male hierarchy, where he speaks of "those who enjoy the passive part" as damnable, men whom one will not give "confidence or respect or friendship" and who although they are men, are "unmanly". Plutarch speaks of young men who have been seduced into pederasty, who have been abused and who hate those who abused them and who take revenge. He mentions examples, especially telling is one that implied an insult by the older man, the tyrant of Ambracia. The tyrant asked his lover if he was not yet pregnant and thereby exposed him to the ultimate insult by treating him like a woman.

Thus, the Platonic ideology of the pederast relationship, built on the idea of masculine friendship as a unique relationship between free men, was for all practical purposes undercut by Plutarch's use of rather coarse and conventional images, we might even say stereotypes of masculinity. It is the sexually aggressive, dominant male who is presented as the realistic representation of masculinity.

Plutarch does not raise the question if there is a conflict between past ideals of masculinity, where male-to-male love was acceptable among heroes, and his present ideal, where such love is excluded, and not even recognised as love. Instead, different images and discourses of masculinity appear to be left side by side. Foucault has suggested that Plutarch changes the concept of love so it excludes relationships between men and youths (Foucault 1986, 202-10). There is something to be said for this suggestion. In his discussion of marriage (see below) Plutarch makes "friendship", a quality that had been the privilege of male relationships, into a characteristic of the relationship between a man and woman. Thus, relationships between an eromenos and his erastes are excluded from this very quality.

Marriage and the masculine character

To return to the argument of *Amatorius:* Plutarch has used the character of the youth, Bacchon, to prove the advantage of a marriage to a pederast relationship. He has rejected a relationship to an older man as a threat to Bacchon's development to become a man. But what then with the alternative — a marriage to Ismenodora? The pederast relationship is not contrasted with a marriage with a young girl. Bacchon is abducted by a rich and resourceful widow and the result is that he will remain in a dependent position, but now with a woman in charge instead of a man. So what is the advantage to Bacchon, and how does this position help him to become a man?

This issue is the point of departure for the criticism from the pederasts' party. Their criticism of Ismenodora and her scheme to have Bacchon marry her turns around conventional views of dangerous women. She is criticised for her wealth and for her determination to command and to dominate. Wealth makes women "frivolous, haughty, inconstant and vain" (*Amat.* 753B). Ismenodora is accused of breaking with the norms of shame. If she had been modest (*aischunesthai*) and wise (*sôphronein*), she would have been sitting at home awaiting suitors. When she now breaks with the modesty that is appropriate for women, it is an indication that she will bring shame on her husband, by commanding and dominating him.

This criticism is part of "popular" masculine views throughout centuries in the Mediterranean world, from the description of Penelope in the Odysseys to expectations from young Bedouin women in modern Egypt (Abu-Lughod 1986, 118-67). There is in this position an element of the traditional fear of women: if they are not controlled, they will break with the modesty that is expected of them and become dangerous to men. In his reply Plutarch appears to agree with the pederasts' party about what constitutes acceptable behaviour in women, but he argues that Ismenodora is different because of her noble character. Thus, she will treat Bacchon well and look after him.

Foucault has pointed out that Plutarch describes her and her behaviour in terms that would fit a male erastes in his relations to his eromenos (Foucault 1986, 196-97). Plutarch appears to take over the ideal characteristics of the pederast relationship and apply them to the relationship between husband and wife. His argument appears to be that this ideal can in fact be better fulfilled in a relationship between husband and wife. His reason is that a woman can participate in traditional male characteristics as friendship and virtue *(aretê)* since many women have shown a great courage that was "truly masculine" *(andreion)* (*Amat.* 769A-B). The traditional picture of woman as a "natural being", and therefore as charming but seductive to pleasure, is balanced by a picture of the wise and chaste woman who can gain the friendship of her husband.

Plutarch gives examples from history that it was slave women, not women of noble character who acted badly and exploited and dominated men (*Amat.* 753D-754A). But these men who became their preys were themselves to blame, it was a result of their own weakness and softness (*malakia*). Plutarch's terminology here reveals that the problem with these men was that although they were powerful and mighty, they did not have a masculine character. Other men, however, who were poor and obscure and who married rich women did not lose their dignity, but enjoyed honour and exercised authority; that is, they showed themselves as true men (*Amat.* 753F-754A). In short, masculinity is a matter of a man's character; he must have self-possession and prudence and must not have a servile mind. It follows that he should not try to humble a rich and beautiful wife; rather, it is through the extra weight of his character that he must turn the scales, and then his wife will be controlled and guided with both profit and justice (*Amat.* 754B). It is only a weak and effeminate man who will try to humble a rich wife, instead of making himself better than her (*Con. praec.* 139B).

Plutarch's discussion shows how "masculine" and "feminine" are character traits that are not exclusively linked to the two genders "man" and "woman". On the other hand, there is a strong association between the "masculine" ideal and the social rôle "man" and men hold a superior position in Plutarch's ideological and social hierarchy (Blomqvist 1995, 181-82). It is only by "becoming male" that women gain significance and can enter a more equal relationship with men, for instance so that they can become "friends". Thus, to share in male characteristics is a way for women to gain honour. There is nothing comparable for men if they share in feminine characteristics and become "soft", that only results in shame.

In Plutarch's emphasis on marriage there is a shift away from the masculine ideals from an older and more heroic age. His examples of marriages where men hold an inferior position shows that true masculinity can be a character issue that is not linked to wealth, power or fame. This form of masculinity represents a form of honour that is not dependent upon status or competition, but more upon quiet qualities, like authenticity and holding one's own ground. But it is nevertheless a strong identity. Plutarch's positive examples are men who under adverse circumstances, facing women who are in a stronger position than themselves, are able to assert themselves. In one way we might say that Plutarch's examples are "democratic". In contrast to Dio's discussion of a masculinity that is restricted to an élite, Plutarch opens up the possibility that men in humble positions can show themselves to be true men vis-à-vis their wives, the most important arena of all where masculinity was put to the test.

Conclusions

There are divergent interpretations of Plutarch's picture of marriage. Foucault (1986, 147-85) has argued that Plutarch represents a new perspective on love and marriage, emphasising the conjugal or dual nature of marriage. Plutarch represents an important stage in the development of "self". Patterson (1991, 4709-23) on the other hand claims that Foucault overestimates the originality of Plutarch's ideas and argues that he is dependent upon popular and traditional ideas. But the important aspect is not that Plutarch has kept many traditional ideas, e.g. pertaining to the inferior position of women, but rather the new framework within which they are placed, viz. that of friendship between men and women. That they can now be partners in friendship ascribes some sort of equality to women (Engberg-Pedersen 1994b), even if it is phrased as participation in a masculine character. Moreover, as noted by Patterson, there is also another new aspect in Plutarch's discussion of marriage, and that is the almost exclusive focus on the relation between husband and wife, apart from a social context. In contrast to e.g. Stoic philosophers, like Plutarch's older contemporary, Musonius Rufus, marriage viewed as household or as part of a social institution in the *polis* does not play an important rôle.

This does not mean that a man's position within the city was unimportant. We have found that both Dio and Plutarch argued that men should play a responsible rôle in the city. The days when men could win honour and status through the warrior rôle were gone, there were now more peaceful ways to gain honour. Both Dio and Plutarch preserved an emphasis on independence; rather than making one's fortune by becoming a retainer of the emperor or his representatives, they encouraged men to stay in their cities and to win honour by governing themselves and showing civic virtues. Thus, there was en emphasis upon what "you can do for yourselves". This put the focus upon the group, of course, but also upon the individual. It is this emphasis on the individual that becomes visible in Plutarch's discussion of marriage between a man and a women. The woman becomes more of a person, since she can now become the "friend" of her husband. This development is still couched in terms of her sharing in a "masculine" character, but it nevertheless represents a shift in emphasis. Friendship is no longer the exclusive characteristic of an all male society. This has repercussions for the evaluation of pederast relationships. They no longer serve as an introduction to friendship among males. In Plutarch's discussion they lose their special character of "friendship"; instead, they are compared to marriage between a man and a woman and found wanting.

Changes in mentality from the classical period to the Hellenistic age may be subtle, but still recognisable. The views found in Dio Chrystostom and Plutarch indicate a development in the same direction: there is more emphasis on the "peaceful" qualities of masculinity, and a man's rôle in marriage and his relations to his wife plays a larger rôle in the definition of what it means to be a man.

University of Oslo
Institute of Biblical Studies
Box 1023, Blindern
N-0315 Oslo
Norway

Bibliography

Abu-Lughod, L. 1986. *Veiled Sentiments. Honor and Poetry in a Bedouin Society.* Berkeley/Los Angeles.

Adkins, A.W.H. 1960. *Merit and Responsibility.* Oxford.

Blomqvist, K. 1995. "Chryseïs and Clea, Eumetis and the Interlocutress. Plutarch of Chaeronea and Dio Chrysostom on Women's Education", *Svensk Exegetisk Årsbok* 60, 173-90.

Brod, H. (ed.) 1987. *The making of Masculinities.* Boston.

Delaney, C. 1987. "Seeds of Honor, Fields of Shame", in: Gilmore (ed.) 1987, 35-48.

Dio Chrysostom 1949-51. *Orations.* 5 vols. Loeb Classical Library. London.

Dover, K.J. 1989 (1978). *Greek Homosexuality.* Cambridge, Mass.

Engberg-Pedersen, T. (ed.) 1994a. *Paul in His Hellenistic Context.* Minneapolis/Edinburgh.

Engberg-Pedersen, T. 1994b. "Two Types of Individualism in Hellenistic Philosophy", paper, Helsinki, 22.8. 1994.

Foucault, M. 1986. *History of Sexuality III. The Care of the Self.* New York.

Gilmore, D.G. 1987. "Honor, Honesty, Shame: Male status in Contemporary Andalusia", in: Gilmore (ed.) 1987, 90-103.

Gilmore , D.G. (ed.) 1987. *Honor and Shame and the Unity of the Mediterranean.* Washington.

Gilmore, D.G. 1990. *Manhood in the Making.* New Haven.

Gleason, M.W. 1990. "The semiotics of Gender: Physiognomy and self-fashioning in the second century C.E.", in: Halperin, Winkler & Zeitlin (eds.) 1990, 387-416.

Gruen, E.S 1984. *The Hellenistic World and the Coming of Rome.* Berkeley/Los Angeles.

Halperin, D.H., Winkler, J.J. & F.I. Zeitlin (eds.) 1990. *Before Sexuality.* Princeton.

Halperin, D.M. 1992. "Historicizing the Sexual Body: Sexual preference and erotic identities in the Pseudo-Lucianic *Erotes*", in: Stanton (ed.) 1992, 236-61.

Halperin, D.M. 1990. *One Hundred Years of Homosexuality.* New York.

Jones, C.P. 1971. *Plutarch and Rome.* Oxford.

Marcus, M.A. 1987. "Horsemen are the Fence of the Land: Honor and History among the Ghiyata of Eastern Marocco", in: Gilmore (ed.) 1987, 49-60.

Martin, L.H. 1994. "The Anti-Individualistic Ideology of Hellenistic Culture", *Numen* 41, 117-40.

Moxnes, H. 1993. "BTB Readers Guide: Honor and Shame", *BiblThB* 23, 167-76.

Moxnes, H. 1994. "The Quest for Honour and the Unity of the Community in Romans 12 and in the Orations of Dio Chrysostom", in: Engberg-Pedersen (ed.) 1994a, 203-30.

Ortner, S.B. & Whitehead, H. (eds.) 1981. *Sexual Meanings*. Cambridge.
Patterson, C. 1991. "Plutarch's 'Advice on Marriage': Traditional Wisdom through a Philosopical Lens", in: *ANRW* II, 33.6, 4709-23.
Russell, D.A. 1972. *Plutarch*. London.
Stanton, D.C. (ed.) 1992. *Discourses of Sexuality: From Aristotle to AIDS*. Ann Arbor.
Winkler, J.J. 1990. *The Constraints of Desire*. New York.

DEATH ON DELOS:
CONVENTIONS IN AN
INTERNATIONAL CONTEXT

Lise Hannestad

No site has offered us more information on life in Greece during the Hellenistic period than Delos. The much reduced habitation during the Roman and Byzantine periods and the virtual lack of post-Byzantine remains have provided very favourable conditions for archaeological work, and the French excavators, working on the island for about 120 years, have responded admirably to this challenge and provided us with a wealth of information in an impressive series of publications.

The fact that Delos was not only perhaps the most important pan-Hellenic sanctuary in Hellenistic times but after 166 BC also "the most celebrated emporium of the Mediterranean world"[1] gives it special importance in research on the late Hellenistic period, on the co-existence and interaction of people from Greece, the Levant and the western Mediterranean.

For several reasons which I will not discuss here, excavations and archaeological research in the past have tended to focus on graves — on the archaeology of death. Delos is one of the few exceptions to this rule. What is particularly well known of the island in the Hellenistic period in addition to the many public buildings are in fact the houses of the living, their decoration, etc. With all this copious information available on *life* in Hellenistic Delos, it may seem somewhat perverse to make the grave reliefs from its necropolis the subject of this paper, all the more so since the level of information on the graves from Delos' necropolis is far from comparable to what we know of the conditions of the living. Many grave reliefs were removed from Rheneia in the Late Antique and Byzantine periods and reused as building material on Delos and have thus been found out of context. Furthermore, the early archaeological explorations on Rheneia in the nineteenth century brought large numbers of grave reliefs to various European museums without the find circumstances being recorded.

On the other hand, the very fact that we are so well-informed on the visual iconography which this multi-ethnic society used in sculpture for other purposes,

public or private, adds a particular dimension to the study of the iconography and
the inscriptions with which they chose to commemorate their dead.

Grave reliefs were widely used in many regions of the Hellenistic world and
in recent years several contributions on this subject have appeared.[2] Thus, there
is also a wider geographical context and a scholarly debate to which the Delian
gravestones can be related.

The population

It has been calculated[3] that before 166 BC the total population of the island did
not exceed ten thousand whereas after the Athenian colonization it amounted to
somewhere between 20,000 and 30,000.[4]

Whereas the cemeteries of a Greek city usually extended outside the city walls
along the main roads, the burials and grave monuments visible to all passers-by,
the situation on Delos was different. In 426 BC the Athenians had declared the
island sacred, and from then on no burials could take place there but only on the
neighbouring island of Rheneia.[5] The prohibition on burial on Delos seems to have
been upheld until the Christian period. The necropolis extends along the eastern
shore of Rheneia opposite Delos (the distance is about 1 km), has a length of
about 1 km and a depth of 100-150 m. In the epigram on the gravestone of the
woman Isias (no. 469),[6] it is said that she rests on a promontory, watching the
many ships pass by. Excavations and research in the necropolis in the 1970s and
1980s show that in one part with fairly large plots there was *c.* 1 epitaph per 22
sq.m. (Couilloud-Le Dinahet 1984, 345). This would give a minimum number
of about 4,500-5,500 monuments. However, the concentration was certainly denser
in other less wealthy parts of the necropolis (Couilloud-Le Dinahet 1978, 863).

That we are able to study in detail the Hellenistic grave reliefs from Delos
is due to the comprehensive studies by Marie-Thérèse Couilloud.[7] Her monumental
monograph from 1974 comprises *c.* 370 relief-decorated stelai, and though some
of these are surely not Delian and others have been added since, I think we may
confidently take this number as a realistic reflection of what has actually been
found. To these may be added a much smaller number (*c.* 50) of stelai with only
inscription and no relief, and five painted stelai. Other types of grave monuments
such as cylindrical altars or free-standing statues are comparatively rare. A relief-
decorated stele thus seems to be the standard gravestone on Hellenistic Delos.
With a calculation of a minimum of *c.* 5,000 monuments in the necropolis, the
preserved number represents less than 10% of the total.

Dating by style is notoriously difficult when it comes to Hellenistic sculpture,
and the chronology of the Delian reliefs depends to a large extent on the

inscriptions. In this paper, the datings proposed by Couilloud (1974, 243ff.) have been adopted. According to her (1974, 307), at least 90% of the inscriptions date to the last decades of the second and the first decades of the first century BC. We may assume that most of them were erected in the period 166-69 BC.

The stele
The predominant stele is rectangular and crowned by a pediment (e.g. pls. 15-17); less common is a curved upper part with a vegetal ornamentation (e.g. pls. 20 and 26) — also typical of the Cycladic stelai of the Classical period — and fairly rare a profiled horizontal top. The relief is either set in a rectangular recess, the so-called "sunk relief" (Cumont 1993) (e.g. pl. 17), or flanked by two pillars carrying an arch (pl. 16), or less often by Corinthian columns carrying a "Doric" or an "Ionic" entablature (e.g. pls. 19 and 28). In contrast to the Attic grave reliefs of the Classical period, the figures in the Hellenistic reliefs from Delos always stay within the "frame". Though there are some fine pieces, the average artistic quality of the reliefs is modest.

The inscriptions
The inscriptions are always placed below the relief. They are very stereotype. Name, patronymic and origin are the three basic pieces of information. From the second half of the third century the salute *chaire* is introduced and also the longer *chrêste chaire*, the most common formula from the second century. Age is mentioned in only a few epigrams, titles or honours hardly ever, and profession never. For women, the name of the husband may be mentioned but by no means so often as her father's name or her origin. Apart from *chrêstos*, the deceased is sometimes also described as *alupos*, whereas other epithets are extremely rare (Couilloud 1974, 256). Only very seldom is the person or persons who erected the stele mentioned in the inscription (nos. 28 (very early), 143 and 348). All the inscriptions, also for *Romaioi*/Roman citizens, are in Greek; only one is bilingual, Greek and Latin.

Dexiôsis
A very common theme is the *dexiôsis*, i.e. two persons joined in a handshake.

I. (Table 1) (nos. 1-45 and 466). In its most simple form the motif consists of only two persons, normally a seated person to the left and a standing one to the right (e.g. pls. 15-16). The majority of the reliefs show a combination of a man and a woman — 25 show the woman as seated, 15 the man. Variations are few: 2

have a boy as the standing person; in another variation (nos. 34-38) the seated and the standing figures are of the same sex.[8]

This simple version of the dexiosis is usually combined with the pediment stele (the favourite type on Delos) and a sunk relief,[9] less often with an architectural setting with pillars carrying an arch. Only no. 13 (pl. 15) has a setting with pediment and columns.

It seems that the stelai with this motif tend to be a little smaller than variants with servants and perhaps more figures (see below). The height of this type is between 96 and 30 cm.

Of the inscriptions, the majority give the name of only one person, but on some of the reliefs the inscription is clearly placed so as to make room for one more.

Patronymic is given for 12 out of 21 commemorated women and for 14 out of 17 men. Roughly two-thirds (= 21) give an ethnikon. Family relations (other than patronymic) mentioned: granddaughter (no. 4); wife (no. 14); no. 28 tells us that the wife erected the stone (name of the man's father not mentioned); mother (no. 35, which does not mention her father). Epithets other than *chrêstos*: *alupos* is used in 5 cases (f and m, the ethnic (3 cases) is Syrian: 1 Laodicea, 2 Apamea), 1 *philomêtôr*.

II. (Table 2) (nos. 46-85 and 467). In a more elaborate version of the dexiosis, a diminutive slave may be appended to one or both the main figures, a female slave for a woman and a male slave for a man (e.g. pl. 17).

On an average these stelai tend to be taller than the variety with only two persons. The height varies between 167 and 68.5 cm.

The dating ranges from the second half of the second century and into the first century.

Again the majority of the inscriptions commemorate only one person. Patronymic is given for 16 out of 21 women, and for 9 out of 11 men, ethnikon in 21 of 28 inscriptions. Family relations other than patronymic: 6 wife, 1 mother. Epithets other than *chrêstos*: 2 *alupos* (f, 1 from Antioch).

Usually in these representations of the dexiosis (Groups I and II), the sex of the seated figure and the person in the inscription correlate, i.e. the seated figure would normally be the deceased. It should also be noted that the dexiosis motif with a seated figure was most popular as a woman's gravestone.

III. (Tables 3a-c). Dexiosis with more persons than the two performing the dexiosis, apart from servants.

One standing person in the middle: *Table 3a: A child or a youth* (nos. 86-90 and 92). On no. 88 (pl. 18) the woman is described as a good wife, which is unusual. The stele is earlier than the main group of stelai and dates from the third century.[10] It is perhaps the earliest of our series and one of the very few specimens from before the Athenian colonization in 166 BC.

Tables 3b: One adult in the middle (nos. 93-100) and *3c: One or two standing extra adults* (nos. 101-110bis). No. 107 (pl. 19) is the finest and best preserved. It is unusual in having three inscriptions: for Mysta, daughter of Mnaseas from Laodicea; for Apollonios, son of Apollonios from Alexandria; and for Apollonios, son of Dionysios from Alexandria: thus for mother, son and father. The inscription for the son seems to have been made before the other two.

The number of this type of dexiosis with added figures other than slaves is so small that we can hardly draw conclusions from it. Perhaps we may suggest — not surprisingly — that the group tends to include inscriptions for more than one person. The height of the stelai of group III varies between 156 and 52 cm.

Also in the more elaborate versions of the dexiosis with slaves and more than one standing person (groups II-III), the pediment and arch and pediment and sunk relief varieties are popular. Flat top combined with sunk relief is seen (nos. 93, 119-20) and also rounded top combined with sunk relief (no. 88, early) (pl. 18) or with columns (nos. 57-58 and 125). Pediment-columns are also more common.

IV. Dexiosis between two standing persons (Table 4) is fairly rare, only 10 examples being preserved (nos. 118-127 plus a couple of fragments) (see pl. 20), and the iconography tends to be rather individual. One of them (no. 120) belongs among the earliest of the reliefs (it is dated to the third century), and its iconography is more closely related to Attic late Classical iconography than most of the reliefs. Thus, one of the two men has a beard and is leaning on a walking-stick. The other reliefs of this group are all dated to the second half or end of the second century, i.e. they belong to the earlier part of the second Athenian domination of Delos.

The preserved inscriptions are all for men.

A seated figure

Table 5 (nos. 130-88 + fragments) illustrates another extremely popular motif. As in the dexiosis scenes, the figure is usually seated on a *diphros*, sometimes covered with a blanket, rarely in a chair. By far the most common is a seated woman accompanied by a female slave (pl. 25), but a woman seated alone (pl. 21) is also quite common. There is a much smaller number of scenes with a man as the seated figure (pl. 22), but there is nothing to suggest that this motif for men indicates a special status such as very old age or specific honours. A few examples show two seated figures, with a standing figure in the middle. No. 185 (pl. 23) is an unusual and very fine example of this — only one inscription with the epithet *alupos* may suggest that the figure in the centre is the first commemorated. Perhaps the son of the two parents flanking him? There is a large variety of combinations with one or two standing figures. The variation with a child (nos. 141-43 and 177-79) seems rather to be an epitaph for the child (3 m inscriptions on the 6 pieces) rather than for the seated woman. In Table 5 the total of preserved stelai is given, but only some of the variations are presented; the calculations of the numbers of patronymics and ethnics are based on the total number of preserved inscriptions.

In the stelai with a seated figure, the predominant architectural setting is pediment and sunk relief, but the other combinations are also seen. In height they vary between 141 and 30 cm, but there tend to be many rather small specimens among them.

Apart from the family relations enumerated in Table 5, one woman is explicitly mentioned as unmarried. Epithets other than *chrêstos* and *alupos* is one *philologos*.

A standing figure

Table 6 (nos. 212-310, 473) shows a definitely male motif. In combination with a pet, usually a dog or cock, it is often used for children (pl. 24). Of the many representations of men, there are two characteristic groups in which attributes, or to use a German term "Beiwerk", play a larger rôle than in the majority of the Delian stelai: (1) with a herm (pl. 29), and (2) with a tree around which coils a snake. The height varies between 175 and 30 cm.

Very few of the men are commemorated without patronymic. On the other hand, ethnic seems to be less common here than in the previous groups, possibly because this group includes many stelai set up for children or very young persons. No other family relations than those enumerated in Table 6 are found.

Man seated on a rock or a ship

Table 7 shows a small but very distinctive group of reliefs with a man seated on a rock or on a ship (rock nos. 327-44, ship nos. 345-47, shipwreck nos. 348-50) (pl. 27). In two cases the motif is combined with dexiosis. Apart from one inscription for m+f, they are all for men. As has been argued convincingly by Couilloud (1974, 295ff.) and other scholars, this motif does not derive from Attic funerary iconography on, for instance, white lekythoi and does not represent the dead in Hades or in Charon's boat. It is a commemoration of men who died at sea, a suitable motif for late Hellenistic Delos. Such an interpretation is confirmed by variations where we see two heads in the sea beside the ship. The motif is also seen in, for instance, Samos, Cos, Chios, and Rhodes.

Warrior standing on the prow of a ship
(Table 7) (nos. 351-359bis) (pl. 26). As suggested by Couilloud (1974, 293f.), the motif probably commemorates a soldier who died in action at sea.

Discussion

This presentation of the relief-decorated grave stelai from Delos is not quite complete,[11] but covers more than 90% of the stelai, enough — I think — for an attempt to interpret the reliefs as evidence for commonly acknowledged values.

Compared with, for instance, the grave reliefs from Smyrna, it is striking that the Delian funerary iconography shows very few examples of 'Beiwerk', but concentrates on the figures themselves.

The Delian *woman*, as she emerges from the reliefs, wears a long chiton and a mantle which normally covers the head (e.g. pls. 16-21 and 28). When seated, she usually sits very upright and holds the mantle in what is often known as the 'bridal' gesture (e.g. pls. 21 and 28). Another frequently seen gesture is with one hand touching the chin. Rather than reflexion,[12] it is probably better interpreted as sorrow, as suggested by the epigram going with one relief of this type (no. 468), which speaks of the particularly sad fate of the dead woman from Ascalon, who is now buried in foreign soil.

A few stelai (nos. 147-49) (the provenances of which are not certain) suddenly reveal a quite different role model (pl. 25): instead of the veiled woman sitting very upright, we see an Aphrodite seated in a relaxed pose with her head uncovered, elegant coiffure, the mantle only covering her hips and legs. But in general the Aphrodite iconography, so beloved by the Delians for the decoration of their houses, held no attraction when it came to funerary iconography and presenting their own women. They preferred the austere Hera.[13]

The *pudicitia* type, so often met with in the Smyrna reliefs and also in portrait sculpture from Delos itself,[14] is only rarely found in the reliefs.

In only a few of the reliefs is the typical female attribute, the wool basket, depicted standing on the ground besides the seated woman (nos. 131, 151-52, 154, 160) (pl. 21). This emblem may, however, be incorporated in the pictorial language of a woman's grave, even if not included in the relief, as is evidenced by Tertia Horaria's sarcophagus (no. 58) (pl. 31), to which I shall return later. But in general this attribute does not seem to be an important part of a woman's image. Even rarer are allusions to love of the arts: in two examples (nos. 144, 161) the seated woman is characterized by a lyre (chitara). By far the most popular attribute is the — often diminutive — female slave, usually holding a casket (pl. 25), sometimes open, sometimes closed, or less often a fan (nos. 78, 82-83, 88, 156, 173, 270, 272), and in two cases (nos. 75, 152) a mirror. Alabastra are depicted on three reliefs (nos. 124, 144, 161) placed on a wall or a piece of furniture covered by a blanket. In one case (no. 128) the slave may be handing the woman a flask.

The image of the Delian *man* is just as stereotypical as that of the woman. He is normally clean-shaven, wears a mantle and normally a chiton with short sleeves underneath (e.g. pls. 16-17 and 20). As in the woman, old age is not depicted, and the realistic portraiture so characteristic of the honorary sculpture of Delos is reflected in only a few of the stelai (e.g. no. 118). With one hand the man usually holds a bunch of folds of his mantle (e.g. pls. 15 and 17) or his arm is held along his body under the mantle. This is the standard gesture in the dexiosis scenes. In the representations of a standing man, the Sophocles-Aeschines pose[15] of the right arm is common (e.g. nos. 174, 280) (e.g. pls. 19 and 23). A kind of combination of Aeschines and "holding a bunch of folds of the mantle" is also seen (e.g. no. 278). The message cannot have been specifically how a man should carry himself in the ekklesia or the boule;[16] it is not the narrow definition of the citizen which is conveyed but a much broader message of how a man should conduct himself in public in the Hellenistic period. A mantle leaving part of the breast bare is clearly a convention signalling youth, education, connection with the gymnasium (e.g. pl. 19). In stele no. 69 showing a seated and a standing man joined in a handshake, the standing man wears the mantle in this fashion, whereas the seated man wears a chiton underneath his mantle. The epitaph of the stele is for two men, father and son from Athens, and the inscription is made for them jointly — the difference in dress in this case clearly signals the different age of the two men. It is interesting to compare this Hellenistic ideal of the young man with the ideal of youth as conveyed by a Classical grave relief made in Athens but found on Delos (no. 286) (pl. 30).

Stronger allusions to the gymnasium are found in the group where the man is standing beside a herm (pl. 29). An epigram on one of these stelai (no. 473) expresses the attitude which lies behind the allusions to the gymnasium. It states that Themistokles, son of Themison from Antioch, died victorious (as an athlete) at the age of twelve with an intellect and a courage comparable to that of his namesake.

Images of the ordinary Delian man in chiton and mantle may also allude to the gymnasium by means of a strigil usually held by his slave (by far the most common attribute, nos. 75, 105, 119, 180, 274-75, 277, 280-81, 285, 287, 294, 301-3). Another attribute to be seen is a book roll (nos. 98, 138, 222-23, 277, 304 and possibly 249) held either by the man himself (e.g. nos. 222-23, 304) (pl. 29) or by his slave (no. 98), suggesting of course intellectual activity. In a single case (no. 269) a tragic mask stands beside the man, and on his other side a cock symbolizing the agon and victory of the theatre.

As with the Delian woman, the most common attribute for the Delian man is in fact the small (male) slave. Usually the slave is merely present (e.g. pls. 22 and 29), but as just mentioned he may be bringing or holding an object, first and foremost the strigil, in a few cases a vase (nos. 75, 281, both combined with a strigil, 288). A rare attribute is the crown, presented by the slave on no. 69 (where the standing man wears a mantle and no tunic, in the fashion of the gymnasium) or held by the older seated man on no. 185. On no. 296 the man is crowned and holds a palm, both attributes clearly indications of victory in agones, since he stands in front of a herm.

Quite a different model of a man is encountered in the small group of pictures commemorating men who died at sea. In these reliefs, the man is either naked or wears a short chlamys (pl. 27) — a touch of realism suddenly enters these scenes: on board a ship you wear work clothes and may even be naked in a shipwreck, there being nothing to suggest that this is heroic nudity. The man seated on the rock or ship supports his head in his left hand. Again this should rather be taken as an expression of a particularly hard fate, not as an indication of an intellectual bent.

As pointed out by Couilloud (1974, 293) the warrior on the ship (pl. 26) is clearly modelled on hoplites or horsemen of Attic funerary stelai of the fourth century.

The slave is the attribute par excellence for a Delian, a female for a woman and a male for a man. A person has only one slave in attendance, not so much because more than one slave was considered bad taste (thus Zanker 1993), but because it was considered an essential part of good life that a slave was always ready to carry your things, take orders, and so on.

The differences in size and quality which we may notice in the reliefs were probably further strengthened not only by the varying sizes of burial plots already mentioned but also by the total decoration of the tomb. Interesting evidence for this is provided by the tomb of Tertia Horaria (pl. 31): stele no. 58 was set up on her sarcophagus, which rested on a platform consisting of a base (profiled like an Ionic column base), a central part with Corinthian columns and pilasters at the corners and an entablature with Doric architrave and frieze and Ionic dentil frieze. Thus the traditional stele has been reduced to a minor, but essential part of the grave monument, perhaps almost a *sine qua non* in funerary iconography. The epigram for Martha, daughter of Demosthenes (no. 466), suggests this when it starts by saying: "A relief stele (*stele glupta*) has been erected to mark my grave."

That the late Hellenistic stelai set up by members of the community on Delos have their roots in the Attic funerary iconography of the fifth and fourth century cannot be doubted, but there are two theories as to how this came about: (1) that it was a deliberate choice of the Athenian cleruchoi after 166 to use the funarary iconography of fourth-century Athens, i.e. to consider them as part of a Classicistic revival, or (2) to see them as a result of a continued tradition in the Cyclades through the third-early second century of a pictorial language strongly influenced from Athens.[17] The second theory seems the most probable, since evidence for a revival of the use of sculptured grave stelai on a larger scale at Athens itself in the second century BC is lacking.[18]

Of the 203 inscriptions listed in tables 1-7, *c.* 56% commemorate a male (rarely two or more), *c.* 39% a female (rarely two or more) while only about 5% commemorate both a male and a female.[19]

The distribution of ethnics in the different motifs shows no preference by specific groups for specific motifs or special phrasing of the inscription. Even the epithet *alupos,* which is usually considered to be used by people from Syria and the East may also be found in an inscription for two Athenians. The same iconography is used by slaves and by freemen.

Compared with the grave reliefs from Smyrna the visual language of the Delian reliefs is simpler. One might perhaps call it a pictorial lowest common denominator of a very heterogeneous society.

Andrew Stewart (1990, 226) has described the iconography of late Hellenistic sculpture from Delos as often unconventional, sometimes bizarre. But it was not for their grave monuments that the multi-ethnic society of the island created this mixed and unconventional sculpture — this effort was made for the living and their city, not for the necropolis on the neighbouring island. In death the Delians preferred to draw on a deep-rooted tradition, on images that could be immediately understood by anyone familiar with Greek tradition, and they transformed this tradition into convention.

The evidence of the grave reliefs thus does not corroborate Niclas Rauh's conclusion on the Delian society in the late Hellenistic period that "groups of foreigners sufficiently large to warrant a collective identity tended to organize themselves religiously as well as ethnically according to the worship of the gods of their homelands." In contrast to this testimony of the conventions of the cosmopolitan society of Delos in its daily life, no matter where they came from, people all tended to prefer the visual language of funerary sculpture of Classical Athens for their burial rituals.

Institute of Classical Archaeology
University of Aarhus
DK-8000 Aarhus C
Denmark

Table 1: Dexiosis with 2 figures: 1 seated, 1 standing

Reliefs 46			*Inscriptions* 33
f	m	23	18 (14 f - 2 m - 2 f+m)
f	b	1	1 (1 f)
f	f	2	2 (1 f - 1 f+f)
?	?	1	1 (1 f)
m	f	10	6 (6 m)
m	b	1	1 (1 m)
m	m	3	3 (2 m+m (father & son) - 1 m)
?	?	1	1 (1 m)

Of the 21 commemorated f, 10 have patronymic, 1 patronymic+wife, 1 patronymic of 2 generations. Of the 17 commemorated m, 14 have patronymic.

Ethnics: 21
Ascalon: 1 (f, patronymic)
Apamea: 1 (m)
Athens: 1 (2 m, patronymics, father and son)
Antioch: 3 (2 x m, patronymic; 1 f, patronymic+wife)
Berytos: 1 (m, patronymic)
Corinth: 1 (m)
Damascus: 1 (f, patronymic)
Delos: 1 (f+m, patronymics)
Laodicea: 2 (f; f, patronymic+wife)
Magnesia: 1 (2 m, patronymics, father and son)
Media: 1 (f, patronymic)
Mykonos: 1 (m)
Ptolemais: 1 (f, patronymic)
Sidon: 1 (? f, patronymic)
Roman *tria nomina*: 4 (3 x f, 1 f+f; 1 is for a slave, 3 for freemen)

Epithets:
alupos: 5 (f and m; 1 Laodicea; 2 Apamea)
philomêtôr: 1 (m)

Table 2: Dexiosis with 1 or 2 slaves

Reliefs 40			*Inscriptions* 28
f	m,	1 female slave 21	15 (14 f - 1 f+m)
f	f,	1 female slave 4	3 (3 f)
f	m,	2 slaves (f and m) 4	2 (1 m - 1 f)
f	m,	1 male slave 2	2 (2 m)
f	f,	2 female slaves 1	1 (1 f)
m	m,	1 male slave 1	1 (1 m+m, father and son)
m	m,	1 male slave 2	1 (1 m+m)
m	f,	1 m and 1 f slave 5	3 (2 m - 1 f+m)

Of the 21 commemorated f, 12 have patronymic, 3 patronymic+wife, 1 patronymic+wife+mother, 2 wife.
Of the 11 commemorated m, 9 have patronymic.

Ethnics: 21
Athens: 3 (1 f, patronymic and wife; 1 m+m patronymics; 1 m, patronymic)
Antioch: 2 (1 f, patronymic+wife; 1 f+m, patronymics, siblings)
Berytos: 1 (1 m, patronymic)
Gaza: 2 (1 m+f, patronymics; 1 m, patronymic)
Laodicea: 3 (1 f, patronymic+wife; 2 f, patronymic)
Naxos: 1 (1 f)
Neapolis: 1 (1 f, patronymic)
Roman *tria nomina*: 8 (including slaves: 1 f; 1 f+m)

Epithets:
alupos: 2 (f; Antioch)

Table 3a: Dexiosis with standing child or a youth in the middle

Reliefs 6			*Inscriptions* 6
f	m	5	5 (2 f - 1 m - 2 f+m)
m	f	1	1 (m+f)

Of the 5 commemorated women, 4 have patronymic.
Of the 4 commemorated men, 3 have patronymic.

Ethnics: 4
Athens & Dardanos: 1 (1 f+m)
Athens & Antioch: 1 (1 f+m)
Ascalon: 1 f
Thasos : 1 f

Table 3b: Dexiosis with adult person in the middle

Reliefs 8			*Inscriptions* 4
f	m	3	3 (1 m - 1 m+m (different patronymics) - 1 f)
m	f	4	1 (m+f, patronymic)
m	m	1	

Ethnics: 3
Chios: 1
Naxos: 1
Roman *tria nomina* : 1

Table 3c: Dexiosis with one or more adults

Reliefs 11			*Inscriptions* 4
f	m	7	3 (1 m+m - 1 f+m+m - 1 m)
m	f	4	1 (m+f)

Ethnics: 3
Alexandria & Laodicea: 1 (m+m+f, parents and son)
Antioch: 1 (1 m+f (without ethnic)
Roman *tria nomina*: 1 (2 m)

Table 4: Dexiosis between two standing persons

Reliefs 10			*Inscriptions* 6
f	m	7	5 (1 m+m - 4 m)
m	m	2	1 (m+m, brothers)
b	m	1	

Of the 7 f-m, 3 have additions in form of slaves, 2 have one or two children between m and f, 1 shows a standing m on either side of the couple, 1 shows a seated m to the left of the couple.

Ethnics: 3
Berytos: 1 (1 m, patronymic)
Roman *tria nomina*: 2

Table 5: Seated figures

Reliefs total 59 + frgs.		*Inscriptions* total 54
Some of the groups:		
f	9	5 (5 f)
f and f slave	20	16 (14 f - 1 m+m+m+m+m - 1 m)
f + c	6	3 (3 m)
m	1	1 (1 m)
m and slave	5	4 (4 m)
f and st f	1	1 (1 f)
f and 2 st f	1	
f and st m	2	1 (1 f)
f ? ?	1	1 (1 f)
f, c, slave, st m, f	1	1 (1 f+f)
m and st m	1	
m and st m and slave	1	1 (1 m)
m and 2 st f	1	
m and st f & m, slave	1	

Inscriptions (total): Of the 32 commemorated women, 14 have patronymic, 1 patronymic+wife, 2 wife, 1 mother, 1 sister (of a man).
Of the 27 commemorated men, 22 have patronymic.

Ethnics:
Ascalon: 1 (1 f)
Anthedon: 1 (5 m)
Antioch: 1 (1 f, patronymic)
Athens: 2 (1 f, patronymic+wife; 1 m, patronymic)
Chalcedon: 1 (1 f, patronymic)
Delos: 1 (1 m, patronymic)
Hierapolis: 2 (1 f, patronymic+wife; 1 f, patronymic)
Laodicea: 3 (1 f, wife; 2 m, patronymic; 1 f, patronymic: combined with inscr. for 1 f, Roman *tria nomina*, slave)
Marathos: 1 (1 f)
Smyrna: 1 (1 m, patronymic)
Tarsos: 1 (1 f)
Roman *tria nomina*: 4 (1 f, slave; 1 f; 1 m, slave, 1 f, slave, sister of a freedman: combined with inscr. for f from Laodicea)

Epithets:
alupos: 8 (f, f+m, m; Apamea, Arethusa, Athens, Laodicea, Roman *tria nomina*)

Table 6: Standing figure

Reliefs 100				*Inscriptions* 62
f (or young girl)	5			4 (4 f)
f and f slave	4			1 (1 f)
m (or child)	36			24 (24 m)
m and slave	24			13 (13 m)
m, herm, slave	4			4 (4 m, all patronymic)
m, tree+serpent, slave	3			3 (3 m, all patronymic)
c and pet	17			8 (1 f - 7 m)
m f	4			4 (1 f+m - 2 f - 1 m)
m f?	1			1 (1 m+f)
f f	1			
? ?	?	1		

Of the 10 women commemorated, 5 have patronymic, 2 patronymic+wife, 2 wife.
Of the 54 commemorated men, 43 have patronymic, 1 adopted son (possibly not Delian).

Ethnics: 25
Alexandria: 2 (2 m, patronymic)
Ascalon: 3 (3 m, patronymic)
Athens: 4 (3 m, patronymic; 1 f+m, patronymics)
Heraclea: 2 (2 m, patronymic)
Laodicea: 2 (1 f, patronymic; 1 m, patronymic)
Laodicea in Phoenicia: 1 (1 m, patronymic)
Seleucia on the Tigris: ?
Stymphale: 1 (1 f)
Syros: 1 (1 m)
Roman *tria nomina*: 7 (3 m, slave; 4 m)

Epithets:
alupos: 5 (m, m slave, f)

Table 7: **Figure seated on rocks or on a ship**

Reliefs 20		*Inscriptions* 15
On rock		
m	4	2 (2 m)
m, slave or child	5	5 (5 m)
m, ship	7	7 (7 m)
m+f, dexiosis, slaves	1	1 (1 m+f)
2 m, dexiosis	1	

Ethnics: 11
Apamea: 1 (patronymic)
Athens: 2 (patronymic)
Berytos: 1 (m (patronymic)+f from Berytus)
Pergamon: 1 (patronymic)
Thessalonike: 1 (patronymic)
Velia: 1 (patronymic+father)
Roman *tria nomina*: 4 (4 m)

Epithets:
alupos: 3 (m, Pergamon, Roman *tria nomina*)

Ship:
3 reliefs   1 inscr. (2 m, patronymics)

Shipwreck:
3 reliefs   3 inscr. (1 m, patronymic - 1 Roman *tria nomina* - 1 m)

No ethnics, apart from the Roman *tria nomina*.

Table 7a: **Warrior on ship**

Reliefs 10	*Inscriptions* 6
	1 m; 3 m, patronymic; 2 m, Roman *tria nomina* (1 slave, 1 freeman)

No ethnics, apart from the Roman *tria nomina*.

Epithets:
alupos: 2 (Antioch, Roman *tria nomina*)

Notes

1. Rauh 1993.
2. An example is Zanker 1993. For an outline of Hellenistic grave reliefs, see Schmidt 1991.
3. Bruneau 1968, 636-37. The calculation is based on the number of citizens participating in the banquets of the Posideia (between 1,500 and 2,000).
4. Roussel (1931, 443) from a list of ephebes (*ID* 2598); also Tréheux 1952, 582 has suggested ca. 25,000.
5. For the necropolis on Rheneia, see Couilloud-Le Dinahet 1978.
6. The numbers in this paper refer to Couilloud's catalogue (1974).
7. Couilloud 1974; 1974a; 1975; 1978; 1984. See also Schmidt 1991, 35ff, in which he correctly attributes nos. 91 and 86 to Byzantium.
8. The majority of this very simple version of the *dexiosis* date to the end of the second and the beginning of the first century, but the motif continues also later in the first century. A few are dated earlier than the end of the second century (no. 17 — never in use as a grave stele — is dated to the end of the third or beginning of the second century BC, and no. 28 to the third century BC or the beginning of the second).
9. Cumont 1993, 41 states that in Classical Athens "the memorials with sunk reliefs are definitely more modest as compared with naiskos stelae."
10. Couilloud 1974 stresses the evidence for the stele being from Rheneia, not from Tinos, as has sometimes been suggested. The arch frame makes a Cycladic origin certain.
11. In fact there is a small group of banquet reliefs and a couple of reliefs with a horseman. Banquet nos. 313-26 = 14
    Varying:
    1 banqueter (no. 313) a woman
    1 banqueter and a servant (no. 314) a man, male epitaph
    1 banqueter (man or woman) and one seated on a chair (nos. 315-17)
    1 banqueter, 1 seated, 1 male servant (nos. 318-22), the banqueter is a man, the seated a woman. The epitaph is for the man or the woman (no. 322)
    2 banqueters, seated person, male servant (no. 323), a male name is inscribed
    1 banqueter, seated woman, standing person, male servant, (nos. 324-25), epitaph for the banqueter.
12. Zanker 1993 interprets the gesture as one of meditation or reflexion, comparing with third-century portraits of philosophers.
13. Nos. 87 and 466 do not make use of the Aphrodite iconography, but show a woman with her head uncovered. No. 466 has an epigram for an unmarried young woman, Martha, daughter of Demosthenes, suggesting that the bare head in these cases refers to the unmarried status of the commemorated woman.
14. E.g. the well-known Cleopatra, see Chamonard 1922, 39ff. and Kreeb 1988, 17ff. and 282ff.
15. See Zanker 1993, 216f.
16. The interpretation given by Zanker 1993 of the Smyrna reliefs.
17. Athenian sculptors emigrating, suggested by Couilloud 1974, 285f., following a hypothesis by Marcadé 1969.
18. See the forthcoming contribution by S. Houby-Nielsen for grave customs in late Hellenistic Athens.
19. Of the stelai without reliefs about two thirds commemorate one male.

Bibliography

Bruneau, Ph. 1968. "Contribution a l'histoire urbaine de Délos à l'époque hellénistique et à l'époque impériale", *BCH* 92, 633-709.

Bulloch, A. et al. (eds.) 1993. *Images and Ideologies, Self-definition in the Hellenistic World.* Berkeley/Los Angeles.

Chamonard, J. 1922. *Le quartier du théatre. Exploration archéologique de Délos* VIII. Paris.

Couilloud, M.-Th. 1974. *Les monuments funéraires de Rhénée. Exploration archéologique de Délos.* Paris.

Couilloud, M.-Th. 1974a. "Reliefs funéraires des Cyclades de l'époque hellénistique à l'époque impériale", *BCH* 98, 397-498.

Couilloud, M.-Th. 1975. "Autels et stéles des Cyclades", *BCH* 99, 313-29.

Couilloud-Le Dinahet, M.-Th. 1978. "Recherches à Rhénée", *BCH* 102, 855-77.

Couilloud-Le Dinahet, M.-Th. 1984. "Nécropole délienne et épitaphes: problèmes d'interprétation", *BCH* 108, 345-53.

Cumont, C.W. 1993. *Classical Attic Tombstones.* Kilchberg.

Kreeb, M. 1988. *Untersuchungen zur figürlichen Ausstattung delischer Privathäuser.* Chicago.

Marcadé, J. 1969. *Au Musée de Délos.* (BEFAR 215). Paris.

Rauh, N. 1993. *The Sacred Bonds of Commerce, Religion, Economy and Trade Society at Hellenistic Roman Delos, 166-87 B.C.* Amsterdam.

Roussel, P. 1931. "La population de Délos à la fin du IIe siècle avant J.-C.", *BCH* 55, 438-49.

Schmidt, S. 1991. *Hellenistische Grabreliefs.* Köln.

Tréheux, J. 1952. "Études d'épigraphie délienne", *BCH* 76, 562-95.

Stewart, A. 1990. *Greek Sculpture, An Exploration.* New Haven/London.

Wolters, C. 1975. *Steles funéraires hellénistiques. La Thessalie. Actes de la Table-Ronde 21-24 Juillet 1975, Lyon*, 81-98. Paris.

Zanker, P. 1993. "The Hellenistic Grave *Stelai* from Smyrna: Identity and Self-image in the Polis", in: Bulloch et al. (eds.) 1993, 212-30.

INDEX OF PERSONS

INDEX OF MODERN AUTHORS

GEOGRAPHICAL INDEX

INDEX LOCORUM

PLATES

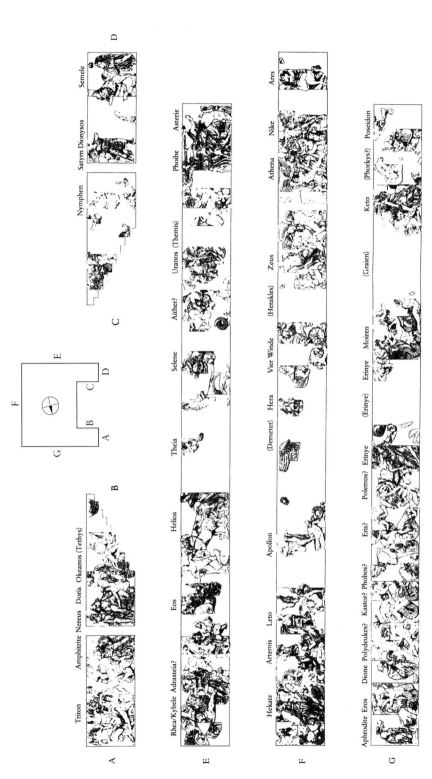

Pl. 1. Pergamum altar. Schematic plan with arrangement of sections A-G of the great frieze (top centre); Great frieze of the Pergamum altar (after Schalles 1986, plate II).

Pl. 2. Pergamum altar. Reconstruction of the east side (after Hoepfner 1989, 632, fig. 33).

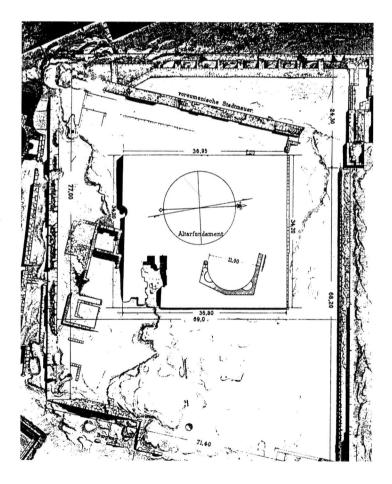

Pl. 3. Plan of the Pergamum altar temenos (after Kunze 1990, 124, fig. 1).

*Pl. 4. Pergamum altar. East
frieze: Hera (after Winnefeld
1910, plate 10).*

*Pl. 5. Pergamum altar. East
frieze: Gê (after Winnefeld
1910, plate 12).*

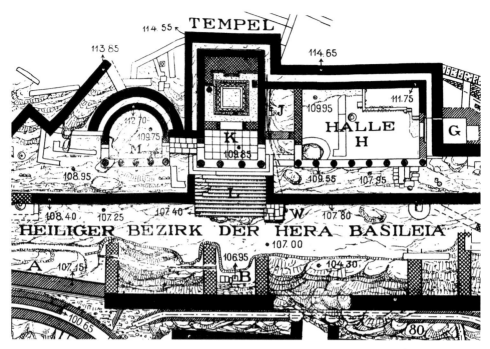

Pl. 6a. Pergamum. Reconstruction of the great gymnasium (after Radt 1988, 132, fig. 40).

Pl. 6b. Pergamum. Plan of the Hera temple and sanctuary above the great gymnasium (after AM 37, 1919, plate 18).

Pl. 7. Roman coin: Juno in biga (after Crawford 1974, plate 48.20).

Pl. 8. Column crater in Vienna showing naked women with strigils grouped around a high-stemmed washbasin (Vienna 2166).

Pl. 9. Hellenistic burial of young woman in Patras buried with an elaborate equipment for embellishment, among other things a mirror (placed on her womb), a strigil placed at her right hand and two silver shells placed at her right shoulder. (After Papapostolou 1982, plate 96).

Pl. 10. Burial in Kerameikos of an infant placed in two amphora halves with grave gifts placed at their side, 5th century bc (Ker. IX, plate 9:1). (Courtesy of the German School at Athens).

Pl. 11. Burial in Kerameikos of an infant placed in an amphora, 5th century bc (Ker. IX, plate 9:7). (Courtesy of the German School at Athens).

Pl. 12. Two silver shells from a rich Hellenistic burial of a young woman in Patras. (After Papapostolou 1982, plate 113: g-d).

Pl. 13. Burial in Kerameikos containing among other things a strigil, a loom-weight and a natural shell, 4th century bc (After Schlörb-Vierneisel 1966, plate 60: 2). (Courtesy of the German School at Athens).

Pl. 14. Hellenistic terracotta of Aphrodite squatting in a double shell and holding a pomegranate in each hand; acquired in Naples. (Courtesy of the Department of Antiquities, The National Museum of Copenhagen, inv. no. 3239; Breitenstein 1941, no. 670).

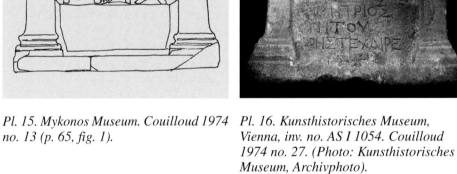

*Pl. 15. Mykonos Museum. Couilloud 1974
no. 13 (p. 65, fig. 1).*

*Pl. 16. Kunsthistorisches Museum,
Vienna, inv. no. AS I 1054. Couilloud
1974 no. 27. (Photo: Kunsthistorisches
Museum, Archivphoto).*

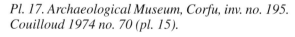

Pl. 17. Archaeological Museum, Corfu, inv. no. 195.
Couilloud 1974 no. 70 (pl. 15).

Pl. 18. National Archaeological
Museum, Athens, inv. no. EM
1028. Couilloud 1974 no. 88.
(Photo: National Archaeological Museum, Athens).

*Pl. 19. National Museum, Athens, inv. no. EM 1194. Couilloud 1974
no. 107. (Photo: National Archaeological Museum, Athens).*

Pl. 20. Mykonos Museum, inv. no. 29. *Couilloud 1974 no. 125 (p. 106, fig. 4).*

Pl. 21. Delos Museum, inv. no. A 7234. *Couilloud 1974 no. 131 (pl. 31).*

Pl. 22. Kunsthistorisches Museum, Vienna, inv. no. AS I 1062. Couilloud 1974 no. 163. (Photo: Kunsthistorisches Museum, Archivphoto).

Pl. 23. National Museum, Athens, inv. no. EM 1218. Couilloud 1974 no. 185 (pl. 43).

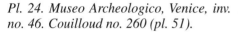

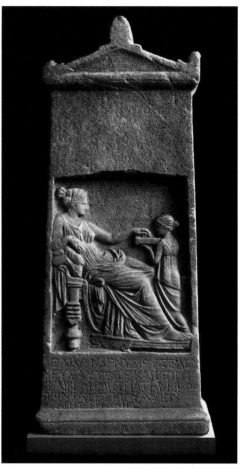

Pl. 24. Museo Archeologico, Venice, inv. no. 46. Couilloud no. 260 (pl. 51).

Pl. 25. Ny Carlsberg Glyptotek, Copenhagen, inv. no. IN 2026. Couilloud 1974 no. 148. (Photo: Ny Carlsberg Glyptotek).

*Pl. 26. Delos Museum. Couilloud 1974
no. 357 (pl. 70).*

*Pl. 27. Collection Roma, Zanthe. Couilloud
1974 no. 341 (pl. 67).*

*Pl. 28. Mykonos Museum. Couilloud
1974 no. 58 (p. 85, fig. 3).*

*Pl. 29. Kunsthistorisches Museum, Vienna,
inv. no. AS I 753. Couilloud 1974 no. 297
(pl. 58).*

Pl. 30. British Museum, London, cat. no. 625. Couilloud no. 286. (Photo: British Museum).

*Pl. 31. Reconstruction of the funeral monument of Tertia Horaria after
Couilloud (p. 227, fig. 9); cf. pl. 28.*